Equipment Fund

METHODS IN PLANT HISTOLOGY

THE UNIVERSITY OF CHICAGO PRESS
CHICAGO, ILLINOIS

—

THE BAKER & TAYLOR COMPANY
NEW YORK

THE CAMBRIDGE UNIVERSITY PRESS
LONDON

THE MARUZEN-KABUSHIKI-KAISHA
TOKYO, OSAKA, KYOTO, FUKUOKA, SENDAI

THE COMMERCIAL PRESS, LIMITED
SHANGHAI

METHODS IN
PLANT HISTOLOGY

By

CHARLES J. CHAMBERLAIN, Ph.D., Sc.D.

Professor Emeritus of Morphology and Cytology
in the University of Chicago

FIFTH REVISED EDITION

THE UNIVERSITY OF CHICAGO PRESS
CHICAGO · ILLINOIS

COMPOSED AND PRINTED BY THE UNIVERSITY OF CHICAGO PRESS
CHICAGO, ILLINOIS, U.S.A.

PREFACE TO THE FIRST EDITION

This book has grown out of a course in histological technique conducted by the author at the University of Chicago. The course has also been taken by non-resident students through the Extension Division of the University. The *Methods* were published over a year ago as a series of articles in the *Journal of Applied Microscopy*, and have called out numerous letters of commendation, criticism, suggestion, and inquiry. The work has been thoroughly revised and enlarged by about one-half. It is hoped that the criticism and suggestion, and also the experience gained by contact with both resident and non-resident students, have made the directions so definite that they may be followed, not only by those who work in a class under the supervision of an instructor, but also by those who must work in their own homes without any such assistance.

More space has been devoted to the paraffin method than to any other, because it has been proved to be better adapted to the needs of the botanist. The celloidin method, the glycerin method, and freehand sectioning are also described, and their advantages and disadvantages are pointed out.

The first part of the book deals with the principles of fixing and staining, and the various other processes of microtechnique, while in the later chapters these principles are applied to specific cases. This occasions some repetition, but the mere presentation of general principles will not enable the beginner to make good mounts.

The illustrations and notes in the later chapters are not intended to afford a study of general morphology, but they merely indicate to students with a limited knowledge of plant structures the principal features which the preparations should show. The photomicrographs were made from the author's preparations by Dr. W. H. Knap, and Figures 52, 57, and 59 (Figs. 61, 66, and 68 of second edition) were drawn by Miss Eleanor Tarrant; all other figures of plant structures were made from the author's drawings.

Corrections and suggestions will be heartily appreciated.

CHARLES J. CHAMBERLAIN

CHICAGO
June 1, 1901

v

PREFACE TO THE SECOND EDITION

It is gratifying to the author to learn that the kindly reception accorded to *Methods in Plant Histology* has exhausted the edition. Since the first edition appeared, a little more than four years ago, laboratory methods have been greatly improved, and systematic experiments have made it possible to give much more definite directions for making preparations.

In the present edition much more attention has been given to collecting material. Professor Kleb's methods for securing various reproductive phases in the algae and fungi have been outlined in a practical way. Methods for growing other laboratory material are more complete than in the earlier edition.

The paraffin method has been much improved, and the glycerin method has been almost entirely replaced by the Venetian turpentine method, to which a whole chapter is devoted. Other new chapters deal with microchemical tests, freehand sections, special methods, and the use of the microscope.

The author is deeply indebted to his colleague, Dr. W. J. G. Land, for numerous suggestions and improvements in methods.

Corrections and suggestions will be heartily appreciated.

CHARLES J. CHAMBERLAIN

CHICAGO
July 1, 1905

PREFACE TO THE THIRD EDITION

The continued appreciation accorded to *Methods in Plant Histology* has exhausted the second edition. Since that edition appeared, methods have become more and more exact, so that the present volume is practically a new book. The general arrangement of the subject matter, and directions for collecting material and for securing reproductive phases in the algae and fungi have been retained, and a chapter on "Photomicrographs and Lantern Slides" (chap. xii) has been added.

Great improvements have been made in the paraffin method, so that sections are easily cut which were impossible ten years ago, while ten years of added experience with the Venetian turpentine method have made it possible to describe it so definitely that even the beginner should find no serious difficulty.

The author is deeply indebted to his colleague, Dr. W. J. G. Land, for numerous suggestions and improvements covering the whole field of microtechnique. He is also greatly indebted to Dr. S. Yamanouchi for many improvements in the methods applicable to algae and mitotic figures.

Corrections and suggestions will be heartily appreciated.

CHARLES J. CHAMBERLAIN

CHICAGO
May, 1915

PREFACE TO THE FOURTH EDITION

It is gratifying to the author that the appreciation accorded to *Methods in Plant Histology*, when it first appeared as a series of articles in the *Journal of Applied Microscopy*, has continued through three editions of the book. While the chapter headings and general arrangement remain about the same as before, the book has been almost entirely rewritten.

Directions for collecting material have been amplified and the preparation of the most familiar laboratory types has received particular attention. While no radical changes have been made in the paraffin method, the process has been shortened and improved; the Venetian turpentine method, introduced in the second edition and improved in the third, has come into such general use that the experience of many laboratories has been added to that of our own, and the directions have become so definite that there is little excuse for failures. The cellulose acetate method, which may do as much for woody structures as the Venetian turpentine method has done for its class of mounts, is outlined in a tentative way, and the chapter on "Photomicrographs and Lantern Slides" has been extended and improved.

The introduction of American stains, which are becoming very accurately standardized, has occasioned some modifications throughout.

The author is even more deeply indebted than before to his colleague, Dr. W. J. G. Land, for suggestions and improvements covering the whole field of microtechnique and photography. He is also indebted to Dr. S. Yamanouchi for improvements applicable to algae and mitotic figures. Dr. Paul J. Sedgwick is responsible for much of the improvement in photomicrography and for many of the photomicrographic illustrations. To Miss Ethel Thomas, who assisted me for many years, I am indebted for improvements, criticisms, and suggestions covering the whole range of the book. Besides, I must thank a host of colleagues and students all over the world for help in all phases of the subject.

Corrections and suggestions will be heartily appreciated.

CHARLES J. CHAMBERLAIN

CHICAGO
October, 1924

PREFACE TO THE FIFTH EDITION

As one edition of this book has followed another, we have tried to keep the methods up to the highest possible standard. We have tried to keep our own technique up to date and have had the pleasure of seeing various phases of microtechnique as practiced in the leading universities of our own country and also in the laboratories of England, Europe, and the Orient.

The directions for collecting material have been still further amplified, and directions for fixing, dehydrating, and staining have been improved.

"Paleobotanical Microtechnique" and "Laboratory Photography" have been amplified and given chapter headings. There is a new chapter on "Illustrations for Publication." The steam method and Jeffrey's vulcanizing method for sectioning hard woods, and Gourley's method for staining living vascular tissues will repay the time one must spend to gain a mastery of these phases of technique.

The paraffin method has been improved for both delicate and hard tissues. Improvements have been made throughout; in fact, the book has had a rewriting, not a mere revision.

The author is even more deeply indebted than before to his friend and colleague, Dr. W. J. G. Land, for suggestions and improvements covering the entire field of microtechnique and photography. He is also indebted to Dr. S. Yamanouchi for refinements in the paraffin method —from fixing to the finished mount—which make 3 and 2 micron sections easy, 1 micron sections not too difficult, and $\frac{1}{2}$ micron sections a possibility. Dr. Paul J. Sedgwick has written the parts dealing with "Botanical Photomicrography" and "Movie Photomicrography." To Miss Ethel Thomas, who assisted me for many years, I am indebted for improvements, criticism, and suggestions covering the entire range of the book. Besides, I must thank a host of colleagues and students all over the world for help in all phases of the subject.

Corrections and suggestions will be heartily appreciated.

CHARLES J. CHAMBERLAIN

CHICAGO
April, 1932

CONTENTS

PART I

CONTENTS xiii

CONTENTS

PART I

INTRODUCTION

From the days of Nehemiah Grew and Robert Hooke to the time of Matthias Schleiden and Herman Schacht, histological technique was in a very primitive condition, each investigator making his own microscope and other apparatus. Stems and similar objects were held in the hand and cut with sharp knives, while things which did not lend themselves to such technique were dissected with needles, even such difficult objects as embryo sacs and embryos being teased out so that fairly accurate views were obtained. Schleiden's cell theory (1838), the "theory" that a plant consists entirely of cells, was developed from such preparations.

Carl Zeiss, one of Schleiden's students, dissatisfied with his microscope, quit the study of botany and proceeded to improve microscopes. His success gave the scientific world immensely better microscopes, and the better microscopes brought improvements in histological technique. By 1850, stains were being used, and improvements came so fast that a history of technique, rather than the practice of it, would be needed if one were to trace the whole subject. Before the end of the century, there were numerous fixing agents, paraffin baths, and microtomes, and staining had reached a high degree of efficiency.

Unfortunately, some of the skill of the older botanists in teasing material and studying it in the living condition had been lost; but this valuable phase of technique is being revived and, with the micromanipulator, results are being obtained which surpass the wildest dreams of Schleiden and Strasburger.

In the fourth edition we stated that the pollen grain of a lily, placed on a dark background, is barely visible to the naked eye; but with modern technique, such a pollen grain can be cut into fifty sections, the sections can be mounted and stained without getting them out of order, a photomicrograph can be made from the preparation and a lantern slide from the photomicrograph, and finally there appears on the screen a pollen grain 10 feet long, with nuclei a foot in diameter, nucleoli as large as baseballs, and starch grains as large as walnuts.

While this is a striking illustration, modern technique shows its efficiency better in demonstrating the structure of chromatin and the

3

finer details of protoplasm and its derivatives. For general morphological work, sections are not cut so thin. About 10 μ is a serviceable
thickness, with 5 μ for oil immersion details. Algae and fungi, with
their small nuclei, usually need 3 or 2 μ sections. With improvements
in microtomes and in technique, the 1 μ section is not so rare, and ribbons of root-tips have been cut at $\frac{1}{2}$ μ. A microscope, giving several
times the magnification of any microscope now on the market, is in
an advanced experimental stage. Should such microscopes get into
use, it would be necessary to regard a 2 μ section as rather thick, and
nothing thicker than 1 μ could be regarded as thin. Such a microscope would bring great improvements in technique.

Every investigator whose work demands a microscope should study
technique until he gains such a grasp of fundamentals that he will be
able to make the modifications which individual problems may require. Those who think that such work is mere mechanical drudgery,
which can be done by an assistant, are likely to become armchair investigators, drawing false conclusions or becoming scholastic grafters,
according as the assistant is mediocre or talented. Besides, there is
always the danger that a talented assistant may "hold out" something. A younger member of a faculty, doing research work for his
superior, may make an important discovery but, knowing that his
superior has little knowledge of the progress of the investigation,
may "hold it out" and, later, publish it himself, preaching the same
sermon from a different text. Benjamin Franklin's advice, "If you
want your business done, go; if not, send," applies very well to investigations involving histological technique.

We strongly advise the student to collect his own material in the
field, for such collecting is a valuable part of a botanical education.
There are details of habitat and behavior which are never described
in books. One learns gradually, by experience, that certain kinds of
plants grow in certain kinds of places; and further, that not only the
season, but even the weather, may be an important factor. A heavy
rain may cause some algae to disappear; while the same rain, followed
by a few days of sunshine, will bring ideal conditions for collecting
Myxomycetes and many other fungi. One learns that while *Lycogala*
is pink, it is in the free nuclear condition, and that *Stemonitis* is in
that condition as long as it is white; and *Volvox* may be abundant at
the bottom of a pond when there is scarcely any in suspension. The
successful investigator learns how a flower bud should look, if it is to

yield floral development, how the flower looks when the embryo sac is mature; and how it looks after fertilization.

Such studies add immensely to the value of a preparation. A considerable part of a botanical education can be gained by collecting material, making and studying preparations, reading what is available, and *thinking*.

Some biologists regard cut and stained sections as a mere mess of artifacts, giving only distorted, misleading views of the actual structures; and it must be admitted that some structures, notably the liquid albuminoids, are changed by the processes of fixing, imbedding, and staining. However, no one knows this better than the expert cytologist. Every student of plant structures should compare the fixed and stained material with the living. Chromosomes in the pollen mother-cells of a lily can be counted and measured and photographed in the living condition; and such details which can be seen in the living condition are so like those in fixed and stained material that we believe that finer details, which can be seen dimly or not at all in living material, are equally well preserved. Chromosomes as small as those in the spore mother-cells of *Osmunda cinnamomea* can be seen in the living condition, the various stages in mitosis can be traced, and chondriosomes can be seen moving vigorously in living cells. Protoplasmic connections can be seen easily in living cells of the endosperm of *Diospyros discolor*, and can be seen, dimly, in the endosperm of a date seed, as one gets it on the market. And so we believe that smaller protoplasmic strands, which cannot be seen in the living condition, but which are easily seen in thin, well-stained sections, are not artifacts produced by fixing, imbedding, and staining, but are real structures which have merely been made visible by these processes. Of all the structures with which the cytologist has to deal, protoplasm suffers most from fixing and imbedding. But even here, protoplasm, like that in the egg of a cycad, shows the large vacuoles and smaller and smaller vacuoles in the living condition, so that still smaller vacuoles, not visible in the living condition, are no more likely to be artifacts than those so easily seen in the living condition.

However, all who make preparations for microscopic investigation should be constantly on guard, and should always compare the living material with that which has been subjected to the various processes of microtechnique.

CHAPTER I

APPARATUS

The microscope is the most important piece of apparatus. It should have a rack and pinion coarse adjustment, a fine adjustment, two eyepieces magnifying about 5 and 10 diameters, a low-power objective of about 16-mm. focus, and a high-power objective of about 4-mm. focus, a double nosepiece, an iris diaphragm, and an Abbé condenser. A cheap and practical form is shown in Figure 1, and similar instruments are for sale by all the leading companies.

The rest of the apparatus is for getting material ready for observation with the microscope. The following list includes only the apparatus necessary for making preparations: a microtome; a razor; a hone and a good razor strop; a paraffin bath; a turntable; a scalpel; a pair of needles; a pair of scissors; a pair of forceps; staining-dishes; solid watch glasses; bottles; a graduate (50 or 100 c.c.); pipettes; slides, 1×3 inches; round covers, 18 mm. or $\frac{3}{4}$ inch in diameter; and square covers, $\frac{7}{8}$ inch. Longer covers will be needed for some of the serial sections.

Keep the apparatus clean, especially the microscope. Since the chemicals used in histological technique are likely to damage the stage and substage of the microscope, it is well to place upon the stage a piece of glass 3 or 4 inches square. A lantern-slide cover is just right for this purpose. It is not necessary to fasten it to the stage, since it is merely for protection while examining slides which are wet with reagents. In our own laboratory we use for examining wet slides a cheap microscope with only a single low-power objective and a single ocular.

Some knowledge of the structure and optics of the microscope is necessary if one is to use it effectively. Why are there so many diaphragms? Why is there an arrangement for raising and lowering the condenser? Why does the mirror bar swing? Why is one side of the mirror plane and the other concave? Everyone who uses even a cheap microscope should know the answers to questions like these. All the leading manufacturers furnish, free of charge, booklets, explaining

7

the construction of the microscope and giving practical directions for its care and use.

Aside from the microscope itself, the microtome is the most important piece of apparatus in the laboratory. In recent years there has been immense improvement in microtomes, but we still have only two general types —the sliding and the rotary.

If there is to be only one microtome, it should be of the sliding type; for all kinds of sectioning can be done with the sliding microtome, while only paraffin ribbons can be cut with the rotary. The rotary microtome is convenient, rapid, and, to a large extent, eliminates the necessity for skill; but a good sliding microtome, in the hands of an expert, will yield paraffin sections superior to any which can be cut with a rotary microtome. Paraffin sections of root-tips have been cut as thin as $\frac{1}{2}\,\mu$ with the medium-priced sliding microtome shown in Figure 2. It should be provided with a clamp which will hold any kind of knife; but we should strongly recommend, in addition, the clamp shown in Figure 3, which will hold

FIG. 1.—An efficient microscope of moderate price. The leading optical companies put the same objectives and oculars upon such instruments as upon their most expensive stands.

any of the thin safety razor blades. For any sections not more than $\frac{3}{8}$ inch square, the safety razor blade is long enough. Paraffin ribbons $\frac{3}{4}$ inch wide can be cut with safety razor blades. Celloidin sections, up to $\frac{3}{8}$ inch square, can be cut with the safety razor blade; but larger sections must be cut with a microtome knife.

Clamps have been devised for holding safety razor blades for cutting with rotary microtomes (Fig. 4).

Fig. 2.—A sliding microtome capable of the best paraffin sectioning, and also good for cutting sections of stems, roots, and other things.

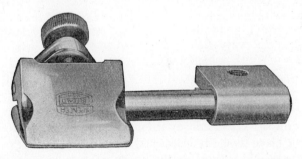

Fig. 3.—Clamp for sliding microtome for holding thin safety razor blades

Success with safety razor blades depends, to a large extent, upon the blade. Many blades, which are fairly good for shaving, are worthless for microtome cutting, because they are too soft. After the leading domestic firm had refused to furnish blades much harder than those on the market, John Watts, 24 Redcross Street, London, E.C. 1. England, furnished blades so hard that they broke when tightened in the ordinary handles used for shaving. These blades are ideal for his-

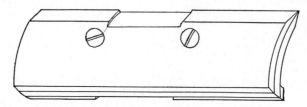

FIG. 4.—Clamp for holding safety razor blades in the Spencer rotary microtome

tological work. In ordering, one should state that he wants blades specially hardened for microtome use.

Many have trouble with safety razor blades, especially when used with the rotary microtome, where the best holder is of the type shown 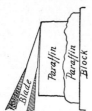 in Figure 4. The blade is bent into a curve, making the angle of the cutting edge look less than it really is. The holder must stand more nearly vertical than a regular microtome knife to give the cutting edge the same angle. Study Figure 5, which shows correct position. If the blade is too nearly vertical, it will rub the paraffin instead of cutting it; while there will be scraping instead of cutting, if the blade is too far from the vertical position. The position will vary slightly with hard and soft, and with thick and thin, sections. If the blade projects too far beyond the holder, it will vibrate; if it does not project enough, the paraffin will hit the holder. Figure 5 will make this clear.

FIG. 5.—The correct relative positions of holder, blade, and paraffin, for both sliding and rotary microtomes.

The stout razors our grandfathers used to shave with are excellent for freehand sectioning and even for cutting sections on the microtome. The blade should be sharpened flat on the under side and beveled on the upper, as shown in Figure 6. If sharpened without this chisel bevel, there will be a "wire" edge, and smooth cutting will be impossible. A satisfac-

FIG. 6.—A grandfather's razor with chisel-edge sharpening.

tory bevel can be secured by merely tilting the knife while finishing the sharpening. The heavier microtome knives have a back which is put on during sharpening, thus getting a proper bevel. Modern razors, ground hollow on both sides, are worthless for histological work.

There should be two good hones: a fine carborundum hone for the preliminary sharpening, and a yellow Belgian hone for finishing. About $10 \times 2\frac{1}{2}$ inches is a good size. If the second hone be quite hard and the finishing skilfully done, little or no stropping may be necessary. The best strops used by barbers are satisfactory for microtome knives.

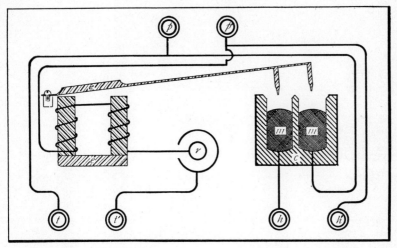

Fig. 7.—Land's electric constant apparatus, showing diagram of the automatic switch, as described in the *Botanical Gazette* of November, 1911.

Great improvements have been made in paraffin baths. A type devised by Dr. Land has never been surpassed in accuracy. The novice is likely to have trouble with it. This bath is not on the market, but, with the help of the diagrams, one can make it and having made it one can use it (Figs. 7 and 8). A detailed description of the thermostat and heater is given in the *Botanical Gazette* of November, 1911. Unless the coil in the heater is perfectly protected, there will be a short circuit; but this danger can be obviated, in large measure, by using oil instead of water in the jacket.

Another form of heater, using long electric bulbs instead of a coil, can be made with less skill. From a sheet of transite $\frac{1}{8}$ inch thick, make a box just the size of the bottom of the bath and about 4 inches deep. In this box put three long electric bulbs. Two of the bulbs, about 250 watt, giving a temperature of about 40° C., should be connected with the regular outlets and should be on all the time. The third bulb, which should be capable of raising the temperature 15° or 20° C., should be connected with a thermostat. An efficient thermo-

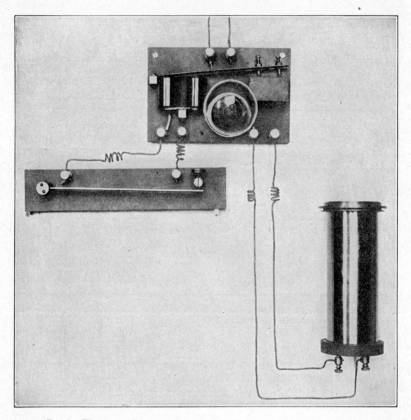

Fig. 8.—Thermostat, heater, and switch of Land's electrical constant apparatus

stat, capable of keeping the variation in temperature within about 1° can be made in a short time. Take a piece of soft steel $\frac{3}{4}$ inch wide and $\frac{1}{16}$ inch thick, and 17 inches long; lay upon it three strips of aluminum of the same width and length, but only $\frac{1}{32}$ inch thick. These four pieces are fastened together by drilling numerous holes, not more than $\frac{1}{16}$ inch in diameter, and riveting with pieces of brass wire. After fastening the four pieces together for about 7 inches, begin to bend all four pieces, fastening them together as the bending continues, so that finally there will be a horseshoe shape with the parallel sides about $1\frac{1}{2}$ inches apart. One end of the horseshoe is fastened to a block of transite or other non-conductor, while the other end moves freely. On this free end is fastened a good platinum contact, which can be bought at any automobile supply store. This contact should be on a screw, so that it may be adjusted. A similar contact is fastened to a post, so that the two contacts are about $\frac{1}{8}$ inch apart. Anyone familiar with

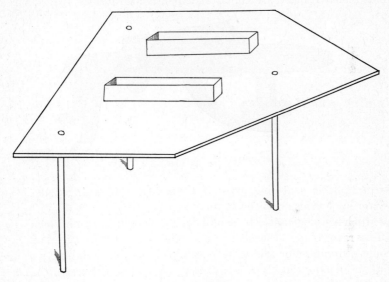

Fig. 9.—Paraffin bath

electricity can make the connections. Various temperatures are secured by changing the distance between the platinum points. To prevent sparking, there must be a condenser in the circuit leading to the thermostat. A telephone condenser (0.500MF) is satisfactory. Possibly, some of the cheap radio condensers would do.

Anyone can make a bath which, if carefully watched, gives excellent results (Fig. 9). It is simply cut from brass, 2 or 3 mm. in thickness, with three legs screwed into it. There should be brass boxes, 10 or 12 cm. long, to contain the paraffin. It is neither necessary nor desirable that the boxes have covers. Boxes are easily made from square brass tubing, 1 inch square. Cut the tubing into pieces 10 or 12 cm. long, saw off one side, and solder pieces into the ends with hard solder. The brass plate can be heated with any kind of flame at the pointed end.

Since the Venetian turpentine method has almost entirely displaced the glycerin method, the turntable is disappearing from the botanical laboratory; but some objects, like *Nemalion* and moss protonema, are still mounted in glycerin or glycerin jelly; and so one still finds occasional use for this once necessary piece of apparatus. A serviceable form is shown in Figure 10. More expensive turntables, with devices

FIG. 10.—Turntable

for automatic centering, present no practical advantages, and the centering devices are often in the way.

Much histological work usually done with scalpels can be done with safety razor blades, especially since holders of the Gits type have become common. For trimming paraffin blocks and handling paraffin ribbons, a more rigid type is necessary. A scalpel with a straight edge is preferable.

Needles are used so constantly that it is well to have clamping holders. However, nothing is quite equal to a rather large handle whittled out from a piece of light pine.

Scissors are seldom used in the botanical laboratory except for cutting out labels. Rather stout scissors, with blades about $2\frac{1}{4}$ inches long, are best for general purposes.

It is convenient to have two pairs of forceps, a strong pair for handling slides and a lighter pair, preferably with broad shovel-shaped points, for handling cover glasses. Curved forceps are not necessary; the cover-glass forceps, used by bacteriologists for staining on the cover, are of no use in botanical histology.

For staining on the slide, Stender dishes are very convenient. The form shown in Figure 11*A*, about 60×90 mm., is in general use. Some prefer the Coplin jar, shown in Figure 11*B*; but it is troublesome to clean, and if slides are placed back to back, as shown in the figure, water is carried up in dehydrating and xylol is carried down. When a large number of slides of the same kind are to be stained at one time, the cheap and practical device, shown in Figure 12, is a time-saver.

It is simply a coil of brass wire, 0.064 inch in diameter (No. 14, Band's gauge), wound so that the coil is about ⅞ inch across. Such a coil, carrying 15 slides, will go into an ordinary Stender dish, except that the coil projects enough to prevent the cover from fitting. Taller

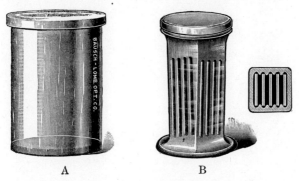

A   B

Fig. 11.—Staining-dishes: *A*, Stender dish; *B*, Coplin jar

glasses, from the five-and-ten-cent store, can be used for the absolute alcohol and xylol, which must be kept well covered. We have been using a coil made from wire 0.051 inch in diameter (No. 16 Band's gauge), wound so that the coil is 1 3/16 inch across. It holds the slides and the ordinary Stender dish can be covered.

Biological supply houses use rectangular staining dishes and holders carrying 50 slides.

Solid watch glasses, or Minots, as they are often called, are always useful. Each student should have a dozen or more.

Each student should have three bottles of about 1-liter capacity for 90 per cent alcohol, absolute alcohol, and xylol. In addition, a half-dozen bottles, holding about 100 c.c., will be useful. There should be two bottles, holding about 50 c.c., for clove oil. If one is doing much research work, it will be convenient to have many more bottles for graded series of alcohols and xylols.

There should be a graduate, preferably 50 c.c. or 100 c.c. If the bottles are of uniform size, 50 c.c., 100 c.c., 500 c.c. and 1,000 c.c., the student should soon be able to estimate with sufficient accuracy for making up reagents which do not require extreme accuracy.

Three or four pipettes, or medicine droppers, will be useful. Occasionally, the glass of an ordinary pipette, thrust into a small camera bulb, will save time in drawing off reagents.

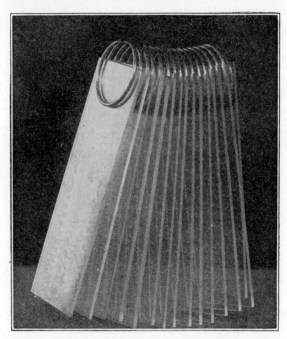

FIG. 12.—Coil of brass wire holding 15 slides

Slides and covers are a constant expense. Many slides now upon the market are imperfect. Beware of slides which are not perfectly flat. Be skeptical in regard to any claim that slides are already clean enough to use. Of course, there should be no bubbles. "White" slides are to be preferred to those which appear greenish in the box. For ordinary class work, slides of medium thickness are more serviceable, but for critical cytological work many investigators prefer very thin slides.

Slides and covers, as you buy them, are *never* clean, no matter how

nice they may look. Leave them overnight or 24 hours in cleaning
fluid:

Dichromate of potash......................	20 g.
Sulphuric acid............................	30 c.c.
Water...................................	250 c.c.

Rinse well in clean water and then leave them overnight or 24 hours
in soapy water with plenty of soap. Rinse thoroughly in clean water
and wipe dry. The cleaning fluid cleans. The soap is necessary on
account of the acid in the cleaning fluid, and rinsing removes the
soap. Unless the acid is completely removed, many stains will fade.

There is never any objection to very thin covers, except that they
require care in cleaning. For mounts which are to be used with an immersion lens, it is better to have the cover of the same width as the
slide. The advantage is evident, since there is no danger of getting
balsam on the cover when wiping off the immersion fluid; besides, one
can put sections to the very edge of the slide and still be sure that they
will be covered. Since most mounts for research work are mounted
under long covers and are intended for examination with immersion
lenses, we should recommend covers of 25×50 mm., or even 25×60
mm. Round covers are desirable only when mounts are to be sealed
on a turntable. Larger slides and correspondingly larger covers are
needed for special purposes.

By consulting a catalogue, which will be furnished by any dealer,
the beginner can determine what he needs to buy, and what he can
find substitutes for, if it is necessary to be very economical.

CHAPTER II

REAGENTS

During the eight years since the fourth edition of this book appeared, practically no new ingredients of formulas have come into general use; but there have been new combinations of ingredients and considerable improvement in the use of reagents. The following account presents not only those reagents which are in constant use but some of those which are used only occasionally. *The Microtomist's Vade-Mecum*, by Lee, is written from the standpoint of the zoölogist, but it contains very complete formulas for stains and other reagents which are equally valuable to the botanist.

For convenient reference, a list of reagents, including stains, is given in chapter xxxi. Stains are treated more fully in chapter iii.

KILLING AND FIXING AGENTS

No process in microtechnique is in more urgent need of improvement than this first step of killing and fixing. In nearly every investigation involving histological technique some fixing agent or other is recommended; but usually so little attention is paid to other factors which may be just as important, that it is doubtful whether the fixing agent is responsible for the excellence or mediocrity of the preparations. If the fixing is bad, it is impossible to get good preparations; but insufficient washing after fixing, too rapid dehydration, too long an immersion in the paraffin bath, or too high a temperature in the bath may result in poor preparations even when the fixing has been good. If material is examined at every stage, mistakes can be corrected—in the next lot of material.

Usually the same reagent is used for both killing and fixing. The purpose of a killing agent is to bring the life-processes to a sudden termination, while a fixing agent is used to fix the cells and their contents in as nearly the living condition as possible. The fixing consists in so hardening the material that the various elements may retain their natural condition during all the processes which are to follow.

Zoölogists often use chloroform or ether for killing an organism, and then use various fixing agents for various tissues.

Most of our formulas are merely empirical, for very few botanists are expert chemists, and those who have some knowledge of chemistry are interested in physiological problems rather than in microtechnique.

The principal ingredients of the usual killing and fixing agents are: alcohol, chloroform, chromic acid, dichromate of potash, potassium iodide, copper acetate, acetic acid, osmic acid, formic acid, picric acid, sulphuric acid, platinum chloride, iridium chloride, corrosive sublimate, and formalin. We shall consider first:

THE ALCOHOLS

a) **Ninety-five per cent alcohol.**—This is in quite general use for material which is needed only for rough work. It is extremely convenient, since it kills, fixes, and preserves at the same time and needs no changing or washing. It really has nothing to recommend it for fine work. It causes protoplasm to shrink, but cell walls usually retain their position, so that 95 per cent alcohol will do for freehand sections of wood and many herbaceous stems, where it is not necessary to preserve cell contents; but even freehand sections of tender stems, like geraniums and begonias, will look better if better reagents are employed. Alcohols weaker than 95 per cent are not to be recommended as fixing agents, although 70 per cent alcohol, or even 50 per cent, will preserve material for habit work. The time required for fixing in 95 per cent alcohol is about the same as for absolute alcohol. The subsequent treatment is the same, except that material to be imbedded in paraffin or celloidin must be dehydrated in absolute alcohol. Material preserved in weaker alcohols and intended only for habit study may be kept in the reagent until needed for use. Unless some glycerin be added, material left in 95 per cent alcohol becomes very brittle. Stems, roots, and similar objects may be kept indefinitely in a mixture of equal parts of 95 per cent alcohol and glycerin.

Methyl alcohol, or wood alcohol as it is commonly called, serves equally well.

b) **Absolute (100 per cent) alcohol.**—This is a fair killing and fixing agent, it causes but little shrinking of the protoplasm, and is a timesaver if material is to be imbedded in paraffin. The time required for fixing in alcohol is very short. For small fungi, like *Eurotium*, 1 minute is long enough. Root-tips of the onion, anthers of the lily, and similar objects require from 15 to 30 minutes. Larger objects may require an hour. No washing is necessary, but all plant tissues contain water; consequently, if material is to be imbedded in paraffin, the alcohol used for fixing should be poured off and fresh alcohol added before proceeding with the clearing. If material is to be mounted in Venetian turpentine, as is likely to be the case in small filamentous fungi, the transfer to the stain may be made directly from the absolute alcohol to any stain dissolved in an alcohol not weaker than 85 per cent. Small forms with no vacuoles may be transferred to a weaker alcoholic stain or even to an aqueous stain; but neither the fixing nor the rude transfer would be at all satisfactory with forms like *Zygnema* or *Saprolegnia*.

Acetic acid is used with alcohols to counteract the tendency to shrink. One of the most widely known of the alcohol combinations is

c) **Carnoy's fluid.—**

Absolute alcohol............................ 6 parts
Chloroform................................. 3 parts
Glacial acetic acid.......................... 1 part

The penetration is very rapid. An object like an onion root-tip is doubtless killed in less than a minute and 15 or 20 minutes is long enough to fix an object of this size. Wash in absolute alcohol, changing frequently, until no odor of acetic acid or chloroform remains. For a root-tip, the entire process does not require more than an hour. It is better to imbed in paraffin at once, but when this is not convenient, the material may be washed in absolute alcohol until the odor of acetic acid and chloroform disappears, cleared in xylol, and, with a block of paraffin about half the bulk of the liquid added, may be left indefinitely. Cyanin and erythrosin, fuchsin and iodine green, and similar combinations stain brilliantly after this reagent.

d) **Acetic alcohol.—**Farmer and Shove recommend for fixing root-tips of *Tradescantia virginica* a mixture of 2 parts absolute alcohol and 1 part glacial acetic acid. The mixture is allowed to act for 15–20 minutes, after which the acid is washed out with absolute alcohol and the material is imbedded as soon as possible.

e) **Formalin alcohol.—**This is one of the most satisfactory alcohol combinations. Various proportions are used by different workers. Professor Lynds Jones, who first brought the combination to my notice, added 2 c.c. of commercial formalin to 100 c.c. of 70 per cent alcohol. We have used a larger proportion of formalin, often as much as 10 c.c. to 100 c.c. of 70 per cent alcohol. Results which seem equally good have been secured by adding from 4 to 10 c.c. of formalin to 100 c.c. of 50 per cent alcohol. Material in this fixing agent may be left until needed for use.

f) **Formalin acetic alcohol.**—This combination, for general anatomical work, might almost be called a universal fixing agent. About 5 c.c. of glacial acetic acid and 5 c.c. of commercial formalin to 90 c.c. of 50 per cent or 70 per cent alcohol is generally satisfactory. If the protoplasm shrinks away from the cell wall, increase the proportion of acetic acid to 7 per cent or even to 10 per cent. We should not recommend more than 10 per cent of acetic acid in any fixing agent.

When one is on a long trip, moving frequently from place to place, with little opportunity to make the numerous changes which are necessary when using the chromic formulas, this is the best fixing agent we have found. It will fix and preserve an amount of material equal to its own weight, and the material may be left in the solution for months. The reagent is good for almost any material, except the unicellular and filamentous algae and fungi, which are more satisfactory in media containing no alcohol.

THE CHROMIC-ACID GROUP

Chromic acid, or solutions with chromic acid as a foundation, are the most generally useful killing and fixing agents yet known to the botanist. A 1 per cent solution of chromic acid in water gives good results, but it is better to use the chromic acid in connection with other ingredients, such as acetic acid, formic acid, osmic acid, etc. Chromic acid does not penetrate well, and this is one reason why it is seldom used alone. Unfortunately it precipitates some liquid albuminoids in the form of filaments and networks, which may be mistaken for structural elements. In botanical work, acetic acid is nearly always mixed with chromic acid. The pickles of the dinner table show that acetic acid is a good preservative, and that it causes little or no shrinking. It penetrates rapidly, and is likely to cause swelling rather than shrinking, thus counteracting the tendency of chromic acid to cause plasmolysis. The swelling is as bad as shrinking. If the proportion of acetic acid is too high, material may even break up; but 2 per cent, or even 6 per cent, may be used to show the topography of an embryo sac of an angiosperm, or the free nuclear stage of the endosperm of a gymnosperm; and for filamentous algae, which are to be mounted whole, 3 per cent is very effective.

It is convenient to have in the laboratory the following stock solution of chromo-acetic acid from which various solutions can be made as they are needed

Chromic acid crystals......................	10 g.
Glacial acetic acid.........................	10 c.c.
Water..................................	1,000 c.c.

Keep the stock solution in a glass-stoppered bottle because the acetic acid evaporates very rapidly.

To make a solution containing 0.5 g. of chromic acid and 2 c.c. of glacial acetic acid to 100 c.c. of water, add 50 c.c. of water to 50 c.c. of the stock solution, and then add to the weakened solution 1.5 c.c. of glacial acetic acid. Any desired proportions can be secured in a similar way. Weighing the crystals for every new proportion is more tedious. The proportions of the various ingredients, for the present at least, must be determined by experiment. With favorable objects like fern prothallia, *Spirogyra*, and other things which can be watched while the fixing is taking place, suitable proportions are rather easily determined, because specimens, after being placed in the reagent, may be examined at frequent intervals, and combinations which cause plasmolysis may be rejected and different proportions tried until satisfactory results are secured. For example, fern prothallia might be placed in the following solution: chromic acid, 2 g.; acetic acid, 1 c.c.; and water, 97 c.c. If plasmolysis takes place, as it probably will, weaken the chromic or strengthen the acetic. In general, it will be better to weaken the chromic, but not to less than $\frac{1}{2}$ per cent. If there is still some shrinking after the chromic has been reduced to $\frac{1}{2}$ per cent, strengthen the acetic. For most fern prothallia, the stock solution, with the addition of 2 c.c. of glacial acetic acid to 100 c.c. of the solution, is satisfactory for material to be mounted whole, and also for sections. A combination may be quite satisfactory for fern prothallia and still fail to give good results with *Spirogyra*, and a combination which is excellent for *Spirogyra* may fail utterly with *Vaucheria*. For critical work the most favorable proportions must be determined for the particular object under observation. In observing the effect of the fixing one can determine whether there is any noticeable plasmolysis or distortion, but whether the fixing is thorough can be determined only by noting how the tissues endure the subsequent processes. When the effect of the reagent cannot be observed directly, it is well to make a freehand section and thus determine whether plasmolysis takes place. It is not safe to judge the action of a fixing agent by the appearance of sections cut from material which has been imbedded in paraffin, because shrinking of the cell contents often takes place during the transfer from absolute alcohol to the clearing agent or during infiltration with paraffin, and sometimes even during later processes. When there is doubt as to proportions, we should suggest 2 g. chromic acid, 3 c.c. acetic acid, and 300 c.c. water as a good formula for most purposes.

A large quantity of the fixing agent is required and it cannot be used again. The volume of the fixing agent should be at least 25 times that of the material to be fixed. We use about 50 volumes of the fixing agents to one of the material.

The time required for fixing undoubtedly varies with different objects, but even a delicate object, like *Spirogyra*, which is penetrated immediately, should remain in the fixing fluid for from 18 to 24 hours. Most botanists leave material like onion root-tips and lily ovaries in the chromo-acetic acid about 24 hours. Two days, or even 3 or 4 days, does no damage, and we should prefer 48 hours rather than to use less than 24 hours.

Christman, in his work on rusts, left material for three days in Flemming's fluid, a much more vigorous agent than the chromo-acetic acid. We have often imbedded material which had been in chromo-acetic acid for several days, and it seemed to have suffered no injury. It is well known that zoölogists allow fixing agents like Müller's fluid and Erlicki's fluid to act for weeks before the material is passed on to the next stage, and it may well be questioned whether botanists have not made a mistake in allowing the chromic solutions to act for so short a time. More rapid penetration, and consequently more immediate killing, can be secured if the reagent is kept warm (30°–40° C.). The warming also shortens the time required for fixing, but, for cytological work, it is quite possible that the danger of producing artifacts may be increased by the heat.

After fixing is complete, all reagents containing chromic acid as an ingredient should be washed out with water. Running water is desirable, and where this is not convenient the water must be changed frequently.

About 24 hours is long enough for complete washing in running water. Shorter periods may be sufficient for some things, but 24 hours will not do any damage even to the most delicate objects, and a shorter time may be insufficient.

Heavy objects which sink promptly may be placed in a Stender dish or wide-necked bottle under a gentle stream of water. There is little

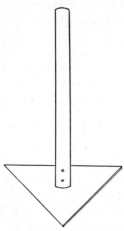

danger in this method if the material is heavy enough to remain at the bottom: the only objection is that much of the water does not reach the bottom. Here is a better method: tie a piece of cheesecloth over the neck of a bottle; slip over the water tap a rubber tube with a piece of glass tube tied in the end, and slip the glass tube through the cheesecloth nearly down to the bottom of the bottle. The washing will then be very thorough. A method devised by Dr. Dudgeon is simple and very efficient, especially for delicate materia or objects which have a tendency to float. A glass tube, 1 inch in diameter, is cut into pieces $2\frac{1}{2}$ inches in length. The glass is then heated to round off the sharp edges and, while the glass is still very hot, one end is flared a little, so that a piece of cloth can be tied over or fastened over it with a rubber band. Bolting cloth or bolting silk is best because water passes through it so readily. For flaring the ends of the tubes a triangular piece of copper $\frac{1}{16}$ inch thick is very convenient (Fig. 13). Heat the copper, cut the edges into a cake of beeswax, and turn the instrument around a little in the end of the hot glass tube. Any number of these tubes can be placed in a jar without any danger of losing material.

FIG. 13.—Instrument for flaring glass tubes.

Another method which we have found satisfactory is to put the material into a tea filter, which can be got at the five-and-ten-cent store. This is good for everything except filamentous forms which stick in the little holes. Any number of the tea filters can be placed in a jar and washed from a single water tap.

Here is still another method: take a box about 6 inches wide, 18 inches long, and 4 inches deep; bore $\frac{3}{8}$-inch holes in the bottom, and into each hole put a piece of rubber tubing about 4 or 5 inches in length. Pipettes can be fastened in the ends of these rubber tubes. Place the box under the tap. In the botanical laboratory at Woods Hole, Massachusetts, large quantities of material are washed at one time by using an ordinary washtub with the bottom arranged as just described for the box. If one is using such a large box or tub and does not need all the streams of water, the tubes not in use may be closed by means of clamps.

Where running water is not available we should recommend the washtub, as just now described. The tub could be filled, and, with a single lot of material, would run for 10 or 12 hours.

With delicate filamentous or branching algae and fungi, extreme care must be taken in the washing, for the material must not get tangled. Put some material—not too much—in a large Petri dish, propped up on an inverted dish and tilted just enough to let the water

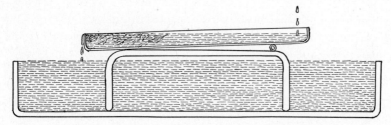

Fig. 14.—Washing delicate filamentous and branched material

run off gently. As a precaution, the supporting dish may be placed in a larger dish (Fig. 14). The stream of water should be from a pipette fastened in the end of the rubber which has been slipped over the water faucet. Drops of water are even better than a small stream. Although some objects might be washed in 10 or 12 hours, it is better to wash for 24 hours. Nothing would be damaged by the longer time and subsequent processes, especially staining, might be improved.

Everyone has his own chromo-acetic acid formulas. Some of those in more general use are the following:

a) **Stock chromo-acetic solution.**—
Chromic acid................................. 1 g.
Glacial acetic acid........................... 1 c.c.
Water....................................... 100 c.c.

This solution has been used quite extensively in embryological work upon the higher plants. It fixes thoroughly, but often causes plasmolysis in cells with large vacuoles.

b) **Weak chromo-acetic solution** (Shaffner's formula).—

Chromic acid............................... 0.3 g.
Acetic acid................................. 0.7 c.c.
Water...................................... 99.0 c.c.

This has also been used in embryological work. It causes little or no plasmolysis. Difficult material, like *Aster* heads and ripe *Capsella* pods, cuts more readily after this reagent than after the stronger solutions.

c) **Strong chromo-acetic solution.**—

Chromic acid............................... 1 g.
Glacial acetic acid......................... 3 c.c.
Water...................................... 100 c.c.

For fern prothallia, most liverworts, moss capsules before they have begun to get reddish or brownish, and most filamentous algae and fungi, this is a good fixing agent.

d) **Licent's formula.**—

One per cent chromic acid.................... 80 c.c.
Glacial acetic acid......................... 5 c.c.
Formalin................................... 15 c.c.

This formula has been recommended for coenocytic algae and fungi and for embryo sacs.

The most famous and, up to the present time, the most satisfactory of all the chromic mixtures, are the Flemming solutions or modifications of them. In his work on mitosis and upon the structure of protoplasm he used two solutions, commonly called the stronger and weaker solutions, which contained osmic acid in addition to the chromic and acetic acids. Various proportions of the three ingredients have been used by various investigators.

While the chromic and acetic acids may be made up in a stock solution, it should be remembered that the acetic acid will evaporate unless kept in a very tightly stoppered bottle. The osmic acid should be kept in a tightly stoppered bottle, always using a glass stopper, and the bottle should be completely covered with black paper. *The osmic acid must not be added to the other two ingredients until you are ready to drop the material into the fixing agent.*

e) **Flemming's fluid** (stronger solution).—

A $\begin{cases} \text{One per cent chromic acid.} \dots\dots\dots\dots \text{ 45 c.c.} \\ \text{Glacial acetic acid.} \dots\dots\dots\dots\dots \text{ 3 c.c.} \end{cases}$

B. Two per cent osmic acid. . . . . 12 c.c.

This formula has been very popular for cytological work, and has been highly recommended for chromosomes, centrosomes, achromatic structures, and mitotic phenomena in general. The fluid should be allowed to act for from 24 to 48 hours, and the washing should be very thorough.

Material should be in very small pieces ⅛ inch square, or in thin slices ⅛ inch or less in thickness, for the fluid penetrates poorly. The blackening due to the osmic acid may be removed by peroxide of hydrogen just before the slide is passed from the alcohol into the stain. Harper and Holden, in their work on *Coleosporium*, recommended 4 hours on the slide in a 3 per cent solution of the peroxide of hydrogen. Some prefer a stronger solution of the peroxide of hydrogen, even 20 per cent. The peroxide should be in water, if one is following it by an aqueous stain, but may be in 50 per cent alcohol if it is to be followed by an alcoholic stain. Yamanouchi has used chlorine for bleaching, and the results are fully equal to those obtained with peroxide of hydrogen, and the chlorine is cheaper. Make the bleacher as follows: Place some potassium chlorate crystals—a group about as large as a grain of wheat—in the bottom of a 100 c.c. Stender dish; add one drop of 25 per cent hydrochloric acid in water; immediately fill the Stender full of 30 per cent alcohol and thus dissolve the fumes in alcohol. This will bleach sections in 10 minutes, or even less. Wash in 30 per cent alcohol 2 or 3 hours before staining. Tröndle uses 1 per cent chromic acid in water for bleaching; it is slow, requiring about 8 hours, but he maintains that material stains better than after bleaching with peroxide of hydrogen. According to Miss Merriman, the linin in the nuclei of onion root-tips is not so well preserved in this solution, but the arrangements of the chromatin granules is brought out with greater distinctness. Flemming's safranin, gentian violet, orange combination gives excellent results after this reagent.

f) **Flemming's fluid** (weaker solution).—

A $\begin{cases} \text{One per cent chromic acid.} \dots\dots\dots\dots \text{ 25 c.c.} \\ \text{One per cent acetic acid.} \dots\dots\dots\dots \text{ 10 c.c.} \\ \text{Water.} \dots\dots\dots\dots\dots\dots\dots\dots \text{ 55 c.c.} \end{cases}$

B. One per cent osmic acid. . . . . 10 c.c.

As in all solutions containing osmic acid, mix A and B only as needed for immediate use.

g) Benda's fluid.—

One per cent chromic acid	16 c.c.
Two per cent osmic acid	4 c.c.
Glacial acetic acid	2 drops

This modification of Flemming's stronger solution has been used in various investigations upon chromatin.

h) Merkel's fluid.—

Equal volumes of a 1.4 per cent solution of chromic acid and a 1.4 per cent solution of platinic chloride. This is also an expensive re-agent. It is recommended for mitotic phenomena, but does not seem to equal Flemming's solution.

i) Hermann's fluid.—

One per cent platinic chloride	15 parts
Glacial acetic acid	1 part
Two per cent osmic acid	4 or 2 parts

This is the most expensive fixing agent yet discovered, and for botanical purposes it does not seem to be any better than the cheaper chromic mixtures. It is mentioned here with chromic mixtures because it originated as a variation of Flemming's fluid, the platinic chloride being substituted for the chromic acid. Recently, it has been resurrected and highly recommended for the structure of the chromosome. Personally, I do not believe it is equal to Flemming's weaker solution; and, even in this weaker solution, the percentage of osmic acid may be too high.

j) Chicago formula.—

Chromic acid	1 g.
Glacial acetic acid	2 c.c.
One per cent osmic acid	6 to 8 c.c.
Water	90 c.c.

The osmic acid, of course, to be added immediately before using.

For a couple of years an extensive series of experiments has been carried on with root-tips of *Vicia faba*, *Allium cepa*, and especially with *Trillium erectum*. The stock chromo-acetic solution was tried with the addition of from 1 to 10 c.c. of 1 per cent osmic acid, fixing from 24 to 48 hours. While the solutions with the lower percentages of osmic acid fixed fairly well, they proved decidedly inferior in staining, especially with Haidenhain's iron-alum haematoxylin. Solutions with 9–10 c.c. of osmic acid are unnecessarily strong. The solution with 8 c.c. of osmic acid produces the best fixing, and the staining is brilliant, especially with Haidenhain's haematoxylin. For some things, especially algae, the chromic acid may be reduced and the osmic acid increased. Some suggestions are made in Part II, in connection with various objects.

PICRIC ACID

Use a saturated solution in water or 70 per cent alcohol. One gram of picric acid crystals will saturate about 75 c.c. of water or alcohol. This reagent penetrates well and does not make the material brittle. It is to be recommended when difficulty is anticipated in the cutting. If used cold, the time varies from 1 to 24 hours, depending upon the character of the tissue and size of the specimen. If used hot (85° C.), 5 or 10 minutes will be sufficient. This fixing agent is used rather extensively by zoölogists, especially for embryological work. Botanists have not given it fair trial. Since it seems worthless for mitotic figures, they have not made a thorough trial of it for other objects. It might be worth while to try it for embryo sacs, free nuclear stages in the female gametophytes of gymnosperms, and similar things for which satisfactory fixing has not yet been devised.

Material should be washed in 70 or 50 per cent alcohol. Water is injurious, and some even go so far as to avoid aqueous stains, unless the material has been thoroughly washed. The washing should be continued until the material appears whitish and the alcohol no longer becomes tinged with yellow. Picro-carmine gives its best results after this reagent. Picric acid can be combined with various other fixing agents, and so we have picro-sulphuric acid, picro-nitric acid, picro-chromic acid, picro-chromic-sulphuric acid, picro-osmic acid, picro-alcohol, and picro-corrosive sublimate. The picric acid in all mixtures should be rather strong.

A picric-acid combination which has gained some popularity for cytological work is

Bouin's fluid.—

> Formalin (commercial)........................ 25 c.c.
> Picric acid (saturated solution in water)......... 75 c.c.
> Glacial acetic acid........................... 5 c.c.

Fix about 24 hours. Rinse in water for a few minutes to remove the more superficial picric acid, and then complete the washing in 35 per cent or 50 per cent alcohol. There is likely to be some swelling, but spindles of mitotic figures stain well. The formula has given good results with early stages in the female gametophyte of *Pinus* and would be worth a trial with the embryo sacs of angiosperms.

CORROSIVE SUBLIMATE

Corrosive sublimate, or bichloride of mercury, is soluble in water and in alcohol. About 5 g. will make a saturated solution in 100 c.c. of water. It is very much more soluble in alcohol, but for practical purposes 5 g. in 100 c.c. of 50 per cent alcohol may be regarded as a favorable solution. Corrosive sublimate used alone does not give as good results as when mixed with acetic acid, chloroform, or picric acid. Fixing is very rapid, the material being fixed almost as soon as it is penetrated by the fluid. Material which is at all transparent, like some ovules and the endosperm of gymnosperms before the formation of starch, becomes opaque as soon as fixed, and so the time needed for fixing is easily determined. From 10 minutes to 30 minutes should be sufficient for onion root-tips or lily ovaries. Smaller or larger objects require shorter or longer periods. When used hot (85° C.), the fixing is much more rapid. While a few minutes' fixing may be sufficient, we let the reagent reach the boiling-point, then remove the flame, and just as soon as the bubbling ceases, put the material in and leave it until the liquid becomes cool. It may be left for 20 minutes, or even 30 minutes, without any damage.

Wash out aqueous solutions with water and alcoholic solutions with alcohol. In either case, the washing must be very thorough, since preparations from incompletely washed material are sure to be disfigured by crystals of corrosive sublimate. After material fixed in the aqueous solution has been washed in water for an hour, add a little of the iodine solution used in testing for starch. The liquid will turn brownish or amber-colored, and then clear up; add a little more, until the liquid fails to clear up completely, a very slight amber remaining for an hour or even permanently. After material fixed in the alcoholic solution has been washed in 50 per cent alcohol for an hour or more, add the iodine solution used in testing for starch or even add, drop by drop, tincture of iodine, until the color fails to disappear. With unicellular forms, filamentous forms, and thin things, like fern prothallia, such washing is likely to be sufficient, but with more bulky material which is to be sectioned, the crystals may appear in the paraffin ribbon. In such cases, the slide should be dipped for a minute in the iodine solution just before staining.

Camphor may be used instead of iodine to hasten the washing, but it does not give any color reaction.

Material should be imbedded as soon as possible, since it gets brittle if allowed to remain in alcohol.

Kinoplasmic structures do not stain well with gentian violet, but safranin and the haematoxylins stain almost as well as after chromic-acid mixtures, and the carmines give their most brilliant stains, as a result of the formation of mercuric carminate.

The following formulas are merely suggestive:

a) **Corrosive sublimate and acetic acid.—**

Corrosive sublimate.........................	3 g.
Glacial acetic acid..........................	5 c.c.
Alcohol (50 per cent) or water...............	100 c.c.

b) **Corrosive sublimate, acetic acid, and formalin.—**

Corrosive sublimate.........................	4 g.
Glacial acetic acid..........................	5 c.c.
Formalin...................................	5 c.c.
Alcohol (50 per cent) or water...............	100 c.c.

This is our favorite formula. For material which is to be mounted in glycerin, glycerin jelly, or Venetian turpentine, use the aqueous solution; for material which is to be imbedded, use the alcoholic. Cilia are caught and preserved; and even delicate organisms, like *Volvox*, do not collapse.

c) **Corrosive sublimate, acetic acid, and picric acid.—**

Corrosive sublimate.........................	5 g.
Glacial acetic acid..........................	5 c.c.
Picric acid, saturated solution in 50 per cent alcohol....................................	100 c.c.

Miss Ethel Thomas recommends this formula for the female gametophyte of *Pinus*.

d) **Corrosive sublimate and picric acid** (Jeffrey's solution).—

Corrosive sublimate, saturated solution in 30 per
cent alcohol............................... 3 parts

Picric acid, saturated solution in 30 per cent
alcohol.................................... 1 part

It would be worth while to try other combinations.

IODINE

Iodine is well known as an antiseptic. It is also a good fixing agent for unicellular, colonial, and filamentous forms. It penetrates rapidly.

To a saturated solution of potassium iodide in distilled water, add iodine to saturation. Filter and dilute with distilled water until the solution has a rich brown color. For fixing, dilute still further to a light-brown color. The solution fixes in 10–24 hours, but material may be left in it for several days. Wash thoroughly in tap water which has stood long enough to give off all excess of air. If the staining of the starch does not disappear, a $\frac{1}{2}$ per cent solution of tannic acid in water will remove any excess color.

FORMALIN

Formalin is an excellent preservative. It has been mentioned already as an ingredient in several formulas. Commercial formalin has a strength of 40 per cent. Throughout this book, a 2, 4, or 6 per cent formalin is understood to mean 2, 4, or 6 c.c. of commercial formalin to 98, 96, or 94 c.c. of water, alcohol or any other ingredient. Commercial formalin is sure to contain some formic acid. For most purposes, it is neither necessary nor desirable to remove the acid. For studying the origin of vacuoles, it is necessary to have neutral formalin, which can be secured from commercial formalin by distillation. Place some sodium bicarbonate in a flask of formalin and distil by heating over a Bunsen flame. It is not worth while to distil more than is needed for immediate use, since the formic acid soon reappears.

For filamentous algae and fungi a 3–6 per cent solution of the ordinary commercial formalin in water is very good. Material is left in the solution until needed for use. For marine algae, sea water should be used instead of fresh water. Both marine and fresh-water material should be washed for an hour in fresh water before staining. Material of *Polysiphonia*, left in a 12 per cent solution of formalin for 10 years, showed scarcely any shrinking of cell contents, the filaments were not breaking up, and even the color had scarcely faded.

A 6 per cent solution will fix one-fourth its volume of material. With material like filamentous algae or leafy liverworts, a 10 per cent solution will fix all one can put into the bottle without crowding.

For class use, material should be washed in water for several minutes, because the fumes are irritating to the eyes and mucous membranes.

For a study of chondriosomes or the origin of vacuoles, the following combination is satisfactory:

Bensley's formula.—

    1. Formalin (neutral) . . . . 10.0 c.c.
    2. Dichromate of potash . . . . 2.5 g.
    3. Corrosive sublimate . . . . 5.0 g.
    4. Water . . . . 90.0 c.c.

Make the solution 2, 3, 4, and then add the neutral formalin. Fix about 24 hours. Wash in water, but use the iodine—necessary on account of the corrosive sublimate—just before staining sections on the slide.

Yamanouchi's formula.—

    Formalin (neutral) . . . . 10 c.c.
    Water . . . . 100 c.c.

This simpler formula brings out the chondriosomes very clearly. Fix overnight or even 24 hours. A thorough washing is easy and staining is brilliant, especially with Haidenhains iron-alum haematoxylin.

GENERAL HINTS ON FIXING

Since it is desirable that a fixing agent penetrate quickly to all parts of an object, the material should be in small pieces.

The best fixing agents do their best work near the surface of the piece. Of course, filamentous algae and fungi, and delicate objects like fern prothallia and root-tips, are simply thrown into the fixing agent. Alcohol, formalin alcohol, or formalin alone may penetrate $\frac{1}{4}$-inch cubes; but the chromic-acid series, which gives the best results in cytological work, penetrates so poorly that cells more than $\frac{1}{16}$ inch from the surface are not likely to be well fixed. Most objects should be trimmed with a razor so that no part shall be more than $\frac{1}{16}$ inch from the surface. Even then, it must be remembered that a waxy or cutinized or suberized surface presents an almost impassable barrier to the chromic series.

Some objects, although small, cause trouble in various ways. Many buds are hairy and will not sink; if such things are dipped quickly in strong alcohol, they will usually sink. If rather large air bubbles prevent the material from sinking, as in case of perichaetical leaves of some mosses and involucral leaves of liverworts, a little dissection or a careful snip with the scissors will often obviate the difficulty. If an air-pump is available, some bubbles are easily removed, but air bubbles in cells may resist even the air-pump. An aspirator fastened to a water tap is very efficient in removing bubbles. Heating followed by rapid cooling is recommended by Pfeiffer and Wellheim for removing air, but, for cytological work, the remedy is worse than the bubbles.

It is often asked whether fixing agents really preserve the actual structure of cell contents. It must be admitted that some things— notably the liquid albuminoids—are much modified in appearance, but the most competent observers are now inclined to believe that such delicate objects as chromosomes, centrosomes, the achromatic figure, and even the structure of protoplasm, can be studied with confidence from material which has been fixed, imbedded, and stained. Extensive investigations upon various objects in the living condition have strengthened this confidence.

It is certain that we have not yet found the ideal fixing agent for cell contents. Such an agent must not be a solvent of any of the cell contents, must penetrate rapidly, must preserve structures perfectly, and must harden so thoroughly that every detail shall remain unchanged during the subsequent processes of dehydrating, clearing, imbedding, sectioning, and staining.

DEHYDRATING AGENTS

Objects which are to be imbedded in paraffin or celloidin, and also all other objects which are to be mounted in balsam or Venetian turpentine, must be dehydrated, i.e., they must be freed from water. The slightest trace of water is ruinous. Alcohol is used almost exclusively for dehydrating. The process must be gradual. If material has been fixed in an aqueous solution, it must pass through a series of alcohols of increasing strength, beginning with about 3 per cent alcohol. Twenty years ago, most botanists were beginning with 35 per cent alcohol; in the second edition of this book (1905) we recommended 15, 35, 50, 70, 85, 95, and 100 per cent as a safe series, since it causes no obvious plasmolysis of the cell contents. As investigations have become more and more critical, especially investigations upon the structure of chromatin, it has been found that even 15 per cent alcohol is too strong for a beginning. It is maintained that, in addition to the damage done by transferring from water to so strong an alcohol, the final dehydration is not so perfect as it is when the series begins with a weaker alcohol. Yamanouchi, whose work upon delicate algae has been particularly successful, uses the following series: $2\frac{1}{2}$, 5, $7\frac{1}{2}$,10, 15, 20, 30, 40, 50, 70, 85, 95, and 100 per cent. After such gradual early stages, there seems to be no objection to the less gradual stages which follow. Of course, there is no particular virtue in the fractions: it is convenient to make a 10 per cent alcohol, then dilute it one-half for the 5 per cent, and dilute the 5 per cent one-half for the $2\frac{1}{2}$ per cent. The $7\frac{1}{2}$ per cent is made with sufficient accuracy by adding a little water to the 10 per cent alcohol.

It is not safe to suggest minimum times for each grade of alcohol. One might as well recognize that in histological technique speed and excellence seldom go together. For the first six grades, three grades a day, morning, noon, and evening, seem to be safe: for 30, 40, 50 and 70, two grades, morning and evening; 85, for 24 hours, changing the alcohol 2 or 3 times, since this is the best place for hardening; 95, for 24 hours; for the absolute alcohol, 24 hours, with 2 or 3 changes, should complete the dehydration.

If pieces are larger than $\frac{1}{4}$-inch cubes, the times should be longer.

In all cases, the absolute alcohol should be changed 2 or 3 times. The grades below 85 per cent can be used repeatedly. The absolute alcohol should not be used again for this purpose, but may be put back into the 95 per cent bottle. It is always well to filter the alcohols when pouring back into the bottle. Otherwise, there would soon be an accumulation of starch grains, pollen grains, spores, and various other things. Waste alcohol as strong as 85 or 95 per cent will be useful for rinsing one's hands when dealing with Venetian turpentine. If it is necessary to be very economical, the stronger alcohols may be filtered into a single large bottle and the strength of the mixture can then be determined by using an alcoholometer. Knowing the strength of the mixture, one can easily make any weaker grade.

Be very sure that bottles or Stenders for absolute alcohol are perfectly dry; also, keep the bottles well corked and keep the lids on the Stenders. The importance of excluding moisture cannot be exaggerated. Tightly fitting corks and closely fitting covers are better than absorbents; prevention is better than cure.

The lower grades are made up from 95 per cent alcohol.

Formulas for alcohols —The following formulas will enable anyone to make the other grades of alcohol from 95 per cent alcohol and water.

95	95	95	95	95	95	95	95	95
10	15	20	30	40	50	60	70	85
85	80	75	65	55	45	35	25	10

The foregoing are the formulas for various alcohols from 10 to 85 per cent. The first column shows the formula for making 10 per cent alcohol. The percentage of alcohol secured in each case is indicated by the middle number in each column. In the first formula, subtract 10 from 95; the result, 85, is the number of cubic centimeters of water which must be added to 10 c.c. of 95 per cent alcohol in order to obtain 10 per cent alcohol. The mixture contains 95 c.c. of 10 per cent alcohol. If more or less than 95 c.c. of the mixture is needed, take proportional parts of 10 and 85. This simple method is a time-saver, but if the bottles or Stender dishes are to be filled frequently, it will be a still further saving of time to use a long label (Fig. 15) and, after pouring in the 95 per cent alcohol, draw a line showing how high it reaches; and then, after pouring in the water, draw another line. The next time it is necessary to fill the bottles merely pour in 95 per cent alcohol until it reaches the first line, and then pour in water until it reaches the second line. It is not necessary to use distilled water if pure drinking-water is available.

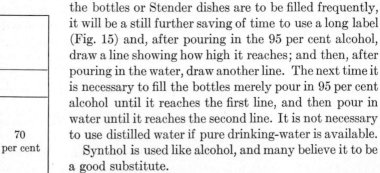

FIG. 15.—
Label for stain-
ing-dish.

Synthol is used like alcohol, and many believe it to be a good substitute.

Acetone has also been used with more or less success for all grades except absolute alcohol.

Some investigators use more or less complicated diffusion apparatus and make the dehydration process extremely gradual. Judging from the finished preparation, we find no advantage in the method. In the diffusion process, the solution is constantly changing. This may not be an advantage.

Some very minute objects, like bacteria and the smaller Cyano-phyceae, may be dehydrated by heating them until all water is drawn off, but, of course, this shows merely the form, with little or nothing of the internal structure.

CLEARING AGENTS

Clearing agents are so named because they render objects transparent. When clearing agents are used to precede infiltration with paraffin, the clearing is merely incidental, the real purpose being to replace the dehydrating agent with a solvent of paraffin. The clearing is useful, even in this case, because it indicates when the replacing has become complete.

When the clearing agent is used to precede infiltration with paraffin, the material should always be most thoroughly dehydrated with absolute alcohol before beginning with the clearing agent. When the clearing agent is used to clear sections or small objects just before mounting in balsam, absolutely perfect dehydration is not necessary with all clearing agents. Bergamot oil, carbolic acid, and Eycleshymer's clearing fluid (equal parts of bergamot oil, carbolic acid, and cedar oil) will clear readily from 95 per cent alcohol. Sections to be cleared in xylol or clove oil should be dehydrated in "absolute" alcohol. If the absolute alcohol is below 99 per cent, xylol will not clear perfectly; but clove oil clears readily from 99 per cent. If the absolute alcohol is not up to 99 per cent it is a good practice to go from the alcohol to clove oil; and then, from clove oil to xylol.

Water may be removed by distilling or by putting a "drier" into the alcohol. Put some calcined copper sulphate into the bottle of "absolute" alcohol, shake, and allow to stand for 24 hours. Then pour off and add fresh copper sulphate, shake, and repeat the operation until the fresh copper sulphate no longer gets conspicuously blue when put into the alcohol. When the alcohol can be mixed with xylol without becoming milky, it may be called absolute alcohol.

Some put a little calcium sulphate into the "absolute" alcohol and keep it there, pouring off the alcohol very gently as it is needed.

By any of these methods, 99 per cent alcohol can be brought up to usable absolute alcohol. Distilling, followed by a drier, will bring 95 per cent alcohol up to a usable absolute alcohol.

Xylol.—In our opinion, xylol is the best clearing agent to precede infiltration with paraffin. After the material has been dehydrated, it should be brought gradually into xylol. Thirty years ago it was customary to bring material directly from absolute alcohol into xylol; twenty years ago, two or three mixtures of absolute alcohol and xylol were used before reaching the pure xylol; at present, those who are doing the most critical work are making this process still more gradual. As cytologists have been studying more and more minute structures, the methods have become more and more critical. As in the case of the alcohol series, the xylol series has its grades closer together at the beginning than at the end. The following series seems to be sufficiently gradual: $\frac{1}{16}$, $\frac{1}{8}$, $\frac{1}{4}$, $\frac{1}{2}$, $\frac{3}{4}$, pure xylol. It is hardly necessary to use a graduate in making up the series. For the $\frac{1}{2}$, use equal parts of xylol and absolute alcohol; for the $\frac{1}{4}$, use equal parts of the $\frac{1}{2}$ and absolute alcohol; for the $\frac{1}{8}$, use equal parts of the $\frac{1}{4}$ and absolute, and for the $\frac{1}{16}$, equal parts of the $\frac{1}{8}$ and absolute. The $\frac{3}{4}$ can be guessed at with sufficient accuracy.

We prefer a closer series of xylols, using $2\frac{1}{2}$, 5, $7\frac{1}{2}$, 10, 15, 20, 30, 40, 50, 75, and 100 per cent. Infiltration with paraffin is more thorough with this closer series. We use it and recommend it. Three grades a day, morning, noon, and night, will do for filamentous algae and fungi, fern prothallia, onion root-tips, and similar objects. For larger pieces the times should be longer. For $\frac{1}{4}$-inch cubes, change morning and evening. For still larger pieces, 24 hours in each grade is not too long. In all cases, the pure xylol should be changed 2 or 3 times. While the pure xylol must not be used again for this purpose, it is still good for dissolving paraffin ribbons when staining on the slide.

Xylol is the best agent for clearing sections just before mounting in balsam. Preparations cleared in xylol harden more rapidly, and this is such a decided advantage that even when sections have been cleared in cedar oil or clove oil it is worth while to give them a minute or two in xylol before mounting. Besides, clove oil is a solvent of many of the most frequently used stains and, consequently, preparations in such stains would fade, if transferred directly from clove oil to balsam.

Xylol evaporates so rapidly that one must take care not to let sections become dry before applying the balsam. Thin sections perfectly dehydrated seem to clear in a few seconds; but, even with very thin sections, it is better to let the xylol act for at least a minute. Sections $20\,\mu$ in thickness should remain in the xylol 5 minutes before mounting in balsam. If there is much moisture in the air, or if the absolute alcohol is not above suspicion, clear sections in clove oil before transferring to xylol.

Chloroform.—Some botanists use chloroform to precede the infiltration with paraffin. In the later stages of infiltration it is more easily removed than xylol. It seems to possess no other advantages, and for clearing sections just before mounting in balsam it is inferior to xylol or clove oil. Its value in hardening celloidin and as a fixing agent entitles it to a place in the histological laboratory.

Cedar oil.—It is not always easy to get good cedar oil. If the stuff offered for sale looks like turpentine and smells like it, it is worthless for histological purposes. Good cedar oil has a slightly amber tint, the color resembling a weak clove oil. It should have the pleasant odor of cedar wood. The very expensive cedar oil used with immersion lenses is not needed for clearing or for preceding infiltration with paraffin. It is claimed that material cleared in cedar oil does not become so brittle as that cleared in xylol or chloroform.

Dr. E. J. Kraus has used cedar oil extensively in clearing large objects—strawberries and gooseberries either whole or cut in two, sections of apple 2 to 4 mm. thick, and similar objects. This method is proving valuable in vascular anatomy, some material showing the course of bundles very clearly in pieces so large as centimeter cubes.

Xylol can be used in the same way, but is so volatile that specimens often dry up. Dr. Land suggests equal parts of xylol and carbon disulphide for clearing large objects which are to be examined without sectioning.

Clove oil.—This is an excellent agent for clearing sections and small objects just before mounting in balsam. It clears more readily than xylol. When the absolute alcohol has deteriorated so that xylol no longer clears the sections, clove oil may still clear with ease. While clove oil will clear from 95 per cent alcohol, it is better to use absolute. Since preparations cleared in clove oil harden slowly, it is a good plan to treat them with xylol before mounting in balsam. Gentian violet is somewhat soluble in clove oil, and this fact makes it possible to secure a beautiful differentiation, because the stain is extracted from some elements more rapidly than from others. The stain may be extracted completely from the chromosomes during the metaphase and still remain bright in the achromatic structures. After the desired differentiation has been attained, the preparation should be placed in xylol to remove the clove oil, since the continued action of the clove oil would cause the preparation to fade. Do not use a Stender dish for clove oil, but keep it in a 50 c.c. bottle. Put on a few drops, and immediately drain them off in such a way as to remove the alcohol as completely as possible. Then flood the slide and pour the clove oil back into the bottle, repeating the process until the proper differentiation has been reached. Replace the clove oil with xylol and mount in balsam. With stains not soluble in clove oil, the xylol is not necessary, except to facilitate the hardening of the preparation.

Clove oil may be used in removing the celloidin matrix from celloidin sections. It is useless as an agent to precede infiltration with paraffin.

Eycleshymer's clearing fluid.—This is a mixture of equal parts of bergamot oil, cedar oil, and carbolic acid. It clears readily from 95 per cent alcohol, and consequently is useful in clearing celloidin sections when it is desirable to preserve the celloidin matrix. In sections stained with haematoxylin, or haematoxylin and eosin, the stain may be removed completely from the matrix by the use of acid alcohol, and the matrix may be preserved by clearing from 95 per cent alcohol.

It is not intended that the mixture should be used to precede infiltration with paraffin.

Other clearing agents.—Bergamot oil, carbolic acid, turpentine, benzine, gasoline, and other reagents have been tried for clearing, but none seem to be worth more than a warning mention.

MISCELLANEOUS REAGENTS

Canada balsam is used almost exclusively for mounting. Very thick balsam is disagreeable to handle and makes unsatisfactory mounts. Very thin balsam, in drying out, allows bubbles to run under the cover. Xylol is cheaper than balsam, and consequently the balsam on the market is likely to be too thin for immediate use. The stopper may be left out until the balsam acquires the proper consistency. Balsam must not be acid. If there is the slightest acid reaction, most stains will fade.

Paraffin should be of at least two grades, a soft paraffin melting at 40° to 45° C., and a hard paraffin melting at 52° to 54° C. Grübler's paraffin and most imported paraffins melt at the temperature indicated on the wrappers. The melting-point indicated on the wrappers of paraffins sold by some American dealers does not enable one to make even a guess as to the real melting-point. Paraffin marked 70° C. may melt at 60° C., and other grades are likely to melt before the temperature indicated on the labels is reached. The fact that the price rises with the melting-point may explain the discrepancy. Test every grade with a thermometer. If it is desired to get a paraffin melting at 52° C. and your sample melts at 50° C., add a little paraffin with a melting-point above 52° C.; if the sample melts at 55° C., add a little with a melting-point below 52° C.

Grübler's paraffins need no modification, but paraffins only slightly inferior can be improved by the addition of bayberry wax. A piece of the wax, not larger than a grain of corn, to a pound of paraffin, is likely to improve the infiltration and cutting.

Paraffin may be used repeatedly. Keeping it in the liquid condition in the bath month after month has an advantage, since it becomes more and more tenacious and homogeneous.

Glycerin, glycerin jelly, Venetian turpentine, and gold size are described in the chapter on "The Glycerin Method" (chap. vii). Celloidin is described in the chapter on "The Celloidin Method" (chap. x), and cellulose acetate in the chapter on "The Cellulose Acetate Method" (chap. xi). The reagents already described are noted further in connection with specific applications. Reagents used in making microchemical tests are described in the chapter on "Temporary Mounts and Microchemical Tests" (chap. v).

A list of reagents will be found in chapter xxxi.

Cleaning fluid.—No matter how nice they may look and no matter what dealers may claim, slides and covers, as you buy them, are *never* clean. This is a good cleaning fluid:

Potassium dichromate	2 g.
Water	10 c.c.
Sulphuric acid	23 cc..

Dissolve the potassium dichromate in water and add the sulphuric acid.

For cleaning slides and covers, this solution may be diluted 25 or even 50 times with water.

Leave slides and covers in the solution for 24 hours, rinse thoroughly in water, and then put them into soapy water and leave them overnight or 24 hours. Rinse thoroughly and wipe dry. If the least trace of acid is left, many stains will fade.

For developing trays and most kinds of laboratory glassware, the solution can be used, full strength, for a few minutes or an hour.

The solution can be used repeatedly.

CHAPTER III

STAINS AND STAINING

As edition after edition of this book has appeared, there has been a decrease rather than an increase in the number of stains in general use; but there has been a notable improvement in the use of some stains which have long been popular. For cytological work Haidenhain's iron-haematoxylin holds more firmly than ever its place at the head of the list, with Flemming's triple stain an easy second.

For anatomical work, safranin still holds first place for the lignified elements of the vascular system, but the claim of Delafield's haematoxylin to first place for cellulose tissues is no longer undisputed, for anilin blue is giving excellent results and light green seems to give more accurate views of the phloem than we were securing with any of the other stains. However, it must be admitted that preparations of coniferous woods, stained in safranin and Delafield's haematoxylin by Thomson and his students at the Toronto laboratory, have not been surpassed.

The fact that excellent preparations can be made, almost without trial, by using combinations already perfected doubtless deters investigators from experimenting with other stains. There is still abundant room for experimenting with various stains, especially in the use of mordants and in the effect of the same stain or combination after various fixing agents. It is to be regretted that botanists who need microtechnique have so little knowledge of chemistry, and that chemists have no interest in developing methods of staining. During the past few years, American stains have been developed until many equal and some even surpass the famous Grübler products; and, besides, the American stains are becoming standardized. The Commission on Standardization of Biological Stains, and especially its able president, Dr. H. J. Conn, cannot be too highly commended for the great improvement in American stains. The first standardized stain, methylene blue, was put on the market in the summer of 1923 and, before the end of the year, safranin was added. By the end of 1929, forty-three stains had been certified. The certification means that the stain has passed spectrophotometric tests, has been tested chemically, and has been tried in actual practice. The advantage to the one who uses stains is that, when he finds a certified stain which is satisfactory, he can always get exactly the same stain again.

The earlier stains, even the Grübler stains, were merely textile dyes, usually more or less modified. A student once asked Professor W. J. G. Land what was the difference between gentian violet and crystal violet, and received the reply, "Gentian violet is crystal violet plus mud." Textile dyes were often weakened or adulterated. *Biological Stains*, an excellent book by Dr. Conn, gives not only an account of the work of the commission but also an interesting history of stains and staining.

Stains may be classified in various ways: e.g., there are three great groups of stains—the carmines, the haematoxylins, and the anilins. Stains may be classified as basic and acid, or they may be regarded as general and specific. A general stain affects all the elements, while a specific stain affects only certain elements, or stains some elements more deeply than others. Stains which show a vigorous affinity for the nucleus have been called "nuclear stains," and those which affect the cytoplasm more than the nucleus have been termed "plasma stains."

Of course, such stains are specific.

We shall consider some of the more important haematoxylins, carmines, and anilins, reserving general directions and theoretical questions for another chapter. The formulas are largely empirical. Some of those given here are taken from *The Microtomist's Vade-Mecum* (Lee), which is easily the most complete compendium of stains and other reagents concerned in microtechnique. *Biological Stains*, although not covering so much ground, is, in many respects, superior, and the formulas are for the standardized stains.

Other formulas are from *Botanical Microtechnique* (Zimmermann) and from Stirling's *Histology*, and still others are from current literature and from our own laboratory. The directions for using a stain apply to stains made up according to the formulas which are given here, and may need modification if other formulas are employed. It is hoped, however, that the directions will give the student sufficient insight into the *rationale* of staining to enable him to make any necessary modifications. Since American stains have come into general use, the need for *rationale* is even greater, especially if the American stains are made up according to standard formulas, which are based largely upon the Grübler products. In general, it would seem that the American stains are purer and that they act more rapidly.

The current practice in staining paraffin sections on the slide differs from the practice in staining freehand sections or small objects which are to be mounted whole. In case of paraffin sections, the cell contents are usually as important and often more important than the cell walls; consequently, extreme care must be given to every detail. With freehand sections the cell contents often drop out, but even when they remain, the cell walls are usually the important features; and so the process is considerably shortened.

For staining freehand sections, it is customary to use solid watch glasses, unless the sections are very large. The details of the method are given in chapter vi, on "Freehand Sections."

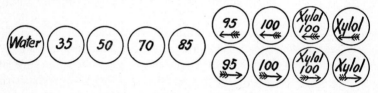

FIG. 16.—Arrangement of staining-dishes

For staining sections on the slide, nothing is better than the ordinary Stender dish. The arrangement of Stender dishes shown in Figure 16 is very convenient. The advantage is obvious. With two dishes each of xylol, xylol-alcohol, absolute alcohol, and 95 per cent alcohol, one set can be used in passing down to the stain, and the other, which is thus kept free from any paraffin in solution, can be used in passing back to the balsam. Even for paraffin sections, some use only three alcohols, 50, 95, and 100 per cent, and the first two may be simply poured over the slide; in this case, only one Stender dish—for the 100 per cent alcohol—is necessary in the alcohol series, the other two alcohols being kept in bottles. This short method gained great popularity because it was used in Strasburger's laboratory at Bonn. It was the influence of this school and its great master which led to the adoption of the short schedule in the second edition of this book. A few years' trial showed the weakness of the method, and we returned to the longer schedule. The crudeness of the short schedule is doubtless responsible for the tenacity with which the Bonn school has clung to the theory of linin and chromomeres. The young investigator should be warned that during the last twenty years of his life, Strasburger, who had been a leader in technique, cut very few sections and did practically no staining, but used preparations made by assistants. Let us now consider a few of the most important stains.

THE HAEMATOXYLINS

The most important haematoxylins are Heidenhain's iron-alum haematoxylin, Delafield's haematoxylin, Mayer's haem-alum, and Boehmer's haematoxylin.

All the haematoxylins mentioned contain alum, and, according to Mayer, who has written the most important work on haematoxylin stains,[1] "the active agent in them is a compound of haematin with alumina. This salt is precipitated in the tissues, chiefly in the nuclei, by organic and inorganic salts there present (e.g., by the phosphates), and perhaps also by other organic bodies belonging to the tissues." These salts are fixed in the tissues by the killing and fixing agent, and when the stain is applied a chemical combination results.

The first American haematoxylin was not satisfactory. It was dark and did not stain well. Manufacturers bleached it, but that made the staining worse. They then made a darker, but better, product. If crystals are dark colored, feel sticky when rubbed between the fingers, and go into solution quickly, the stain is not likely to be satisfactory. Crystals of a light yellowish sand color, dissolving slowly and requiring about six weeks to ripen, are much better. Haematoxylins stain well after any of the fixing agents described in the preceding chapter, but they are most effective when used after members of the chromic-acid series.

Heidenhain's iron-alum haematoxylin.—This stain, introduced by Heidenhain in 1892, immediately gained great popularity and now, after more than 40 years' constant use, still maintains first place in cytological investigations. Two solutions are used, and they are never mixed:

A. Four per cent aqueous solution of ammonia sulphate of iron.

B. One-half per cent aqueous solution of haematoxylin.

In making solution A, use the violet ferric crystals, not the ferrous. The first solution acts as a mordant, i.e., it does not stain, but pre-

---

[1] "Ueber das Färben mit Hämatoxylin," *Mittheilungen aus der Zoologischen Station zu Neapel,* **10**:170–186, 1891, and "Ueber Hämatoxylin, Carmin und verwandte Materien," *Zeitschrift für wissenschaftliche Mikroscopie,* **16**:196–220, 1899.

pares the tissue for the action of the second solution. It is better to make a 4 per cent solution and dilute it when a 2 per cent or weaker solution is needed. The bottles and also the Stender dishes containing the ammonia sulphate of iron nearly always become coated with a yellowish film of iron oxide. This film also forms on sections or on material to be mounted whole, but is so thin that it would be overlooked unless one compared the sections with others without any film, just as ordinary glass looks all right unless you compare it with fine cut glass. This film forms only when the temperature of the fluid rises above 18° C. So, keep the solution below 18° C. while using it.

Solution A is at its best as soon as the crystals are completely dissolved and it remains in practically perfect condition for about two months, after which it gradually deteriorates.

The haematoxylin crystals for solution B should be dissolved in distilled water. This will require about 10 days, during which time the bottle should be shaken often and vigorously. The solution must then be allowed to ripen for a month before it is ready for use. During the ripening, which is an oxidation process, a cotton plug should be used instead of a cork, to facilitate the oxidation; but as soon as the stain is ripe, a cork—preferably a closefitting glass stopper—will prolong the maximum efficiency. If kept in a cool place, away from strong light and kept *quiet*, the stain may retain its efficiency for six months. When needed, pour out *very gently*. The same solution, on a table in the laboratory, poured out as one pours other stains, would lose its efficiency in less than a month. As soon as the rich wine color begins to disappear, the solution is worthless. Some prefer to dissolve the haematoxylin crystals in alcohol—about 10 g. in 100 c.c. of absolute alcohol. This solution should stand until it has a deep wine-red color. This will require 4 or 5 months, and a year is not too long. From this stock solution, make up small quantities as needed. About 4 or 5 c.c. of this stock solution in 100 c.c. of water gives a practically aqueous solution, and it is already ripe.

The general method is as follows: treat with A, stain in B, and then return to A to reduce and differentiate the stain. Never transfer directly from A to B, or from B to A; always wash in water before passing from one of the solutions to the other.

While all follow the general method just indicated, no two investigators would prepare exactly the same schedule, even for staining the same object, e.g., root-tips; neither investigator would use the same schedule for a root-tip and an embryo sac; an alga might require different treatment, and all the preceding variations might fail miserably with the pollen tubes of cycads. This stain is so important that every worker must learn it, and the only way to learn it is to become acquainted with the general outline of the process and then adapt every step to the case in hand.

For the sake of illustration, I asked a prominent cytologist, Dr. S. Yamanouchi, who has been notably successful in staining mitotic figures, to write a schedule indicating his methods of using this stain. While he protested that the practice could not be written down, he kindly prepared the following schedule, not for the instruction of his colleagues, but to introduce the method to beginners. The schedule is for paraffin sections. Throughout the schedule, I have interpolated comments and suggestions.

Yamanouchi's schedule.—

1. Xylol, 5 minutes, to dissolve the paraffin.

    Do not heat the slides to melt the paraffin. However, a gentle warming which does not approach the melting-point of the paraffin does no damage and makes the paraffin dissolve more readily. The xylol soon has considerable paraffin in solution, but 100 c.c. of xylol should remove the paraffin from at least 100 slides with ribbons 25 mm. long and 10 μ thick. If the ribbons are only 5 μ thick, 200 slides can be treated.

2. Xylol and absolute alcohol, equal parts, 5 minutes.

3. Absolute alcohol, 5–7 minutes.

4. Ninety-five, 85, 70, 50, and 35 per cent alcohol, 5 minutes each.

    If material has been fixed in a reagent containing osmic acid, it should be bleached. For this purpose, 10–15 c.c. of hydrogen peroxide may be added to 100 c.c. of the 50 per cent alcohol, where the slides should remain until the blackening disappears.

5. Water, 10–20 minutes.

    If any alcohol is left in the sections, the staining will not be brilliant. Change the water several times.

6. Iron-alum.

    Use the 4 per cent solution. For many objects, like the archegonia of gymnosperms and the embryo sacs of angiosperms, 1 hour is usually enough. For chromosomes in root-tips and anthers, 2 hours may be long enough; but for algae, 2 hours is generally a minimum.

7. Wash in water, 5 minutes.

    The water should be changed several times. If the washing is not thorough, the differentiation will not be sharp.

8. Haematoxylin.

Many objects, like the archegonia of gymnosperms and the embryo sacs of angiosperms, will stain sufficiently in 5 or 6 hours; most algae require at least 20 hours.

9. Wash in water, 5 minutes, changing as often as the water shows any color.
10. Iron-alum, 2 per cent solution.

No time can be indicated here. The preparation must be watched under the microscope. After some experience, one can form some judgment from the color tone, as the slide stands in the Stender dish of iron-alum, but the finishing must always be done under the microscope. In general, if it requires more than 2 hours to secure good differentiation, use a stronger iron-alum; if the differentiation is reached in less than $\frac{1}{2}$ hour, use a weaker iron-alum. A 3μ section of a root-tip from material fixed in chromo-acetic–osmic acid, with 8 c.c. of 1 per cent osmic acid to 100 c.c. of the stock solution, should be perfectly differentiated in 2 hours. If the stain comes out too rapidly, use 2 per cent iron-alum for an hour and finish in a 1 per cent solution. The less the proportion of osmic acid, the faster will the stain be extracted. If the stain is coming out rather slowly, as it should, one can handle from 6 to 10 slides at one time. Put the slides on a 5×7 glass plate and put the plate on the stage of the microscope. The iron-alum can be added or removed with a pipette. As slide after slide reaches the proper differentiation, it is placed in water.

11. Water, 30 minutes.

The water should be changed several times. If this washing is not thorough, the preparation will fade, on account of the continued action of the iron-alum. If an aqueous counter-stain is used, apply it at this point.

12. Thirty-five, 50, 70, 85, 95, and 100 per cent alcohol, 5 minutes in each.

If an alcoholic counter-stain is used, apply it near the alcohol of the same strength as the stain.

13. Absolute alcohol and xylol, equal parts, 5 minutes.
14. Xylol, 2–5 minutes.
15. Balsam.

While this schedule should enable the student to apply the method not only to sections but to objects to be mounted whole, like filamentous algae and fern prothallia, an additional schedule for such things is given in chapter viii on "The Venetian Turpentine Method."

The times given above must not be accepted as final. Many prefer to wash 3 or 4 times as long after the first immersion in iron-alum. Some think that 4 hours is enough for the entire process. In staining with iron-alum haematoxylin for protoplasmic connections, 24 hours in 4 per cent iron-alum, with 1 or 2 minutes washing in water, 2 days in haematoxylin, 5 minutes washing in water, and 1 minute in 1 per cent iron-alum may be a good schedule to start with. The times must be determined for each case. Many put the slide into iron-alum in the morning and finish the process in the afternoon. These short schedules are not likely to prove satisfactory with mitotic figures. A plan which has proved convenient and very successful is to put the slide into the iron-alum in the morning, wash in water for an hour at some convenient time in the afternoon, leave it in the ½ per cent haematoxylin overnight, and finish the preparation the next morning. It is a long process, requiring care, patience, and judgment, but it is worth the effort.

Chromosomes, centrosomes, and pyrenoids take a brilliant black; or, if the second treatment with iron-alum be more prolonged, a blue black or purple. Achromatic structures stain purple, but the stain can be extracted while it is still bright in the chromosomes. Lignified, suberized, and cutinized structures stain lightly or not at all. Cellulose does not stain so deeply as with Delafield's haematoxylin. Archesporial cells and early stages in sporogenous tissue stain gray. Many details which are not so brilliantly colored often show good definition.

If a counter-stain is desired, anything which gives a serviceable contrast may be used. In any case, the haematoxylin stain must be complete and the washing thorough before the second stain is applied. An aqueous stain should be applied just after the final washing in water; an alcoholic stain should be applied during the process of passing the slides through the alcohols, staining in a solution of safranin in 50 per cent alcohol from the alcohol of a concentration nearest that of the stain; and staining after the final absolute alcohol, if the stain is dissolved in clove oil.

A stain of 3 or 4 minutes in safranin adds an excellent differentiation in case of many algae and does not obscure nuclear details. The exine of pollen grains may take a brilliant red with safranin in 5 or 10 minutes, contrasting sharply with the mouse gray of the intine. Orange G, in clove oil, often gives a pleasing contrast.

Delafield's haematoxylin.—"To 100 c.c. of a saturated solution of ammonia alum add, drop by drop, a solution of 1 g. of haematoxylin dissolved in 6 c.c. of absolute alcohol. Expose to air and light for one week. Filter. Add 25 c.c. of glycerin and 25 c.c. of methyl alcohol. Allow to stand until the color is sufficiently dark. Filter, and keep in a tightly stoppered bottle" (Stirling and Lee). The addition of the glycerin and methyl alcohol will precipitate some of the ammonia alum in the form of small crystals. The last filtering should take place 4 or 5 hours after the addition of the glycerin and methyl alcohol.

The solution should stand for at least 2 months before it is ready for using. This "ripening" is brought about by the oxidation of haematoxylin into haematin, a reaction which may be secured in a few minutes by a judicious application of peroxide of hydrogen. However, we prefer to let the haematoxylin ripen naturally. There is no objection to making this stain in considerable quantity, since it does not deteriorate. We have used Delafield's haematoxylin which had been in a cork-stoppered bottle for 20 years, and it still gave the rich characteristic stain.

Transfer to the stain from 50 or 35 per cent alcohol or from water. The length of time required is exceedingly variable. Sometimes sections will stain deeply in 3 minutes, but it is often necessary to stain for 30 minutes or even longer. This stain may be diluted with several times its own volume of water; when this is done, the time required is correspondingly long, but the staining is frequently more precise. The length of time required will be fairly uniform for all material taken from the same bottle. This fact indicates that the washing process, which follows killing and fixing, is an important factor; if the washing has been thorough, the material will stain readily; but if the washing has been insufficient, the material may stain slowly or not at all. The washing is particularly important when the fixing agent contains an acid. Transfer from the stain to tap water. Distilled water is neither necessary nor desirable. Some writers recommend washing for 24 hours, but this is entirely unnecessary; for paraffin sections on the slide, 5 or 10 minutes is long enough, and even for rather thick free-hand sections 20 or 30 minutes is sufficient. Use plenty of water and keep changing it as often as it becomes in the least discolored. Precipitates are often formed when slides are transferred directly to alcohol from this stain, and sometimes even after washing in water. A few gentle dips in acid alcohol (2 drops of HCl to 100 c.c. of 70 per cent alcohol) will usually remove the precipitates. This extracts the stain more rapidly from other parts than from the nuclei, and hence gives a good nuclear stain, while at the same time it removes any disfiguring precipitates. Some prefer to stain for a very short time and use no acid alcohol, but, as a rule, it is better to overstain and then differentiate in this way, because sharper contrasts are obtained. Transfer from acid alcohol to 70 per cent alcohol and leave here until a rich purple color replaces the red due to the acid. Since small quantities of the acid alcohol are carried over into the 70 per cent alcohol, it is well to add a *drop* of ammonia now and then to neutralize the effect of the acid. Too much ammonia is to be avoided, for it gives a disagreeable bluish color with poor differentiation, probably on account of the precipitation of alumina. The preparation is now dehydrated in 95 per cent and then in absolute alcohol, cleared in xylol or clove oil, and mounted in balsam.

The following is a general schedule for staining paraffin sections on the slide in Delafields' haematoxylin:

1. Stain (from water or from 35 or 50 per cent alcohol) 10 minutes
2. Rinse in water................................ 10 minutes
3. Thirty-five and 50 per cent alcohol.......... 3 minutes each
4. Acid alcohol................................. 5 seconds
5. Seventy per cent alcohol..................... 3 minutes
6. Eighty-five per cent alcohol.................. 3 minutes
7. Ninety-five per cent and 100 per cent alcohol. . 3 minutes each
8. Xylol and 100 per cent alcohol, equal parts....... 3 minutes
9. Xylol....................................... 3 minutes
10. Mount in balsam.

If, after rinsing in water, the stain is evidently too weak, put the slide or section back into the stain until it appears overstained. Place the slide in acid alcohol. If an acid alcohol with 2 drops of HCl to 100 c.c. of 70 per cent alcohol reduces the stain too much in 10 or 15 seconds, use less acid or stain longer. Transfer to 70 per cent alcohol without any acid. As soon as the color changes from red to purple, examine under the microscope. If it is still overstained, return to the acid alcohol; if the stain is too weak, return to the haematoxylin and try it again. After the haematoxylin is just right, apply a contrast stain, if you wish to double stain. Before transferring to the xylol wipe the alcohol from the back of the slide, or at least rest the corner of the slide upon blotting-paper for 2 or 3 seconds, in order that you may not carry over so much alcohol into the xylol. Add a drop of balsam and a cover. Since the xylol is very volatile, this last step must be taken quickly. If blackish spots appear they are usually caused by the drying of sections before the balsam and cover are added; if there are whitish spots or an emulsion-like appearance, the clearing is not thorough; this may be caused by poor xylol (or other clearing agent); by absolute alcohol which is considerably weaker than its name implies (the absolute alcohol must test at least as high as 99 per cent, and ought to test as high as 99.5 per cent, if xylol is to be used for clearing); or by passing too quickly through the absolute alcohol and xylol, or even by moisture on the cover glass. The last danger is easily avoided by passing the cover quickly through a Bunsen or alcohol flame before laying it on the balsam.

Delafield's haematoxylin is the most generally useful stain in the haematoxylin group. It brings out cellulose walls very sharply, and consequently is a good stain for embryos and the fundamental tissue system in general. With safranin it forms a good combination for the vascular system, the safranin giving the lignified elements a bright red color, while the haematoxylin stains the cellulose a rich purple. It is a good stain for chromatin, and the achromatic structures show up fairly well, but can be brought out much better by special methods. Archesporial cells and sporogenous tissue are very well defined if proper care be taken. Lignified and suberized walls and also starch and chromatophores stain lightly or not at all. Whenever you are in doubt as to the selection of a stain for general purposes, we should advise the use of Delafield's haematoxylin.

Mayer's haem-alum.—Haematoxylin, 1 g., dissolved with gentle heat in 50 c.c. of 95 per cent alcohol and added to a solution of 50 g. of alum in a liter of distilled water. Allow the mixture to cool and settle; filter; add a crystal of thymol to preserve from mold (Lee).

It is ready for use as soon as made up. Unless attacked by mold, it keeps indefinitely. Transfer to the stain from water. It is seldom necessary to stain for more than 10 minutes, and 4 or 5 minutes is generally long enough. As a rule, better results are secured by diluting the stain (about 1 c.c.–10 c.c. of distilled water) and allowing it to act for 10 hours or overnight.

This is a good stain for the nuclei of filamentous algae and fungi, since it has little or no effect upon cell walls or plastids. Wash thoroughly in water, transfer to 10 per cent glycerin, and follow the Venetian turpentine method, as described in chapter viii.

Erlich's haematoxylin.—

Distilled water	50 c.c.
Absolute alcohol	50 c.c.
Glycerin	50 c.c.
Glacial acetic acid	5 c.c.
Haematoxylin	1 g.
Alum in excess.	

Keep it in a dark place until the color becomes a deep red. If well stoppered, it will keep indefinitely. Transfer to the stain from 50 per cent or 35 per cent alcohol. Stain from 5 to 30 minutes. Since there is no danger from precipitates and the solution does not overstain, it is not necessary to treat with water or with acid alcohol, but the slide may be transferred from the stain to 70 per cent alcohol. Eosin, erythrosin, or orange G are good contrast stains. Jeffrey uses safranin and Erlich's haematoxylin for woody tissues.

Boehmer's haematoxylin.—

A {	Haematoxylin	1 g.
	Absolute alcohol	12 c.c.
B {	Alum	1 g.
	Distilled water	240 c.c.

The solution A must ripen for two months. When wanted for use, add about 10 drops of A to 10 c.c. of B. Stain from 10 to 20 minutes. Wash in water and proceed as usual.

Cellulose walls take a deep violet. The closing membrane (torus) of the bordered pits of conifers will usually stain deeply in about 15 minutes. Lignified, suberized, and cutinized structures stain slightly or not at all. When they do stain, the color is not violet, but a light yellow or brown.

THE CARMINES

Botanists have never given the carmines a fair trial, doubtless because the stains were not considered worth it; but the splendid preparations by Professor Powers of various members of the Volvocaceae, and by Belling in staining pollen mother-cells whole, prove that we should pay more attention to this group. Only a few of the multitudinous formulas will be considered.

The carmine solutions keep for several years, some of them even improving with age, if distilled water has been used in the formulas and the stains have been kept in tightly stoppered bottles. If the solution becomes turbid, it should be filtered.

Greenacher's borax carmine.—

Carmine...................................	3 g.
Borax......................................	4 g.
Distilled water............................	100 c.c.

Dissolve the borax in water and add the carmine, which is quickly dissolved with the aid of gentle heat. Add 100 c.c. of 70 per cent alcohol and filter (Stirling).

The following is a slightly different method for making this stain from the ingredients mentioned above: Dissolve the borax in water, add the carmine, and heat gently for 10 minutes; after the solution cools, add the alcohol and filter; let the solution stand for 2 or 3 weeks, then decant and filter again.

Stain the material in bulk from 50 per cent alcohol 1–3 days, then treat with acid alcohol (50 c.c. of 70 per cent alcohol+2 drops of hydrochloric acid) until the color becomes a clear red; this may require only a few hours, but may take 2 or 3 days. The material may then be passed through the rest of the alcohols (6–24 hours each), cleared, imbedded, and cut. After the sections are fastened to the slide, the paraffin should be dissolved off with xylol. The balsam and cover may be added immediately, or the xylol may be rinsed off with alcohol and a contrast stain may be added.

Alum carmine.—A 4 per cent aqueous solution of ammonia alum is boiled 20 minutes with 1 per cent of powdered carmine. Filter after it cools (Lee).

Stain from 12 to 24 hours and wash in water. No acid alcohol is needed, since the solution does not overstain.

Carmalum (**alum lake**).—Use 1 g. of the powdered stain to 100 c.c. of very dilute ammonia water. Filter, if there is any precipitate.

Mayer's carmalum.—

Carminic acid..............................	1 g.
Alum.......................................	10 g.
Distilled water............................	200 c.c.

Dissolve with heat; decant or filter and add a crystal of thymol to avoid mold.

With material of Volvocales fixed in weak aqueous potassium iodide,

so weak that the solution has a light brown color, or fixed in weak osmic acid, only 4 or 5 drops of 1 per cent osmic acid to 50 c.c. of distilled
water, this carmalum is good for material to be mounted whole. Dilute the stain considerably, put in a crystal of thymol to prevent mold,
and allow the stain to act for weeks, or even a couple of months. It is
not likely to overstain.

Alum cochineal.—

Powdered cochineal.	50 g.
Alum.	5 g.
Distilled water.	500 c.c.

Dissolve the alum in water, add the cochineal, and boil; evaporate
down to two-thirds of the original volume, and filter. Add a few drops
of carbolic acid to prevent mold (Stirling).

Stain as with alum carmine. It used to be a common practice to
stain in bulk in alum cochineal and counter-stain on the slide with
Bismarck brown.

Belling's iron aceto-carmine 1.—For counting chromosomes in pollen
mother-cells mounted whole, Belling used a modified aceto-carmine
method. The preparations are good for an immediate count, but do
not last longer than a few days or a week.

"Ordinary aceto-carmine is prepared by heating a 45 per cent solution of glacial acetic acid to boiling with excess of powdered carmine,
cooling, and filtering. The young anthers are teased out with steel
blades or needles in a drop of this until it changes slightly toward bluish red. An excess of iron spoils the preparation."

Belling's iron aceto-carmine 2.—"To a quantity of aceto-carmine a
trace of solution of ferric hydrate dissolved in 45 per cent acetic acid is
added until the liquid becomes bluish red, but no visible precipitate
forms. An equal amount of ordinary aceto-carmine is then added.
The anthers are teased out with nickled instruments." A cover-glass
is then added and sealed with vaseline. The preparation lasts only a
few days, but is much superior to any obtained by the usual *intra
vitam* processes.

The method is not as easy as it might seem to be. Much time will be
saved by reading the detailed account given in Belling's book, *The
Use of the Microscope.*

McClintock's iron aceto-carmine.—Dr. Barbara McClintock's
modification of the Belling method makes the preparations permanent.

1. Fix anthers in 1 part glacial acetic acid and 3 parts absolute alcohol from 12 to 24 hours.
2. Squeeze contents of an anther into a drop of Belling's iron aceto-carmine. Remove all structures except the pollen mother-cells, which must come into contact with both cover and slide. Otherwise they will be washed off. Place a cover glass over the drop.
3. Heat over an alcohol flame for a second, repeating 4 or 5 times. The drop must not boil.
4. Place the slide in a Petri dish filled with 10 per cent acetic acid until the cover rises from the slide. Some of the pollen mother-cells will stick to the slide and some to the cover.
5. Place both slide and cover in equal parts of absolute alcohol and acetic acid.
6. Pass through 1 part acetic acid to 3 parts absolute alcohol, 1 part acetic to 9 parts absolute alcohol, absolute alcohol, equal parts absolute alcohol and xylol, pure xylol, a few minutes in each.
7. Mount in balsam.

Dr. McClintock used certified carmine (NCa2).

THE ANILINS

Many of the most brilliant and beautiful stains yet discovered belong to this group. These stains are very numerous, but not so numerous as their names; for different names have been given to the same stain, and the same name has been given to different stains. Fortunately, the Committee on Standardization of Biological Stains is doing a good work in standardizing the nomenclature as well as the stains themselves. A valuable list of synonyms, with the preferred designations, was published in *Science*, **57**:743–746, 1923, and other references to the work of the commission are given in the Bibliography on page 341, and brought up to 1929 in Dr. Conn's book, *Biological Stains*.

General formula.—Make a 10 per cent solution of anilin oil in 95 per cent alcohol, shaking frequently until the anilin oil is dissolved; then add enough water to make the whole mixture about 20 per cent alcohol; then add 1 g. of cyanin, erythrosin, safranin, gentian violet, etc., to 100 c.c. of the solution. Solutions containing anilin oil do not keep so well as aqueous or alcoholic solutions. Personally, we hardly ever use solutions containing anilin oil.

The anilins keep well in balsam, but not so well in glycerin. Xylol is a good clearing agent for all of them; but clearing in clove oil improves stains like gentian violet, which are more or less soluble in clove oil. Even in such cases, xylol should follow the clove oil, or the preparation will fade.

While the anilins are not as permanent as the haematoxylins, most of them keep fairly well if the staining has been carefully done. Preparations fade if exposed long to bright sunlight. Keep the slides in the box when not in use, and even when in use, do not leave them on the laboratory table, exposed to the sun. We have preparations, made more than 30 years ago, in which the safranin and gentian violet are still bright; and others made more than 15 years ago, in which Magdala red and anilin blue have not faded.

Some of the anilins are acid, some basic, and some are neutral.

The rapidity with which sections must be transferred from one fluid to another makes many of them more difficult to manage than the haematoxylins or the carmines, but the stains are so valuable that even the beginner should spend most of his time with the anilins.

Many anilins stain quite deeply in from 1 to 20 minutes, but if the stain washes out during the dehydrating process, stain longer, even 10–24 hours if necessary. Often the brilliancy of the stain can be increased by leaving the slide for 5 minutes in a 1 per cent solution of permanganate of potassium before staining. The permanganate acts as a mordant.

The following are the more important anilins now in use by botanists. The directions apply to solutions made up according to the formulas given with the different stains.

Safranin.—For the botanist, safranin is the most useful of all the anilin stains, and safranin O is practically the only safranin he needs. This stain, although certified, still has a certain measure of variability, but is comparatively uniform. In the fourth edition of this book we advised making the stain by mixing equal parts of an alcohol-soluble and a water-soluble safranin. We thought we generally got a better stain and probably we did, sometimes, because the stains were not uniform, and, by this method, we had two chances, instead of only one, for getting a good stain. The certified safranin O is equally soluble in water or alcohol. A 1 per cent solution in 50 per cent alcohol, or in water is best for general work and can be diluted when desirable.

Flemming, who developed the famous triple stain—safranin, gentian violet, orange—dissolved 0.5 g. of alcoholic safranin in 50 c.c. of absolute alcohol and, after 4 days, added 10 c.c. of distilled water.

The first American safranins were very unsatisfactory; but there have been great improvements, and one company, the National Anilin and Chemical Company, has produced a safranin with 90 per cent dye content, much stronger than any of the European stains. This is the safranin which has been certified by the Committee on Standardization of Stains. Other companies are also improving. Coleman and Bell's Safranin Y, for bacilli, is good for staining xylem.

All safranins keep indefinitely, solutions 20 years old staining as well, or better, than when fresh.

An anilin safranin may be made according to the general formula.

The transfer to the stain depends upon the formula. If the stain is aqueous, transfer to the stain from water; if made up in 50 per cent alcohol, transfer to the stain from 50 per cent alcohol.

Sections of woody tissues, cut from living material, should be put into 95 per cent alcohol for about 1 hour and then transferred to the alcoholic stain. If cut from formalin material, sections should be left in water for $\frac{1}{2}$ hour, changing the water several times; then in 15, 35, and 50 per cent alcohol, about 5 minutes in each grade; and then be stained in alcoholic safranin. If cut from formalin alcohol acetic-acid material, the sections should be placed in 50 per cent alcohol for at least 10 minutes, changing once or twice before being placed in the alcoholic stain. These are minimum times: longer times are just as good and may be better.

The time required for staining varies with the tissue, the fixing agent, and the quality of the stain. In general, it may be said that 2 hours is a minimum and 24 hours a maximum. If the staining be too prolonged, delicate structures, like starch grains, crystals, and various cell constituents, may wash out. The mere fact that the whole section does not wash off does not mean that everything is fastened to the slide. On the other hand, with a short period, it is difficult to get a sharp differentiation. In staining a vascular bundle, one should be able to wash the safranin from the cellulose walls and still leave a brilliant red in lignified structures. For paraffin sections, 3–6 hours will usually be sufficient. It is a good practice to put the slides into the stain in the morning and finish the mounts any time in the afternoon. For freehand sections of woody tissues, 24 hours is not too long, and in a 50 per cent alcoholic safranin, the sections may be stained for a week.

From the stain, transfer to 50 per cent alcohol. If the sections are deeply stained, and sufficient differentiation is not secured within 5 or 10 minutes, a drop of hydrochloric acid added to 50 c.c. of the alcohol will hasten the extraction of the stain. If staining vascular tissue, draw the stain from the cellulose walls, but stop before the lignified walls begin to fade. If a contrast stain is to be added, like light green, which weakens the safranin; or anilin blue or Delafield's haematoxylin, which need to be followed by an acid; the safranin should be strong enough to allow the necessary reduction. If staining mitotic figures, draw the stain from the spindle, but stop before the chromosomes begin to weaken. When the desired differentiation has been reached, wash out the acid in 50 per cent alcohol, if acid has been used. About 5 minutes should be sufficient for the washing.

If safranin is to be used alone, pass through 50, 70, 85, 95, and 100 per cent alcohol, through the xylol-alcohol, then through xylol to balsam. If clove oil is used, omit the xylol-alcohol, but follow the clove oil with xylol to hasten the hardening of the preparation.

If a second stain is to be added, transfer from the 50 per cent alcohol to any alcoholic stain. If the second stain is an aqueous stain, rinse the slide or sections for a minute in water before applying the stain.

Safranin is the most generally useful of all the red stains, and, fortunately, it is quite permanent. Lignified, suberized, cutinized, and chitinized structures stain red, as do also the chromosomes, nucleoli, and centrosomes.

Directions for using safranin in combination with other stains will be given in connection with various objects.

Acid fuchsin.—Use a 1 per cent solution in water or in 70 per cent alcohol. The solution in alcohol is preferable if sections are to be mounted in balsam. This stain often acts with great rapidity, 2 or 3 minutes being sufficient. The method for using acid fuchsin with woody tissues is given in the chapter on "Freehand Sections" (chap. vi). In staining embryo sacs, pollen grains, and such structures, longer periods are better. Stain 1 or 2 hours, and then differentiate in a saturated solution of picric acid in 70 per cent alcohol. This may require 30 seconds, or even several minutes. Rinse in 70 per cent alcohol until a bright red replaces the yellowish color due to the acid, and then proceed as usual.

Basic fuchsin.—This stain has become valuable to botanists through the researches of Gourley, who used it to stain the vascular system of living plants. It does not diffuse during dehydration or clearing. Detailed directions are given on page 151.

Dissolve 0.5 g. basic fuchsin in 20 c.c. of 95 per cent alcohol and dilute with 1,000 c.c. of tap water. A smaller quantity can be made by dissolving 50 mg. in 2 c.c. of 95 per cent alcohol and diluting with 100 c.c. of tap water.

Congo red.—This is an acid stain resembling acid fuchsin. For cytological work use a ½ per cent aqueous solution; for anatomical work use a saturated solution. It is a good stain to use after malachite green or anilin blue. Transfer to the Congo red from water, stain 15 minutes, wash in water, transfer—for wood sections—to 85 per cent alcohol, and wash until the green or blue color of the previous stain begins to show through the red. Then treat quickly with absolute alcohol, clear in xylol, and mount in balsam.

Eosin.—This has long been a favorite stain, but for most purposes it has been replaced by similar stains giving better differentiation. The dry stain is made in two forms, one for aqueous and the other for alcoholic solution. Each should be used with its intended solvent. Make a 1 per cent solution in alcohol or water. It is worth mentioning that the aqueous solution is an excellent red ink.

For material to be mounted whole in glycerin, glycerin jelly, or Venetian turpentine, stain overnight or, better, 24 hours; pour off the stain, which may be used repeatedly; treat, without washing in water, with a 2 per cent aqueous solution of acetic acid for 5 or 10 minutes, changing 2 or 3 times; transfer to 10 per cent glycerin without washing in water, since the stain will be brighter if the whole solution is slightly acid. When the glycerin becomes thick, mount in glycerin jelly. If the Venetian turpentine method is to be used, wash the glycerin out in alcohol slightly acidulated with acetic acid (a couple of drops of acetic acid to 50 c.c. of alcohol), and do not drain off the last alcohol too completely before transferring to the 10 per cent Venetian turpentine. According to Lee, the glycerin should be slightly alkaline. The alkalinity can be brought about by adding half a gram of common salt to 100 c.c. of the 10 per cent glycerin. We have found that eosin keeps better when the media are slightly acid.

For staining paraffin sections, the alcoholic solution is better and the time may not be more than a few minutes, especially if the eosin is being used as a contrast stain.

We have found the Eosin Y, of Coleman and Bell, very satisfactory, especially for fungi to be mounted whole. With the rapid improvement in the manufacture of stains, it is very probable that other dealers will have equally good products. Investigators will save time and money by keeping track of the findings of the commission on Standardization of Biological Stains.

Haematoxylin and eosin and methyl blue and eosin are good combinations. The eosin should follow the other stain.

Erythrosin.—This is really an eosin, but there is some difference in the method of manufacturing. It is more precise and a more transparent stain than eosin and is to be preferred for nearly all staining of paraffin sections. Make a 1 per cent solution in distilled water or in 70 per cent alcohol. It gives good results when made up according to the general formula.

Erythrosin stains rapidly, from 30 seconds to 3 minutes being sufficient. When used in combination with other stains, erythrosin should come last.

Magdala red.—The name, Magdala red, is too indefinite to mean anything. The Magdala red *echt* (genuine), of Grübler, is worth nothing as botanical stain. Sometimes a bottle labeled simply Magdala red gave fine results. It would seem that the occasional stains which succeeded are practically the same as the American stain, phloxine; at least, a stain called Phloxine B (color index number 778), made by the National Anilin and Chemical Company, behaves like the best "Magdala red" and seems to give uniform results.

Phloxine B.—Probably the occasional lots of Magdala red which proved to be so satisfactory in the Magdala red and anilin blue combination were phloxine.

Phloxine.................................... 1 g.
Ninety per cent alcohol...................... 100 c.c.

This stain is particularly valuable for staining algae which are to be mounted whole. In this case it should be followed by anilin blue. Full directions are given in chapter viii.

For staining sections to be mounted in balsam, dilute the phloxine one half with water. Stain for 24 hours, dehydrate in 95 and 100 per cent alcohol, clear in clove oil, transfer to xylol, and mount in balsam.

Phloxine stains lignified, suberized, and cutinized structures, and also chromosomes, centrosomes, nucleoli, and pyrenoids. It is likely to overstain, but the differentiation is easily secured by placing the finished mounts upon a white background in the direct sunlight. When the desired differentiation has been reached, it is better to avoid direct sunlight, although the mounts do not seem to fade in the ordinary light of a room.

Except for special purposes, it is better to use this stain in combination with blue, green, or violet.

Gentian violet.—Dissolve in the anilin oil solution as directed in the general formula. Although it does not keep as well as the aqueous solution, it stains better, especially when dealing with the achromatic structure of the mitotic figure. Often the brilliancy of the stain can be increased by leaving the slide for about 5 minutes in a 1 per cent aqueous solution of permanganate of potassium before applying the stain, or in Gram's iodine solution (1 g. iodine, 2 g. potassium iodide, 300 c.c. water) after staining in violet.

The greatest objection to the aqueous and anilin-oil solutions of gentian violet is that the stain washes out so rapidly in alcohols that it is impossible to run the slide up through the series. The usual practice is to dip the slide in water to remove most of the stain and thus avoid carrying it into the alcohol: then transfer directly from water to 95 per cent alcohol, allowing the alcohol to act for only 2 or 3 seconds, then allow the absolute alcohol to act for 5 or 6 seconds, and then, while the stain is still coming out in streams, begin the treatment with clove oil. Holding the slide in one hand, pour on a few drops of clove oil, and immediately drain off in such a way as to carry off the alcohol. This clove oil should not be used again. Then flood the slide repeatedly with clove oil, pouring the clove oil back into the bottle. A 50-c.c. bottle of clove oil is large enough. About 100 mounts can be cleared with 50 c.c. of this oil. The clove oil is a solvent of gentian violet, but it dissolves the stain from some structures more rapidly than from others; e.g., the stain may be completely removed from the chromosomes while it is still bright in the achromatic structures. As soon as the stain is just right, drain off the clove oil and put the slide into a Stender dish of xylol for a couple of minutes. The xylol will soon take on an amber color, but this will not reduce its efficiency in clearing; on the contrary, its efficiency will improve. However, the least trace of clove oil, carried over into the balsam, will finally cause the stain to fade. Therefore, transfer the slide to fresh, clear xylol and let it remain for 2 or 3 minutes before mounting in balsam.

As may be inferred from what has preceded, alcohol would soon extract the stain, without any application of clove oil. The clove oil is used, not only because it extracts the stain more slowly, but because it dissolves the stain from some structures more rapidly than from others; e.g., the stain may be completely removed from the chromosomes while it is still bright in the achromatic structures, so that with safranin and gentian violet one can get red chromosomes on a violet spindle.

Many use the gentian violet dissolved in clove oil. Dissolve 1 g. gentian violet in 200 c.c. absolute alcohol and pour into 200 c.c. of clove oil. Stir thoroughly or shake in a bottle, then pour into an open dish and keep warm until the mixture evaporates down to about 200 c.c. Then keep in a well-stoppered bottle. Put a little on the slide with a pipette, allow it to stain for 2–10 minutes and then drain back into the bottle, for the stain can be used repeatedly. If gold orange or orange G, dissolved in clove oil, is to be used, put it on at this point and allow it to act for 10–20 seconds. Then drain it off into its bottle and put the slide into a Stender dish of xylol. Transfer to a Stender dish of clear xylol, and mount in balsam.

Some still use cedar oil to follow the clove oil. This stops the action of the clove oil, but the preparations harden slowly.

Gentian violet or, better, crystal violet, is an excellent stain for achromatic structures in all stages of development. Chromatin, in many of its stages, is also stained. In metaphase and anaphase one should be able to get red chromosomes and violet spindles with safranin and gentian violet. If the chromosomes also persist in retaining the violet, shorten the stain in gentian violet. Cilia stain well; starch grains stain deeply, chromatophores less deeply, and lignified walls may not stain at all. One should be able to get red lignified walls and violet cellulose walls with safranin and gentian violet.

Cyanin.—This stain is also called Quinolein blue and Chinolin blue. Dissolve 1 g. of cyanin in 100 c.c. of 95 per cent alcohol and add 100 c.c. of water. The cyanin would not dissolve in 50 per cent alcohol. We have not found Grübler's cyanin at all satisfactory with the foregoing formula. With the general formula the Grübler's cyanin will not dissolve. We use a cyanin prepared by H. A. Metz and Company, 122 Hudson Street, New York. This cyanin dissolves completely when made up according to the general formula. It stains rapidly, 5–10 minutes usually being sufficient. Chromosomes take a deep blue, but the spindle is only slightly affected. Lignified structures stain blue, while cellulose walls are scarcely affected and the stain is easily washed out.

Iodine green.—Use a 1 per cent solution in 70 per cent alcohol. Stain for an hour, rinse in 70 per cent alcohol, dehydrate in 95 per cent alcohol and absolute alcohol, clear in xylol or clove oil, and mount in balsam. If the stain washes out too rapidly and does not give sufficient differentiation, stain longer, overnight or even 24 hours.

Lignified structures stain green, but, after proper washing, cellulose is scarcely affected. A bright green may be left in the chromosomes after all the stain has been washed out from the spindle.

Acid fuchsin, erythrosin, and eosin are good contrast stains for mitotic figures. Acid fuchsin or Delafield's haematoxylin are good for cellulose walls.

Light green (*Licht Grün*).—Light green is an acid stain, soluble in water, alcohol, or clove oil. It stains quickly and forms a sharp contrast with safranin or phloxine.

Stain in safranin and then, with little or no washing out, stain in a weak alcoholic solution of acid green (about 0.2 g. in 100 c.c. of 95 per cent alcohol). From 20 seconds to about 1 minute may be sufficient. The green rapidly reduces the safranin, and consequently the staining must not be too prolonged. A successful preparation should show red chromosomes and green spindle. Lignified walls should be red, and cellulose walls, green.

Malachite green.—A 1–3 per cent aqueous solution is good for cellulose walls. The stain contrasts well with Congo red.

Methyl green.—A 1 per cent solution in water is good for staining lignified structures. Lee recommends that the solution be acidulated with acetic acid. This is not necessary for staining lignified membranes nor for staining chromosomes. Methyl green has long been a favorite stain for living tissues. It is more easily controlled than iodine green, especially in double staining to differentiate lignified and cellulose walls.

Acid green.—Make a solution according to the general formula, or simply make a 1 per cent solution in water. This stains cellulose walls and achromatic structures, but scarcely affects lignified walls or chromosomes.

Anilin blue.—Strong alcoholic solutions are best for botanical work. Even though the dry stain may be intended for aqueous solution, make a 1 per cent solution in 85 or 95 per cent alcohol.

This stain can be recommended for cellulose walls, achromatic structures of mitotic figures, for cilia, and it is particularly valuable for algae. Directions for using it with algae are given in chapter viii.

Orange G.—Make a 1 per cent solution in water, in 95 per cent alcohol, or a $\frac{1}{10}$ per cent solution in clove oil. We prefer the solution in clove oil.

The orange dissolves very slowly if put directly into clove oil. It is better to dissolve $\frac{1}{2}$ gram of orange in 50 c.c. of absolute alcohol. In a well-corked bottle in the paraffin oven at 52° C., this much orange may go into solution. Then remove the cork and allow about half of the alcohol to evaporate. Pour on 200 c.c. or more of clove oil and let it stand for several hours. If any of the stain has not gone into solution, pour off the clear fluid, which is now ready for use, and pour some more clove oil on the residue, allowing the residue to go slowly into solution. In staining, we use a small bottle of the orange, pouring it on the slide and draining it back into the bottle. The absolute alcohol, carried into the clove oil in this way, does no damage, except that it dilutes the stain a little.

Transfer to the aqueous stain from water; to the alcoholic stain from 85 per cent alcohol, since the stain is always applied as a second or third stain; use the solution in clove oil after the dehydration in absolute alcohol. Times are always short and are to be reckoned in seconds rather than in minutes. If the solution in clove oil has been used, the slide should be transferred to xylol before mounting in balsam.

This is a plasma stain. It is distinctly a general rather than a selective stain, but is valuable as a background for other structures which have been stained violet or blue or green. It first came into prominence as the third member of the triple stain—safranin, gentian violet, orange.

Gold orange.—This stain, which many incorrectly suppose to be the same as orange G, is much more readily soluble in clove oil and stains with much greater rapidity.

DOUBLE STAINS AND TRIPLE STAINS

Occasionally one uses a single stain to bring out some particular structure, but in most cases two, or even three, stains are used.

In staining a vascular bundle, one stain may be selected which stains the xylem, but not the phloem, while another of a different color stains the phloem, but not the xylem, thus affording a sharp contrast. In staining mitotic figures, one stain may stain the chromosomes, while another of a different color may be used to stain the spindle.

One stain may affect another, the second stain often weakening the first. There is not likely to be much success without patience and constant observation.

Flemming's safranin, gentian violet, orange.—Safranin has long been a famous stain for mitosis. This triple combination was published in 1891, but its value in plant cytology was not thoroughly appreciated until five or six years later, when its application was developed to a high degree of perfection by various investigators of the Bonn (Germany) school. Three methods, which may be designated as A, B, and C, will be described.

A. According to Flemming, stain 2 or 3 days in safranin (dissolve 0.5 g. safranin in 50 c.c. absolute alcohol, and after 4 days add 10 c.c. distilled water); rinse quickly in water; stain 1–3 hours in a 2 per cent aqueous solution of gentian violet; wash quickly in water, and then stain 1–3 minutes in a 1 per cent aqueous solution of orange G. Transfer from the stain to absolute alcohol, clear in clove oil, and mount in balsam. We are indebted to Flemming for the chromo-acetic–osmic fixing agent. No cytologist has made a greater or more permanent contribution to cytological technique, but his method of using the triple stain is mentioned only as a matter of history: no one uses it today.

B. The following formulas and method seem to be better for mitotic phenomena in plants: Make a 1 per cent solution of safranin in 50 per cent alcohol, a 1 per cent aqueous solution of gentian violet, and a 1 per cent aqueous solution of orange G.

Transfer paraffin sections to the stain from 50 per cent alcohol after the xylol or turpentine used in dissolving away the paraffin has been rinsed off. Stain from 3 to 24 hours. If the period be too short, the washing out is so rapid that it is difficult to stop the differentiation at the proper point, and, besides, the red is likely to be less brilliant. Rinse in 50 per cent alcohol until the stain is washed out from the spindle and cytoplasm, but stop the washing before the chromosomes begin to lose their bright red color. If the washing out takes place too slowly, treat with slightly acidulated alcohol (one drop of HCl to 50 c.c. of 50 per cent alcohol) for a few seconds. The acid must be removed by washing for 15–30 seconds in alcohol which has not been acidulated.

Wash in water for a couple of minutes and then stain in gentian violet.

The time required is so variable that definite instructions are impossible. The gentian violet should stain the spindle, but not the chromosomes. If the stain be too prolonged, it may be impossible to get it out from the chromosomes and still leave it bright in the spindle. If the period be too short, the stain will wash out from the spindle. For mitotic figures in the germinating spores of the liverwort, *Pellia*, 30 minutes is not too long. In this case, the stain washes out easily from the chromosomes without the use of acid, and the spindle takes a rich violet which is not easily washed out. In embryo sacs of *Lilium* try 10 minutes. In pollen mother-cells try 5–10 minutes. For root-tips try 2–10 minutes. Chromatin in the early prophases and in telophases will stain with the violet, and the violet will not wash out, but in phases in which fully formed chromosomes are visible the violet can be washed out if the period has not been too long. If the aqueous gentian violet or crystal violet fails to stain the spindle, try the anilin oil solutions.

Remove the slide from the gentian violet and dip it 5 or 6 times in water and then stain from 30 seconds to 1 minute in orange G. The orange stains cytoplasm and at the same time washes out gentian violet.

Transfer from the orange G to 95 per cent alcohol, dipping the slide a few times in this merely to save the absolute alcohol. Dehydrate in absolute alcohol 3–30 seconds.

Clear in clove oil, as already described in the paragraph on gentian violet. Transfer to xylol and mount in balsam.

Safranin and gentian violet are often used without the orange. In this case, transfer from the gentian violet directly to 95 per cent alcohol, and proceed as before.

An objection to both these methods is that the gradual series of alcohols cannot be used, because the gentian violet washes out so rapidly. If one should try a filament of *Spirogyra* with either of these methods, it would hardly be recognizable when it reaches the balsam; but with thin sections, especially when well fastened to the slide, conditions are different and there does not seem to be much damage. With any aqueous solution of gentian violet or crystal violet, the violet is less likely to be lost, if permanganate of potash is used before the stain, or Gram's iodine after it.

We are using a third method which seems to be better than either of the two just described. Slides can be run up, through the alcohols in the usual way.

C. Use the safranin solution described in B, but use clove oil solutions of gentian violet and orange G, or gold orange. Make the orange solution as described on page 65. The solution of gentian violet is prepared in the same way, but it does not take as long to get a good solution.

After staining in safranin and dehydrating in absolute alcohol, flood the slide with the clove oil solution of gentian violet or crystal violet and stain for 5–30 minutes, or even for hours if necessary. Drain the stain into the bottle, for it can be used repeatedly. Put pure clove oil on with a pipette and watch until the stain is satisfactory. In a mitotic figure, the chromosomes should be red, and the spindle, violet. Pour off the clove oil and put on the orange. About 10–30 seconds will usually be long enough. Pour the orange back into its bottle, rinse with pure clove oil, and place the slide in a Stender dish of xylol. This xylol will soon take on an amber color. Transfer to clear xylol and mount in balsam.

With freehand sections, which are likely to be much thicker, the process is the same but the times will be longer.

Safranin and light green.—Stain in 50 per cent alcoholic safranin, wash in 50 per cent alcohol, but stop while the safranin is still somewhat stronger than desired in the finished mount; then stain in light green (1 g. in 100 c.c. of 90 per cent alcohol) for 10–30 seconds. The light green not only stains vigorously but reduces the safranin. Pass through 95 and 100 per cent alcohol, clear in xylol, and mount in balsam.

The light green can be dissolved in clove oil. With a pipette, flood the slide with light green, stain for 30 seconds, pour the light green back into its bottle, rinse with pure clove oil, transfer to xylol, and mount in balsam.

Used in either way, this combination is very good for anatomical work, especially for vascular anatomy.

Cyanin and erythrosin.—Both solutions may be made according to the general formula for anilins, or 1 per cent aqueous solutions may be used. Miss Thomas recommends 1 gram dissolved in 100 c.c. of 95 per cent alcohol. After the solution is complete, add 100 c.c. of distilled water. Since the combination is used only for paraffin sections or for small organisms dried down on the slide, her formula is preferable. Transfer to the alcoholic cyanin from 50 per cent alcohol, stain 5–10 minutes or longer; rinse quickly in 50 per cent alcohol, transfer to erythrosin, and stain 30 seconds to one minute. Rinse quickly in 50 per cent alcohol, then in 95 per cent and absolute alcohol. Clear in xylol and mount in balsam.

If aqueous stains are used, transfer to the cyanin from water, rinse in water, stain in erythrosin, rinse in water, and transfer directly to 95 per cent alcohol. If the cyanin washes out, stain for 1 hour, and if it still washes out, omit the rinsing and transfer directly from the cyanin to the erythrosin.

The erythrosin may be used first; in this case stain for 5 minutes in erythrosin, transfer directly to cyanin, and stain for about 10 seconds. Dehydrate in 95 per cent and in absolute alcohol, clear in xylol or in clove oil, and mount in balsam.

The stains wash out so rapidly that the series of alcohols cannot be used.

Chromosomes and nucleoli stain blue, and achromatic structures, red. Lignified structures stain blue, and cellulose walls, red. The various cell constituents are often sharply differentiated. It was this combination which suggested the now obsolete terms, "cyanophilous" and "erythrophilous."

Phloxine and anilin blue.—In the fourth edition, this combination was described under the heading, Magdala red and anilin blue, but the occasional lots of the red stain which gave satisfactory results were probably phloxine. Make both solutions as directed in chapter viii on "The Venetian Turpentine Method."

For paraffin sections, stain 3–24 hours in phloxine, dip in 95 per cent alcohol to rinse off the stain, and then stain 2–10 minutes in the anilin blue. Dip in 95 per cent alcohol to rinse off the stain, and treat for a few seconds with alcohol slightly acidulated with hydrochloric acid (one drop to 50 c.c. of 95 per cent alcohol). In the acid alcohol the blue will become more intense, but the red would soon be extracted. Wash in 95 per cent alcohol to remove the acid. If the acid has weakened the phloxine put a pinch of sodium carbonate into the 95 per cent alcohol. The red may brighten. If the red is too weak, return to the phloxine and try again. From the 95 per cent alcohol transfer to absolute alcohol, to xylol, and then mount in balsam.

For staining algae, more complete directions are given in chapter viii.

Acid fuchsin and iodine green mixtures.—Two solutions are kept separate, since they do not retain their efficiency long after they are mixed:

A { Fuchsin acid........................... 0.1 g.
    Distilled water........................ 50.0 c.c.

B { Iodine green.......................... 0.1 g.
    Distilled water....................... 50.0 c.c.

C { Absolute alcohol....................... 100.0 c.c.
    Glacial acetic acid..................... 1.0 c.c.
    Iodine................................ 0.1 g.

Mix equal parts of A and B. Transfer to the stain from water. The proper time must be determined by experiment. For a trial, 24 hours might be recommended. Transfer from the stain directly to solution C and from C to xylol.

A. Acid fuchsin............. 0.5 g. in 100 c.c. of water
B. Iodine green............. 0.5 g. in 100 c.c. of water

Mix a pipette full of A with a pipette full of B; stain 2–8 minutes; transfer to 85 per cent or 95 per cent alcohol, dehydrate rapidly, clear in xylol, and mount in balsam. Both these formulas are good for mitosis.

Acid fuchsin and methyl green.—Both may be used in 1 per cent aqueous solutions.

For mitotic figures, stain in green for about an hour, wash in water or alcohol until the green is extracted from the spindle, and then stain for about 1 minute in the fuchsin. Dehydrate in 95 and 100 per cent alcohol, clear in xylol or clove oil, and mount in balsam. If the green washes out, stain longer; if it is not readily extracted from the spindle, shorten the period. If the fuchsin stains the chromosomes, shorten the period, and lengthen it if the fuchsin washes out from the spindle. The chromosomes should take a brilliant green, and the spindle, a bright red.

Delafield's haematoxylin and erythrosin.—Stain first in the haematoxylin, and after that stain is satisfactory, stain for 30 seconds or 1 minute in erythrosin. This is a good combination, and, for most plant structures, gives a far better differentiation than the traditional haematoxylin and eosin, since the erythrosin has all the advantages of the eosin and is more transparent. Orange G is also a good stain to use with Delafield's haematoxylin.

Directions for staining in safranin and Delafield's haematoxylin are given in the chapter on "Freehand Sections" (chap. vi).

Heidenhain's iron-haematoxylin and orange G.—This haematoxylin is very satisfactory when used alone. A light staining in orange G, however, sometimes improves the mount. After the last washing in water, stain for about 30 seconds in orange G; or, if the orange is in clove oil, stain after dehydrating in absolute alcohol.

Eosin, erythrosin, and most plasma stains fail to increase the effect of a good stain in iron-haematoxylin; but staining overnight in safranin and reducing the stain until it becomes a faint pink in the protoplasm may still show a distinct red in the nucleoli. Then stain in iron-alum haematoxylin in the usual way.

Combinations might be described almost without limit. Several more will be suggested in Part II in connection with various groups of plants.

We have not tried to make the list of stains complete, but we have described more than any botanist will learn to use critically. Master two or three good combinations and don't spend much time with the rest.

CHAPTER IV

GENERAL REMARKS ON STAINING

The function of a stain is to make structures visible which cannot be seen without staining, or to bring out clearly structures which are only faintly visible. A filament of *Spirogyra* shows the chromatophore clearly if merely mounted alive in a drop of water; the nucleus is visible and the pyrenoids can be distinguished. Such a study is necessary if one is to understand anything about the plant and, for an elementary class, this much is sufficient; but a drop of iodine solution applied to the edge of the cover would emphasize certain details, e.g., the starch would appear blue, the nucleus a light brown, and the cytoplasm a lighter brown. This illustrates at least one advantage to be gained by staining; it enables us to see structures which would otherwise be invisible, or almost invisible. Much of the recent progress in morphology and cytology has been due to the development of critical methods of staining. Some of the combinations and methods recommended by various workers are good in themselves, while others, not so good, have yielded results because they have been so skilfully used.

CHOOSING A STAIN

Some stains which are excellent in differentiating certain structures are worthless for others; but the worthless stain may be the best one for something else. Beautiful and instructive preparations sometimes result from some happy chance, as when a slide is passed through alcohols which have become tinged with various stains. Such slides may show four or five stains well balanced; but uniform success demands skill and judgment in manipulation, and also a knowledge of the structures which are to be differentiated. Let us take a vascular bundle for illustration. Safranin stains the xylem a bright red, but, with judicious washing, is entirely removed from the cambium and cellulose elements of the phloem. A careful staining with Delafield's haematoxylin now gives a rich purple color to the cellulose elements which were left unstained by the safranin, thus contrasting sharply with the lignified elements. If cyanin and erythrosin be used, the xylem takes the blue while the cambium and phloem take the red.

The mere selection of two colors which contrast well is not sufficient. Green and red contrast well, but safranin and iodine green would be a poor combination, for both would stain chromosomes and neither would stain the spindle; both would stain lignified structures and neither would give satisfactory results with cellulose walls. Both stains are basic. Acid green would have given a contrast in both these cases, because it stains achromatic structures and cellulose walls. In general, an acid stain should be combined with a basic one, but there are so many exceptions that it is hardly worth while to learn a list of basic and acid stains. Stains which stain chromosomes are likely to be basic, and those which do not stain chromosomes are likely to be acid or neutral. If it were true that acid stains affect only basic structures, and basic stains affect only acid structures, a classification of stains would be of great value. Safranin and gentian violet are both basic but, with the safranin properly washed out and the gentian violet properly applied, chromosomes stain red while the spindle stains violet. Lignified cell walls stain red, while cellulose walls stain violet. The exine of a pollen grain stains red while the intine stains violet. It is very evident that, to secure a contrast, it is not necessary that one stain be basic and the other acid. The only way to insure success is to become familiar with the action of each stain upon the various structures.

THEORIES OF STAINING

The history of staining does not go back to Aristotle, but a carmine was used for microscopic purposes as early as 1770. Even in 1838, when Schleiden announced his cell theory, staining had not become an important part of histological technique, although some use was being made of carmine and iodine. Beginning with 1850, stains were used more and more and, during the last thirty years of the century, demands for better stains became so insistent that in Germany companies were formed to furnish stains for microscopic use. The famous Grübler Company is still furnishing excellent stains, some of which, like their haematoxylin, have not been surpassed. During the World War, stains were produced in America and, when the Commission on Standardization of Biological Stains was organized, stains improved rapidly and many of them have become not only excellent but uniform, so that, when a stain has become valuable for some particular purpose, one can get more exactly like it.

A short history of staining is given in Dr. Conn's book on *Biological Stains*, in which one can find references to more extensive works on the subject.

As soon as staining became recognized as a necessary part of histological technique, theories began to appear, some of them suggestive, some instructive, and some only amusing.

In 1890 Auerbach, a zoölogist, published the results of his studies upon spermatozoa and ova. He found that, if preparations containing both spermatozoa and ova were stained with cyanin and erythrosin, the nuclei of the spermatozoa took the cyanin, while the nuclei of ova preferred the erythrosin; hence he proposed the terms "cyanophilous" and "erythrophilous." Auerbach regarded these differences as an indication of sexual differences in the cells.

Rosen (1892) supported this theory, and even went so far as to regard the tube nucleus of the pollen grain as female, on account of its erythrophilous staining. In connection with this theory it was suggested that the ordinary vegetative nuclei are hermaphrodite, and that in the formation of a female germ nucleus the male elements are extruded, leaving only the erythrophilous female elements; and, similarly, in the formation of a male nucleus the female elements are extruded, leaving only the cyanophilous male elements.

As long ago as 1884 Strasburger discovered that with a mixture of fuchsin and iodine green the generative nucleus of a pollen grain stains green, while the tube nucleus stains red. In 1892, in his *Verhalten des Pollens*, he discussed quite thoroughly the staining reactions of the nuclei. The nuclei of the small prothallial cells of gymnosperm microspores are cyanophilous like the male generative nuclei. The nuclei of a nucellus surrounding an embryo sac are also cyanophilous, while the nuclei of structures within the sac are erythrophilous. His conclusion is that the cyanophilous condition in both cases is due to poor nutrition, while the erythrophilous condition is due to abundant nutrition. A further fact in support of the theory is that the nuclei of the adventitious embryos which come from the nucellus of *Funkia ovata* are decidedly erythrophilous, while the nuclei of the nucellus to which they owe their food-supply are cyanophilous.

In division stages nuclei are cyanophilous, but from anaphase to resting stage the cyanophilous condition becomes less and less pronounced, and may even gradually change to the erythrophilous.

An additional fact in favor of this theory is that in *Ephedra* the tube nucleus, which has very little cytoplasm about it, is cyanophilous. Strasburger claimed that there is no essential difference between male and female generative nuclei, and subsequent observation soon showed that within the egg the sex nuclei rapidly become alike in their reaction to stains.

Malfatti (1891) and Lilienfeld (1892–93) claim that these reactions are dependent upon the amount of nucleic acid present in the structures. During mitosis the chromosomes consist of nearly pure nucleic acid and are intensely cyanophilous, but the protoplasm, which has little or no nucleic acid, is erythrophilous. There is a gradual transition from the cyanophilous condition to the erythrophilous, and vice versa, the acid structures taking basic stains, and basic structures, the acid stains.

The terms "erythrophilous" and "cyanophilous" soon became obsolete, and many claimed the affinity is for basic and acid dyes, rather than for blue or red colors. That the terms were misnomers became evident when a combination like safranin (basic) and acid green (acid) was used, for the cyanophilous structures stained red, and the erythrophilous, green.

According to Fischer (1897 and 1900), stains indicate physical but not chemical composition. Fischer experimented with substances of known chemical composition. Egg albumin was shaken until small granules were secured. These were fixed with the usual fixing agents, and then stained with Delafield's haematoxylin. The extremely small granules stained red, while the larger ones became purple. Since the granules are all alike in chemical composition, Fischer concluded that the difference in staining must be due to physical differences. With safranin, followed by gentian violet, the larger granules stain red and the smaller, violet; if, however, the gentian violet be used first, then treated with acid alcohol, and followed by safranin, the larger granules take the gentian violet and the smaller, the safranin. In root-tips similar results were obtained. Safranin followed by gentian violet stained chromosomes red and spindle fibers violet, while gentian violet followed by safranin stained the chromosomes violet and the spindle red. One often reads that chromosomes owe their strong staining capacity to nuclein, and especially to the phosphorus, but, according to Fischer, this is shown to be unfounded, since albumin gives similar results, yet contains no phosphorus, and is not chemically allied to nuclein.

Probably the most important reason which led Fischer to undertake this series of experiments was the claim that certain granules of the Cyanophyceae should be identified as chromatin because they behaved like chromatin when stained with haematoxylin. Fischer's experiments not only proved that chromatin cannot be identified in this way but raised the question whether staining reactions ever indicate chemical composition. At present, it would seem that, in most cases, the staining indicates only physical differences. However, in some cases there is a chemical reaction, e.g., when material fixed in bichloride of mercury is stained in carmine, mercuric carminate is formed.

It would be very convenient if we knew just how much dependence should be placed upon staining reactions as a means of analysis. If two structures stain alike with Delafield's haematoxylin, does this mean that they have the same chemical composition; or if, on the other hand, they stain differently, must they necessarily be different in their chemical composition? Delafield's haematoxylin, when carefully used, gives a rich purple color, but a careful examination will often show that in the same preparation some structures stain purple, while others stain red. Does this mean that the purple and red structures must have a different chemical composition? Many people believe that structures which stain differently with a given stain must be chemically different, but they readily agree that structures which stain alike are not necessarily similar in chemical composition. Chromosomes of dividing nuclei and lignified cell walls stain alike with safranin; chromosomes and cellulose cell walls stain much alike with Delafield's haematoxylin; but everyone recognizes that the chromosome is very different in its chemical composition from either the cellulose or the lignified wall.

However, in an indirect and somewhat uncertain way, one can infer the nature of certain structures from the staining. For instance, if sections of various objects have been stained with safranin, we may draw the following inferences with more or less confidence: if cells in the xylem region of a vascular bundle stain red, their walls are lignified; if cortical cells, which may appear quite similar in transverse section, stain red, they are likely to be suberized; if the outer walls of epidermal cells stain red, they are cutinized; but if the outer boundary of the embryo sac of a gymnosperm stains red, it is chitinized. Of course, these inferences can be made only because the various structures have been tested by more accurate methods.

Whatever doubt or uncertainty there may be in regard to theories of staining or in regard to the value of stains as a means of analysis, there is no doubt that stains are of the highest importance in differentiating structures, and in bringing out details which would otherwise be invisible.

PRACTICAL HINTS ON STAINING

The number of stains in the catalogues is becoming so great that it is impossible to become proficient in the use of all of them. As we have already intimated, it is better to master a few of the most valuable stains than to do indifferent work with many. An experienced technician knows that it is impossible to judge from a few trials whether a given stain or combination is really valuable or not. As a matter of fact, some of the most valuable combinations, like Haidenhain's iron-alum haematoxylin and Flemming's safranin, gentian violet, orange, require patient study and long practice before they yield the magnificent preparations of the trained cytologist. The beginner, especially if somewhat unacquainted with the details of plant structure, may believe that he has an excellent preparation when it is really a bad, or at most an indifferent, one. To illustrate, let us suppose that sections of the pollen grain of a lily have been stained in safranin and gentian violet. If the preparation merely shows a couple of dense nuclei and a mass of uniform cell contents surrounded by a heavy wall, the mount is poor. If the two nuclei are quite different and starch grains are well differentiated in the tube cells and the wall shows a violet intine contrasting sharply with a red exine, the mount is good. Anything intermediate is indifferent. If mitotic figures have been stained with cyanin and erythrosin, a first-class preparation should show blue chromosomes and red spindles; if stained with safranin and gentian violet, the chromosomes should be red and the spindles, violet.

In staining growing points, apical cells, young embryos, antheridia, archegonia, and many such things, the cell walls are the principal things to be differentiated, if the preparations are for morphological study. As a rule, it is better in such cases not to use double staining, but to select a stain which stains the cell walls deeply without obscuring them by staining starch, chlorophyll, and other cell contents. For example, try the growing point of *Equisetum*. The protoplasm of such growing points is very dense. If Delafield's haematoxylin and erythrosin be used, the haematoxylin will stain the walls and nuclei, and will slightly affect the other cell contents, but the erythrosin will give the cytoplasm such a dense stain that the cell walls will be seriously obscured. It would be better to use haematoxylin alone. For counting chromosomes, it is better to stain in iron-alum haematoxylin alone, or in safranin alone. The same suggestion may well be observed in tracing the development of antheridia, archegonia, embryos, and similar structures.

In using combinations, it must be remembered that the second stain often affects the first, e.g., if safranin is to be followed by Delafield's haematoxylin, in staining a vascular bundle, it will not do to make the safranin just right and then apply the haematoxylin, for the acid which must be used to differentiate the haematoxylin and to avoid precipitates will also reduce the safranin, and the red will be too weak. You must overstain in safranin so that the reduction will finally leave it just right. The same hint will apply if safranin is to be followed by anilin blue, since, here, also, acid must be used; if light green is to follow the safranin, the stain itself is so acid that the safranin must be rather strong before the light green is applied. Orange, whether in water or in clove oil, reduces many stains and, consequently, such stains must be strong enough to allow the weakening. These hints are only samples: the student must observe the behavior of the various stains when used singly and when used in various combinations.

With perfect confidence, we can give advice to the beginner and to the seasoned investigator: *master a few stains*. With Haidenhain's iron-alum haematoxylin, stain sections of root-tips until you can see the finest details of the chromatin. When you can make a perfect preparation of a root-tip with this stain, you will have made a good start toward a satisfactory histologial technique. Gentian violet is often used to stain the cilia of sperms; but Haidenhain's iron-alum haematoxylin will stain the cilia of cycad sperms so critically that the base of the cilium, as it passes through the *Hautschicht* (plasma membrane), will be differentiated from the part projecting beyond the *Hautschicht*. Master this haematoxylin stain and then, with sections of root-tips, practice the safranin, gentian violet, orange combination until you can stain the chromosomes red, the spindle violet, and the cytoplasm orange. For vascular anatomy, learn to stain xylem with safranin; and, for a contrast, stain cellulose walls with Delafield's haematoxylin, gentian violet, light green, or anilin blue. For filamentous algae and fungi, master the iron-alum haematoxylin method; and

then try the phloxine and aniline-blue combination. Do not pass judgment against a standard method or even a new method just because
you fail to get results at the first trial. After you have become proficient with the iron-alum haematoxylin for mitotic figures in higher
plants, you are sure to fail if you try the same procedure with *Rhizopus;* but, nevertheless, the stain is just as good for *Rhizopus* as for
figures in pollen mother-cells or root-tips.

Permanent preparations are such a necessary part of most advanced
work that one is in danger of delaying the critical observation until he
has made a permanent mount. It cannot be repeated too often that
one should develop also the technique of studying the living structures.
It is impossible to make a permanent mount of the rotation of protoplasm. Study motile spores while they are moving before you make
permanent preparations. The difficult and complicated histological
technique loses much of its value unless it is accompanied by a thorough study of living material.

CHAPTER V

TEMPORARY MOUNTS AND MICROCHEMICAL TESTS

Skill in making freehand sections, without any microtome, and in teasing with needles, and in making delicate dissections under the simple microscope are absolutely necessary in any investigation dealing with the structure and development of plants. Preliminary study with the aid of such methods not only gives a broader view of structures in all dimensions and helps the interpretation of stained microtome preparations but is necessary in determining whether material is worth all the labor of making permanent mounts. That particular class of temporary mounts intended only for chemical tests is considered separately in the second part of this chapter.

TEMPORARY MOUNTS

A preliminary examination of almost any botanical material may be made without any fixing, imbedding, or staining. If a little starch be scraped from a potato, and a small drop of water and a cover-glass be added, a very good view will be obtained, and if a small drop of iodine solution be allowed to run under the cover, the preparation, while it lasts, is better than some permanent mounts. The unicellular and filamentous algae can be studied quite satisfactorily from such mounts. The protonema of mosses and the prothallia of ferns should be studied in this way, even if a later study from sections is intended. The addition of a little iodine identifies the starch and makes the nucleus more plainly visible. If the top of a moss capsule be cut off at the level of the annulus, a beautiful view of the peristome may be obtained by simply mounting in a drop of water, or, in a case like this where no collapse is to be anticipated, the object may be mounted in a small drop of glycerin—just enough to come to the edge of the cover without oozing out beyond—and the preparation may be made permanent by sealing with balsam, gold size, or any good cement. The antheridia and archegonia of mosses may be examined if the surrounding leaves are carefully teased away with needles. Freehand sectioning with a sharp razor and judicious teasing with a pair of needles will give a fair insight into the anatomy of the higher plants without demanding any further knowledge of technique. This rough work is a very desirable antecedent to the study of microtome sections, because most students see in a series of microtome sections *only* a series of sections when, in the mind's eye, they ought to see the object building itself up in length, breadth, and thickness as they pass from one section to another.

The movements of protoplasm can, of course, be studied only in the living material. Every laboratory should keep *Chara* growing at every season of the year. Mount a small portion and note the movements in the internodal cells. Avoid any pressure and any lowering of the temperature. A gentle raising of the temperature will accelerate the movements. A leaf of *Elodea* shows the movements very clearly, especially in the midrib region. The stamen hairs of *Tradescantia* have long been used, their color, resembling a faint haematoxylin stain, making them particularly favorable. Stinging hairs show a brisk movement if they are mounted quickly and without injury. Fortunately, the common onion always furnishes favorable material for demonstrating the movements of protoplasm. Strip the epidermis from one of the inner scales of the bulb and mount in water. The granules may appear to better advantage in yellow light, like that of an ordinary kerosene lamp.

In studying the movements of protoplasm, a drop of aqueous carmine, allowed to run under the cover, will bring the protoplasm more clearly into view. The protoplasm is often so nearly colorless that one recognizes it only by the movement of plastids and various granules which are carried along in the current.

The discharge of spores and gametes should be observed in the living material: the difference in the behavior of spores and gametes is very striking and can be appreciated only while they are alive. Most aspects of growth and movement can be studied best in the living condition. In short, it is well to make a preliminary study of everything.

The development of the micromanipulator has brought such an immense improvement in the technique of studying living material that some investigators can make tiny glass needles which they can insert into a cell, hook a needle into each end of a chromosome, stretch it, and allow it to contract. This remarkable instrument, which can be used with any high-grade microscope, opens an attractive field for work in cytology and microchemistry.

The germination of spores and the growth of pollen tubes can be studied in the hanging drop. For facilitating such cultures there are many devices, such as hollow-ground slides, glass rings, rubber rings, etc. (Fig. 17). A device which is better for most purposes, and which is easily made by any student, is to cut a square or round hole $\frac{5}{8}$ inch in diameter in a piece of pasteboard $\frac{1}{8}$ inch thick, 1 inch wide, and $1\frac{1}{2}$ inches long. The pasteboard is then boiled to sterilize it and to make it fit more closely to the slide. While the pasteboard is still wet, press it to the slide, make the culture in a drop of water or culture solution on the cover, and invert the cover over the hole. A little water added at the edge of the pasteboard from time to time will keep it from warping and will at the same time provide a constant moist chamber.

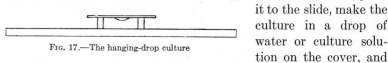

FIG. 17.—The hanging-drop culture

In collecting material for mitotic figures in anthers it is necessary to examine fresh anthers, if one wishes to avoid a tedious and uncertain search after the anthers have been imbedded. By teasing out a few cells from the apex and a few from the base of the anther the stage of development is readily determined, and anthers which do not show the desired stages can be rejected. By allowing a drop of eosin or methyl green to run under the cover, the figures are more easily detected. The actual progress of mitosis has been observed in the stamen hairs of *Tradescantia*. If care be taken not to injure the hairs or let the temperature drop, a mount in water, or in 1 per cent sugar solution, or in the juice of the plant, may live long enough for a study of a complete mitosis, which takes 2 or 3 hours.

MICROCHEMICAL TESTS

Botanical microchemistry has developed to such an extent that it has become an independent subject, like bacteriology. We shall consider only the commonest tests which are needed constantly by students of morphology. For a thorough presentation of the chemistry of the cell, we are still looking forward with great anticipation to a forthcoming book by Dr. Sophia Eckerson, whose critical tests and analyses we have observed for many years. In the meantime, *Pflanzenmikrochemie*, by Dr. O. Tunmann (Gebrüder Bornträger, Berlin), is recommended to those who read German. Zimmerman's *Botanical Microtechnique* (Henry Holt & Co., New York) is still recommended to those who must rely upon English. We shall give only a few tests, but in considering the various stains we shall indicate the effect of each stain upon the various plant structures.

Starch.—Mount the starch or starch-containing structures in water, and allow a drop of iodine solution to run under the cover. Starch assumes a characteristic blue color. The solution may be prepared by dissolving 1 g. of potassium iodide in 100 c.c. of water and adding 0.3 g. of sublimed iodine. A strong solution of iodine in alcohol (about 1 g. in 50 c.c. of absolute alcohol) keeps well. A drop of this solution added to 1 c.c. of water is good for testing. With too strong a solution, the starch first turns blue but rapidly becomes black.

Grape-sugar.—In cells containing grape-sugar, bright-red granules of cuprous oxide are precipitated by Fehling's solution. It is better to keep the three ingredients in separate bottles, because the solution does not keep long after the ingredients are mixed. The solutions may be labeled A, B, and C.

A	Cupric sulphate	3 g.
	Water	100 c.c.
B	Sodium potassium tartrate (Rochelle salt)	16 g.
	Water	100 c.c.
C	Caustic soda	12 g.
	Water	100 c.c.

When needed for use, add to 10 c.c. of water 5 c.c. from each of the three solutions. The sections, which should be two or three cells in thickness, are warmed in the solution until little bubbles are formed. Too much heat must be avoided. Mount and examine in a few drops of the solution. The twig or organ may be treated with the solution, and the sections may be cut afterward. Other substances precipitate copper, and may be mistaken for grape-sugar by the beginner.

Cane-sugar.—Cuprous oxide is not precipitated from Fehling's solution by cane-sugar, but after continued boiling in this solution the cane-sugar is changed to invert-sugar and the copper is precipitated. The solution becomes blue.

Proteins.—The proteins turn yellow or brown with the iodine solution. It is better to use a stronger solution than when testing for starch. It must be remembered that many other substances also turn brown when treated with iodine.

When proteins are warmed gently in concentrated nitric acid, the acid becomes yellow. The color may be deepened by the addition of a little ammonia or caustic potash.

When proteins are heated with Millon's reagent, the solution becomes brick-red or rose-red. This reaction takes place slowly even in the cold. The following is one formula for this reagent:

Mercury..................................... 1 c.c.
Concentrated nitric acid...................... 9 c.c.
Water....................................... 10 c.c.

Dissolve the mercury in the nitric acid and add the water.

Fats and oils.—The fatty oils are not soluble in water and are only slightly soluble in ordinary alcohol. They dissolve readily in chloroform, ether, carbon disulphide, or methyl alcohol.

Alcannin colors oils and fats deep red. The test is not decisive, because ethereal oils and resins take the same red color. Dissolve commercial alcannin in absolute alcohol, add an equal volume of water, and filter. The fats and oils in sections left in this solution for 24 hours should be bright red. The reaction is hastened by gentle heating.

Osmic acid, as used in fixing agents, colors fats and oils brown or black, and the black remains even after all the processes of the paraffin method. The black can be bleached out in hydrogen peroxide, or chlorine (see p. 27).

In case of fats and oils, solubility and color reactions are useful, but must be regarded as corroborative evidence, not as decisive proof. For more critical and detailed methods, consult the book by Tunmann, which will also give the literature of the subject.

The middle lamella.—Even the origin and development of the middle lamella are none too well known; its microchemistry has progressed but little beyond the color-reaction stage. The middle lamella consists largely of pectin or pectic compounds. The easy isolation of cells, when treated with Schultze's maceration, depends upon the ready solubility of pectins in this reagent. Many intercellular spaces arise through the natural solution or gelatinization of the lamella.

In polarized light, with crossed Nicols, the middle lamella is resolved into three lamellae, the middle one appearing dark, and the two outer lamellae, light.

Ruthenium red is a good stain, since it gives as good results as any and has the advantage of keeping well in balsam or glycerin jelly. Make a very weak solution—1 g. to 5,000 c.c. of water, or even weaker —and keep it in the dark. It stains many other things besides the lamella, but is, nevertheless, a good stain.

Pectin is not at all confined to the middle lamella, but is found in other membranes, particularly in spore coats.

Cellulose.—In concentrated sulphuric acid cellulose swells and finally dissolves. It is also soluble in cuprammonia. The cuprammonia can be prepared by pouring 15 per cent ammonia water upon copper turnings or filings. Let the solution stand in an open bottle. It does not keep well, but its efficiency is readily tested. Cotton dissolves almost immediately as long as the solution is fit for use.

With iodine and sulphuric acid, cellulose turns blue. Treat first with the undiluted iodine-potassium-iodide solution described in the test for starch, then add a mixture of two parts of concentrated sulphuric acid and one part of water.

With chloroïodide of zinc, cellulose turns violet. Dissolve commercial chloroïodide of zinc in about its own weight of water and add enough metallic iodine to give the solution a deep brown color.

The cell walls of fungi consist of *fungus cellulose*. When young, they give a typical cellulose reaction; when older, they become insoluble in cuprammonia and, with iodine and sulphuric acid, show only a yellow or brown, instead of the typical blue. With chloroïodide of zinc, the wall stains yellow or brown, instead of violet.

Reserve cellulose, which is common in thick-walled endosperm of seeds, shows the same microchemical reactions as ordinary cellulose.

Callose.—The thickening on the sieve plate differs from cellulose in its staining reactions, and in its solubility. It is insoluble in cuprammonia, but will dissolve in a 1 per cent solution of caustic soda.

Stain in a 4 per cent aqueous solution of soda (Na_2CO_3) for 10 minutes, and transfer to glycerin. The callus should take a bright red. If stained very deeply and then transferred to a 4 per cent soda (without the corallin), the stain is extracted from the cellulose but remains in the callus. Unfortunately, the preparations are not permanent.

If stained for about an hour in a dilute aqueous solution of anilin blue, the stain may be extracted with glycerin until it remains only in the callus. After the blue is satisfactory, a few minutes in aqueous eosin will afford a good contrast. The preparation may be mounted in balsam and is fairly permanent.

Lignin.—Lignified walls are insoluble in cuprammonia. The iodine and sulphuric acid or the chloroïodide of zinc, used as in testing for cellulose, give the lignified walls a yellow or brown color. After a treatment with Schultze's maceration fluid, lignified membranes react like cellulose.

Phloroglucin in a 5 per cent aqueous or alcoholic solution applied simultaneously with hydrochloric acid gives lignified walls a reddish-violet color. The preparations do not keep.

Cutinized and suberized walls.—These are insoluble in cuprammonia or concentrated sulphuric acid. They are colored yellow or brown by chloroïodide of zinc, or by iodine and sulphuric acid, when applied as in testing for cellulose or lignin. With alcannin, they take a red color, but the red is not as deep as in case of fats and oils. After soaking in an aqueous solution of caustic potash, suberized membranes take a red-violet color when treated with chloroïodide of zinc.

If a strong, fresh alcoholic solution of chlorophyll be allowed to act upon suberized membranes for 15–30 minutes in the dark, they stain green, while lignified and cellulose walls do not take the stain. The preparations are not permanent.

A solution of alcannin in 50 per cent alcohol stains suberized and cutinized walls red, but the color may not be very sharp.

Cyanin can be recommended. First, treat with *Eau de Javelle* (potassium hypochlorite), which can be obtained ready for use at any drug-store. This destroys tannins, and the lignified walls lose their staining capacity. Make a 1 per cent solution of cyanin (Grübler's) in 50 per cent alcohol and add an equal volume of glycerin. This should show blue suberized walls, while the lignified walls remain unstained.

Gum, mucilage, and gelatinized membranes.—These are all soluble in water and are further characterized by their strong power of swelling. They are insoluble in alcohol. A series of forms with various color reactions is included under this heading.

Crystals.—Nearly all crystals which are found in plants consist of calcium oxalate. Crystals of calcium carbonate, calcium tartrate, and calcium sulphate also occur. Calcium oxalate is soluble in hydrochloric acid or nitric acid. It is better to use the concentrated acids. The crystals are insoluble in water and acetic acid. Sulphuric acid changes calcium oxalate into calcium sulphate. When treated with barium chloride, crystals of calcium sulphate become covered with a granular layer of barium sulphate, while crystals of calcium oxalate are not affected.

Calcium carbonate, when treated with hydrochloric acid or acetic acid, dissolves with effervescence. The acetic acid should be rather dilute.

CHAPTER VI

FREEHAND SECTIONS[1]

The real freehand sections of pre-microtome days, cut by holding the object in one hand and the knife in the other, are becoming less and less frequent in well-equipped laboratories. Since the subsequent technique for such sections is the same as for those cut with a microtome without imbedding, both kinds of sections can be treated together. However, every student should learn to cut real freehand sections: the laboratory is no place for one who is awkward with his hands; manual dexterity must be acquired if there is to be any success in morphological studies, which demand critical preparations. Not only freehand sections, but other small thin objects which can be treated like sections, will be considered in this chapter.

The beginner should start with the freehand section because the processes are rapid and it is easy to find the causes of imperfections and failures.

For cutting sections of small twigs, roots, rhizomes, and similar objects, we use a safety razor blade, either held directly in the fingers or in the type of clamp shown in Figure 3. For those who use the old-fashioned razor, the grandfather type, shown in Figure 6, is the best.

In cutting, brace the forearms against the sides, hold the object firmly in the left hand, and cut with a long, oblique stroke from left to right. The edge of the razor and the direction of the stroke should be toward the body, not away from it as in whittling. If the material is fresh, the object and the razor should be kept wet with water, the razor being dipped in water for every stroke. For hard objects, like twigs of oak or maple, the grandfather razor will need sharpening after cutting a dozen sections. It is a waste of time to put off sharpening until the razor has become noticeably dull, for all sections except those cut when the razor is perfectly sharp are sure to be inferior. With softer material the razor may hold its edge for hundreds of sections. Those sections which seem to be worth further treatment should be

[1] Before attempting the freehand sectioning, the beginner should read the paragraphs on killing, fixing, washing, hardening, dehydrating, and clearing, beginning on pp. 18 and 112.

87

placed at once in water or in a fixing agent and, of course, the choice of a fixing agent should be determined before the sections are cut.

With the advent of a cheap, efficient sliding microtome, the hand microtome began to fall into disuse and, today, it has almost disappeared.

The sliding microtome (Fig. 2) reduces to a minimum the necessity for manual dexterity, but it is a more complicated machine. Study the various parts before you begin to cut sections. How is the knife adjusted? How is the object clamp raised and lowered? How is the thickness of the section determined? In case of a simple microtome like the one shown in Figure 2, the student should soon answer such questions without any help from the instructor. In case of more complicated microtomes, a demonstration by the instructor will save both time and machine.

In cutting sections of wood or herbaceous stems, the knife should be set obliquely so as to use as much as possible of the cutting edge. In most cases it is neither necessary nor desirable to cut very thin sections by this method; 10 μ is very thin, and 20, 30, or even 40 μ is usually thin enough.

Cut with a firm, even stroke, wetting both knife and object after every section. Use water, if the material is fresh; if preserved, use the preservative. Some use a brush in removing sections from the knife, but nothing is quite equal to one's finger; anyone who is in danger of a cut while performing this act is in need of this little practice in manual dexterity.

WOODY AND HERBACEOUS SECTIONS

Safranin and Delafield's haematoxylin.—In order to make the directions as explicit as possible, let us follow the processes from collecting the material to labeling the slide. The rhizome of *Pteris aquilina* is a good object to begin with. Dig down carefully until the rhizome is exposed; then with a sharp knife cut off pieces a foot in length, wrap them in wet paper, and bring them into the laboratory. If the rhizome has been cut carelessly or pulled up, as is usually the case, the finished mount will show ruptures between the bundles and bundle sheaths, disfiguring what should have been a beautiful preparation.

While the material is still fresh and moist, cut the sections, placing them in water as fast as they are cut. When through with the cutting rinse the sections in water and transfer to 95 per cent alcohol, where they should remain for at least 30 minutes—an hour, or even over-night, does no damage. Pour off the alcohol and pour on a 50 per cent alcoholic solution of safranin (a 1 per cent solution of safranin in 50 per cent alcohol). Stain overnight, or even for 24 hours.

Pour off the safranin (which may be used repeatedly) and pour on 50 per cent alcohol. The alcohol will gradually wash out the safranin, but this stain is washed out more rapidly from cellulose walls than from those which are lignified. The sections should remain in the alcohol until the stain is nearly—but not quite—washed out from the cellulose walls, while still showing a brilliant red in the large lignified tracheids. If 5 or 10 minutes in the alcohol draws the safranin from the lignified walls as well as the cellulose, stain longer; if the differentiation is not secured in 5 or 10 minutes, a small drop of hydrochloric acid added to the alcohol will hasten the process. Some recommend staining for only 1 or 2 hours, but the washing-out process is likely to be rapid and uncertain.

Pour off the alcohol and wash the sections thoroughly in ordinary drinking-water. The washing should be particularly thorough if acid has been used to hasten the previous process, for the preparations will fade if any acid remains.

Stain in Delafield's haematoxylin 3–30 minutes. Usually 5 minutes will be about right. Delafield's haematoxylin will stain the cellulose walls, but will have little or no effect upon lignified structures.

Transfer to drinking-water, not distilled water. The red color of the whole section, as it appears to the naked eye, will be rapidly replaced by a rich purple. Continue to wash in water for 2 or 3 minutes after the purple color appears. If the cellulose walls show only a faint purplish color, put the sections back into the stain and try a longer period. If the color is a deep purple or nearly black, add a little hydrochloric acid (1 drop to 50 c.c. is enough) to the water. It is better to put the drop into a bottle of water and shake thoroughly before letting the acidified water act upon the sections. As soon as the sections begin to appear reddish, which may be within 4 or 5 seconds, pour off the acidified water and wash in drinking-water, changing the water 3 or 4 times a minute, until the reddish color caused by the acid has been replaced by the rich purple color so characteristic of haematoxylin. The acid not only secures differentiation by dissolving out the stain from lignified structures more rapidly than from cellulose walls but it also removes the disfiguring precipitates which almost invariably accompany staining with Delafield's haematoxylin. The acid also washes out the safranin; it is for this reason that the washing after safranin should be stopped while there is still some red color in the cellulose walls. The acid should not only reduce the density of the haematoxylin and remove precipitates but should also remove the little safranin which may remain in the cellulose walls. After the purple color has appeared, the sections should be left in water for 20 or 30 minutes, changing frequently. They might be left in the water for several hours. The acid must be washed out thoroughly or the stains will fade.

Now place the sections in 50 per cent alcohol for 1 minute, then in 95 per cent alcohol for 1 minute, 100 per cent alcohol for 5 minutes, and then transfer to xylol. As soon as the sections become clear—in about 1–5 minutes—they are ready for mounting in balsam. If the

FIG. 18.—The label

sections do not clear readily, as may be the case if the air is damp, or if the alcohol or xylol is not quite pure, transfer from the absolute alcohol to clove oil, which will clear, even if the absolute alcohol is rather poor. Then transfer from clove oil to xylol; the objection to mounting directly from clove oil is that preparations harden more slowly than when mounted from xylol. With a section-lifter, or scalpel, or brush, transfer 3 or 4 sections to a clean, dry slide, put on 1 or 2 drops of balsam, and add a cover, first heating it gently to remove moisture. If xylol has been used for clearing, it is necessary to work rapidly; for the sections must never be allowed to dry. Use square or oblong covers for such mounts, reserving round covers for glycerin mounts. If material is abundant, use as many sections as you can cover conveniently. If you have used several stains with the same material, select for each mount sections from the different stains. In ordinary wood sections each mount should show the three most important views, transverse, longitudinal radial, and longitudinal tangential sections. It is wasteful to use three slides and three covers to show these three views, or to make a mount containing only a single section of the rhizome of *Pteris*.

Put the label at the left. Write first the genus and species; then indicate what part of the plant has been mounted. The date on which the material was fixed is often valuable. In many cases, the date of collecting the material is desirable. The beginner is likely to write also the stains used, and other details, which he will find quite unnecessary after a little experience. Figure 18 illustrates a good style of labeling and mounting.

The following is a convenient summary of the foregoing processes, beginning with the sections in 95 per cent alcohol:

1. Sections in 95 per cent alcohol.
2. Safranin, 12–24 hours.
3. Fifty per cent alcohol, with or without acid, until color is right, generally about 2–10 minutes.
4. Water, 5 minutes, changing frequently.
5. Delafield's haematoxylin, 3–30 minutes.
6. Water, 5–10 minutes, changing frequently.
7. Water slightly acidulated, 5–10 seconds.
8. Water, to wash out acid, 20–30 minutes.
9. Fifty per cent alcohol, 5 minutes.
10. Ninety-five per cent alcohol, 5 minutes.
11. One hundred per cent alcohol, 5 minutes.
12. Xylol, 5 minutes.
13. Balsam.
14. Cover and label.

If clove oil seems necessary, finish as follows:

12. Clove oil, 2–5 minutes.
13. Xylol, 5 minutes.
14. Balsam.
15. Cover and label.

Another method has given excellent results, especially with old stems, pieces of dry boards, etc. Cut pieces 5–10 mm. square and 2–3 cm. long, boil in water 10–24 hours and, when cool, transfer to equal parts of 95 per cent alcohol and glycerin. Material may be left in this mixture indefinitely. Hard woods should remain here for at least two weeks before cutting, since the mixture is a good preservative and hard woods left in it for a year are easier to cut.

After sections have been cut, wash them in tap water, then in distilled water, and stain half an hour or more in weak Delafield's haematoxylin—about 5 parts of the solution, as given in the formula, to 100 parts of water—and then wash in distilled water. Stain in weak safranin—about 2 parts of the stock solution to 100 parts of water—overnight or even for several days. Wash in tap water, then wash in 95 per cent alcohol for 30 seconds or longer, according to the appearance of the stain. Dehydrate in absolute alcohol, clear in clove oil, transfer to xylol, and mount in balsam. This method is very good for gymnosperm woods.

Since it usually happens that processes are commenced, but cannot be completed, at a single laboratory period, it is necessary to know where sections may be left for several hours or until the next day without suffering injury. At 1, 2, or the pure water of 8 in the schedule given above, sections may be left until the next day. If it is not desirable to mount all of the sections which have been prepared, they may be kept indefinitely in clove oil or xylol. If the sections are to remain for a year or more in the clearing agent, xylol is to be preferred. Shells with good corks are best for keeping such material.

For the study of vascular anatomy, this is the most permanent stain which has come into general use.

More recently, safranin combined with anilin blue or with light green has been coming into favor. Both these methods will be described.

Safranin and anilin blue.—Use the alcoholic safranin already described, and a 1 per cent solution of anilin blue in 90 per cent alcohol.

With this combination we should recommend a long stain in safranin, not less than 24 hours. Wash in 50 per cent alcohol, but do not extract all the safranin from the cellulose walls. Stain 2–10 minutes in anilin blue. Rinse a few seconds in 95 per cent alcohol, then treat for about 5 seconds with 95 per cent alcohol slightly acidulated with hydrochloric acid—one drop in 50 c.c. of alcohol may be enough. The weak blue should at once change to a bright blue and, at the same time, the acid will remove some of the safranin. It is for this reason that we proceed while the sections are still somewhat overstained in safranin. Wash for 1 or 2 minutes in 95 per cent alcohol to remove the acid. A trace of sodium carbonate, just enough to make the alcohol alkaline, may be added to the 95 per cent alcohol. If any acid remains, the safranin will fade. Dehydrate in absolute alcohol 5 minutes, clear in xylol, or first in clove oil and then in xylol, and mount in balsam.

For convenient reference, the process may be summarized, but it must be remembered that all the schedules are intended merely to introduce the beginner to the method.

1. Sections in 95 per cent alcohol.
2. Stain in safranin, 24 hours.
3. Fifty per cent alcohol until the stain becomes weak in cellulose walls, but not until it is removed entirely.
4. Anilin blue, 2–10 minutes.
5. Ninety-five per cent alcohol, 2–5 seconds.
6. Ninety-five per cent alcohol, slightly acidulated with hydrochloric acid, 5 seconds.
7. Ninety-five per cent alcohol, with or without a trace of sodium carbonate, 1 or 2 minutes.
8. Absolute alcohol, 1–5 minutes.
9. Xylol, 5 minutes. The xylol may be preceded by clove oil.
10. Mount in balsam.

Lignified and suberized walls should stain bright red, and cellulose walls, bright blue. To make this beautiful combination a success, it is necessary to be very careful. If too much safranin is extracted at stage 3, the acid at stage 6 will still further weaken the red stain and the contrast will not be sharp.

Safranin and light green (Land's schedule).—This is another beautiful combination, and the student should be successful from the first, since the light green is simpler to apply than either Delafield's haematoxylin or anilin blue.

Land uses either aqueous, anilin, or alcoholic safranin, and uses the light green in clove oil, or in a mixture of clove oil and absolute alcohol. Make a saturated solution of light green in clove oil. Since the solution takes place slowly, the mixture should stand several days before using. If a small quantity of absolute alcohol be added to the clove oil, the stain dissolves more readily. For some structures the stain is more brilliant than with the simple clove-oil solution.

Sections from fresh material are fixed in 95 per cent alcohol; sections from preserved material are rinsed in alcohol or water before staining. The following schedule will summarize the method:

1. Safranin, 2–24 hours.
2. Fifty per cent alcohol, until differentiated.
3. Dehydrate in 95 and 100 per cent alcohol.
4. Light green (in clove oil), 3–30 minutes.

5. Xylol: 2 or 3 c.c. of absolute alcohol may be added to each 100 c.c. of xylol, if the free light green shows a tendency to precipitate.

6. Mount in balsam.

This stain is particularly good for phloem. Since the light green is not likely to overstain and only slightly weakens the safranin, the combination is a rather easy one, so that even the beginner can hardly fail to get a good preparation.

Malachite green and Congo red.—I am indebted to Dr. Sharp for this method, which has been popular in Professor Grégoire's laboratory at Louvain.

Sections of fresh material should be treated with 95 per cent alcohol and then transferred to water.

1. Three per cent aqueous solution of malachite green or methylene blue, 6 hours or more.

2. Wash in water.

3. Congo red, 1 per cent aqueous solution, 15 minutes.

4. Wash in water.

5. Rinse in 80 per cent alcohol. As soon as the malachite green or anilin blue color appears through the red, transfer quickly to

6. Absolute alcohol.

7. Xylol.

8. Balsam.

Iodine green and acid fuchsin is another good combination for such sections. The stain will be particularly brilliant if sections from fresh material are fixed in 1 per cent chromo-acetic acid for 24 hours; and then washed for an hour in water. Beginning with the sections in water, the procedure is as follows:

Stain in aqueous iodine green for 12–24 hours. Then wash in water until the stain is nearly all washed out from the cellulose walls but is still brilliant in the lignified walls. If the stain acts for too short a time, the washing-out process necessary to remove the stain from the cellulose walls will leave only a pale green color in the lignified walls. Stain in aqueous acid fuchsin for 2–10 minutes. This should stain the cellulose walls sharply, but should not act long enough to affect the lignified tissues. Pour off the stain (which may be used repeatedly), and pour on 95 per cent alcohol, and immediately pour it off and add absolute alcohol. The 95 per cent alcohol should not act for more than 5 or 10 seconds, its only function being to save the more expensive absolute alcohol. From 10–30 seconds will usually be long enough for the absolute alcohol. Too long a period in the alcohols will weaken the stain. Clear in xylol or clove oil, and mount in balsam.

If a 50 or 70 per cent alcoholic solution of iodine green has been used, the stain should be washed out in 50 per cent alcohol; otherwise the treatment is the same.

Methyl green (aqueous solution) **and acid fuchsin** is a good combination, and the student may find it easier to get a good differentiation than with iodine green. Follow the directions for the aqueous iodine green and acid fuchsin. It may be necessary to wash more rapidly, since the methyl green is easily extracted.

Safranin and gentian violet.—This is a good combination for vascular anatomy. Stain overnight in safranin, rinse in 50 per cent alcohol until the stain is reduced to a light pink color in the cellulose walls; then rinse in water and stain 5–10 minutes in aqueous gentian violet or crystal violet. Rinse in water, dehydrate in 95 and 100 per cent alcohol, differentiate and clear in clove oil, transfer to xylol, and mount in balsam.

Orange may be added to this combination, making a triple stain. In this case, do not reduce the safranin at all, but rinse quickly in 50 per cent alcohol, then in water, stain in gentian violet, rinse in 95 per cent alcohol, and stain for 1 or 2 minutes in orange dissolved in clove oil. This will not only reduce and differentiate the gentian violet, but will reduce the safranin. Transfer to xylol and mount in balsam. If the safranin is drawn out too rapidly, stain for 15–30 seconds in the orange, transfer to clove oil without any orange until the gentian violet is satisfactory; then transfer to xylol and mount in balsam.

Both the violet and the orange may be used in clove oil. In this case, transfer to the violet from absolute alcohol, and from the violet to the orange; then to pure clove oil until the violet looks right. Transfer to xylol and mount in balsam.

The bordered pits of conifers, the Bars of Sanio, and the middle lamella are beautifully stained by this method. For the Bars of Sanio, it may be necessary to stain in the clove oil violet over night, or even for 24 hours.

Other combinations might be suggested, e.g., iodine green or methyl green with Bismarck brown, methyl green with Delafield's haematoxylin; orange G might be added after the safranin and Delafield's haematoxylin, and various other stains might be tried. In double staining it is usually best to combine a basic with an acid stain.

Green and red make a good contrast, but a section stained with iodine green and safranin would be a failure, because both stains would stain the xylem and neither would stain the cellulose. Both stains are basic. Red lignin and green cellulose could be secured by using safranin and acid green. Green lignin and red cellulose as already indicated, can be got with iodine green and acid fuchsin.

The time required for the different processes varies greatly, and the time required for a subsequent process is often more or less dependent upon the time given to processes which preceded it. Good mounts of sections of the petiole of *Nuphar advena* have been secured from material which had been cut, fixed, stained in safranin and Delafield's haematoxylin, and mounted in balsam, the entire time being less than 30 minutes. This is an extreme case, and nothing is gained, except time, and the saving of time is apparent rather than real, for the histologist always has something to do while the sections are in the stain.

Preserved, fresh, and dry material.—If sections are to be cut from material preserved in formalin, the piece should be washed in water, since the odor is annoying and the fumes are injurious to the eyes, and the acid in the formalin interferes with most stains.

The sections are placed in the stain from water. Sections from alcoholic material are transferred directly to the stain. If the material is in a mixture of alcohol and glycerin, the sections should be washed in water or 50 per cent alcohol until the glycerin has been removed before transferring to the stain.

Some material cuts well when fresh, but cuts with difficulty when preserved. On the other hand, some material cuts well when preserved, but hardly at all when fresh. Some material which is too soft to cut when fresh can be cut with ease after it has been in formalin alcohol for a week or more.

Oak, hickory, maple, and other hard woods need special treatment because they are so hard to cut. It is a good practice to boil the material in water and treat with hydrofluoric acid before any sectioning is attempted. The following is the usual method when this acid is used: Cut the material into blocks 5 or 6 mm. square and 2 or 3 cm. long and boil in water for several minutes; then transfer to cold water and, after several minutes, repeat the boiling. The alternate boiling and cooling, which should be repeated several times, drives out the air. Transfer to equal parts of commercial hydrofluoric acid and water. From 1 to 3 weeks will be enough for most woods. Some oaks, ebony, apple, etc., may require a longer time and the acid may be used pure. Three days in 10 per cent acid may be enough for corn stems. Wash thoroughly in water for a day or two. Then leave in equal parts of 30 per cent alcohol and glycerin for several days before cutting. Material may be left indefinitely in the mixture of glycerin and alcohol.

An article by Dr. La Dema M. Langdon, dealing with the preparation and sectioning of hard, woody tissues, appeared in the *Botanical Gazette* of July, 1920. By her method, hard, woody tissues are softened so that they cut readily and can even be imbedded in paraffin and cut successfully.

OBJECTS MOUNTED WITHOUT SECTIONING

Fern prothallia, mounted without sectioning, make very useful preparations. Select desirable stages and fix in chromo-acetic acid for 24–48 hours (chromic acid, $\frac{1}{2}$ g.; acetic acid, 3 c.c.; water, 100 c.c.). Wash in running water 6 hours or overnight; stain in Delafield's haematoxylin for 5–30 minutes; wash in water slightly acidulated with hydrochloric acid for a few seconds, and then wash thoroughly in tap water. The prothallia must now be brought through a graded series of alcohols—$2\frac{1}{2}$, 5, $7\frac{1}{2}$, 10, 20, 35, 50, 70, 85, 95, and 100 per cent. About 2 hours should be the minimum in each grade, except 85, where 24 hours is better, since this is the best place to complete the hardening. About 2 hours will be long enough for the 95 and 100 per cent. Then use mixtures of alcohol and xylol. Then use a series of xylol-alcohol, beginning with 5 parts xylol to 95 parts absolute alcohol. The following series seems to be close enough: 5, 10, 20, 35, 50, 75, pure xylol. An hour in each may be sufficient.

Then bring the prothallia into a mixture of xylol and balsam, using at least 10 parts of xylol to 1 of balsam. If left in a shell, without corking, the xylol will soon evaporate, so that in a few days the prothallia may be mounted. Use the balsam in which the material has been standing, because any other balsam may have a different concentration. At every step in the process the prothallia should be examined under a microscope, so that any shrinking may be detected. If each succeeding step is tested with a single prothallium, a general disaster may be avoided. If plasmolysis takes place, weaken the reagent and try another prothallium. When a safe strength is found, bring on the bulk of the material, and use the same method with succeeding steps. The dangerous places are likely to be the transfer from alcohol to xylol and the transfer from xylol to balsam. The process is tedious, but the mounts are very firm and durable. The Venetian turpentine method is less tedious and is likely to produce better results than the method just described. Fix in the chromo-acetic mixture just mentioned. Stain some prothallia in iron-alum haematoxylin and some in phloxine and anilin blue. When both have reached the thick turpentine, fine preparations can be made by mounting prothallia from both lots under the same cover.

Sori of ferns.—Instructive mounts of sori or of individual sporangia may be made without sectioning. It is better to choose ferns with thin leaves, since leaves thicker than those of *Asplenium thelypteroides* are likely to be unsatisfactory. If this fern is at hand, cut off several of the small lobes which bear from three to six pairs of sori. Fix in chromo-acetic acid; wash in water; stain in Delafield's haematoxylin, or omit staining altogether; pass through a series of alcohols, allowing each grade to act for at least 10 minutes; clear in clove oil; and mount in balsam. If the sori have begun to turn brown, better views of the annulus will be obtained without staining.

Mosses and liverworts.—Nearly all mounts are more successful by other methods, for which the student should consult the chapters on Bryophytes (chaps. xxi and xxii). Excellent mounts of the peristome of the moss can be made as follows: From fresh or preserved capsules cut off the peristome just below the annulus. Treat with 95 per cent alcohol 10 minutes, absolute alcohol 10 minutes, clear in clove oil or xylol, and mount in balsam. It is a good plan to put at least three peristomes on a slide, one with the outside up, one with the inside up, and another dissected to show details of the teeth.

Fairly good unstained mounts of the archegonia and antheridia of small mosses can be obtained by following the directions for mounting the sori of ferns.

Beautiful and instructive mounts of the more delicate foliose Jungermanniaceae can be made by staining lightly in Delafield's haematoxylin whole plants, or pieces as long as can be covered conveniently. The method is that just given for fern prothallia. The mount should show both dorsal and ventral views.

The epidermis shows its best surface views without sectioning. Select some form with large stomata, like *Lilium* or *Tulipa*, strip pieces of epidermis from both sides of the leaf, and place them immediately in absolute alcohol for 10 minutes. Stain in Delafield's haematoxylin;

after this stain is satisfactory and all acid has been washed out, stain for 1 or 2 minutes in aqueous eosin, erythrosin, or acid fuchsin; place directly into 95 per cent alcohol for a few seconds (merely to save the absolute alcohol), then into absolute alcohol for about 30 seconds, and then into clove oil. Mount in balsam. The epidermis is likely to curl and, unfortunately, patience seems to be the only remedy. In mounting, be careful to get pieces from both sides of the leaf, and be sure that the pieces are outside up. The inside of the epidermis is usually more or less rough, on account of the mesophyll torn off with it. *Sedum purpurascens* will show various stages in the development of stomata, even in epidermis stripped from mature leaves. The epidermis of the *Sedums* strips off very easily. If the large *Sedum maximum* is available, it is not difficult to strip off pieces 2 or 3 centimeters wide and several centimeters long. There is not much tendency to curl. The pieces may be spread out flat in a Petri dish, fixed in the chromo-acetic-osmic solution, just recommended for fern prothallia, or in this solution without the osmic acid. Wash in water, stain in Delafield's haematoxylin and eosin, or in safranin and gentian violet. Then wash in water and run up through a series of alcohols—5, 10, 20, 35, 50, 70, 85, 95, and 100 per cent—about 30 minutes in each grade, except 85, which should be allowed to act for a couple of hours or overnight. Then transfer to clove oil, xylol, and balsam. This is a more tedious method, but it is worth the trouble. We have had the best results with the haematoxylin and eosin combination.

Other objects.—The cases just given will suggest other objects which might be mounted by such methods. Nearly all objects which used to be mounted in balsam without sectioning are now handled successfully by the Venetian turpentine method.

CHAPTER VII

THE GLYCERIN METHOD

Mounting in glycerin, once a very popular method, has become almost obsolete. In its day, it was very good for unicellular and filamentous forms and for various small objects; and we still use it for moss protonema, which keeps the natural green and brown colors for years. The transfer from glycerin to glycerin jelly is easy and safe, and glycerin jelly has considerable consistency, so that it is easy to seal. We almost never mount in glycerin, but transfer to glycerin jelly. The glycerin method, except the final mounting, also constitutes the first part of the Venetian turpentine method and, consequently, it is necessary to learn the capabilities and limitations of glycerin.

The method, from fixing to mounting, as used in connection with staining and without staining, will now be described.

Stained preparations.—The familiar *Spirogyra* is a good form to begin with. Fix in chromo-acetic-osmic solution ($\frac{1}{2}$ g. chromic, 3 c.c. acetic acid, 6 c.c. 1 per cent osmic acid, and 90 c.c. water); or in a chromo-acetic solution without osmic acid (1 g. chromic, 3 c.c. acetic acid, and 96 c.c. water). Fix 24 or 48 hours and wash in running water for 24 hours. At this point it is the usual practice to stain and transfer to 10 per cent glycerin; but preparations are more nearly perfect if the material receives more hardening than the chromic fixing agents can give it, before it goes into the stain. Therefore, run it up, as if it were to be imbedded in paraffin, until it reaches 85 per cent alcohol. The following series is recommended: $2\frac{1}{2}$, 5, $7\frac{1}{2}$, 10, 15, 20, 30, 40, 50, 70, and 85 per cent, with $\frac{1}{2}$ hour in each of the first five grades; 2–4 hours each in 20 and 30; 5 or 6 hours each in 40 and 50; all day or overnight in 70; 24 hours in 85. The 85 per cent completes the hardening so that, with reasonable care, the subsequent processes do little or no damage. After the hardening in 85 per cent alcohol, run back to water through the same series of alcohols, with one hour in each grade down to 30; below 30, 20 minutes in each grade; water, 20 minutes, and then stain.

The most generally satisfactory stain is Haidenhain's iron-alum haematoxylin. If there was any osmic acid in the fixing agent the

100

material must be bleached in hydrogen peroxide or in chlorine before proceeding with the stain (see p. 27). After bleaching and washing in water, treat with 2 per cent iron-alum, 4 hours; wash in water, 30 minutes; stain in ½ per cent haematoxylin overnight or 24 hours; wash in water, 30 minutes; and transfer again to iron-alum. This time, the iron-alum will extract the stain. The rapidity of the action of the iron-alum will now depend upon the fixing agent. If it contained 6 or 7 c.c. of 1 per cent osmic acid to 100 c.c. of the solution, it may require an hour, or even more, to make a satisfactory differentiation of the stain. If there was no osmic acid in a chromic fixing agent, the differentiation may be complete in 10 minutes. If the stain becomes too weak in 4 or 5 minutes, use 4 per cent iron-alum as a mordant, stain longer, and use 1 per cent iron-alum for the second treatment. Haidenhain's iron-alum haematoxylin gives its most brilliant results when chromic mixtures with 5–7 c.c. of 1 per cent osmic acid to 100 c.c. of the chromo-acetic acid have been used.

Different species of *Spirogyra* and even different collections, fixed in the same reagent, will differ in their reaction to stains; and different unicellular and filamentous forms in different fixing fluids, will present so much difference in times that only general suggestions can be given. When the stain is satisfactory, wash in running water for an hour. If this second iron-alum is not washed out thoroughly, its continued action will cause the preparation to fade.

Put the material into 10 per cent glycerin (1 part glycerin and 9 parts water), and then allow the water to evaporate gradually in a place as free from dust as possible. Nothing is better than a Petri dish for this purpose, because it presents a large surface for the evaporation of the water in the mixture. If there is much dust, cut a piece of filter paper just the size of the dish and let it float on the 10 per cent glycerin. The liquid will soak through the paper and evaporate without exposing the material itself to the dust. The process may be hastened, safely, by warming up to 35° C. The temperature of a paraffin bath—45° to 52° C.—causes such rapid evaporation that the material is likely to shrink. The concentration from 10 per cent glycerin to pure glycerin should not require less than three days. This time is easily regulated by the amount of 10 per cent glycerin and the size of the exposed surface.

When the glycerin has become about as thick as pure glycerin, the material is ready for mounting. Place a small drop of glycerin, with

the material, in the center of the slide, taking care not to put on so much that there will be a confusing tangle. Use scissors constantly so as not to injure filaments by trying to tease them out. Put on a round cover. There should be *just enough* glycerin to come to the edge of the cover-glass, but *not any more*, for it is impossible to seal a mount if glycerin has oozed out beyond the cover.

The mount should now be sealed. Canada balsam, various asphalts, cements, flat varnish, gold size, and other things have been used. Canada balsam is always at hand and seems to be as good as any. Preparations which had been sealed with gold size more than fifty years before have been exhibited in perfect condition, but they must have been hidden away in some museum, for a glycerin mount would never survive fifty years of laboratory use. The gold size, as painters

FIG. 19.—Slide, natural size, showing size and form of ring

use it, is likely to be too thin for sealing mounts. Put some of it in a 1-ounce bottle with a wide neck and leave the cork out until the gold size thickens a little. Should it become too thick, thin it with turpentine.

Nothing but practice will enable one to spin a good ring, but a good camel's-hair brush, a good turntable, and a balsam neither too thick nor too thin will facilitate matters. Gently touch the cover and slide at three or four points with the tip of the brush, so that a very small drop of balsam will bind the cover to the slide. In half an hour the tiny drops of balsam will have hardened sufficiently for the next step, the spinning of the ring. Clip the slide to the turntable so that the cover glass is perfectly concentric with the rings, give the turntable a gentle spin, and with the brush touch the slide as far out from the cover as you wish the ring to extend, then gradually approach the cover. Dip the brush in the balsam again, and gradually extend the ring until it is about $\frac{1}{16}$ inch wide on the cover. The touch must be extremely gentle or the cover will be moved. Do not try to put on a thick ring the first time, but let a thin ring harden for an hour (months would do no damage), and then a thicker ring can be added without any danger. Thin rings are too likely to be broken, and thick rings are in the way if the preparation is to be examined with high powers. A medium ring is best, and it should consist of two coats, for a crack would seldom appear at the same place in both coats. A good shape and thickness for a ring are shown in Figure 19.

The following is a summary of the foregoing processes:

1. Fix in chromo-acetic-osmic acid, 24 hours.
2. Wash in water, 24 hours.
3. Alcohols, $2\frac{1}{2}$–85 per cent.
4. Alcohols, 85–$2\frac{1}{2}$ per cent.
5. Wash in water, 30 minutes.
6. Iron-alum, 4 hours.
7. Wash in water, 30 minutes.
8. Haematoxylin, $\frac{1}{2}$ per cent, 24 hours.
9. Wash in water, 30 minutes.
10. Iron-alum until the stain is satisfactory.
11. Wash in water, 30 minutes.
12. Ten per cent glycerin.
13. Mount and seal.
14. Label.

The times just given may seem unnecessarily long, but one can always do something between times. The following summary, taken from the fourth edition of this book, is much shorter and it gives good results, unless you compare the slides with those made by the longer schedule, just as ordinary glass looks good, unless you put it side by side with plate glass:

1. Fix in chromo-acetic-osmic acid, 24–48 hours.
2. Wash in water, 24 hours. Bleach and wash in water.
3. Iron solution, 2 hours.
4. Wash in water, 10 minutes.
5. One-half per cent haematoxylin, 3–24 hours.
6. Wash in water, 10 minutes.
7. Iron solution until stain is right.
8. Wash in water, 1 hour.
9. Ten per cent glycerin.
10. Mount and seal.

If material has been fixed in formalin, it should be washed in water for 30 minutes before starting with stage 3 of the long schedule, or the first iron-alum of the short schedule. Material preserved in formalin–alcohol–acetic acid, with 70 per cent alcohol, should be run down to water before staining. If the alcohol is only 50 per cent, put the material in 70 and 85 per cent, a day in each, and then run down to water.

Mayer's haem-alum is also a good stain for filamentous algae and fungi which are to be mounted in glycerin. The process, after fixing and washing in water, is as follows:

1. Transfer to the stain from water.
    It is seldom necessary to stain longer than 10 minutes. As a rule, it is better to dilute the stain (about 1 c.c. to 10 c.c. of distilled water) and allow it to act for 10 hours or overnight.
2. Wash in water, 20 minutes.
3. Ten per cent glycerin until sufficiently concentrated.
4. Mount and seal.

Eosin is a good stain for many algae and fungi which are to be mounted whole, if sharp outlines rather than cell contents are to be brought out. After material has been fixed and washed in water, run it up to 85 per cent alcohol and back to water. Stain in an aqueous solution of eosin for 24 hours; pour off the eosin, which can be used repeatedly, and pour on a 1 or 2 per cent solution of acetic acid in water. Pour this off and pour on some more of the acid, until very little stain washes out. The process may require 2–5 minutes. Then place in 10 per cent glycerin containing about $\frac{1}{2}$ per cent acetic acid, and allow the glycerin to concentrate. The acetic acid is to prevent the stain from washing out. When the glycerin has reached the proper concentration, mount and seal as before.

The following is a rapid method for forms like *Aspergillus* and *Penicillium*: Fix in 100 per cent alcohol about 2 minutes; stain in aqueous eosin 5 minutes; wash in water about 1 minute; fix in 1 per cent acetic acid 1 minute; then mount directly in 50 per cent glycerin to which about 1 per cent acetic acid has been added. It is hardly worth while to try this method with forms which have large cells; they are sure to collapse. If a form like *Eurotium* passes through the earlier processes without danger, but collapses when put into the 50 per cent glycerin, put it into the 10 per cent glycerin and allow the glycerin to concentrate.

Mounting without fixing or staining.—It is sometimes desirable to retain the natural color of an object. The chlorophyll green can usually be preserved by mounting directly in glycerin without any previous fixing. Other colors also are often preserved in this way. Moss protonema makes beautiful preparations by this method. If possible, select protonema showing the very young moss plants. The brown protonema and brown bulbils preserve their color perfectly. Wash the dirt away from the protonema, which is then placed in 50 per cent glycerin. Let the glycerin concentrate, transfer to glycerin jelly, and mount in the usual way.

The method is very useful when one finds a single specimen of *Pediastrum*, or any small form which would be lost in the more complicated processes. Place a large drop of 10 per cent glycerin on a slide; with a pipette, transfer the object to the drop, and allow the glycerin to concentrate. Then add a cover and seal the mount.

GLYCERIN JELLY

It is almost never necessary to mount anything in glycerin, because material can be transferred directly from glycerin to glycerin jelly. If the glycerin jelly is well made, it is quite firm and mounts will last for a year or two, without sealing; but it is better to seal them with balsam. A very good formula is known as *Kaiser's gelatin*. It is made as follows: One part by weight of the finest French gelatin is left for about 2 hours in 6 parts by weight of water; 7 parts of glycerin are added, and for every 100 grams of the mixture, 1 gram of concentrated carbolic acid. The whole is warmed for 15 minutes, stirring all the while until all the flakes produced by the carbolic acid have disappeared. Filter while warm through a fine-mesh cheesecloth.

To make a mount, take a small piece of the glycerin jelly, not more than half as large as a grain of wheat—the exact size will depend upon the material—warm it until it melts, and then transfer to it the material which has already been brought into thick glycerin. It is a good plan to touch the material to filter paper in order to remove as much glycerin as possible; for the less glycerin the firmer the mount will be. The mount may be sealed as soon as it is cool; but some prefer to let it stand for a week or two before sealing. In any case, it is a fairly firm mount, so that there is no danger of moving the cover.

Everything which can be brought safely into pure glycerin can be mounted in glycerin jelly, and the preparation is much more stable than a glycerin mount.

CHAPTER VIII

THE VENETIAN TURPENTINE METHOD

Venetian turpentine is made from the resin of *Larix europea*. It looks like Canada balsam and in many ways behaves like it; but it is readily soluble in absolute alcohol. Consequently, material can be transferred directly from absolute alcohol to Venetian turpentine, without passing through xylol or any similar reagent. The mounts are as hard and durable as balsam mounts and they become as transparent as if a clearing agent had been used.

While the method was described by Pfeiffer and Wellheim in 1894, it received no recognition in the United States or even in Europe. I made a casual trial of it when preparing the first edition of this book more than thirty years ago; but the preparations were such miserable failures that the process did not seem worth mentioning.

The method was next brought to my attention during a demonstration in Strasburger's laboratory at Bonn. He was using preparations of *Zygnema* and *Spirogyra*, the staining of which surpassed anything I had ever seen. He remarked that it was not worth while to consult Pfeiffer and Wellheim's lengthy article, because his preparations had been made by the authors and no one else had made a success of the method. However, when I returned, I made a careful study of the process, and finally learned to use it successfully. The details as given in that paper were too indefinite for practical use, but, after one has learned the method, the article can be read with profit.

The practical advantages of the method are the elimination of the dangerous xylol stage, the hard durable mounts, and a greater variety of stains than can be used with glycerin.

After fixing, washing in water, running up in alcohols from $2\frac{1}{2}$ to 85 per cent, running back to water, and staining in an aqueous stain, e.g., iron-alum haematoxylin, the process is as follows:

1. Ten per cent glycerin until concentrated.
2. Wash the glycerin out thoroughly in 95 per cent alcohol.
3. Complete the dehydration in 100 per cent alcohol.

106

4. Ten per cent Venetian turpentine in an exsiccator until the turpentine becomes thick enough for mounting.
5. Mount in the Venetian turpentine.

Even after the method became established, there occurred a period of several years during which it was practically impossible to get a Venetian turpentine suitable for histological use. Consequently, it was necessary to resort to glycerin jelly or to try various schemes for bringing material into Canada balsam; but good Venetian turpentines are again available and are even more satisfactory than those which established the method in popular favor. We have tested two brands which are giving uniform and excellent results: these are the "Venice Turpentine (True)," sold by the Fuller-Morrison Company, of Chicago; and the "Turpentine Venetian" (No. 2605), sold by the National Anilin and Chemical Company, of New York. There are probably other good turpentines and still others are likely to appear.

The general outline, just given, is not sufficiently definite for a working introduction. The following concrete examples, describing the use of Venetian turpentine with an aqueous stain, with an alcoholic stain, and with a combination of aqueous and alcoholic stains, will be more practical than general directions. The steps from fixing to mounting, used with an aqueous stain, will be described first, since this will introduce the method in its least complicated form.

Heidenhain's iron-haematoxylin.—Using *Spirogyra* as a type, proceed as follows:

1. Fix 24 hours in chromo-acetic acid.
   1 per cent chromic acid...................... 100 c.c.
   Glacial acetic acid............................   3 c.c.
   The volume of the fixing agent should be at least 50 times that of the material to be fixed.
2. Wash in running water 24 hours. (After this washing in water, the material may be run up to 85 per cent alcohol for hardening, and then back to water.)
3. Two per cent aqueous solution of iron-alum (ammonia sulphate of iron), 4 hours.
4. Wash in running water, 20 minutes.
5. Stain overnight, or 24 hours, in $\frac{1}{2}$ per cent aqueous solution haematoxylin.
6. Wash in water, 20 minutes.

7. Two per cent aqueous solution of iron-alum, until the stain is satisfactory. This can be determined only by examining frequently under
the microscope.

8. Wash in water, 2 hours. If this washing is not thorough, the continued
action of the iron-alum will cause the preparations to fade.

9. Transfer to 10 per cent glycerin, and allow the glycerin to concentrate
until it has the consistency of pure glycerin. It is not necessary to use
an exsiccator. Merely put the glycerin into shallow dishes, and leave
it exposed to the air, but protected from dust. If the material is in Petri
dishes or other dishes with a large surface, 3 or 4 days will be sufficient.
This process may be hastened by warming, if the temperature does not
go above 35° C. If the reduction from 10 per cent glycerin to pure
glycerin is accomplished in less than 48 hours, the change in the concentration is so rapid that material is likely to suffer.

10. Wash out the glycerin with 95 per cent alcohol. It will be necessary
to change the alcohol several times. From 10 to 20 minutes will be
sufficient if the alcohol is changed frequently. This alcohol cannot be
used again for the same purpose, but it will be useful in cleaning one's
hands and in cleaning dishes which have contained Venetian turpentine.

11. Complete the dehydration in 100 per cent alcohol: 10 minutes should
be sufficient.

12. *Most failures are now ready to occur.*

From the absolute alcohol the material is transferred to a 10 per
cent solution of Venetian turpentine in absolute alcohol. The turpentine thickens as the alcohol evaporates, and when it reaches the consistency of pure glycerin the material is ready for mounting. *The 10
per cent Venetian turpentine is very sensitive to moisture,* and most
failures are due to this characteristic; consequently the concentration
cannot be allowed to take place with the turpentine exposed to the air
of the room. Use an exsiccator. This will not only absorb the moisture
from the air, but will soon remove the alcohol from the turpentine
mixture. Make an exsiccator as follows: Place a saucer full of soda
lime (sodium hydroxide with lime) on a plate of glass, and cover with
a bell jar. This is a simple and effective exsiccator. Instead, you may
simply scatter soda lime in the bottom of any low museum jar with
tight-fitting cover. The tin cans, with tight covers, in which you get
your pound of "Improved Vacuum Coffee" make good exsiccators for
small amounts of material. You may improvise other forms; the essen-

tial thing is to provide a small, air-tight place in which the soda lime may work.

Instead of soda lime you may use fused calcium chloride or the white sticks of sodium hydroxide.

We are now ready for the transfer from absolute alcohol to the 10 per cent Venetian turpentine. *Make the transfer quickly.* Pour off the absolute alcohol and place the dish, with the material, in the exsiccator; then pour on the 10 per cent turpentine, *and immediately put on the cover.* This is better than to pour on the turpentine and then try to get the dish well placed in the exsiccator.

The greater the surface of soda lime exposed, the more rapid will be the concentration of the Venetian turpentine. The concentration must not be *too* rapid. Not less than 2 days should be allowed for the concentration of 30 c.c. of the turpentine in an ordinary Minot watch glass.

Great care must be taken not to let any of the soda lime, or other drier, get into the turpentine.

When the lime has become saturated, it may be heated until dry, and then used again. If material is put into an exsiccator with nearly saturated lime, the turpentine becomes milky. If the material is very valuable, wash in absolute alcohol until entirely free from any milky appearance, and start again in 10 per cent turpentine. If the material can be replaced, throw away the milky stuff and start at the beginning. It may teach one not to put material into an exsiccator with half-saturated lime.

In Tucson, Arizona, the Venetian turpentine method is easy, with no need for an exsiccator. Dr. J. G. Brown tells me that the air is so dry that the 10 per cent Venetian turpentine can be left exposed to the air until it concentrates, just as we leave the 10 per cent glycerin.

As soon as the turpentine has attained the consistency of pure glycerin, it may be exposed to the air without any danger from moisture; but the turpentine would soon become too thick for mounting. If the turpentine has become too thick, thin it with a few drops of absolute alcohol or with 10 per cent or any thin solution of Venetian turpentine.

Mount the material in a few drops of the Venetian turpentine and add a cover. Tapping on the cover with the handle of a needle or scalpel will often separate the filaments so that they are more convenient for examination. Square covers may be used since it is entirely unnecessary to seal the mounts, which are as hard and durable as those mounted in balsam.

Material in the thickened Venetian turpentine, when not needed for immediate mounting, may be put into small bottles. The corks should be of the best quality; otherwise the turpentine will become too thick. While it can be thinned by adding thin turpentine, it is better, for easy mounting, not to let the turpentine become too thick. If the turpentine is only a little too thick, warming it gently will thin it enough for making mounts; but if any material is to be put away, a few drops of absolute alcohol or of a thin Venetian turpentine should be added. Material in Venetian turpentine, well corked and kept in the dark, does not fade or deteriorate in any way.

Phloxine and anilin blue.—Fix in chromo-acetic acid and wash in water, as described in the previous schedule. Transfer from water to 10 per cent glycerin and allow the glycerin to concentrate. It is not necessary to use an exsiccator since there is no danger from moisture in the air. When the glycerin attains the consistency of pure glycerin, wash the glycerin out with 95 per cent alcohol. This washing must be very thorough; otherwise the staining will not be satisfactory.

1. Stain in phloxine. A double stain in Magdala red and anilin blue has sometimes given very satisfactory results; but, just as often, has been entirely worthless. The reason for the discrepancy seems to be that stains sold under the name of Magdala red are of various composition, some of them containing no Magdala red at all. The standardized stain, phloxine, seems to be identical with successful lots of Magdala red and results are rather uniformly successful. Make a 1 per cent solution of phloxine in 90 per cent alcohol and stain for 24 hours.

2. Rinse the material for a minute in 90 per cent alcohol.

3. Stain in anilin blue, using a 1 per cent solution in 90 per cent alcohol. We prefer to make a fresh solution every time we have anything to stain. It is not necessary to measure it. A little of the powder—about half the bulk of a grain of wheat—in 30 c.c. of 90 per cent alcohol, will give an efficient solution. The time required for successful staining will vary from 3 to 30 minutes. Do not put all the material into the anilin blue at once, but, by trying a few filaments at a time, find out what the probable periods may be.

4. Rinse off the stain in 90 per cent alcohol, and then treat for a few seconds in acid alcohol (1 very small drop of HCl to 30 c.c. of 90 per cent alcohol). The acid alcohol fixes and brightens the anilin blue, but extracts the phloxine. If the anilin blue or the acid alcohol acts for too short a time, the blue will be weak; if they act too long, the red is lost entirely. If the blue overstains too

much, wash it out in 95 per cent alcohol. The phloxine is not likely to over-stain.

5. Absolute alcohol, 5 or 6 seconds.

6. Transfer *quickly* to 10 per cent Venetian turpentine and proceed as in the previous schedule.

The surprising beauty of successful preparations will compensate for whatever failures may occur. Nuclei and pyrenoids should show a brilliant red, while the chromatophores and cytoplasm should be dark blue. The cell walls should show a faint bluish color.

Heidenhain's iron-alum haematoxylin and eosin.—Follow the schedule for iron -haematoxylin until the glycerin has been washed out in 95 per cent alcohol. Then stain for an hour in a solution of eosin in 95 per cent alcohol. Wash for a minute in 95 per cent alcohol, then a minute in absolute alcohol, and then transfer to the 10 per cent Venetian turpentine.

Heidenhain's iron-alum haematoxylin and safranin.—Follow the schedule for iron-haematoxylin until the glycerin has been washed out in alcohol, and then add to the 95 per cent alcohol several drops of a solution of safranin in 95 or 100 per cent alcohol and allow the stain to act for 30 minutes or an hour. Then dehydrate in absolute alcohol and transfer to 10 per cent Venetian turpentine.

Other stains may be used. Aqueous stains should be used before starting with 10 per cent glycerin. Alcoholic stains should be in strong alcohol—about 90 per cent—and should be applied just after washing out the glycerin.

This method is equally good for filamentous fungi and also for the prothallia of *Equisetum* and ferns, for delicate liverworts and mosses, and similar objects.

If you have a good turpentine, good stains, *and avoid moisture*, the Venetian turpentine method should not be difficult, and the results with filamentous and unicellular forms and other small objects surpass anything yet secured by other processes.

CHAPTER IX

THE PARAFFIN METHOD

For studies which demand very thin, smooth sections, the paraffin method still holds the first place, with no near competitor. Some have added to the paraffin a little of this or that or the other, and these additions have corrected, somewhat, the imperfections of poor paraffins. A thoroughly good paraffin will yield smooth ribbons at 1 μ and, in cold weather, ribbons $\frac{7}{10}$ μ and even $\frac{1}{2}$ μ in thickness have been cut in our laboratory. Modern microtomes, while rather complicated, give wonderful results and, to some extent, eliminate the element of skill. The microtome, shown in Figure 20, with the cooling attachment designed by Dr. Land, has cut even ribbons, 1μ in thickness, from the antheridial receptacles of *Marchantia*. With the comparatively inexpensive sliding microtome shown in Figure 2, page 9, smooth, even ribbons of root-tips have been cut as thin as $\frac{1}{2}$ μ. It is doubtful whether any other microtome, however expensive, has ever cut thinner or smoother sections. Both of these microtomes were designed by Mr. H. N. Ott, president of the Spencer Lens Company. With these microtomes, especially with the small sliding one, serial sections can be cut of pollen grains and spores too small to be seen by the naked eye.

Many of the principles involved in this method are general in their application, and some of the processes are common to other methods. One who has mastered the paraffin method should have little trouble with any other method of preparing plant material for microscopic examination.

The following are the stages from fixing material to the finished mount:

KILLING AND FIXING

As stated in the chapter on "Reagents" (chap. ii), the purpose of a killing agent is to bring the life-processes to a sudden termination, while a fixing agent is used to fix the cells and their contents in as nearly the living condition as possible. The fixing consists in so hardening the material that the various elements may retain their natural condition during all the processes which are to follow. Usually the same re-

agent is used for both killing and fixing. Zoölogists, from humane mo-
tives, may use chloroform for killing, while other reagents are used for
fixing. In fixing root-tips, anthers, and other material for a study of
mitotic figures, it is necessary that killing be very prompt. In a weak
solution of chromo-acetic acid, nuclei which have begun to divide may
complete the division, although the reagent might hinder nuclei from

Fig. 20.—Spencer rotary microtome with electric motor, and Land's apparatus for temperature
control.

entering upon division. A strong chromo-acetic solution will increase
the number of mitotic figures, and the chromo-acetic–osmic solution,
given on page 28, will still further increase the number, and the proportion of anaphases will be greater.

· Take the killing and fixing fluids into the field. If one waits until
the material is brought to the laboratory there may be some fixing,
but it will, in many cases, be too late to do much killing. Material
which has begun to wilt is not worth fixing. Material like *Spirogyra*,
however, may be wrapped in several thicknesses of newspaper, placed

in a botany can and brought into the laboratory. Before fixing, it should be placed in water for half an hour. Such forms suffer more from lack of air when placed in a bottle or a can than from lack of water when wrapped in wet newspaper. Branches with developing buds may be brought in and kept in water. Cones of the cycad, *Ceratozamia*, sent from Jalapa, Mexico, have arrived in Chicago with cell division still going on at a rapid rate. But such cases are extremes; as a rule, take the killing and fixing fluids into the field.

Always have the material in very small pieces, in order that the reagents may act quickly on all parts of the specimens. Pieces larger than cubes of 1 cm. should be avoided whenever possible. While one sometimes needs sections 2 or even 3 cm. long, it is not likely to be necessary to fix pieces more than 4 or 5 mm. in thickness. For very fine work no part of the specimens should require the reagent to penetrate more than 1 or 2 mm.

For fixing agents of the chromic-acid series, the volume of the reagent should be about 50 times that of the material.

Fixing agents with alcohol as an ingredient will fix a larger proportion of material. It must be remembered that the water, which is always present in living tissues, weakens the fixing agent.

The time required for fixing varies with the reagent, the character of the tissue, and the size of the piece. About 24 hours is a commonly recommended period for chromic-acid solutions, but 2 or even 3 days will do no harm.

Directions for making and using the various fixing agents are given in the chapters on "Reagents" (chaps. ii, xxxi).

WASHING

Nearly all fixing agents, except the alcohols, must be washed out from the material as completely as possible before any further steps are taken, because some reagents leave annoying precipitates which must be removed, and others interfere with subsequent processes. Aqueous fixing agents with chromic acid as their principal ingredient are washed out with water; aqueous solutions of corrosive sublimate are also washed out with water. Use running water whenever possible and, whenever running water is not available, change the water frequently. With both methods, the tubes with bolting silk on each end, or the tea filters from the five-and-ten-cent store will facilitate the washing. Very effective "bottles" for washing can be made of wire gauze. With shears, cut a piece about 8 cm. square; bend it into a cylinder; solder along the edge; and solder in a circular piece for a bottom. Stand several of these in a dish about 6 cm. deep; let a gentle stream of water come in at the bottom, and wash for 24 hours.

Alcoholic solutions should be washed out with alcohol of about the same strength as the fixing agent; picric acid, or fixing agents with picric acid as an ingredient, must not be washed out with water, but with alcohol, whether the picric acid be in aqueous or alcoholic solution.

HARDENING AND DEHYDRATING

After the material has been washed, it is necessary to continue the hardening and also to remove the water. Alcohol is used almost entirely for these purposes. It completes the hardening and at the same time dehydrates, that is, it replaces the water in the material, an extremely important consideration, for the least trace of moisture interferes seriously with the infiltration of the paraffin.

The process of hardening and dehydrating must be gradual; if the material should be transferred directly from water to absolute alcohol, the hardening and dehydrating would be brought about in a very short time, but the violent osmosis would cause a ruinous contraction of the more delicate parts. In recent years, cytologists have been making the dehydration process more and more gradual. Twenty years ago most workers began the dehydration process with 35 per cent alcohol and used the series 35, 50, 70, 85, 95, and 100 per cent alcohol. Some placed an intermediate grade between water and 35 per cent alcohol. If plasmolysis—the tearing away of the protoplast from the cell wall—was avoided, the series was thought to be sufficiently gradual; but a series which may avoid plasmolysis may not be adequate if one is to study the finer details of cell structure. The following series is recommended: $2\frac{1}{2}$, 5, $7\frac{1}{2}$, 10, 15, 20, 30, 40, 50, 70, 85, 95, and 100 per cent. There is no particular virtue in the fractions: it is convenient to make 10 per cent alcohol, dilute with an equal volume of water for the 5 per cent, and dilute the 5 per cent with an equal volume for the $2\frac{1}{2}$ per cent. It will be noted that the series begins with very close grades and that the intervals are gradually increased. The claim is that, by beginning with very weak alcohols in close grades, more perfect dehydration can be secured at the end of the series. Various devices, like constant drip and osmotic apparatus, have been proposed to secure a more gradual transfer; but these have no advantages, unless the mixture is very complete before it reaches the material. If the drops fall near the material, the liquid is in a constant turmoil.

In passing through the graded series, it is not necessary to use a large amount of alcohol: 2 or 3 times the volume of the material is sufficient.

The grades of alcohol may be used several times, but it must be remembered that pollen grains, fungus spores, starch grains, and various granules are likely to be left in the alcohol, so that it is wise to pour back through a filter each time, thus keeping the alcohols clean.

As the alcohols absorb water from the material, they become weaker and weaker. If the various alcohols be poured in a large "waste alcohol" bottle, when a couple of liters have been accumulated, the strength may be determined by testing with an alcoholometer. Then any grade of less strength can be made from this stock.

The time necessary for each of the stages has not been determined with any certainty. We recommend three grades a day, morning, noon, and evening, for the first six grades; for the 30, 40, and 50, change twice a day, morning and evening; 85, at least 24 hours and better 48 hours, for this is the best grade in which to complete the hardening which will make the material able to withstand the subsequent processes; 95, overnight or 24 hours; absolute, 24 hours, changing two or three times. Material may be left in any of the grades overnight, or 24 hours. If it is to be kept in alcohol, leave it in 85 per cent but, where labor is no object, it is better to go on and imbed it in paraffin.

CLEARING

Let us suppose that the material has been thoroughly dehydrated, so that not the slightest trace of water remains. If the supposition chances to be contrary to fact, all the work which has preceded, as well as all which is to follow, is only an idle waste of time. The purpose of a clearing agent is to make the tissues transparent, but clearing agents also replace the alcohol. At this stage the latter process is the essential one, the clearing which accompanies it being incidental. The clearing, however, is very convenient, since it shows that the alcohol has been replaced and that the material is ready for the next step.

Various clearing agents are in use. Xylol is the most generally employed, and for most purposes it seems to be the best. Bergamot oil, cedar oil, clove oil, turpentine, and chloroform are used for the same purpose. Cedar oil and chloroform may, in some cases, be as good as xylol.

Only a small quantity of the clearing agent is necessary, enough to cover the material being sufficient; but since the grades, except pure xylol, can be used repeatedly, it is better to use four or five times the bulk of the material. Filter as in case of the alcohols.

The transfer from absolute alcohol to the clearing agent should be *gradual*, like the hardening and dehydrating processes. The most successful workers have been making this transfer more and more gradual. Thirty years ago it was customary to transfer from absolute alcohol directly to xylol; then a mixture of equal parts of absolute alcohol and xylol was interpolated; in the second edition of this book three grades were placed between the absolute alcohol and xylol. It is undoubtedly better to make the transfer still more gradual. The following series seems to be safe, $2\frac{1}{2}$, 5, 10, 15, 25, 50, 75, and 100 per cent xylol. These mixtures of absolute alcohol and xylol can be made with sufficient accuracy without measuring in a graduate. The 50 per cent grade is made by mixing equal parts of absolute alcohol and xylol; the 25 per cent, by adding to the 50 per cent an equal volume of absolute alcohol; make the 10 per cent grade from the 25 per cent by adding a little more than an equal volume of absolute alcohol; in the same way, make the 5 per cent from the 10 per cent, and the $2\frac{1}{2}$ per cent from the 5 per cent. The different grades may be kept in bottles and may be used repeatedly. A couple of drops of safranin dissolved in absolute alcohol, added to the 50 or 75 per cent xylol, will color the material a little and will often be helpful in orienting after the imbedding in paraffin.

Three grades a day, morning, noon, and night, will do for all the grades, except pure xylol. It will do no harm to leave the material overnight in any of the grades. The pure xylol should be allowed to act for 10–24 hours, with 3 or 4 changes. This xylol can be used to make up any of the lower grades.

Throughout the dehydrating and clearing it is a good plan to keep the material in Number 4 shells, which are made from glass tubing about 25 mm. in diameter. Other clearing agents may be used, but the process must be just as gradual.

THE TRANSFER FROM CLEARING AGENT TO PARAFFIN

This should also be a *gradual* process. The most convenient method is to place a small block of paraffin in the pure clearing agent with the material, but the block of paraffin should not rest directly upon the objects. Dr. Land uses coarse wire gauze, cut into strips about 15 mm. wide and tapered at both ends. The strip is then bent so that the pointed ends rest upon the bottom of the Number 4 shell, while the middle portion forms a flat table upon which the paraffin may rest. Dip the wire gauze table into xylol and then slip it carefully into the Number 4 shell. The table portion should be 10 or 15 mm. above the material, and there should be enough xylol to extend a few millimeters above the table. Place on the table a block of paraffin about equal to the volume of the xylol in the shell. The table not only prevents the paraffin from injuring the material by mechanical pressure but insures considerable diffusion before the mixture of paraffin and xylol reaches the specimens. After 24 hours (or several days, if time permits) at room temperature, place the shell on a pasteboard box—slide boxes are good—on top of the paraffin bath. Do not place the shell directly upon the metal of the bath, since it is better to minimize heat. As soon as the paraffin is dissolved, add some more, this time leaving the cork out, in order that the xylol may evaporate. About 24 hours on the top of the bath should be sufficient.

THE PARAFFIN BATH

This step is usually called infiltration, but when the transfer from the clearing fluid to paraffin is made gradually, as has just been indicated, the process of infiltration is already begun. It is now necessary to get rid of the xylol or other clearing agent. This is accomplished, to a considerable extent, by pouring off the mixture of xylol and paraffin and replacing it with pure melted paraffin. Pour off the pure paraffin *immediately*. This is important. You will notice that often, when the pure paraffin is poured on, a froth or scum will appear on the surface. Much of the xylol will be in this scum, and, if allowed to remain, it would diffuse into the mass and greatly prolong the time needed for infiltration. So, pour it off and add more pure paraffin, for some xylol remains in the tissues and must be removed. Dot not put the shell into the bath, but use a flat dish of some sort. The main object is to have a fairly large surface exposed, so that the remaining xylol may evaporate as rapidly as possible. Change the paraffin 3 or 4 times. A good 52° C. paraffin will yield smooth sections from $\frac{1}{2}$ μ up to 20 μ. Where thicker sections are needed, a 45° C. paraffin should be used. For many years we have used only a 52° C. paraffin.

A good paraffin is an absolute necessity, if preparations are to be of the highest grade. Some brands of parowax are fairly good if sections do not need to be thinner than 10 μ. For critical work, with sections from 5 μ down to $\frac{1}{2}\mu$, Grübler's 52° C. paraffin stands at the head of the list. It melts at the temperature indicated on the package. Since the price rises with the melting-point, many paraffins are marked higher than they really are.

Some paraffins can be improved by heating almost to the boiling point for several hours. If any scum appears, skim it off; if anything settles to the bottom, pour the paraffin off gently and throw away the sediment. If, with prolonged heating, the paraffin takes on a slightly amber color, keep that paraffin for your best work, for it is likely to be good.

The addition of bayberry wax—a piece about a centimeter square and 5 mm. thick—to a pound of paraffin is likely to improve any paraffin except the best.

Dr. Land added asphalt and secured a paraffin which yielded 1 μ ribbons with a rotary microtome.

Do not throw away the paraffin which you pour off, but put it in a waste jar or beaker, or, still better, in a small tin lard pail, in which you have made a lip to facilitate pouring. This can be placed in the bath, or, in winter, on the radiator, and the xylol will gradually evaporate. After long heating, the paraffin not only becomes as good as new but even better, since it becomes more homogeneous and tenacious. If it contains dust or débris of any kind, it may be filtered with a hot filter.

The time required varies with the character of the material and the thoroughness of the dehydrating and clearing. If this schedule has been followed up to this point, the time will be much shorter than most investigators now deem necessary. In dehydrating and clearing, material could be left overnight at any stage; but in the paraffin bath, the time must be reduced to the minimum. If 30 minutes is enough, an hour may be ruinous; if an hour is right, 2 hours may mean disaster. A few hints may be helpful. Fern prothallia of average size infiltrate perfectly in 20–25 minutes; onion root-tips, in 30–45 minutes; ovaries of *Lilium philadelphicum* or *L. canadense* at the fertilization stage, from 45 minutes to 1 hour; 5 or 6 mm. cubes of the endosperm of cycads, containing archegonia, 2–3 hours; median longitudinal sections of the ovulate cones of *Pinus banksiana*, 4 or 5 mm. thick, may require 6 or 8 hours; if serial sections through the entire cone are wanted, Dr. Hannah Aase found that the time must be prolonged to 24 or even 48 hours. Some particularly difficult material which will be mentioned in the chapter on "Special Methods," may require several days.

When one is dealing with many lots of the same kind of material, as in research work, the time required for infiltration is easily determined. As a rule, *minimize heat.* It is, probably, never necessary to use paraffin with a melting-point higher than 52° C. With Land's cooling device sections 1 μ in thickness can be cut from 52° C. paraffin.

A few final hints may not be amiss. If the dehydration is not complete, it is practically impossible to replace the alcohol *completely* with xylol. Unless this replacement is *complete*, the infiltration with paraffin will be imperfect. Students are likely to prolong the time in the paraffin bath in a vain attempt to force paraffin into a tissue which still contains some xylol. When the alcohol series and xylol series have done their work perfectly, the time in the bath is likely to be shorter than most investigators allow for this stage.

IMBEDDING

Material may be imbedded in paper trays or any apparatus made for the purpose. A satisfactory imbedding-dish is a thin rectangular porcelain dish glazed inside. This dish, called a *Verbrennungsschale*, is made by the Königliche Porzellan-Manufactur, Berlin, Germany. The most convenient sizes are $40\times50\times10$ mm., $68\times45\times10$ mm., and $91\times58\times15$ mm. As listed, these dishes are not glazed; care should be taken to indicate that the dishes must be glazed inside (*innen glasiert*). The paper tray, if well made, is as good as anything. Thick ledger linen or thin, smooth cardboard makes good trays.

Smear the dish or tray with glycerin or soapy water to prevent sticking. Another way to prevent sticking is to put a piece of tissue paper in the dish, pour on water and make the tissue paper fit the inside of the dish, and then pour on the paraffin with the material to be imbedded. The paraffin will not stick to the paper. If several objects are to be imbedded in one dish, it is best to have the dish as near the temperature of melted paraffin as possible; otherwise, the objects may stick to the bottom, and it will be impossible to arrange them properly. Hot needles are good for arranging material. Great care should be taken not to have the dish too hot, since too high a temperature not only injures the material but also prevents a thorough imbedding. Pour the paraffin with the objects into the imbedding-dish and arrange them so as to facilitate the future cutting-out from the paraffin cake. Or, keeping the imbedding tray at the temperature of the paraffin bath—*never hotter*—the objects may be picked out gently and arranged as they are placed in the paraffin in the tray. Look at Figures 21 and 22, representing the arrangement of root-tips in a paraffin cake. From a cake like that in Figure 21 it is easy to cut out tips for sectioning. The arrangement, or rather the lack of it, shown in Figure 22 should be remembered only as an exasperating example.

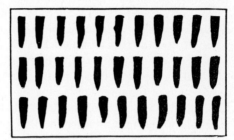

Fig. 21

After the objects have been arranged, cool the cake rapidly by allowing the bottom of the dish to rest upon cold water. As soon as a sufficiently firm film forms on the surface of the cake, let water flow gently over the top. After the cake has been under water for a few minutes, the paraffin will either come out and float on the

Fig. 22

Figs. 21 and 22.—Paraffin cakes of root tips, the upper (Fig. 21) showing a good arrangement; the lower (Fig. 22) showing fewer tips and most of these not in position to be blocked without injury.

water or, at least, it will be easily removed from the dish. If paraffin cools slowly it crystallizes and does not cut well. The layer of paraffin should be just thick enough to cover the objects, not only as a matter of economy, but because a thick layer retards the cooling. Very small objects, like the megaspores of *Marsilea*, ovules of *Silphium*, etc., may simply be poured out upon a *cool* piece of glass, which has been smeared with glycerin or soapy water. In this way, thin cakes are made which harden very rapidly.

If one is doing much imbedding, it is worth while to have the paraffin cakes uniform in size and to have a convenient method of filing.

In our own collection, there are more than 6,000 paraffin cakes. They are filed in pasteboard boxes 28 cm. long, 10 cm. wide, and 2 cm. deep. With the generic name written on the box, and the boxes arranged alphabetically or, preferably, taxonomically, it is easy to find anything in the large collection.

CUTTING

As soon as the paraffin is thoroughly cooled, it is ready for cutting. Trim the paraffin containing the object into a convenient shape, and fasten it upon a block of wood. Blocks of pine $\frac{3}{4}$ inch long and $\frac{3}{8}$ inch square are good for general purposes. Put paraffin on the end of the block so as to form a firm cap about $\frac{1}{8}$ inch thick. Warm the cap and the bottom of the piece containing the object, and press them lightly together; then touch the joint with a hot needle, put the whole thing into cold water for a minute, and it is ready for cutting. Cutting can be learned only by experience, but a few hints may not come amiss:

a) The knife must be *sharp*. This condition, which used to be the most difficult, has become the easiest; for any paraffin section, up to 2 cm. square, can be cut with a safety razor blade. The holder shown in Figure 3, with the sliding microtome shown in Figure 2, with a *hard* safety razor blade, preferably the Watts blade described on page 10, will furnish relief from the tedious sharpening of microtome knives which, at their best, are not equal to a good safety razor blade. The "Gem" or "Star" blade is good for paraffin sections and is unequaled for wood sections, but the back must be broken off to make it fit the holder shown in Figure 3. Fortunately, The American Safety Razor Corporation, Brooklyn, N.Y., will furnish the Gem blade, specially tempered and tested, and with the back removed for microtome use, at 50 cents for a package of 10 blades.

Some students have trouble with safety razor blades. There must be a good holder. The holders shown in Figures 3 and 4 eliminate any trouble from this factor. The *angle* must be right. A study of Figure 5 should eliminate any trouble from this source. In general, the safety razor blade should project farther beyond the holder, and the angle between the blade and paraffin should be greater for thin sections (1–5 μ) than for thicker sections. The blade should project the least, and the angle should be the least, for hard sections and thick sections.

Find the thickness at which the paraffin and object cut best. When in doubt as to the proper thickness, cut at 10 μ. When the room temperature is at zero centigrade, onion root-tips in 52° C. paraffin should yield good ribbons at 2 and 3 μ, on a rotary microtome; and on a good sliding microtome, should yield good sections at 1μ, or even thinner. The ideal temperature for 1–0.5 μ sections, with 50° or 52° C. paraffin, is —2° C. In warm weather, the microtome should be cooled on a block of ice and the knife and object must be kept cool by holding a small piece of ice against them every two or three minutes. A small piece of ice can be kept against the knife or holder by a rubber band. The ice is only a necessary evil. Try to arrange your time so as to do your cutting in cold weather. Let the room get cold, put on a warm coat, and go to work.

If you are still in the microtome knife stage, get two good hones, one for use when the knife is rather dull and the other for finishing. For the first hone, nothing equals a fine carborundum hone. About 5.5×22.5 cm. is a good size. A hard Belgian hone, of the same size, may be a little better for finishing. Flood the stone with water, and rub it with the small slip which accompanies all high-grade hones; this not only makes a lather, which facilitates the sharpening, but it also keeps the surface of the hone flat. As soon as the edge of the knife appears smooth and even under a magnification of 30 or 40 diameters, the sharpening is completed with a good strop. It is better to sharpen the knife every time you use it. A first-class microtome knife, in perfect condition, will cut good sections, but it requires both time and skill to keep the edge perfect. Of course, for large sections, more than 18 mm. in diameter, a regular microtome knife is necessary. To get the right bevel, use a "back." For knives longer than 4 inches, we prefer to have a back only on the upper side. For blades 4 inches or less in length, the tube-like back, giving a bevel like that of a safety razor blade, is satisfactory.

With the Watts safety razor blade in the holders shown in Figures 3 and 4, we have cut smooth ribbons of *Selaginella strobili*, sections through the sporangium region of the whole plant of *Isoetes*, sections of stems of *Cucurbita*, in fact, we have not used an ordinary microtome knife for cutting paraffin ribbons for more than 15 years. Many fail at the first attempt and go back to the continual drudgery of sharpening microtome knives. If the holder shown in Figure 4 is placed in the rotary microtome at the angle used for a microtome knife, failure is certain; for the blade, which is bent into a curve, will scrape rather than cut. A study of Figure 5 should enable anyone to secure the proper angle.

b) Keep the microtome well cleaned and oiled. Xylol is good for cleaning a microtome and the oil used for sewing machines is thin and efficient. Three-in-one oil is all right if the microtome is in constant use, but not so good if the microtome is to remain idle through a long vacation.

c) Trim the block so that each section shall be a *perfect rectangle.*

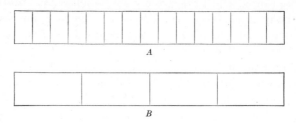

FIG. 23.—Ribbons

A ribbon of sections like that shown in Figure 23 *A* is much better than one like *B* of the same figure, because sections will usually come off in neater ribbons if the knife strikes the longer edge of the rectangle, so that the sections are united by the longer sides rather than by the shorter. Crooked ribbons are caused by wedge-shaped sections,

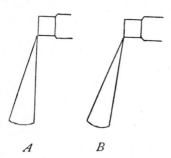

A   *B*

FIG. 24.—Position of the knife

and are always to be avoided, because they make it difficult to economize space, and also because they present such a disorderly appearance. The knife, which should be placed at a right angle to the block and not obliquely, should strike the *whole edge* of the block at once, and should leave in the same manner.

If sections stick to the knife, it may be that the knife is too nearly parallel with the surface of the block, as in Figure 24 *A*. By inclining the knife as in Figure 24 *B*, this difficulty is often obviated. A split or scratch in the paraffin ribbon may be caused by a nick in the knife. Use some more favorable position of the edge, or sharpen the whole knife. A split or a scratch in the ribbon is often caused by some hard granule which becomes fastened to the inner side of the edge of the knife. This is the most common cause of the difficulty. Simply wipe the under side of the knife with a gentle stroke of the finger, slightly moistened with xylol. For the best results, the knife should be wiped in this way *after every section*. The sliding microtome is more convenient for wiping than the rotary. Ribbons 1 μ and even 0.5 μ thick and nearly transparent can be cut on the sliding microtome shown in Figure 2. Such a thin ribbon is not likely to be more than 10 cm. long; but at 10 μ, ribbons 15 or 20 cm. long can be cut on a sliding microtome. It is a good plan to put a piece of ledger linen paper on the holder or knife. The paper, long enough to hold a short ribbon, will probably stick for a minute or two if merely moistened. If it comes off, a little mucilage or a little piece of gummed paper, overlapping a small part of the holder and paper, will keep the paper in position.

Sometimes hard paraffin does not ribbon well. This difficulty may be remedied by dipping a hot needle in soft paraffin and applying it to the opposite edges of the block to be cut. Often the mere warming of the opposite edges of the block with a hot needle is sufficient.

Another method, suggested by Dr. Land to facilitate the cutting of difficult material, has come into general use, and is very effective.

Paraffin absorbs a small amount of water, or water penetrates between the crystals of paraffin. At any rate, water reaches cell walls and, perhaps, other structures which have not been completely infiltrated, and thus softens them. The paraffin cakes may be left for weeks in water. Cakes of class material may be put in water in a fruit can and kept until ready for use. After such treatment, smooth ribbons may be cut from material which would hardly cut at all without it.

If the failure to ribbon well is due to electricity, a *very small* drop of water on the knife will hold the sections and not prevent them from slipping along in a ribbon.

After cutting, the ribbons may be kept for a few weeks, on filter paper, in a closed box; but no time is better for mounting than immediately after cutting.

A ribbon carrier is very convenient. A good carrier can be made by mounting a couple of spools 20 or 30 cm. apart, with a strong piece of cloth for a band. More elaborate carriers may be made if one has tools.

FIXING SECTIONS TO THE SLIDE

Mayer's fixative.—Sections must be firmly fixed to the slide, or they will be washed off during the processes involved in staining. Mayer's albumen fixative is excellent for this purpose. Formula:

White of egg (active principle)................. 50 c.c.
Glycerin (to keep it from drying up)............ 50 c.c.
Salicylate of soda (antiseptic, to keep out bacteria,
    etc.)....................................... 1 g.

Shake well and filter through cheesecloth. It will keep from 2 to 6 months, but, to say the least, it is never better than when first made up.

Put a small drop of fixative on the slide, smear it evenly over the surface, and then wipe it off with a clean finger until only a scarcely perceptible film remains; then add several drops of distilled water and float the sections or ribbons on the water. Warm gently until the paraffin becomes smooth and free from wrinkles. Wrinkled or curved ribbons may be straightened by touching with a needle at each end and pulling gently, just as the ribbon begins to smooth out in the warming.

When the water is warmed, the ribbon almost always stretches. Theoretically, it should not stretch at all, if the cutting has been perfect. If a ribbon cut at 10 μ does not lengthen more than 10 per cent, the cutting is *fairly* good; if it lengthens 20 per cent, cut thicker sections or lower the temperature, using ice if necessary. If a 5μ ribbon does not lengthen more than 10 per cent, the cutting may be regarded as good; at 1 μ or 0.5 μ, if it does not lengthen more than 20 per cent, the cutting has been good. Be very careful not to melt the paraffin, because the albumen coagulates with less heat than is required to melt the paraffin. Consequently, there would be nothing to fix the ribbon to the slide.

After the sections become smooth, remove as much of the water as possible. This precaution is usually neglected. Drain off what you can. Then, by touching filter paper to the edge of the sections, get rid of some more water. As the water is removed by the filter paper, the edge of the ribbon comes first into contact with the slide and thus seals in some water. Touch the edge of the ribbon with a hot needle and use the filter paper again. If care be taken at this point, there is no danger later, even when using stains requiring 24 or even 48 hours in liquids. This may seem slow and tedious, but when you compare a slide of mitosis in root-tips, or the reduction divisions in pollen mother-cells put up this way, with the usual hasty preparations, you will see a difference.

If you should heat the ribbon so hot as to melt it, some things can be saved by cooling the ribbon and floating it off to another slide smeared with fixative. Of course, since the ribbon had not got into contact with the fixative, much would be lost. It is a good plan to put the slide on a metal bath with a piece of corrugated pasteboard under the slide. Very convenient warming plates, which can be kept at a constant temperature, are sold by most dealers in laboratory supplies. A very convenient warming plate is easily made. Simply take a box, or make one, about 2 feet long, 1 foot wide, and 6 inches deep, using a piece of glass or a piece of brass $\frac{1}{8}$ inch thick for the top. Heat it by putting in such an electric bulb as will give the temperature desired. With the bulb in one end of the box, there will be various temperatures in different parts of the box. This is fine for straightening ribbons and for use during imbedding. It can even be used as a paraffin bath where the times are so short that the temperature can be watched constantly.

After the sections have become smooth and the surplus water has been removed, leave the slides where they will be warm, but well under the melting-point of the paraffin, overnight or for 24 hours. If free from dust, they may be kept for several days, or even weeks, before staining. If the sections are very thick, so that they do not need to be smoothed out on water, they may be laid carefully on the fixative, patted down with the finger and they are ready for staining. Sections may stick to the beginner's finger, but he should soon learn to avoid such troubles.

Land's fixative.—Mayer's fixative is so easily prepared and it keeps so well that it is in universal use; but, in many cases, it will not hold the section to the slide. Moss archegonia and moss capsules are likely to wash off, especially if cut rather thick. Large sections of cones of conifers are almost sure to float off as soon as the slide comes into the xylol or alcohol. Sections of ovules of cycads, as soon as they attain a length of 1.5–2 cm., are likely to wash off. For handling these more difficult cases, Dr. Land devised a fixative which has proved satisfactory, even in such extreme cases as sections of ovulate cones of *Pinus banksiana* 2 cm. long. Formula:

Gum arabic............................... 1.0 g.
Dichromate of potash..................... 0.2 g.
Water.................................... 100.0 c.c.

The mixture will not keep; the formula is given merely to indicate its composition. Make a 1 per cent solution of gum arabic in water, which will keep as well as Mayer's fixative; but make the dichromate solution immediately before using. Do not make the solution stronger than 1 per cent; usually 0.2 per cent is strong enough. Dr. Land does not measure, but simply adds enough dichromate crystals to make the water pale yellow.

Smear a few drops of the 1 per cent solution of gum arabic on the slide; flood with the dichromate solution; warm to straighten the ribbons; drain off the excess water and let the preparation dry in the light. The exposure to light renders the gum insoluble in water. LePage's glue or Mayer's albumen fixative may be used instead of gum arabic.

The foregoing directions are taken from Dr. Land's notes.

With the ordinary Mayer's albumen fixative, the dichromate of potash, without the gum arabic, may be used in floating out ribbons, and makes a stronger fixative than the Mayer's formula.

Szombathy's fixative.—

Gelatin	1 g.
Distilled water	100 c.c.
Salicylate of soda (a 2 per cent solution)	1 c.c.
Pure glycerin	15 c.c.

Dissolve the gelatin in water at 30° C., add the salicylate of soda, shake well, cool, and filter through cheesecloth; then add the 15 c.c. of glycerin. The solution should be perfectly clear.

A couple of drops of the fixative, with a couple of drops of 2 per cent formalin, is rubbed on the slide. The sections are then added, and straightened out. The formalin makes the gelatin insoluble. The fixative is much like Land's and is used for difficult material which is not held by Mayer's fixative.

Haupt's fixative.—

Gelatin	1 g.
Phenol crystals	2. g
Glycerin	15 c.c.
Distilled water	100 c.c.

This is a modification of Szombathy's formula. The gelatin is dissolved at 30° C. Gelatin which will not dissolve at this temperature is not satisfactory.

Place a small drop of the fixative on the slide and smear with the finger until the film is very thin. Flood the slide with a 2 per cent solution of formalin in distilled water, put on the ribbon, warm it, and proceed in the usual way.

REMOVAL OF THE PARAFFIN

To remove the paraffin, place the slide in a Stender dish of xylol. About 5 minutes will be sufficient for sections 10 μ thick, but 10 or 20 minutes will do no harm. While a gentle heating will hasten the process and will do no harm, you should *never heat the slide enough to melt the paraffin. Never attempt to warm the paraffin over a lamp.* Overheating is ruinous.

REMOVAL OF XYLOL OR TURPENTINE

To remove the xylol, place the slide in equal parts of xylol and absolute alcohol in a Stender dish. After 5 minutes, transfer to absolute alcohol, which should also be allowed to act for 5 minutes. A little of the paraffin will unavoidably be carried into the xylol-alcohol; a smaller quantity may be carried into the absolute alcohol. The arrangement shown in Figure 15 will completely remove the paraffin before staining.

TRANSFER TO THE STAIN

After the paraffin has been removed with xylol or turpentine, and the xylol or turpentine has been rinsed off with alcohol, the next step is the staining. If the stain is a strong alcoholic one (85–100 per cent alcohol), transfer directly to the stain. If the stain is in 70 per cent alcohol, pass through 95 and 85 per cent alcohol, 5 minutes in each, before staining. If an aqueous stain is to be used, pass down the whole series—95, 85, 70, 50, 35, and water—5 minutes in each, before placing the slide in the stain.

This is rather tedious, but, for cytological work, it seems to be necessary, and one might as well learn early that rapid work and good preparations seldom go together.

DEHYDRATING

After the sections have been stained, they must be dehydrated. If they have been stained in a strong alcoholic solution, transfer to 95 and then to 100 per cent alcohol, 2 minutes in each, if the stain does not wash out too rapidly. If stained in an aqueous solution, pass through the series—water, 5, 10, 20, 35, 50, 70, 85, 95, and 100 per cent alcohol—about 2 minutes in each.

With stains which wash out rapidly, the times must be shortened and some of the alcohols must be omitted. With aqueous gentian violet, all must be omitted except the 95 and 100 per cent, and even in these the time must be shortened to a few seconds.

CLEARING

After the sections have been dehydrated, they must be cleared, or made transparent by some clearing agent. The clearing agent must be a solvent of balsam, but it is not at all necessary that the balsam shall be dissolved in the particular clearing agent which has been used. Xylol balsam is used, not only when preparations have been cleared in xylol, but also when they have been cleared in clove oil, cedar oil, bergamot oil, or other clearing agents.

Xylol is the most generally useful clearing agent. Place the slide in equal parts of xylol and absolute alcohol and then in pure xylol, allowing each to act for about 2–5 minutes.

Clove oil is also an excellent clearing agent. The clove oil should follow the absolute alcohol, without any mixtures. Pour on a few drops of clove oil, and drain them off at once in such a way as to carry with them whatever alcohol may still remain. Then flood the slide repeatedly with clove oil, draining the clove oil back into the bottle. If judiciously used, 50 c.c. of clove oil is enough to clear 50 preparations. Sections are usually cleared in a few seconds. The only objection to clove oil is that mounts harden slowly. To overcome this difficulty, the slide should be dipped in xylol for a minute before mounting in balsam.

Synthetic oil of wintergreen is much less expensive and some claim that it is just as good as clove oil. We prefer clove oil.

For clearing sections on the slide, other clearing agents are hardly worth mentioning.

MOUNTING IN BALSAM

After the sections are cleared, wipe the slide on the side which does not bear the sections. Put on a drop of Canada balsam and add a clean,[1] thin cover. Before the cover is put on, pass it through the flame of an alcohol lamp to remove moisture, for it would be a pity

---

[1] Slides and covers should be treated with hydrochloric acid, or equal parts of hydrochloric acid and water, for several hours. They should then be thoroughly rinsed in water and wiped with a cloth perfectly free from lint. After rinsing in water, they may be kept in 95 per cent alcohol. When a cover is needed for use, it is Dr. Land's practice to rest the corner of the cover on a piece of filter paper to remove the drop of alcohol; then pass the cover through the flame of a Bunsen or alcohol lamp. The film of alcohol will burn and the cover may warp, but it will usually straighten, and it will be clean and dry.

The mixture of sulphuric acid and dichromate of potash, used for cleaning laboratory glassware, is equally good for slides and covers.

indeed to injure a preparation at this stage of the process. Add a label, and the mount is complete.

A TENTATIVE SCHEDULE FOR PARAFFIN SECTIONS

It will be useful to give several tentative schedules for the use of beginners. It cannot be too strenuously insisted that *these schedules are only tentative*, their sole object being to give the beginner a start. The following is a tentative schedule for the ovary of a lily at any period before fertilization. The pieces should not be more than 12 mm. in length.

1. Chromo-acetic acid, 1 day.
2. Wash in water, 1 day.
3. Two and one-half, 5, 10, 15, 20, and 35 per cent alcohol, three grades a day, morning, noon, and night; 50 and 70 per cent, change morning and evening; 85 per cent, 24 hours; 95 per cent, all day or overnight; absolute alcohol, 24 hours, changing 2 or 3 times.
4. Mixtures of absolute alcohol and xylol; $2\frac{1}{2}$, 5, 10, 15, 25, 50, and 75, 3 grades a day, morning, noon, and night; pure xylol, 24 hours, changing 2 or 3 times.
5. Paraffin and xylol, 48 hours.
6. Melted paraffin in the bath, 30–40 minutes, changing 2 or 3 times.
7. Imbed.
8. Section; about 10 μ is a good thickness.
9. Fasten to the slide.
10. Dissolve off the paraffin in xylol, 5 minutes.
11. Xylol and absolute alcohol, equal parts, 5 minutes; 100, 95, 85, and 70 per cent alcohol, 5 minutes each.
12. Stain in safranin (alcoholic), 6 hours or overnight.
13. Rinse in 50 per cent alcohol, using a trace of HCl if necessary; then in 70, 85, 95, and 100 per cent alcohol, 5 minutes each.
14. Stain in gentian violet dissolved in clove oil (or in clove oil with a little absolute alcohol), 10 minutes.
15. Treat with pure clove oil until the gentian violet stain is satisfactory.
16. Rinse in xylol, 1 minute.
17. Mount in balsam.
18. Label.

That the paraffin method is tedious and complicated is universally recognized. Many substitutes have been tried, but without enough success to justify even a reference.

CHAPTER X

THE CELLOIDIN METHOD

The celloidin method has almost disappeared from botanical micro-technique, because material too hard for imbedding in paraffin can be cut without any imbedding at all, and material too delicate to be cut without a supporting medium can be imbedded in paraffin. But these two categories do not cover all the ground; celloidin still has its advantages. Stems too hard for the paraffin method, which lose the cortex or, at least, suffer breaks with the steam method or when cut freehand and cold, can often be cut successfully in celloidin.

Years ago, a piece of rotten wood from an ancient Egyptian mummy case was brought to the writer for identification. It could be rubbed into powder in the fingers, and had to be handled gently to keep it from falling to pieces. It was cut very successfully in celloidin. Stems too hard for paraffin may be cut in celloidin when it is desired to preserve cell contents. Celloidin is still very valuable for most of the sections used in medical schools, because the sections can be prepared in great numbers and each student can take a section, add a drop of balsam and a cover, and have a preparation of his own ready to study. Where serial sections are necessary, as in most morphological and cytological work, the method is too tedious to be worth even a trial, unless the sections cannot be cut in any other way. Besides, most of the more valuable stains color the celloidin matrix, and if the matrix be removed, the more delicate elements may be displaced or even lost.

Celloidin and collodion are forms of nitro-cellulose. They are inflammable, but do not explode. Schering's celloidin, which is only a collodion prepared by a patented process, is in general use for imbedding. Granulated and shredded forms of celloidin are on the market, but the tablets are more convenient. Directions for making the various solutions accompany the celloidin. To make a 2 per cent solution, add to 1 tablet enough ether-alcohol to make the whole weigh 2,000 g. To make a 4 per cent solution, add another tablet, and to make a 6 per cent solution, add an additional tablet, and so on.

The collodion method was published by Duval[1] in 1879. Celloidin

[1]Duval, *Journal de l'anatomie*, 1879, p. 185.

was recommended by Merkel and Schiefferdecker[1] in 1882. The principal features of the method are as follows: Material is dehydrated in absolute alcohol, treated with ether-alcohol, infiltrated with celloidin, imbedded in celloidin, hardened in chloroform or alcohol; after which, it is cut, stained, and mounted.

Eycleshymer, who brought the celloidin method to a high degree of efficiency, published in 1892 a short account, which may be summarized as follows: Put the celloidin tablet, or fragments, into a wide-mouthed bottle, and pour on enough ether-alcohol (equal parts ether and absolute alcohol) to cover the celloidin. Occasionally shake and add a little more ether-alcohol until the celloidin is all dissolved. The process may require several days. The solution should have the consistency of a very thick oil. Label this solution Number 4. Solution Number 3 is made by mixing 2 parts of solution Number 4 with 1 part of ether-alcohol. Solution Number 2 is made by mixing 2 parts of Number 3 with 1 part of ether-alcohol. Solution Number 1 consists of equal parts of ether and absolute alcohol.

After dehydrating, the material is placed successively in solutions 1, 2, 3, and 4. For an object 2 mm. square, 24 hours in each solution is sufficient; for the brain of a cat, a week is not too long.

A paper tray may be used for imbedding. Pour the object, with the thick solution, into the tray and harden in chloroform for 24 hours; then cut away the paper and place the block in 70 per cent alcohol for a few hours. The material may be left indefinitely in a mixture of equal parts of 95 per cent alcohol and glycerin.

Before cutting, the object is mounted upon a block of wood. A block, suited to the microtome clamp, is dipped in ether-alcohol, which removes the air and insures a firmer mounting. Dip the end of the block of wood in solution Number 3, and the piece of celloidin containing the object in solution Number 1. Press the two firmly together, and place in chloroform until the joint becomes hardened.

Set the blade of the microtome knife as obliquely as possible. Both the object and the knife should be kept flooded with 70 per cent alcohol, and the sections, as they are cut, should be transferred to 70 per cent alcohol.

Stain in Delafield's haematoxylin for 5–30 minutes. Wash in water for about 5 minutes, and then decolorize in acid alcohol (2–5 drops of hydrochloric acid to 100 c.c. of 70 per cent alcohol) until the stain is

[1] Merkel and Schiefferdecker, *Archiv für Anatomie und Physiologie*, 1882.

extracted from the celloidin, or at least until the celloidin retains only a faint pinkish color. Wash in 70 per cent alcohol (not acid) until the characteristic purple color of the haematoxylin replaces the red due to the acid. Stain in eosin (preferably a 1 per cent solution in 70 per cent alcohol) for 2–5 minutes. Dehydrate in 95 per cent alcohol for about 5 minutes. Absolute alcohol must not be used, unless it is desirable to remove the celloidin matrix. Eycleshymer's clearing fluid (equal parts of cedar oil, bergamot oil, and carbolic acid) clears readily from 95 per cent alcohol. Mount in balsam.

If serial sections are necessary, arrange the sections upon a slide, using enough 70 per cent alcohol to keep the sections moist, but not enough to allow them to float. Cover the sections with a strip of thin toilet paper, which can be kept in place by winding with fine thread. After the sections have been stained and cleared, remove the excess of clearing fluid by pressing rather firmly with a piece of blotting-paper. Then remove the toilet paper and mount in balsam.

With occasional slight modifications, we have used the method as presented by Eycleshymer in his classes. Instead of the graded series of celloidin solutions, we use a 2 per cent solution, which is allowed to concentrate slowly by removing the cork occasionally, or by using a cork which does not fit very tightly. The material is imbedded when the solution reaches the consistency of a very thick oil. If the material is to be cut immediately, we prefer to imbed it and fasten it to the block at the same time. The blocks should have surface enough to accommodate the objects, and should be about $\frac{1}{4}$ inch thick. White pine makes good blocks; cork is much inferior. Tie a piece of ledger linen paper around the top of the block, letting it project above the top of the block far enough to make for the object a little tray with the end of the block for a bottom.

Place the block for a moment in ether-alcohol and then dip into the 2 per cent celloidin the end of the block which was left rough by the saw. With the forceps remove a piece of the material from the thick celloidin and place it upon the block, taking care to keep it right side up. Dip the block with its object first in thick celloidin, then in thin, and after exposing to the air for a few minutes drop it into chloroform, where it should remain for about 10–20 hours. It should then be placed in equal parts of glycerin and 95 per cent alcohol, where it may be kept indefinitely. If the material is hard, like many woody stems, it will cut better after remaining in this mixture for a couple of weeks.

The following schedules, beginning with the celloidin sections in 70 per cent alcohol, will give the student a start in the staining:

Delafield's haematoxylin and eosin.—

1. Seventy per cent alcohol, 2–5 minutes.
2. Delafield's haematoxylin, 5–30 minutes.
3. Wash in water, 5 minutes.
4. Acid alcohol (1 c.c. hydrochloric acid+100 c.c. of 70 per cent alcohol) until the stain is extracted from the celloidin, or at least until only a faint pinkish color remains.
5. Wash in 70 per cent alcohol (not acid) until the purple color returns.
6. Stain in eosin (preferably a 1 per cent solution in 70 per cent alcohol), 2–5 minutes.
7. Dehydrate in 95 per cent alcohol, 2–5 minutes. Do not use absolute alcohol unless you wish to dissolve the celloidin, which is not necessary with this staining.
8. Clear in Eycleshymer's clearing fluid, usually 1–2 minutes, but sometimes 5–10 minutes.
9. Mount in balsam.

Safranin and Delafield's haematoxylin.—

1. Seventy per cent alcohol, 2–5 minutes.
2. Safranin (alcoholic), 6–24 hours.
3. Acid alcohol (a few drops of hydrochloric acid in 70 per cent alcohol) until the safranin is removed from the cellulose walls.
4. Wash in 50 per cent alcohol, 5–10 minutes to remove the acid.
5. Delafield's haematoxylin, 2–5 minutes.
6. Wash in water, 5 minutes.
7. Acid alcohol, a few seconds.
8. Dehydrate in 95 per cent alcohol, 2–5 minutes, then in absolute alcohol, 2–5 minutes, which will partially dissolve the celloidin.
9. Clear in clove oil, which will complete the removal of the celloidin.
10. Be sure that the sections are free from fragments of celloidin and then mount in balsam.

Stains which can be used with celloidin are limited because they stain the matrix; but some material can be stained in bulk with an aqueous stain while the material is in water, or with an alcoholic stain while passing through the alcohols. Safranin is good for xylem, alum carmine is more generally useful, and borax carmine is good for some animal tissues. A second stain, like Delafield's haematoxylin, which can be extracted from the matrix, can be used after the sections have been cut.

Jeffrey's improvements in the celloidin method have been described in considerable detail by Plowman.[1] Sections of hard stems and roots cut by this method could hardly be surpassed, and they are perfectly adapted to the requirements of photomicrography. The following is a brief abstract of Plowman's paper:

1. **Preparation of material.**—Dead and dry material should be repeatedly boiled in water and cooled to remove air. An air-pump may be used in addition. Living material may be fixed in a mixture of picric acid, mercuric chloride, and alcohol:

Mercuric chloride, saturated solution, in 30 per cent alcohol . 3 parts
Picric acid, saturated solution, in 30 per cent alcohol . . . . . . 1 part

Fix 24 hours, and wash by passing through 40, 50, 60, 70, and 80 per cent alcohol, allowing each to act for 24 hours.

2. **Desilification, etc.**—Silica and other mineral deposits are removed by treating with a 10 per cent aqueous solution of commercial hydrofluoric acid. The material is transferred to this solution from water or from the 80 per cent alcohol. The process may require 3 or 4 days, with one or two changes of the acid and frequent shaking of the bottle. An ordinary wide-mouthed bottle, coated internally with hard paraffin, should be prepared, since the acid is usually sold in bottles with narrow necks. The bottles are easily prepared by filling them with hot paraffin and simply pouring the paraffin out. Enough will stick to the bottle to protect the glass from the acid. Wash in running water 3 or 4 hours.

3. **Dehydration.**—Use 30, 50, 70, 90, and 100 per cent alcohol, allowing 12 hours in each grade.

4. **Infiltration with celloidin.**—There should be ten grades of celloidin: 2, 4, 6, 8, 10, 12, 14, 16, 18, and 20 per cent. Transfer from absolute alcohol to the 2 per cent celloidin. (We should prefer a previous treatment with ether-alcohol.) The bottle should be nearly filled, and the stopper should be clamped or wired in place. Put the bottle on its side in a paraffin bath at 50°–60° C. for 12–18 hours. Cool the bottle quickly in cold water, taking care that the water does not get into the bottle. Pour out the 2 per cent solution (which, as well as all other solutions, may be used repeatedly), and replace it with the 4 per cent, and proceed in the same way with the other grades. When the 20 per cent solution is reached, a further thickening is gained by adding a

[1] A. B. Plowman, "The Celloidin Method with Hard Tissues," *Botanical Gazette*, **37**:456–461, 1904.

few chips of dry celloidin from time to time until the mixture is quite stiff and firm. Remove each block with the celloidin adhering to it and harden it in chloroform for 12 hours. Then transfer to a mixture of equal parts of glycerin and 95 per cent alcohol, where the material should remain for a few days before cutting.

Cutting, staining, and mounting.—Although 10 μ is usually thin enough, sections are readily cut as thin as 5 μ by this method. Remove the celloidin before staining by treating 10–15 minutes with ether; then wash in 95 per cent alcohol and transfer to water, and then to the stain. Stain to a fairly dense purple in an aqueous solution of Erlich's haematoxylin; wash in dilute aqueous solution of calcium or sodium carbonate, and then in two changes of distilled water. Add a few drops of alcoholic solution of equal parts of Grübler's alcoholic and aqueous safranin, and stain to a rich red. A dilute stain acting 1–2 hours is better than a more concentrated stain acting for a shorter time. Transfer directly to absolute alcohol, clear in xylol, and mount in balsam.

Haidenhain's iron-haematoxylin is a very satisfactory stain for photographic purposes.

The celloidin method has its disadvantages as well as its advantages. It is extremely slow and tedious, and it is rarely possible to cut sections thinner than 10 μ while, on the other hand, it gives smoother sections.

Succulent tissues, which are usually damaged by the paraffin method, are easily handled without any injury in celloidin. The fact that the method may be used without heat is often a further advantage. Stems and roots, which cannot be handled at all in paraffin, cut well in celloidin, and much larger sections can be cut than in paraffin, but most material of this kind can be cut without any imbedding.

When material is to be imbedded, use celloidin as a last resort. Use paraffin when you *can*, celloidin when you *must*.

CHAPTER XI

THE CELLULOSE ACETATE METHOD

When the cellulose acetate method first appeared, more than ten years ago, we hoped that it was destined to be as successful with hard woody tissues as the Venetian turpentine method has been with unicellular and filamentous forms; but, up to date, American investigators have found nothing to arouse any enthusiasm for this method, which seems to be at its best in the fogs of London. We have obtained the cellulose acetate from Cellon and tried it repeatedly with hard and soft woods, but have never secured sections which could be compared with those obtained by other methods. However, no one but the authors got good results with Venetian turpentine for many years after the method was published; so, let us hope that the method will yet yield as good sections on this side of the Atlantic as it does on the other.

Hard woods like oak, and even harder material, have yielded smooth thin sections. Cellulose acetate does not injure the finer details of structures and, on that account, is superior to hydrofluoric acid. We are quoting, in full, Mrs. Williamson's account in the *Annals of Botany* for January, 1921.

A NEW METHOD OF PREPARING SECTIONS OF HARD VEGETABLE STRUCTURES

In order to prepare sections of hard vegetable structures it is essential that some method should be devised by which the structure is not only embedded but softened, so that sections can be cut easily and smoothly. After various methods had been tried, the cellulose acetate method successfully used by Dr. Kernot for embedding and sectioning the fabric of aeroplane wings was used. It was discovered that this method not only embedded hard vegetable structures, but also softened them so that sections are easily obtained. It proved best to use cellulose acetate of French manufacture made from pure cellulose, as the viscosity is more uniform than that of English manufacture, which is obtained from the cellulose of wood.

In the preliminary experiments pieces of oak and beech, cut into half-inch cubes, were passed through strengths of alcohol, then placed in pure acetone for two hours and finally into a 12 per cent solution of cellulose acetate in acetone. There they were left for two months, and excellent sections were obtained. Further experiments showed that the passage through alcohols was unnecessary. In the final experiments the pieces of wood were placed in water and the air removed from them, after which they were put into pure acetone for 1–2 hours and finally into the solution of cellulose acetate. It was found that the length of time of immersion in the solution of cellulose acetate necessary for softening the tissues varied with the hardness of the wood, the minimum time for soft woods being two days; for woods such as oak and beech, at least six days are required. Experiments were tried with sâl (*Shorea robusta*) and Pyingadu (*Xylia dolabriformis*), one of the Indian ironwoods, which is extremely hard. After fourteen days in the cellulose acetate solution it was possible to obtain transverse sections of these hard woods. The cellulose acetate solution is therefore capable of softening even the hardest wood in a relatively short time.

In order to stain sections—either hand or microtome—obtained by this method, it is necessary to wash them in pure acetone for 1 to 2 minutes to remove the cellulose acetate, wash in alcohol 1 to 2 minutes, and pass on to the stains selected. Various staining methods for cell walls—such as anilin chloride, methylene blue, and Congo red, ammoniacal fuchsin and Kleinenberg's haematoxylin, etc.—were tried with success. A comparison with stained sections of untreated wood revealed no differences. Delicate tissues in the wood and hyphae of fungi infecting the wood also stain well and are unaffected by the treatment.

A satisfactory method of preparing sections of hard vegetable structures is therefore supplied by the use of a 12 per cent solution of cellulose acetate in pure acetone for softening and embedding.—H. S. WILLIAMSON, Imperial College of Science and Technology.

Correspondence with Mrs. Williamson indicates that the various brands of cellulose acetate behave differently. Cellulose acetate obtained from wood is unsatisfactory. We found that cellulose acetate made from photographic films was also unsatisfactory. Mrs. Williamson used a cellulose acetate sold by Cellon (Richmond) Ltd., 22 Cork Street, London, England, and manufactured by the Société Chimique des Usines du Rhône. The time may be shortened by keeping the temperature at 40° C.

In making the solution, use 12 g. of cellulose acetate to 100 c.c. of pure acetone.

CHAPTER XII

SPECIAL METHODS

It has been the object of the preceding chapters to give the student an introduction to the principal methods of preparing plant material for microscopic study, and to afford him such a grounding in fundamentals that he will be able to develop methods which may be necessary in special cases.

A few methods designed to meet special difficulties are given in this chapter and others are mentioned in the second part of the book, in connection with various laboratory types.

VERY LARGE SECTIONS

It is sometimes desirable to cut very large sections. Sections as large as a cornstalk may be cut freehand, but cut better when imbedded in paraffin or celloidin. Even when cutting a paraffin section of a corn stem, have the knife somewhat oblique, and if the section shows a tendency to curl, as it probably will, a gentle touch with the finger will prevent the curling. If the knife, for the best cutting, is too oblique for ribbons, take each section off separately and put it in a box.

A section of a stem of *Zamia* 5 or 6 cm. in diameter is difficult to handle by the usual methods. If a large microtome, such as is used in cutting complete sections of large brains, is available, the piece of stem is easily held for the cutting. Some of the medium-sized sliding microtomes now have a rigid clamp which will grip a block 3 cm. square. The lower part of the piece can then be trimmed to fit the clamp, leaving the upper part round, so that sections across a stem 6 or 7 cm. in diameter may be cut without much difficulty. With a rather soft stem, like *Zamia*, the surface must be flooded with 95 per cent alcohol after each section, if it is desirable to cut thin sections. From stems 3 cm. in diameter, sections can be cut at about 20 to 30 μ. If the section is not more than 3 or 4 cm. in diameter, it can be mounted on a 50×75 mm. slide. Sections 6 or 7 cm. in diameter can be mounted on lantern slides; if large covers are not available, use another lantern slide for a cover. It will be easier to get neat mounts if the cover is cut down so as to leave a margin 2 or 3 mm. wide. It is not easy to mount a thick section between 2 lantern slides of the same size, on account of the balsam which oozes out at the edges. Such preparations may be used directly as lantern slides. Large sections of the stem of a tree fern make good mounts without any staining.

STONY TISSUES

Sections of the stony tissues of hickory nuts, walnuts, peach stones, and similar refractory substances cannot be cut by ordinary methods.

With a fine saw, saw sections about 1 mm. in thickness. Put some fine carborundum on a piece of plate glass, wet it, lay the section on it and, with the finger on the section, rub with a circular motion until one side of the section is quite smooth. Turn the section over and rub the other side. When the section has become quite thin (about half a millimeter) use a piece of plate glass, about 10 cm. square, instead of the finger. When the section is thin enough, wash it thoroughly, dehydrate, clear, and mount in balsam.

The long, narrow pores show better without any clearing. In this case, dry the section thoroughly, heat a few drops of balsam on the slide to drive off the solvent, put the section into the balsam, and add a cover. The air caught in the long, narrow pores will make them appear as black lines. Sections of most nuts show excellent detail without any staining. Thin sections, however, may be stained in the usual way.

STEAM METHOD FOR HARDWOOD SECTIONS

In 1926 Dr. Josef Kisser published a useful method for cutting sections of hard woods. The method consists, essentially, in letting steam play upon the block as the sections are being cut. The hot steam is easily secured by a simple apparatus which can be set up in a few minutes in any laboratory. All that is needed is a flask, holding about 300 c.c., and some glass tubing (Fig. 25). The temperature of the steam should be about 90° C. If the steam is too hot, the material dries; if the temperature is much below 90° C., there is little advantage from the steam.

The Spencer Lens Company's holder for thin safety razor blades, while excellent for thin paraffin sections, does not hold the thin blade so well for wood sections. However, the holder holds the Durham duplex blade very well, and the Gem or Star blade, with the back broken off, is ideal for wood sections. Of course, if one likes to sharpen microtome knives, they are long and will cut while they are sharp.

It is a good plan to cut the wood into pieces suitable for cutting, so that the sections will be about 5×7 mm. Boil these pieces for 24 hours and then put them into equal parts of 95 per cent alcohol and glycerin for at least a week. After the boiling, very hard woods should be treated with 25 per cent hydrofluoric acid for a week and then washed

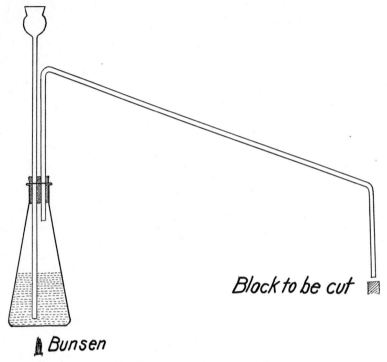

Block to be cut

Bunsen

FIG. 25.—Apparatus for steam method

thoroughly in water before being placed in glycerin and alcohol. A soft wood, like *Pinus strobus*, needs no steam or previous treatment, except a few hours' soaking in water.

Kisser cut transverse sections, 5 mm. square, of ebony. Sections of cocoanut shell 2 mm. square and 6 μ thick were cut smoothly.

JEFFREY'S VULCANIZING METHOD

Jeffrey cut very thin sections of the hardest woods and even such refractory material as peach stones and the shells of various nuts.

Tissues are softened at a temperature of about 320° F., in an ordinary dental vulcanizer. The time required varies. For a three- or four-year-old branch of oak, an hour is usually enough; but for a piece of seasoned oak wood, the time is likely to be 4 or 5 hours.

Brass pipe $\frac{3}{4}$–1 inch in diameter is cut into lengths to fit the vulcanizer, and the ends are threaded for brass caps. On one end, the cap is made tight by "sweating" lead solder into the thread. The other end is made tight by putting into the cap a piece of cardboard and, on top of the cardboard, a circular piece of lead. The tube is then placed in a vise, the water or alcohol, with the material, is put into the tube, and the cap is screwed on tight with a wrench.

After vulcanizing, the material is allowed to cool slowly, and then is treated for a few days in a mixture of 2 parts water and 1 part hydrofluoric acid. Wash well, run up through the alcohols, and preserve in equal parts glycerin and 95 per cent alcohol, until needed for cutting.

By this method, Jeffrey cut transverse sections of cocoanut shells and hard woods as thin as 2 or 3 μ.

CLEARING THICK SECTIONS OR SMALL OBJECTS

It is sometimes desirable to make very thick sections to show general topography rather than detail. A longitudinal section of the fully grown ovule of *Ginkgo* or a cycad may be cut as thick as 3–5 mm. so as to include the entire group of archegonia. A slab can be cut from each side of the ovule with a fine saw, and a razor can be used for smoothing. If the section is from fresh material it should be fixed, washed, etc., with about the same periods as if it were to be imbedded in paraffin. When thoroughly cleared in xylol, the section should be put into a flat museum jar of suitable size and kept in xylol. Before the stony coat of a cycad or *Ginkgo* ovule becomes too hard to cut readily with a safety razor blade, the ovule should be run up to 85 per cent alcohol before cutting the slabs off from the sides, because the turgidity of the endosperm would cause distortion. If the base of the living ovule be placed in basic fuchsin, the vascular system will be stained. Then fix in alcohol and follow Gourley's method, described later in this chapter. Such preparations, when cleared and placed in a smooth glass dish with a light beneath, are very instructive.

Sections of *Zamia* or other cycad stems, 2 mm., or even 5 mm. thick, make instructive mounts, since they show the peculiar course of the bundles, a feature which is largely lost in thin sections.

Kraus prepared large objects very effectively by dehydrating, clearing in xylol, and then transferring to cedar oil. Sections of an apple, either longitudinal or transverse, about 3 or 4 mm. thick, cleared in this way, are very instructive. Strawberries, gooseberries, and similar objects treated in this way afford a kind of study which is too often neglected.

Dr. LaDema M. Langdon cleared 15 mm. cubes of mature wood of *Dioon spinulosum* in this way, but used equal parts of xylol and carbon disulphide for clearing. By placing a light under the dish containing the object, the bundles could be traced perfectly.

LAND'S GELATIN METHOD

It is sometimes desirable to get sections of partly disorganized material. A matrix is necessary to hold the parts in place, but dehydration may make the tissue unnecessarily hard to cut.

Soak ordinary gelatin (which can be obtained at the grocery) in water until no more is taken up. Then drain off the excess water and liquefy the gelatin by heating. Place the material—previously soaked in water—in the melted gelatin and keep it there for several hours. Place also in the gelatin some small blocks of hard wood to serve as supports in the microtome. The material to be sectioned is oriented in a gelatin matrix on the supporting blocks, cooled until the gelatin sets, and then placed in strong formalin to harden the gelatin. In cutting, flood the knife with water.

If the material is to be stained, stain it in bulk before putting it into the gelatin, since the gelatin stains very deeply. Of course, the gelatin could be dissolved with hot water, or hot water and acetic acid, but all the advantage of a matrix would be lost.

It would be worth while to try this method thoroughly with soft, succulent tissues and with hard tissues which become still harder if dehydrated.

SCHULTZE'S MACERATION METHOD

Various solutions are used to separate a tissue into its individual cells. These solutions dissolve or weaken the middle lamella so that the cells are easily shaken or teased apart. Schultze used strong nitric acid and potassium chlorate. Put the material, which should be in very small pieces, into a test-tube; pour on just enough nitric acid to cover it, and then add a few crystals of potassium chlorate. Heat gently until bubbles are evolved, and let the reagent act until the material becomes white. Four or five minutes should be sufficient. The fumes are disagreeable and are very injurious to microscopes. Pour the contents of the tube into a dish of water. After the material is thoroughly washed in water, it may be teased with needles and mounted, or it may be put into a bottle of water and shaken until many of the cells become dissociated.

After a thorough washing in water, the material may be stained. The large tracheids of ferns, dissociated in this way and stained in safranin or methyl green, make beautiful preparations.

JEFFREY'S MACERATION METHOD

A method which I saw at Toronto and which gives much better results was credited to Professor Jeffrey. Wood is cut or split into sections about 300 μ thick, which are then boiled and cooled until free from air. The macerating fluid consists of equal parts of 10 per cent nitric acid and 10 per cent chromic acid. The time will vary with different woods, but is likely to be about 24–48 hours if the temperature is about 35° C. When properly macerated the cells may be shaken apart or are very easily teased apart. Before staining, the material should be very thoroughly washed to remove the acid. A study of such material is very valuable in modern anatomical work.

Maceration methods which act in a few minutes are likely to be so violent that fine details will not be preserved.

PROTOPLASMIC CONNECTIONS

As a rule, protoplasmic connections are not likely to be seen in an ordinary preparation. It used to be thought that the rather large protoplasmic strands seen at the sieve plates of the pumpkin and other Cucurbitaceae were exaggerated examples of protoplasmic continuity; but, as a matter of fact, the large strands do not extend entirely through the plate. The real continuity, through the middle lamella, is scanty and hard to demonstrate.

Very satisfactory material for the demonstration of the connecting strands is furnished by the endosperm of the Japanese persimmon, *Diospyros kaki*. Usually, as you get this persimmon at the grocery store, it is seedless, but occasionally it has seeds. Fix in 10 per cent formalin, or in formalin-alcohol (10 c.c. formalin to 50 c.c. of 50 per cent alcohol); or in glycerin-alcohol (equal parts 95 per cent alcohol and glycerin) for a week. The endosperm of the American persimmon,

Diospyros virginiana, is good, but small and harder to hold. Best of all is the endosperm of the Philippine *Diospyros discolor* (Fig. 26).

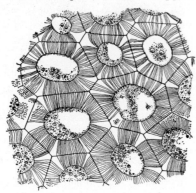

In *Diospyros discolor* the best view will be obtained in sections cut parallel with the flat surface of the seed. Imbedding is neither necessary nor desirable. Clamp the endosperm in the microtome directly and cut sections 8–10 μ thick. For cutting pieces of endosperm too small to be clamped directly, fasten the piece to a convenient block with cellulose acetate, which is easily made by dissolving a photographic film (with the emulsion removed by keeping it a little while in hot water) in

Fig. 26.—*Diospyros discolor:* section of endosperm fixed in formalin and stained in Haidenhain's iron-alum haematoxylin. ×1135.

acetone. The solution should have the consistency of thick syrup. Celloidin or even glue will hold the piece to the block. Put the sections in ether and leave them there for 24 hours, changing once or twice to remove any oily or fatty substances. *If oils and fats are not removed completely, a good stain will be impossible.* Staining is not difficult, if all oils and fats have been removed and the display of protoplasmic connections is very striking (Fig. 26).

1. Fix in formalin, formalin-alcohol, or in glycerin-alcohol for a week.
2. Cut sections 8–12 μ thick.
3. Chloroform or ether, 24 hours.
4. Absolute alcohol, 95 per cent and 50 per cent alcohol, 20 minutes each.
5. Wash in water, 5 minutes.
6. Iron alum, 4 per cent, 8–24 hours.
7. Wash in water, 30 minutes.
8. Stain in ½ per cent haematoxylin, 24 hours.
9. Wash in water. At this stage, examine carefully, because it may not be necessary to reduce the stain in iron-alum. If the connections are not too deeply stained, simply dehydrate, clear, and mount in balsam.

After the first 5 stages, a strong stain in Delafield's haematoxylin, 10–24 hours, followed by a very weak hydrochloric acid, has given good results. A sharp stain in crystal violet, differentiated with orange in clove oil, often fails, but sometimes succeeds; and, when successful, the connections stand out beautifully.

The endosperm of *Phytelephas* (vegetable ivory), of dates, and many other palms, and probably most hard endosperms, will show the connections by the methods just described; but in many cases it is necessary to resort to special methods in order to demonstrate the continuity. In these special methods a reagent is used which causes the membranes to swell before the stain is applied. It is only by such an exaggeration that the more delicate connections can be shown.

Put thin sections of fresh material into a mixture of equal parts of sulphuric acid and water and allow the reagent to act for 2–10 seconds. Wash the acid out thoroughly in water and stain in anilin blue. According to Gardiner, this stain should be made by adding 1 g. of the dry stain to 100 c.c. of a saturated solution of picric acid in 50 per cent alcohol. The staining solution is then washed out in water, and the sections are mounted in glycerin. The sections may be dehydrated, cleared in clove oil, and mounted in balsam. The anilin blue may be used in 50 per cent alcohol acidulated with a few drops of acetic acid.

Chloroïodide of zinc may be used instead of sulphuric acid. Treat the fresh sections for 2 hours with the iodine and potassium iodide solution used in testing for starch; then treat about 12 hours with chloroïodide of zinc. Wash in water and stain in anilin blue. Examine in glycerin.

Try Meyer's pyoktanin method with seeds from dates as you get them on the market. Remove any oils and fats with ether, transfer to absolute alcohol, 95, 85, 70, 50, 35, and 20 per cent alcohol, about 5 minutes in each; then wash well in water and use the following reagents:

1. Iodine, potassium iodide solution: iodine 1 part, potassium iodide 1 part, water 200 parts.
2. Sulphuric acid 1 part, water 3 parts; this mixture to be saturated with iodine.
3. Pyoktanin coeruleum 1 g., water 30 c.c. This pyoktanin is a very pure methyl violet obtained from E. Merck in Darmstadt.

Put sections of the date seed into a watch glass full of the first solution, and allow it to act for a few minutes; then mount in a drop of the solution. The connections will be only very faintly stained, showing a slightly yellowish color. At the edge of the cover, add a drop of the second solution. The preparation will darken a little. Then allow a small drop of the third solution to run under the cover. Allow the stain to act for about 3 minutes. Then plunge the whole preparation into water. The action should be stopped before the entire section has become blue. Now wash the section quickly. If there are annoying, granular precipitates, remove them with a soft brush. Mount in glycerin. The membrane should be a clear blue, while the protoplast and connections should be a blue-black.

The following is Strasburger's modification of Meyer's method, and shows the connections with great distinctness; and the preparations are permanent.

1. Treat the fresh sections with 1 per cent osmic acid, 5–7 minutes.
2. Wash in water 5–10 minutes.
3. Treat with a solution of iodine in potassium iodide (0.2 per cent iodine and 1.64 per cent potassium iodide), 20–30 minutes.
4. Transfer to 25 per cent sulphuric acid, which should act for at least half an hour; 24 hours may be necessary.
5. Bring the sections into 25 per cent sulphuric acid which has been saturated with iodine. Add a drop of Meyer's pyoktanin solution (1 g. pyoktanin coeruleum as sold by E. Merck in Darmstadt in 30 c.c. of water).

In about 5 minutes the sections will be stained sufficiently and can be examined in glycerin. If there are annoying precipitates, remove them with a soft brush.

According to Meyer, the swelling is an advantage only when the walls are very thin. When the walls are thick, the connections show better without any previous swelling.

Try the following method with the seeds of *Diospyros, Latania, Chamerops, Phoenix,* or *Phytelephas*: Soak in water and cut thin sections. Extract the oily and fatty substances with ether; wash in 95 per cent, or in absolute alcohol; stain in anilin blue (Hoffman's blue 1 g. dissolved in 150 c.c. of 50 per cent alcohol) for a few minutes. Examine in glycerin. This method succeeds very well with seeds of the date.

Permanent preparations may be secured by the following method:

1. Fix in 1 per cent osmic acid, or in absolute alcohol, 5–10 minutes.
2. Stain for 24 hours in Delafield's haematoxylin.
3. Wash for a few minutes in acid alcohol (5 drops of hydrochloric acid in 50 c.c. of 70 per cent alcohol).
4. Wash for a few minutes in ammonia alcohol (5 drops of ammonia to 50 c.c. of 70 per cent alcohol).
5. Dehydrate in absolute alcohol, clear in xylol, and mount in balsam.

STAINING CILIA

The cilia of the large spermatogoid of *Gingko* and the cycads stain beautifully in iron-alum haematoxylin, which not only stains the cilia but even differentiates the free portion from the part between the blepharoplast and the surface.

The cilia of sperms of Bryophytes and Pteridophytes stain better with gentian violet or crystal violet. The periods are long; not less than 30 minutes, and often several hours will be required.

The cilia of the motile spores of Thallophytes may often be demonstrated by allowing a drop of the iodine solution used in testing for starch to run under the cover.

Zimmermann gives the following method: Bring the objects into a drop of water on the slide and invert the drop over the fumes of 1 per cent osmic acid for 5 minutes. Allow the drop to dry. Then add a drop of 20 per cent aqueous solution of tannin, and after 5 minutes wash it off with water. Stain in a strong aqueous solution of fuchsin (or carbol fuchsin) for 5 minutes. Allow the preparation to dry completely, and then add a drop of balsam and a cover. The cilia should take a bright red.

Zimmermann also found the following method satisfactory for the cilia of the zoöspores of algae and fungi: Fix by adding a few drops of 1 per cent osmic acid to the water containing the zoöspores; then add an equal amount of a mixture of fuchsin and methyl violet. The fuchsin and methyl violet should be 1 per cent solutions in 95 per cent alcohol. In a few seconds the cilia stain a bright red.

The brilliant staining of the cilia of motile sperms of cycads with iron-alum haematoxylin would warrant a trial in any other form. Skilfully used, this stain will give good results with almost anything.

CHONDRIOSOMES

During the past twenty years the terms chondriosomes, mitochondria, *Chondriokonten*, and about fifty others, have become increasingly frequent in botanical literature. These chondriosomes, although extremely small, can often be seen in living cells. They move as actively as bacteria and very effective moving picture photomicrographs have been made. While probably present in most cells, they are not differentiated by the methods usually employed for other purposes. Most of them bear a superficial resemblance to coccus, bacillus, and spirillum forms of bacteria (Fig. 27).

Many fixing agents either destroy the mitochondria or make it almost impossible to demonstrate them. Fixing agents containing alcohol or any considerable percentage of acid are to be avoided.

We recommend neutral formalin, with 10 c.c. of formalin to 90 c.c. of distilled water. Get the neutral formalin from commercial formalin by distilling with sodium carbonate. It is not worth while to distil more than you need within the next 24 hours, because the formalin will not remain neutral. Formic acid appears in it and its value as a fixing agent for chondriosomes is at an end. Fix for 48 hours, wash in water, and follow the regular procedure for Haidenhain's iron-alum haematoxylin. The chondriosomes should stain black.

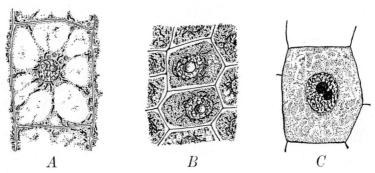

FIG. 27.—Chondriosomes. *A*, periblem of root tip of *Allium cepa*. Fixed in 10 per cent neutral formalin and stained in iron-alum haematoxylin. Preparation by Yamanouchi. *B*, cells in young megasporangium of *Asparagus officinalis*. Fixed in formalin chromic acid and stained in iron-alum haematoxylin. Both ×1135. *C*, canaliculi in root tip of *Allium cepa*, fixed in Bensley's solution and stained in iron-alum haematoxylin. ×1200.

Benda's solution, followed by Haidenhain's iron-alum haematoxylin, will give good results. A solution recommended by Bensley is good also for plant material.

Bensley's solution.—

> Osmic acid, 2 per cent...................... 1 part
> Corrosive sublimate (HgCl₂), 2½ per cent........ 4 parts

Add 1 drop of glacial acetic acid to 10 c.c. of this solution. Fix for 24–48 hours and wash thoroughly in water. On the slide, bleach with hydrogen peroxide; wash in water; treat with the iodine solution used in testing for starch; then wash in water. The slide is now ready for staining. We recommend the usual Haidenhain's iron-alum haematoxylin.

Bensley recommends the following method which we have found rather uncertain, but which, when successful, yields magnificent preparations: On the slide, bleach for 2 or 3 seconds in a 1 per cent aqueous solution of permanganate of potash; then treat with a 5 per cent aqueous solution of oxalic acid until the preparation becomes white (a few seconds); wash in water, and then stain as follows:

1. Copper acetate (neutral) saturated solution in water, 5–10 minutes.
2. Wash in water.
3. One-half per cent haematoxylin, 5–10 minutes.
4. Wash in water.
5. Potassium dichromate (neutral), 5 per cent solution in water until the preparation blackens, usually 30 seconds or less.
6. Differentiate in Weigert's ferricyanide solution.

   Borax.................................... 2.0 g.
   Ferricyanide of potassium................. 2.5 g.
   Water.................................... 200.0 c.c.
7. Wash in water and proceed as usual.

Yamanouchi's method.—Fix in a 10 per cent solution of neutral formalin in water for 24 hours; wash in water, 24 hours; dehydrate, leave objects as small as onion root-tips at least 24 hours in the 85 per cent alcohol; clear in xylols; imbed; stain in iron-alum haematoxylin.

CANALICULI

By using special methods, Bensley has obtained views of the protoplasm of plants, quite different from those seen in ordinary preparations. In the cell of a root-tip a series of small canals, or vacuoles, appears, which is much more definite and extensive than the usual display of vacuoles and which appears before any vacuoles can be recognized in preparations made in the usual way (Fig. 27C). Being a zoölogist, he called these vacuoles *canaliculi*.

GOURLEY'S METHOD FOR VASCULAR SYSTEM

It is well known that if stems be cut under water in which there is a dilute solution of aqueous eosin, the stain will rise in the bundles, making them very prominent, but the material cannot be fixed and cleared because the stain diffuses. In the fourth edition of this book it was stated that such preparations would be still more valuable if they could be fixed and cleared. Dr. Gourley has developed such a method which is valuable, not only for stems, but for various other things. He used basic fuchsin, prepared as follows: 50 mg. basic fuchsin is dissolved in 2 c.c. of 95 per cent alcohol and diluted with 100 c.c. of tap water. Dr. Gourley used two lots of basic fuchsin, one from the Will Corporation and the other from Coleman and Bell. Neither lot has been certified by the Commission on the Standardization of Biological Stains. Young or old plants of *Coleus*—tomato, bean, etc.—are lifted from the soil and the roots are washed free of adhering material. The root system is then immersed in the stain and a part cut off beneath the surface of the solution. In 24–48 hours the bundles will be well stained. Gourley succeeded with plants 6 feet in height.

Cut off the upper 6 inches of a *Coleus* plant, immerse the lower end in the stain and cut off 5 mm. of the stem under the surface of the stain. In 24 hours, rinse off any surface stain in water. Transfer to 50, 60, 70, 85, 95, and 100 per cent alcohol, at least 12 hours in each. Better change only once a day, especially with large pieces. Clear in $\frac{3}{4}$ absolute alcohol and $\frac{1}{4}$ xylol, $\frac{1}{2}$ xylol and $\frac{1}{2}$ alcohol, $\frac{1}{4}$ alcohol and $\frac{3}{4}$ xylol, and pure xylol, 24 hours in each. The material is now ready for study but, since xylol evaporates so rapidly, add cedar oil or carbon disulphide. In a glass dish with a smooth bottom and an electric bulb underneath, the vascular system can be traced in great detail.

An ovule of a cycad, cut from the sporophyll under the staining solution, will have the vascular system well stained within 24 hours. When dehydrated and cleared, the simple outer, and much-branched inner, vascular supply are very striking.

Small fruits and other objects can be studied in this way. In bottles with wide mouth and glass corks, such preparations should keep for years.

After the stain has been taken up, material may be boiled in water or in a very dilute solution of potassium hydrate. After partial disintegration, pieces can be dissected so that the larger vascular units are easily followed.

Gourley's method is at its best where transpiration is strong and the vascular system simple.

STAINING LIVING STRUCTURES

Some stains will stain living structures. Cyanin, methyl blue, and Bismarck brown have been recommended for this purpose. The solutions should be very dilute, not stronger than 1:10,000 or 1:500,000. The solutions should be very slightly alkaline, never acid. It is claimed that such solutions never stain the nucleus, and that if the nucleus stains at all, it is an indication that death is taking place.

Campbell succeeded in staining the living nuclei in the stamen hairs of *Tradescantia* by using dilute solutions of dahlia and of methyl violet (0.001–0.002 per cent in water). Dividing nuclei were stained.

For determining the stage of development of fresh material it is often necessary to use a stain. For this purpose stronger stains may be used, since it is unimportant whether the tissue is killed or not. An aqueous solution of methyl green or eosin can be recommended. With 1 per cent solutions, diluted one-half with water, mitotic figures can be recognized with ease.

CHAPTER XIII

PALEOBOTANICAL MICROTECHNIQUE

During the past three or four years, new methods in paleobotanical microtechnique have greatly minimized the drudgery of making preparations for microscopic examination. The subject of paleobotany has been making such rapid progress that scarcely any problem involving the anatomy of living vascular plants can be investigated intelligently without some knowledge of Mesozoic and Paleozoic forms. Material, especially that of Paleozoic pteridophytes and gymnosperms, is becoming available in the United States, largely through the discoveries of Dr. Noé and his students. Consequently, it is increasingly necessary for laboratories to have apparatus and technique for making rock-sections.

SECTIONS

The outline of the process of cutting a rock-section is very simple:

1. Saw the rock into two pieces.
2. Polish the cut surface.
3. Fasten the cut surface to a piece of glass with hot shellac.
4. With the saw, make another cut, as close to the glass as possible, so as to leave a thin section firmly fastened to the glass.
5. Grind and polish until the section is as thin as possible, or as thin as you want it.
6. Wash all polishing powder off with water.
7. Dry completely and, either with or without moistening in xylol, mount in balsam.

A word of suggestion in regard to these various points may not be amiss.

1. Most rock-sections are cut with a rather expensive and quite complicated instrument, called a "petrotome." The saw is of the circular type, is made of tin or other soft metal, has no teeth, but has diamond dust driven into the margin. A rigid clamp holds the object, and the saw, constantly cooled by a stream of water, gradually cuts through the specimen. If the piece to be cut is more than 5 or 6 cm. in diameter, a band saw is better; and if the piece is 10 or 20 cm. in diameter, the band saw is necessary. The "saw" is not of the type

used in sawing wood, but is a plain band of metal which must not be too hard. To be ideal, it should have diamond dust driven into the margin; but, since the expense would be considerable, carborundum powder and water can be used instead. A band saw is a dangerous piece of apparatus and the operator should be thoroughly protected from a broken, whipping saw.

2. The cut surface can be polished on a revolving brass plate, kept wet, and liberally powdered with fine carborundum.

Or, the cut surface can be rubbed by hand on a piece of plate glass, with plenty of carborundum. This is a more rapid method and most investigators prefer it. When the surface has become even and smooth the specimen is ready for the next step.

3. Fasten the polished surface to the glass slide upon which the section is to be mounted. Plate glass 3 or 4 mm. thick is best for sections larger than 3 or 4 cm. square. Gradually heat the slide until it is quite hot. Melt upon the slide the thin flakes of white shellac used by painters; heat the object and press the polished surface *very firmly* into the melted shellac. Canada balsam, from which the xylol has been driven off by heating, can be used instead of shellac. Much of the Paleozoic material is in the form of coal balls. After the ball has been cut in two, it is often difficult to hold the hemispherical piece in a clamp, especially if the piece is small. In such cases, it is better to fasten the polished surface to a convenient piece of marble, about 2.5 cm. thick, and 5 or 6 cm. square. The marble is easily held in the clamp. As soon as the slide, or marble, and object are cool, the next cut can be made.

4. Fasten the object in the clamp and saw as close to the glass, or marble, as possible, thus leaving a thin section cemented to the slide or marble. If marble has been used, the section is removed by heating or by dissolving it off with xylol. It can then be fastened to the glass slide for grinding and polishing. Anyone who can handle tools should soon be able to cut a section 1 mm. thick. A skilled technician can cut sections as thin as 0.5 mm.

5. The second grinding must be very careful and accurate. This can be done on the revolving brass disc; but here, again, a piece of plate glass, with plenty of carborundum, and water, is gaining favor over the more expensive revolving disc. The glass slide allows one to note how the process is progressing.

6. When the section becomes thin enough, or even before if it begins to crack, wash off the powder.

7. It is usually a good plan to use rather thick balsam for mount-

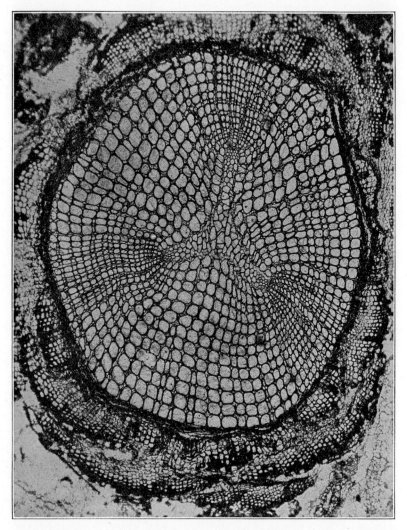

Fig. 28.—*Sphenophyllum pleurifoliolatum:* transverse section of a stem cut from a coal ball of the Upper Carboniferous. Eastman Commercial Ortho film, Wratten E filter (orange), J. Swift and Son 1-inch lens; arc light; exposure, 1 second. Slide by Lomax, negative by Sedgwick. ×19.

ing, even if it should be necessary to heat it a little to make it flow well.

By this method, sections of fossils 10×15 cm. have been cut thin enough for examination with a 4 mm. objective. Sections 3 or 4 mm. square have been cut thin enough for satisfactory examination with a 2 mm. oil immersion lens. Figure 28 shows that a reliable study can be made from sections cut from the solid rock.

Of course, this method can be used for such objects as walnut and hickory shells.

It is not really necessary to cover the section. Just polish the surface with fine carborundum and then polish still smoother with a fine powder of tin oxide. The section will look as if mounted in balsam.

A fine view can be secured without making any section. Merely polish the cut surface as described in the preceding paragraph and examine by reflected light. Excellent photomicrographs can be made from such surfaces.

PEELS

Peels seems to be as good a name as any for a type of "section" which is saving the paleobotanist a lot of time and is making possible a near approach to serial rock-sections. Peels are made with celloidin or with gelatin.

Celloidin peels.—Probably every investigator has his own method of making a celloidin peel. The following method, written by Dr. Fredda Reed, applies to calcified petrifactions:

1. After cutting a coal ball in two, polish the surface of the petrifaction with fine carborundum powder.
2. Wash surface.
3. Treat with 5 per cent hydrochloric acid 2–5 minutes. The thickness of the plant tissue peeled depends upon the length of the acid treatment.
4. Wash gently in running water.
5. Dry.
6. When thoroughly dry support the rock in a horizontal position and pour over the surface a solution of equal parts of absolute alcohol and ether quickly (before the alcohol-ether solution has had time to evaporate):
7. Pour on 25 per cent celloidin (dissolved in equal parts of absolute alcohol and ether).
8. Peel. When the absolute alcohol and ether have evaporated, the celloidin is left as a thin film which may be peeled off by inserting a scalpel under the edge.

9. Wash the film in 5 per cent hydrochloric acid to remove any excess mineral, then wash gently in water.

10. Dry in blotting paper under pressure, otherwise the peel curls badly.

11. The entire film, or only desirable portions of it, may be cleared in xylol and mounted in balsam.

After every peel, polish the surface before making another.

The following variations, used by various investigators, are worth trying: After the peel has been taken off, cleaned, and washed (stage 9 of Dr. Reed's schedule), instead of drying and using blotting paper, put the peel into 50, 70, 85, and 95 per cent alcohol, about 15 minutes in each. If the celloidin appears to soften in 95 per cent alcohol, shorten the time. Transfer to Eycleshymer's clearing fluid (which does not cause such curling as the xylol), and mount in balsam.

Silicified material is treated in the same way, except that hydrofluoric acid (10 per cent in water) is used instead of hydrochloric and is allowed to act longer, about 3 or 6 minutes.

Gelatin peels.—In *Nature*, of March 15, 1930, John Walton describes peels of gelatin. The rock surface is prepared and etched with acid, as in case of celloidin peels, and allowed to dry. Then a hot solution of jelly, containing formalin and glycerin, is poured on the surface. The amount of the mixture poured on will depend upon the size of the object and the desired thickness of the peel. To cover a surface 1 square decimeter in area, use about 2 g. of the pure gelatin used in making bacteriological cultures, 50 c.c. water, 0.5 c.c. glycerin, and 0.5 c.c. formalin. The surface must be surrounded before the etching process with a rim of plasticene, or some other substance, and should be leveled with a spirit level. The water and glycerin are mixed, heated, and the jelly stirred until dissolved. Heat to 60°–80° C., stir in the formalin quickly, and immediately pour the mixture over the surface of the petrifaction. Let the jelly set and remove to a warm well-aired place to dry. Avoid dust. When the jelly is dry, peel it off. It may be hard to start the peel but, once started, it comes off rather easily. Clear in xylol and mount in balsam.

It used to be claimed that in petrifactions all organic matter has been replaced by the mineral. The fact that a peel can be made proves that the old claim is incorrect. The mineral matter is etched down by the acid, the organic matter remaining and coming off in the peel.

CHAPTER XIV

BOTANICAL PHOTOGRAPHY

The only field of photography with which histology is directly concerned is photomicrography, together with paper prints and lantern slides made from photomicrographic negatives; but this field is so difficult that time, temper, and money will be saved by beginning with pictures of trees, flowers, buildings, maps, graphs, lantern slides, and such experimental apparatus as one needs in illustrating investigations.

It is assumed that the student knows something about an ordinary camera and that he knows the usual routine of making negatives and paper prints.

The first step is to get a good negative. Begin with a tree or a building. The most important factor in securing a good negative is correct exposure. The professional photographer does not need any meter, but the rest of us had better use one to determine the length of exposure.

The Watkins Bee Exposure Meter is good and inexpensive. The sensitive paper is reliable for a year, even in the tropics. The Wynne Infallible Exposure Meter lives up to its name. The Harvey and the Voigtlander are good meters of the mechanical type. The Bewi and the Justaphot are more expensive, but they almost remove the necessity for judgment in making exposures. The American Photography Exposure Tables are very convenient and instructive, since the various factors, light, stop, plate, latitude, and time of day, are estimated separately. The tables give also practically all the formulas and directions an amateur needs. An amber-colored filter, increasing the exposure about three times, will keep the clouds, which would otherwise be lost, and will give much better color values.

Next, select a good plate or film. Professor Land, when asked his opinion of the comparative merits of film packs and cut films, said, "Packs cost twice as much as cut films and are only half as good: plates are better than either." But films are improving and the cut film now has an emulsion as good as that on a plate. Such an emulsion cannot be put on a roll film or film pack, because the film has to be pulled over a small roller. The "commercial ortho" cut film is very satisfactory; but, as one learns to get the right exposure, the panchromatic film can be used. Mr. Charles H. Carpenter, the veteran photographer of the Field Museum in Chicago, gave this advice to a beginner: "Pick out a good plate or film, and one developer, and stick to them for the first ten years."

LANTERN SLIDES

After securing a good negative, the method of making a lantern slide or paper print depends upon the size of the negative. Slides and paper prints of the same size as the negative are printed by contact. It is hardly worth while to make a lantern slide by enlargement from a tiny negative; the best lantern slides are made by reduction from larger negatives. On the other hand, excellent paper prints can be made by enlargement.

Lantern slides by contact.—From a $3\frac{1}{4}\times4\frac{1}{4}$ negative a lantern slide can be printed by contact, just as one would make a contact print on paper, because the lantern-slide plate ($3\frac{1}{4}$x4) is so nearly the size of the negative. If one wants a lantern slide of some feature of a larger negative, the lantern-slide plate can be placed over the desired portion and a contact print can be made. The negative can be placed in a printing frame and the lantern-slide plate placed over it, emulsion side against emulsion side. If the printing frame is larger than the negative, put a piece of clear glass in the frame. If the negative is a glass plate, remember that you are dealing with three thicknesses of glass and do not use too much pressure.

Hold the frame in the left hand, as far from the bulb as possible, and snap on the light for a second. If the plate is overexposed, use a weaker bulb or increase the distance. If the plate is completely developed within a minute, the exposure was too long. The exposure should be such that full development will require about 1 minute and 45 seconds. The prominent features should show clearly when viewed from the back of the slide.

If the negative is uneven, the distance from the light may be increased so as to lengthen the exposure to several seconds, thus giving time to shade the weak parts. If a negative is harsh and shows too much contrast, hold it closer to the light and shorten the exposure; if weak and lacking in contrast, hold it farther away and lengthen the exposure.

Dealers in photographic supplies sell a box for making paper prints. It is equally good for making lantern slides, but rather expensive. A box which will give just as good results can be made in a few hours (Fig. 29).

Find or make a box about 18 inches high and large enough to have a glass top 9×11 inches fitted into it. Fit a ground glass into it, about 8 inches from the clear glass in the top. On the bottom, put a red bulb in the middle, with four white bulbs (50 or 60 watt) around it. The red light can be plugged in separately and the four white bulbs can be wired so as to glow only when the switch is closed; or the lights can be wired so that, with only one plug, the red light will be on as long as the plug is in, but the white lights will come on only when the switch is closed (Fig. 29).

For holding the lantern-slide plate firmly against the negative—the dull emulsion side of the lantern-slide plate and the negative should always be in contact with each other—the device shown in Figure 30 is better than a hinged lid.

With this box, the exposure can be estimated very accurately, since the distance between the negative and the light is constant. With only a ground glass to diffuse the light, the exposure is likely to be too short. Put one or two sheets of white paper on top of the ground glass. With both ground glass and paper to diffuse the light, the exposure should be about 2 seconds for a good negative. The number of sheets of white paper should be increased or diminished until 2 seconds gives an exposure which will develop fully in $1\frac{3}{4}$ minutes. With a dense negative, the time will be longer; with a thin negative, it is better to add one or more sheets of paper, so that 2 seconds will be about right for the exposure.

After the plate, film, or paper has been developed and rinsed for about 10 seconds in the acid stop, place it in "hypo."

The hypo removes the silver which was not acted upon by the exposure to light.

Lantern slides by reducing and enlarging.—If a slide is to be made from a 4×5 or larger negative, there must be a reduction. A camera is necessary. A $3\frac{1}{4}\times4\frac{1}{4}$ camera is large enough. If any larger size is used, the plateholder must be "kitted" down to $3\frac{1}{4}\times4$, the standard size of lantern slides in America. In using the larger cameras, mark upon the ground glass the exact size and location of the lantern-slide plate. Fasten the negative in some convenient place where the

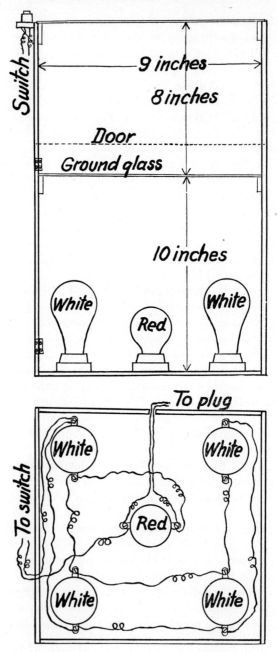

Fig. 29.—Box for making lantern slides and paper prints. Above, view of front; below, view of bottom.

light may shine through it: diffuse daylight is good. Then arrange the camera just as in taking any ordinary picture. The board shown in

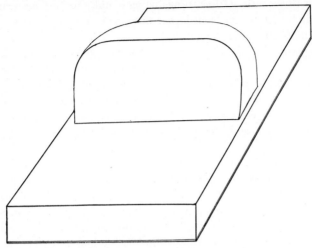

FIG. 30.—Block to press lantern slide plate against the negative

Figure 31 will be just as useful in making lantern slides as in making photomicrographs. At one end of the board fasten a frame which will hold an 8×10 negative and also hold kits for smaller negatives (Fig. 31B and C). The long slot in the board will allow the camera to be fastened at the proper distance. If buildings, trees, or shadows are in the way, tilt the board so as to have a clear sky for a background.

Be very careful in focusing; it is best to examine, with a pocket lens, the image on the ground glass. In general, use a rather small stop, F16 is good. If reducing from an average

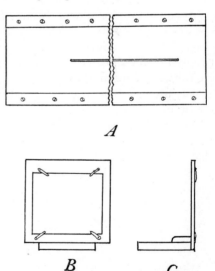

FIG. 31.— A, board for photomicrographic and lantern slide work; B, end view with clips to hold negatives; C, side view of block to be used on board when making lantern slides.

5×7 negative, in good daylight, with an F16 stop, try 2 or 3 seconds. If enlarging from a negative somewhat smaller than a lantern slide, try 8 or 10 seconds. Other things being equal, the best lantern slides are made by reduction from larger negatives and the poorest, by enlargement from smaller negatives.

The superiority of the larger negative is easily demonstrated. With a 5×7 camera, make a negative of some elaborately ornamented building, making the building just cover the plate. Then with a vest-pocket camera, or even a $2\frac{1}{4}\times3\frac{1}{4}$, make a similar negative, so that the building just covers the plate. Make lantern slides from both negatives, so that the building is of the same size on both lantern slides. While the building, as it appears on the screen, is of the same size, no matter which slide is used, the one from the larger negative will show finer detail. The same is true for all kinds of plant subjects. Small cameras are easy to carry and their small films are cheap, but they have no other recommendation. A $3\frac{1}{4}\times4\frac{1}{4}$, with a high grade 4.5 anastigmatic lens, is good, even for scientific work; but a 5×7 is better. If you are strong and ambitious or have some one to carry the heavy load, take an 8×10.

Staining lantern slides.—Some of the stains used in staining microscope slides will give a pleasant tone to lantern slides. Light green gives a clear, moonlight effect. Phloxine gives a transparent, rosy tint. Sepia and other tones could doubtless be imitated by this easy method.

Clearing lantern slides.—Sometimes a slide will seem perfectly clear, just as it comes from the fixing bath, especially from an acid fixing bath; usually, however, it will be better to transfer the slide from the fixing bath to a weak solution of acetic acid—just enough acid to give the solution the taste of weak vinegar—and then rock for a minute before washing.

The following clearing fluid may be used in the same way:

	Metric	Apothecaries'
Alum	20 g.	(1.3 gr.)
Iron sulphate	20 g.	(1.3 gr.)
Citric acid	20 g.	(1.3 gr.)
Water	500 c.c.	(17 oz.)

Coating lantern slides.—After the slide has become thoroughly dry, a coat of balsam or shellac will add much to its brilliancy. Dilute the Canada balsam with xylol until it becomes almost as thin as water; balance the slide on the thumb and first, second, and third fingers, holding it as level as possible; pour the balsam over it, letting the balsam flow evenly over the whole surface; then tilt the slide and pour the balsam back into the bottle. Put the slide in the rack to dry.

Mounting.—Add a suitable mat and a clean lantern-slide cover. Remember that the effect of a first-class lantern slide may be impaired or even ruined by an inartistic mat. Bind the slide and cover together with a lantern-slide binding strip. Paste on the label, or, if you prefer, paste the label on the mat before binding, so as to have it protected by the cover. Lay the slide down so that the positions are just as they were in the original, and then paste the "thumb mark" in the lower left-hand corner.

The Gevaert lantern slide plates are used by many botanists. They are good for general work and the formulas for sepias, purples, and reds by direct development make them attractive for lantern slides of scenery.

Developers.—

For Lantern Slides from Strong Negatives		For Lantern Slides from Weak Negatives	
Distilled water	1,000 c.c.	Distilled water	1,000 c.c.
Metol	3 g.	Metol	$1\frac{1}{2}$ g.
Hydrochinon	1 g.	Hydrochinon	6 g.
Sodium sulphite (crystal)	40 g.	Sodium sulphite (crystal)	50 g.
Sodium carbonate (crystal)	50 g.	Sodium carbonate (crystal)	100 g.
Potassium bromide	1 g.	Potassium bromide	1 g.

The time of development will be about 2–$2\frac{1}{2}$ minutes for black tones, and 1–$1\frac{1}{4}$ minutes for warm tones.

For sepia, purple and red tones.—Use the Gevaert warm tone lantern-slide plates and expose as for ordinary tones. Use the following developer.

A		B	
Distilled water	1,000 c.c.	Distilled water	250 c.c.
Metol	$1\frac{1}{2}$ g.	Ammonium carbonate	30 g.
Hydrochinon	6 g.	Ammonium bromide	30 g.
Sodium sulphite (crystal)	50 g.		
Sodium carbonate (crystal)	100 g.		
Potassium bromide	1 g.		

The ammonium carbonate evaporates so rapidly that it must be kept in closely stoppered bottles, preferably in emery stoppered bottles.

The different tones are obtained by mixing A and B in different proportions.

Cold sepia, 8 parts A to 1 part B. Develop, 5–8 minutes.
Warm sepia, 10 parts A to 3 parts B. Develop, 12–15 minutes.
Purple-red, 8 parts A to 5 parts B. Develop, 20–30 minutes.

Do not try to shorten the time of development by giving a longer exposure.

Rinse thoroughly and fix in an acid fixing bath. The following is recommended for all plates:

Hypo . . . . 150 g.
Sodium bisulphite . . . . 15 g.
Water . . . . 1,000 c.c.

MAPS AND GRAPHS

One often needs a lantern slide of a map. An easy but very unsatisfactory method is to copy from an atlas or, not quite so bad, from a base map. The atlas will have so many places named that what you want to show will be obscured. The best way is to trace a rather large map of the desired region, rub the underside of the tracing paper with a soft pencil and then, by following the lines with a hard pencil, transfer the outline to pure white cardboard. Ink it with dead black India ink making the lines very bold. If the map is 38 cm. wide, lines 1 mm. wide are not too coarse for the outlines of coasts and islands. When they appear on the lantern slide, they will not be more than 0.2 mm. wide. Lettering should be correspondingly bold. Letters less than 1 cm. high on a map 38 cm. wide will not be very conspicuous when they appear on the screen.

In copying a map 38 cm. wide, using a contrast lantern-slide plate (red label plate, if Cramer's is used), with F16 in fair diffuse light, try 20 seconds. If such work is always done in the same place, you will soon know whether to use 15, 20, or 30 seconds. If artificial light is used, there should never be a mistake after you have once determined the proper exposure.

Develop in a contrast or process developer. Use hydrochinon: there should not be any metol in the formula.

Maps are more satisfactory when colored, if there are both land and water areas. After washing out the hypo, stain the slide in an aqueous anilin blue or light green for 10 or 15 minutes. When dry, use a brush to color the land areas orange or any desired color. The second color is likely to be more satisfactory if very dilute.

With all slides which are to be colored, it is better to omit alum from the hypo solution.

For graphs, use the same method, except that hypo solutions with alum and acid may be used.

Lantern slides can be made from typewritten tables in the same way. The paper should be pure white and the letters, dead black. Illustrations in books can be copied in the same way.

While nothing surpasses a process plate for negatives from which you wish to get dead black and clear glass in the lantern slide, or dead black and pure white in a paper print, process films are very good and convenient for filing and are in no danger from breaking.

ENLARGEMENTS

Lantern-slide plates are often used in making photomicrographs of histological preparations, but even when a 5×7 plate is used, an 8×10 enlargement, or even an 11×14, is better for reproduction, assuming, of course, that the negative is good enough to stand enlargement. If the negative is sharp and has no defects, a glossy paper can be used; but if the negative lacks a little in sharpness or has defects, a paper with a velvet surface is better, for the large print can then be touched up with a pencil or pen and, when reduced to the size used in scientific journals, the reproduction will be better than the engraver could have obtained from a small print. Any prints as small as $3\frac{1}{4} \times 4\frac{1}{4}$ or even 5×7, should be on glossy paper and should be squeegeed, if they are to be only 4 inches wide when reproduced. The engraver recommends glossy paper for all prints.

While the enlargement from photomicrographs is the kind which comes within the range of histology, it is better to practice with negatives of trees, flowers, and people. Select your best negatives and use a paper with a velvet surface to begin with.

The negative can be placed in your camera where you place a plate for exposure. You can cut the partition out from the plate holder—except a small border to hold the plate—and then put the negative in as you would a plate; or you can make a frame, just the size of a plate holder to hold the glass negative. For films, use two clear glass plates bound together along one edge with a piece of lantern-slide binding tape.

The relative positions of light, ground glass, negative, and paper are shown in Figure 32.

A 200-watt light or, better still, four or five 60-watt lights, will be sufficient for most work. There should be a reflector behind the light.

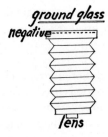

The ground glass, about 2 inches from the negative, is to diffuse the light.

Almost any camera which takes ordinary plate holders will do, but we should advise a strong 5×7 camera of the general Primo pattern. The vertical position is better, because the paper is easier to manipulate. If you prepare your own apparatus, it will save time to look at enlarging cameras on the market, or at least to study the illustrations of them in catalogues.

The time of exposure will vary with the light, the negative, the paper, and the amount of enlargement. With a 200-watt bulb, or a group of 60-watt bulbs, a good negative, an average paper, and an enlargement of three diameters, try 20 seconds. It will save time and money if you use a full sheet of paper and expose for 5 seconds; then cover a strip about an inch wide with a piece of black paper or a metal squeegee plate and expose the rest for 5 seconds more; then cover another inch and expose for 5 seconds; and so on across the paper. When you develop, you will see which exposure was best and, after a few trials, you will be able to estimate the exposure without any trial or, at least, will be able to estimate by trying a small piece of paper.

FIG. 32.—Relative positions of reflector, light, ground glass, negative, lens, and table. At top, above light, there should be holes for ventilation.

There are various developers, but the one given below seems to be as good as any.

H_2O 1,250   c.c.
Metol   1   g.
Sodium sulphite   15   g.
Hydrochinon   4   g.
Sodium carbonate   15   g.
Potassium bromide ....   1.8 g.

There is a relation between the length of exposure and the time of development. Suppose that with a good negative an exposure of 10 seconds with 2 minutes of development gives the best results. Then an exposure of 5 seconds, with 4 minutes of development, or an exposure of 20 seconds with 1 minute of development, should yield prints nearly as good. Too long an exposure gives dark, unsatisfactory prints; while, with too short an exposure, the paper becomes gray or spotted in the effort to get pictures by prolonging the development.

With uneven negatives, the exposure can be controlled, more or less, by holding a suitably shaped piece of cardboard between the lens and the paper, keeping the cardboard in motion to avoid sharp contrasts.

Transfer from the developer into the stop. Here again, there can be some control, because—with the trays close together—part of the print can be slipped into the stop, while the rest develops a little longer, so that a sky with clouds can be developed after the development of the foreground has been stopped. By applying the stop with a tuft of cotton, good prints can be secured from negatives which would yield only flat prints without such treatment.

Then transfer to hypo. Many prefer a plain fixing bath:

Water ....   1 liter
Hyposulphite of soda .... 250 g.

It does not keep well and must not be used if it shows the least brownish color. Make it fresh every day.

A single print would be fixed in 15 or 20 minutes; but prints are almost always piled, one on top of another, in a tray of hypo. They should be moved frequently, taking the one from the bottom and putting it on top. With such movement, half an hour, or even an hour, is not too long.

Then wash in running water for half an hour, or even an hour. If the prints are in a sink, a rubber tube can be fastened to the faucet, and one can pinch the end of the tube so as to spray the prints. In this way, prints may be washed thoroughly in 15 minutes. The most expensive rotary washers have no advantage over this method, except that they save your time.

The prints are then spread out to dry. Let the print drain until the water comes off only in drops; then lay the prints down, face up, on blotting paper or newspaper and wipe off surplus water with a large tuft of cotton. When almost dry—not quite "bone dry"—they can be piled up, one on top of another, or with a thin piece of white blotting paper between, and put under gentle pressure. A board with two or three bricks will be enough. If put under pressure too soon, prints are likely to wrinkle.

If glossy paper is used, place the prints face down upon a clean squeegee plate, and press them with a rubber roller or with a rubber like a window cleaner. When dry, they should come off easily.

OVEREXPOSURES AND UNDEREXPOSURES

Negatives, lantern slides, and paper prints which have been over-exposed or underexposed can often be reduced or strengthened until they are as good as if the exposures had been correct.

Reducing overexposures.—The reducing solution should be applied as soon as the negative, lantern slide, or paper print comes from the fixing bath. If they have been washed and dried, they should be soaked in water for five or ten minutes before using the reducing solution.

The following is a good reducing solution for most purposes:

		Metric	Apothecaries'
A	Water......................	473 c.c.	(16 oz.)
	Hyposulphite of soda..........	31 g.	(1 oz.)
B	Water......................	473 c.c.	(16 oz.)
	Red prussiate of potassium......	31 g.	(1 oz.)

Solution B must be protected from the light. Cover the bottle with black paper and keep it in the dark when not in use.

Mix only for immediate use 8 parts of A to 1 of B and use in rather subdued light. A darkroom is not necessary, but avoid bright light.

When the negative or lantern slide becomes satisfactory, wash it in water as thoroughly as if it had just come from the ordinary hypo fixing solution.

The reduction can be done locally with a tuft of cotton.

When possible, it is better to make a new, correct exposure than to reduce or intensify an incorrect one.

Intensifying underexposures.—Even if a negative or lantern slide has been considerably overexposed, it can be reduced quite satisfactorily; if much underexposed, little can be done for it; if only slightly underexposed, it may be greatly improved by the following solution:

		Metric	Apothecaries'
A	Bichloride of mercury.........	2 g.	(31 gr.)
	Water......................	100 c.c.	(4 oz.)
	Bromide of potassium.........	2 g.	(31 gr.)
B	Sulphite of soda crystals.......	10 g.	(154 gr.)
	Water.....................	100 c.c.	(4 oz.)

The solutions keep indefinitely and may be used three or four times.

Apply the intensifier after fixing in hypo and washing in water. If the negative or slide has been allowed to dry, soak it in water for half an hour before intensifying.

Place the negative or slide in A, rocking the tray as in developing, until it becomes gray or even white. Wash in water for 5 minutes and then transfer to B and leave until the dark color can be seen on the back of the negative or slide. Wash in water as thoroughly as after fixing in hypo.

Some use a saturated aqueous solution of the bichloride of mercury, without the bromide of potassium; and, instead of solution B, use water to which ammonia has been added—about 1 part ammonia to 40 parts water. Excellent sepia tones may be secured in this way. Wash well in water.

After the plate has been thoroughly washed in water, wipe it gently with a tuft of cotton. The cotton must, of course, be thoroughly wet; it is better to hold the plate under a stream of water while wiping. *This should always be done before placing a negative or slide in the rack to dry, after a washing in water.*

PHOTOMICROGRAPHS

By Dr. Paul J. Sedgwick

For the making of photomicrographs at the highest magnifications a regular photomicrographic camera, consisting of a heavy, rigid, optical bed to which are attached the camera proper, the microscope, the condensing lenses, the filters, and the light source, is almost a necessity. Such an outfit certainly facilitates the making of photomicrographs at any magnification, and the worker who is required to make any considerable number of photomicrographs should be so equipped. In the absence of such equipment very satisfactory work can be done with any ordinary camera, microscope, and suitable light source if the worker will exercise sufficient care in their arrangement and alignment. If the camera has a long bellows draw, it should be possible to make pictures with magnifications as great as 1,000 diameters. Without regular photomicrographic equipment it is scarcely worth attempting higher magnifications.

In arranging the equipment for taking a photomicrograph it is absolutely essential that all the equipment be in perfect alignment. This is taken care of in the expensive photomicrographic cameras by providing a heavy metal bed or track to which all of the equipment can be attached and along which the various parts can be shifted as necessary in arriving at the correct optical adjustment. A satisfactory substitute for this rigid optical bed can be constructed from a board of sufficient length to accommodate all of the equipment. A guideway for the camera can be made of wooden strips and screwed to the board. The microscope can be bolted to the board by long bolts with butterfly nuts. The microscope is inclined at 90°. The guideway for the camera must be of a sufficient height to raise the camera to a level which will center it with the microscope. If a table can be spared, it might be found to be more convenient to have one table set apart for photomicrographic work (Fig. 33). A guideway could be fastened to the table, and holes could be bored in the table for bolting down the microscope.

In the discussion that follows it will be assumed that a photomicrograph of a part of a vascular bundle is desired and that the photograph is to have a magnification of approximately 400 or 500 diameters. Furthermore, it will be assumed that the section has been stained in safranin and anilin blue.

The apparatus is arranged as follows. The microscope is inclined at the inclination joint. The lens of the camera is removed, and the tube of the microscope is inserted through the hole in the lens board. Some sort of light-tight arrangement must be made where the tube of the microscope enters the camera. A piece of black velvet will serve if carefully wrapped around the tube of the microscope. The microscope is lined up with the camera as accurately as possible and bolted in place. The mirror of the microscope is removed and the light source is placed in line with the camera and the microscope. The light source may be an arc light, a gas lamp with incandescent mantle, a concentrated filament mazda projection bulb, or a lamp designed especially

FIG. 33.—Apparatus for photomicrography. Expensive apparatus can be seen in catalogues

for photomicrographic work. The light should be lined up as accurately as possible. One or more condensing lenses should be inserted between the light and the condenser of the microscope in order to concentrate the rays. For this, one may use a spherical flask filled with water, or a simple hand reading glass will serve. The condensing lenses of a small stereopticon can be adapted. If a round flask filled with water is used, it will serve both as condenser and heat-absorbing unit. If lenses are used for the auxiliary condensing system, it will be necessary to provide a flat-sided flask or small battery jar with water to absorb the heat and thus protect the slide that is to be photographed. The auxiliary condensing system should be placed in such a position as to project a magnified image of the light source on the iris diaphragm of the condenser of the microscope.

The slide which is to be photographed is next brought into focus on the ground glass of the camera with the coarse and fine adjustments of the microscope. The substage condenser is focused to obtain critical illumination. This will bring the light to a focus on the section to be photographed. An image of the source of light will now be seen on the ground glass superimposed upon the image of the object. By examining the ground glass of the camera, any further adjustments that may be necessary can be made in order to bring the light source, the auxiliary condensing system, the substage condenser, the microscope tube, and the camera into perfect alignment. After all of the adjustments have been correctly made, move the substage condenser a very short distance either toward or away from the slide so as to remove the image of the light source from the ground glass. This adjustment should be very slight and will not appreciably affect the quality of the image of the object to be photographed.

It will now be necessary to decide upon the plate or film to be used for the photograph and it will also be necessary to choose an appropriate light filter. The yellow filters which are used in ordinary photography will be found to be useful, but, if a great amount of photomicrographic work is to be done, the worker should have a set of light filters such as the set of 9 Wratten filters for photomicrography sold by the Eastman Kodak Company. This set includes the filters that will be found to be most useful. In choosing the plate or film and the light filter it is necessary to come to a decision in regard to the effect that is desired in the picture. The choice of plate, or film, and filter will depend upon whether it is desired to obtain the maximum contrast between the object being photographed and the background or whether it is desired to obtain the maximum detail within the object. For the beginner, perhaps the most confusing part of the procedure comes in choosing the proper filter. The yellow and orange filters will probably be the ones most frequently used, for when they are used with a good orthochromatic or panchromatic plate or film the result will be an approximately correct rendering of the color values in black and white. It is not possible to state just which filters will serve for each set of conditions but certain rules will aid in determining. To obtain the greatest amount of contrast between the specimen and the background use a filter or a combination of filters which transmits only that part of the spectrum completely absorbed by the specimen. This will cause the specimen to appear black in the picture. If the result is unsatisfactory because detail within the specimen has been sacrificed in favor of contrast between the background and the specimen, try a filter or a combination of filters whose spectral transmission is not exactly limited to the part of the spectrum absorbed by the object. To eliminate the contrast between the object and the background use a filter or combination of filters transmitting that portion of the spectrum which is also transmitted by the object. After a little experience one will be able to estimate the probable photographic result by making a visual examination with first one and then another of the filters in place.

We started with the assumption that a photograph was to be made of a part of a vascular bundle in a section that had been stained with safranin and anilin blue. If the photograph were to be made without a light filter and on an ordinary uncorrected plate or film which is oversensitive to the blue portion of the spectrum and completely insensitive to the red part, the picture would not be satisfactory. The red-stained part of the specimen would appear black and the parts stained in anilin blue would hardly appear in the photograph. This effect would result from the insensitiveness of the ordinary plate or film to red and the oversensitiveness to blue which gives blue almost the value of white light. Instead, a good color-corrected plate or film should be used and a combination of filters such as the Wratten "B" and "E" filters. This combination of filters will increase the contrast of the part of the specimen stained in blue since the spectral transmission of the combination is included within the absorption band of anilin blue. While these filters will not give the maximum contrast for the safranin-stained portion of the specimen, the contrast will be sufficient and the result will be more satisfactory than if the safranin stain had photographed as pure black, because all detail in the vessel walls would then have been lost.

A booklet, *Photomicrography*, published by the Eastman Kodak Company, includes a table showing the spectral absorption bands of some of the stains used in botanical microtechnique. It also gives data on the transmission spectra of the Wratten filmers ordinarily used in photomicrographic work. Three other booklets published by the Eastman Kodak Company will be helpful though they do not pertain directly to photomicrography. These are, *Wratten Light Filters*, *The Photography of Colored Objects*, and *Color Films, Plates and Filters for Commercial Photography*.

The final focusing of the microscope should be accomplished after the light filter is in place in the path of the light and close to the substage condenser. The plate or film holder should be inserted, the light turned off, the dark slide removed from the plate or film holder, and the exposure made by turning on the light and turning it off. Making the exposure in this way obviates the necessity for using a shutter in the set-up of equipment. During the time of the exposure the table on which the camera is resting should not be touched and no one should be permitted to walk across the floor. These precautions are necessary to prevent a blurring of the image. The time of the exposure will have to be determined by trial. After a correct exposure has been obtained it will be possible to compute further exposures with different filters from the factors given in the booklet, *Photomicrography*.

In the preceding discussion it was assumed that a photomicrograph was to be made at fairly high magnification. For photographs at lower magnifications the ocular is removed from the microscope, and it will probably be best to remove also the draw tube. Care must be exercised to avoid reflections within the microscope. A tube of dull, black paper may have to be inserted in the microscope. A microscope with a large barrel is useful for low-power work. When using 48 mm., 32 mm., and possibly 16 mm. objectives it will be necessary to remove the substage condenser of the microscope in order to get the complete field illuminated. It may also be necessary to insert a piece of ground glass in the path of the light to give even illumination. Critical illumination will be lost in this way, but for low-power work it will not matter.

The relative positions of the various parts of the equipment as set up for high-power work are given below:

Ground glass
Camera bellows
Microscope
Slide
Substage condenser
Light filter
Auxiliary diaphragm
Auxiliary condenser
Water-cooling cell
Auxiliary condenser
Light

MOVIE PHOTOMICROGRAPHS

By Dr. Paul J. Sedgwick

Before the advent of the now popular 16 mm. amateur motion picture film, the cost of making motion pictures was prohibitive for most workers. In screen time 100 feet of the amateur size film is equivalent to 250 feet of the standard 35 mm. film. A further economy is brought about by the fact that the 16 mm. film is a reversal film. There is no extra cost for the making of a positive. The original film is developed as a negative and then immediately converted into a positive by a process of reversal. The entire charge for processing is included in the original purchase price for the film.

The 16 mm. film is being widely used in the preparation of teaching material and is finding some use in the recording of the results of research. Photomicrography with the motion picture camera is not very different from ordinary photomicrography. For movie photomicrographs at normal speed any good amateur motion picture camera will serve. Most of the amateur cameras are equipped with spring motors which operate the shutter so as to take 16 pictures or frames per second. Many of the cameras have half-speed attachments and some have slow motion attachments. With the half-speed attachment 8 frames are exposed each second, and when the finished pictures are later projected, the speed of the action is then seen to be doubled. The slow motion attachments found on some cameras expose either 64 or 128 frames per second which permits the slowing down of fast action. Where time-lapse pictures are desired of such subjects as the germination of a spore, or the conjugation in *Rhizopus*, it is necessary to arrange a motor and a gear system to operate the camera so as to make exposures of individual frames at intervals of several minutes (Fig. 34). For this type of work the most adaptable camera is the original Eastman Model A amateur motion picture camera which is a hand-crank camera and does not have a spring motor. Indeed, the Bausch and Lomb time-lapse mechanism is designed to be used with the Eastman Model A camera.

In making movie photomicrographs, the microscope is generally used in its normal vertical position. The lens of the camera is removed and the camera is connected to the microscope with some sort of an optical connector or double ocular. The Zeiss Company makes a special optical attachment for this purpose in which most of the light from the object is reflected into the camera by a silvered prism and a small amount of light passes through to the inspection ocular. The Bausch and Lomb Company also provides such an attachment with the equipment that they sell for movie photomicrography. In the absence of a special attachment any double ocular such as the demonstration oculars used in elementary teaching may be substituted. Some sort of double ocular is necessary so that it will be possible to watch the action during the time that the picture is being made. It will be necessary to adjust accurately the inspection ocular so that the image seen through it will be in focus when the image formed on the film by the other ocular is also in focus. To accomplish this adjustment, remove the film gate in the camera and place a piece of onion-skin paper which is 16 mm. in width against the aperture plate. If it is preferred, a piece of ground glass cut to a width of 16 mm. may be used instead. Be sure to have the ground surface forward. Focus the microscope very carefully on some object until a sharp image is seen on the onion-skin paper or ground glass which is against the aperture plate. Examine this image with a magnifying lens to verify the focus. After this image is sharp, examine the object through the inspection ocular and bring the inspection ocular into focus by adjusting the ring or collar provided for this purpose. Be very careful not to alter the position of the objective while doing this. After adjusting the inspection ocular so that it is in focus, re-examine the image formed in the camera to make certain that it is still in focus. When both of the images are in focus, the gate may be replaced in the camera and the camera threaded with film. Further focusing as

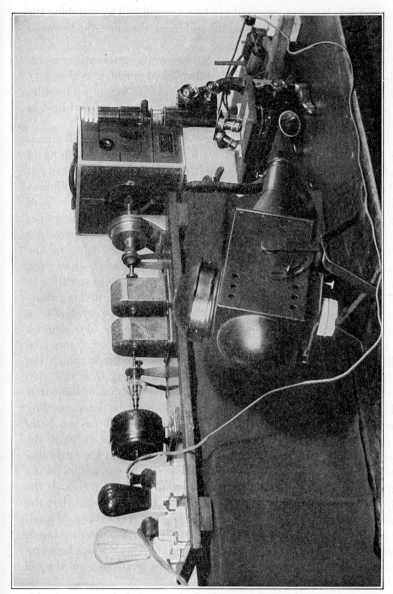

FIG. 34.—Apparatus used in the Botany Department of Syracuse University for making time-lapse movie photomicrographs. The time-lapse mechanism was designed by Professor O. A. Carnahan, of the College of Applied Science, Syracuse University. With this gear system it is possible to make the exposures at any desired interval between one frame per minute and one frame every three hours.

the object is being photographed can be accomplished by watching the action through the inspection ocular and using the fine adjustment of the microscope as necessary.

Because of the running of the mechanism in the automatic cameras or the turning of the crank in the hand-cranked model, it is necessary that the support for the camera be very rigid. In one set up used by the writer the camera is braced with heavy two-by-fours and held in place by large bolts.

The lighting system must be arranged with care. Strong illumination is needed for normal speed work as in the photographing of zoöspores and gametes of the algae, or in photographing the movement of the cytoplasm in a cell of *Elodea*. It is necessary to have sufficient light to give ample exposure in the brief period of approximately $\frac{1}{32}$ of a second that the camera shutter is open when making 16 frames per second. If too much light is used the living cells may be damaged. A water-cooling cell should always be used between the light and the mirror of the microscope. It may be advisable to use the superspeed panchromatic film as this is approximately three times as sensitive to artificial light as is the regular panchromatic film. In making time-lapse pictures as in photographing the growth of the hyphae of a fungus with perhaps one frame exposed every three or four minutes the amount of light that is used may be very small. Each frame is in reality a time-exposure in any time-lapse mechanism in which the shaft of the camera is turned continuously at a very slow rate. No exact information can be given in regard to the amount of light that will be necessary for a correct exposure. This must be determined by experiment. Upon the basis of numerous experiments one can build up in time an experience that will make it possible to estimate the amount of light that will be needed for any subject. At the beginning of each experiment it will be well to expose a foot or two of film on the subject and then remove the film and develop it as a negative. If the strip shows good quality as a negative, it is safe to assume that the exposure is correct and that the reversal positive will have good quality when it is returned from the processing station. If this procedure is followed, it will be necessary that the camera and microscope be set up in a dark room, so that the strip of film can be removed from the roll without fogging the rest of the film.

Motion picture photomicrographs find one of their most valuable applications in making possible the slowing down of action that is too fast to be studied at normal speed and in the speeding up of action that is too slow to be studied at normal speed. The following table will indicate the apparent rate of action as seen on the screen according to the rate at which the frames were exposed in the camera.

Rate of Exposure of Frames	Rate of Action on Screen
128 frames per second	$\frac{1}{8}$ normal
64 frames per second	$\frac{1}{4}$ normal
32 frames per second	$\frac{1}{2}$ normal
16 frames per second	normal
8 frames per second	2 times normal
1 frame per second	16 times normal
1 frame per minute	960 times normal
1 frame every 4 minutes	3,740 times normal
1 frame every 6 minutes	5,760 times normal
1 frame every 10 minutes	9,600 times normal
1 frame every 15 minutes	14,400 times normal

PHOTOGRAPHIC FORMULAS

The makers of photographic plates, films, and papers know what they have put into their emulsions and, consequently, it is better to use their formulas in developing their products.

In making solutions, dissolve the ingredients in the order in which they appear in the formulas, making sure that each one is dissolved before another is added. Remember that metol should be dissolved in *warm* water. A vigorous use of the stirring rod is always worth while and, with sodium sulphite or sodium carbonate, a hard cake will form unless the salts are added slowly with constant stirring. If metol is not completely dissolved before the sulphite is added, they combine and form an inert mass which makes the developer just that much weaker. Use distilled water whenever possible. When distilled water is not available, boil the water—but not in an iron kettle—and then cool and filter it.

Ingredients of formulas.—Many of the formulas in common use have the same ingredients, but in different proportions. Those in most common use are metol, hydrochinon, pyrogallic acid, pyrocatechin, sodium sulphite, sodium carbonate, and potassium bromide, with potassium metabisulphite, carbonate of potassium, sodium sulphide, acetone, sulphuric acid, and citric acid appearing less often.

Hyposulphite of soda, commonly called "hypo," with or without a hardener to harden the emulsion and an acid to counteract the effect of the alkaline developer is used to dissolve the silver which has not been affected by light.

Acetic acid is often used as a "short-stop" between the developer and the "hypo."

Metol.—Metol should be completely dissolved in *warm* water before adding any sulphite. It is a vigorous developer, bringing the entire image up so quickly on the surface of the plate or film that the beginner might stop development too soon. Turn the plate over and look at the other side to make sure that development has taken place throughout the entire thickness of the film. Potassium bromide restrains the rapidity of the action, allowing the metol to soak through the emulsion before the surface development is too extreme. It is almost always used in combination with hydrochinon. Elon, pictol, and rhodinol are about the same as metol and may be substituted for it in formulas.

Hydrochinon.—This developer comes in needle-like crystals which can be dissolved in water at room temperature. If the temperature is below 50° F., it does not act. It develops best at temperatures from 65° F. to 70° F. It is not used alone except for maps, graphs, and such things, where dead black lines and dots with a clear glass background are desired. It is generally used in combination with metol, forming the famous M.Q. developer, in which the metol softens the harshness and gives detail even in the shadows, so that the result is an artistic picture, whether you want a print on paper or a lantern slide. A much larger proportion of hydrochinon is needed for paper prints than for plates or films.

Pyro.—This is often called pyrogallol or pyrogallic acid. Professional photographers generally use pyro. Combined with metol it is widely used in tank development of films. Properly used, it produces splendid negatives; but it has been replaced to a great extent, by newer developers.

Sodium sulphite.—In a tight can or a well-stoppered bottle, this reagent will keep for years. It takes no part in the developing but acts as a preservative, its function being to prevent too rapid oxidation of the metol or other developing agent. Weigh carefully, because too much or too little may cause fog, especially with hydrochinon.

Potassium metabisulphite.—This acid salt is probably the best preservative when pyro is the developing agent, for pyro keeps only in an acid solution. Citric acid, sulphuric acid, and oxalic acid are also used as preservatives with pyro.

Sodium carbonate.—This makes the emulsion swell and thus allows the metol and other developing agents to penetrate more rapidly. The dry granular form is better than the crystal or anhydrous forms. Weigh carefully because too much carbonate will cause fog. Stir vigorously until dissolved.

Potassium carbonate.—Hydrochinon works faster with potassium carbonate than with sodium carbonate, but the potassium carbonate is more likely to cause fog, and it may cause blistering and frilling, especially in warm weather. Sodium carbonate is to be preferred.

Potassium bromide.—The bromide retards the action and keeps down fog. It restrains the developing agent from acting upon the silver which has not been affected by light. Too much bromide retards the action so much that details are not likely to be brought out in the shadows. The right amount checks chemical fog and produces contrast and clearness by retarding the development of the shadows, a desirable result, especially in case of overexposed negatives.

Hyposulphite of soda.—There is great difference of opinion in regard to the composition of the "hypo" bath. Many prefer plain hypo, about 100 g. hypo to 400 c.c. of water. Professor W. J. G. Land, whose negatives, lantern slides, and paper prints could hardly be surpassed, uses this plain hypo bath, which is also preferred by many of the best English photographers. With this bath, there should be an acid "short-stop" between the developer and the bath. Pour acetic acid into water until it tastes about like a weak vinegar. If too strong, it will cause pimples. If no short-stop is used, the alkaline developer is carried over into the hypo and soon spoils it. About 10 or 15 seconds in the short-stop will usually be long enough.

The addition of alum to the hypo is desirable for negatives because it hardens the emulsions; but it is undesirable for lantern slides or paper prints if you wish to color them, because the alum makes them hard to color, so that various "sizing" solutions have to be used.

FORMULAS

For convenient reference some well-known photographic formulas have been brought together here. There will be a still further saving of time if the formula is pasted on the bottle and coated with shellac to keep it from getting wet. While the scientist has no use for antiquated weights and measures, these are so often the only ones given by makers of plates and films that we have added them, often approximately, in parentheses. Grains are in apothecaries' weight and ounces are in avoirdupois.

Developers for plates, films, lantern slides, and papers.—The following standard formulas can be recommended. Many others, some of which may give better results for special cases, will be found in the references at the end of this chapter.

Metol-hydrochinon for lantern slides (Cramer).—

A

	Metric	Apothecaries'– Avoirdupois
Water	750 c.c.	(25 oz.)
Metol (or Pictol, Elon or other substitutes)	2 g.	(30 gr.)
Hydrochinon	6 g.	(90 gr.)
Sulphite of soda	30 g.	(1 oz.)

B

	Metric	
Water	750 c.c.	(25 oz.)
Carbonate of soda	15 g.	(½ oz.)

Mix A and B in equal parts. This developer keeps well even when mixed and can be used repeatedly. When fresh, add one drop of a 10 per cent bromide of potassium solution to each 30 c.c. of the developer. This is a good developer for lantern slides.

Metol-hydrochinon for negatives and papers (Wall).—

	Metric	Apothecaries'– Avoirdupois
Water	1,000 c.c.	(32 oz.)
Metol (or substitutes)	2.25 g.	(34 gr.)
Sodium sulphite (dry)	45 g.	(1½ oz.)
Sodium carbonate (dry)	35 g.	(1⅙ oz.)
Hydrochinon	4.7 g.	(70 gr.)

For negatives, dilute with an equal volume of water. For paper, use 1 part to 3 parts of water and add 0.02 g. (about ⅓ gr.) of potassium bromide to each 30 c.c. of the diluted developer.

Cramer's Pyro-Soda for negatives.—

A

	Metric	Apothecaries'– Avoirdupois
Water	640 c.c.	(16 oz.)
Sodium bisulphite	4.5 g.	(75 gr.)
Pyrogallol	30 g.	(1 oz.)

B

Water	640	c.c.	(16 oz.)
Sodium sulphite (dry)	60	g.	(2 oz.)

C

Water	640	c.c.	(16 oz.)
Sodium carbonate (dry)	30	g.	(1 oz.)

Mix 1 part of each of the three solutions and 8 parts of water.

Developer for line work (Cramer).—

A

	Metric	Apothecaries'–Avoirdupois
Water	1,000 c.c.	(32 oz.)
Hydrochinon	45 g.	(1½ oz.)
Sodium sulphite	30 g.	(1 oz.)
Sulphuric acid	4 c.c.	(60 minims)

B

Water	1,000 c.c.	(32 oz.)
Sodium carbonate	30 g.	(1 oz.)
Potassium carbonate	90 g.	(3 oz.)
Potassium bromide	8 g.	(120 gr.)
Sodium sulphite	90 g.	(30 oz.)

Use equal parts of A and B. This is good for maps and graphs and also for lantern slides where considerable contrast is desired.

Land's Contrast Developer for negatives and lantern slides.—

Hydrochinon	20 g.
Sodium sulphite (dry)	60 g.
Sodium carbonate (dry)	140 g.
Potassium bromide	12 g.
Water	1,000 c.c.

If kept tightly stoppered, with no air space between the liquid and the cork, this developer keeps almost indefinitely. When some is taken out for use, the rest should be put into a smaller bottle, so that there shall be no air between the liquid and the cork.

Another formula, developed by Dr. Land to meet the trying conditions of the tropics, is also useful for lantern slides.

Land's Tropical Developer for negatives and lantern slides.—

Hydrochinon.........................	8 g.
Metol................................	3 g.
Sodium sulphite (dry)..................	30 g.
	(60 g. if crystals are used)
Sodium carbonate (dry)................	30 g.
	(90 g. if crystals are used)
Potassium bromide....................	2 g.
Water...............................	1,000 c.c.

This formula will develop an underexposed plate when the usual developers fail. With this developer, the image flashes into sight with surprising suddenness, but do not become startled and remove the slide too soon, lest you fail to secure details. In the tropics, where it is often impossible to get reasonably cool water, this developer is a boon to the scientist who cannot wait until he gets into a favorable place for developing.

Process Developer for negatives, films, lantern slides, and paper.—

A

	Metric	Apothecaries'–Avoirdupois
Water........................	500 c.c.	(16 oz.)
Hydrochinon..................	22 g.	(176 gr.)
Sulphuric acid................	2 c.c.	(30 gr.)
Sodium sulphite..............	15 g.	(½ oz.)

B

Water........................	500 c.c.	(16 oz.)
Sodium carbonate.............	15 g.	(½ oz.)
Potassium carbonate...........	45 g.	(1½ oz.)
Potassium bromide.............	4 g.	(32 gr.)
Sodium sulphite..............	45 g.	(1½ oz.)

With a process plate, a process film, or a "red-label" Cramer lantern-slide plate, or similar plate by other makers, this developer is ideal for maps, graphs, typewritten tables, and similar subjects. In making copy for the negative, use smooth, pure white paper and dead black ink. The wretched lantern slides, seen so often at scientific meetings, result from using the same plates and developers which are used for landscapes.

Developer for bromide enlargements (Agfa).—

	Metric	Apothecaries'-Avoirdupois
Water	1,250 c.c.	(40 oz.)
Metol	1 g.	(15 gr.)
Sodium sulphite	15 g.	($\frac{1}{2}$ oz.)
Hydrochinon	4 g.	(60 gr.)
Sodium carbonate	15 g.	($\frac{1}{2}$ oz.)
Potassium bromide	1.8 g.	(26 gr.)

The time required for exposure and development depends upon several factors, but, assuming that, with a good negative and Agfa Velvet Cyco paper, 10 seconds is about right for the exposure, two minutes will probably be the maximum time required for complete development. Some papers will require much less exposure and some will require more.

Plain hypo bath.—Many prefer a plain hypo bath, because the addition of a hardener makes lantern slides and prints more difficult to color. With this bath, we strongly recommend an acetic acid "short-stop"—water with enough acetic acid to make it taste like a weak vinegar—to be used between the developer and the hypo. About 10–20 seconds is long enough. As developer is carried into the short-stop, add a few drops of acetic acid occasionally to maintain the acidity. If a lantern slide should not look bright and snappy as it comes from the hypo, rock it in the acetic acid solution until it brightens. This bath is good for plates, films, lantern slides, and papers.

	Metric	Avoirdupois
Water	1,000 c.c.	(32 oz.)
Hyposulphite of soda	250 g.	(8 oz.)

Acid-fixing and hardening bath.—

A

	Metric	Avoirdupois
Water	1,000 c.c.	(32 oz.)
Hyposulphite of soda	250 g.	(8 oz.)

B

	Metric	Avoirdupois
Water	250 c.c.	(8 oz.)
Sulphite of soda	22 g.	($\frac{3}{4}$ oz.)
Sulphuric acid	4 c.c.	($\frac{1}{8}$ oz.)
Powdered chrome alum	15 g.	($\frac{1}{2}$ oz.)

Pour B into A, stirring vigorously. This is then a one solution bath, with a greenish color, which can be used repeatedly. It hardens the emulsion and does not stain. Plates should be left in the bath for 15 minutes after the silver seems to have been dissolved.

Short-stops.—After development, a plate, film, or paper should be rinsed in water or, preferably, in a short-stop before going into the hypo. Enough acetic acid added to the rinsing water to give it the taste of weak vinegar will stop the development immediately and will save the hypo. If the acetic acid is too strong, it will cause pimples on the emulsion. Small blisters are often caused by a direct transfer from the developer to the hypo.

Hardener for plates and films.—In the tropics, and in warm weather anywhere, it is desirable to harden the emulsion.

	Metric	Avoirdupois
Water	300 c.c.	(10 oz.)
Chrome alum (granular)	30 g.	(1 oz.)

After development, transfer to the hardener without previous rinsing in water and rock for 15 seconds; then transfer *directly* to the hypo. The hardener may be used repeatedly. Even if washing must be done in water at 80° or 85° F., the emulsion will not be damaged after treatment with this hardener.

Sepia tones.—Hypo must be washed out *thoroughly* before bleaching.

Stock Bleaching Solution			Stock Toning Solution		
	Metric	*Avoirdupois*		*Metric*	*Avoirdupois*
Potassium bromide....	30 g.	(1 oz.)	Sodium sulphide	30 g.	(1 oz.)
Potassium ferricyanide.	90 g.	(3 oz.)	Water.........	300 c.c.	(10 oz.)
Water..............	300 c.c.	(10 oz.)			

Bleach in 1 part stock bleaching solution to 9 parts water until the print is light brown. Rinse in water 1 minute. Tone in 1 part stock toning solution to 20 parts water. There is no danger in prolonging either bleaching or toning. Wash as thoroughly as after hypo.

Sepia tones may be obtained by bleaching in a saturated solution of bichloride of mercury with 3 drops HCl to 30 c.c. (after hypo has been washed out); washing in water and toning in 1 part ammonia to 10 parts water. Wash thoroughly.

MISCELLANEOUS HINTS

1. Keep all chemicals in a dark, cool, dry place.
2. Keep bottles tightly stoppered and packages tightly closed.
3. Store ammonia, sodium sulphide, and ammonia sulphide away from the rest of the chemicals.

4. Do not keep plates, films, or papers in the same room with the chemicals.
5. Keep everything clean. Dust may be removed from a plate by tapping it gently on the table. If a brush is used at all, keep it clean, for it is as likely to distribute dust as to remove it.
6. If hypo is spilled or even rocks over a little, wipe it up, preferably with a rag wet with potassium permanganate. If allowed to dry, the hypo dust may cause spots on negatives and prints.
7. A temperature of 65°–70° F. is about right for most photographic work.
8. Developers keep longer if made up in two solutions, with the developing agents in one and the carbonate of soda in the other.
9. Be skeptical about "safe lights," even when dealing with lantern slides, slow plates, or even with papers.
10. Most spots are due to dirt, in the dark room, in the camera, on the lens, or on the emulsion.

REFERENCES

Some of the references are advertising pamphlets, but since they are intended to bring the best results with their products, such directions are worth studying.

CRAMER, Manual on negative-making and formulas. St. Louis, Mo., or 30 E. Randolph St., Chicago, Ill.: Cramer Dry Plate Co. (Furnished free.)

FRAPRIE, FRANK R., American photography exposure tables and manual. Boston, Mass.: American Photographic Publishing Co. (About $1.00.)

MALLINCKRODT CHEMICAL WORKS, The chemistry of photography. St. Louis, Mo.: Mallinckrodt Chemical Works. (50 cents.)

EASTMAN KODAK COMPANY, Lantern slides; how to make and color them. Color plates and filters.

WALMSLEY, W. H., The A.B.C. of photomicrography. New York City, N.Y.: Tennant & Ward.

DUNCAN, F. MARTIN, First steps in photomicrography, a handbook for novices. London, E.C. 4., England: Iliffe & Sons, Ltd., 20 Tudor St.

GLOVER, B. T. J., Print perfection, how to attain it. London, E.C., 4., England: British Periodicals, Ltd. 19, Cursitor St. (About 50 cents.)

WALL, E. J., Photographic facts and formulas. Boston, Mass.: American Photography Publishing Co.

————., Practical color photography. Boston, Mass.: American Photography Publishing Co.

HAMPTON, M. MONROE, Photo coloring and tinting. Chicago, Ill.: Central Camera Co., 230 S. Wabash Ave. ($1.00.)

BAILEY, R. CHILD, Photographic enlarging. Dorset House, Tudor St., London, E.C. 4, England: Iliffe & Sons.

CHAPTER XV

ILLUSTRATIONS FOR PUBLICATION

Illustrations will be made from some of the preparations used in the course of any histological or cytological investigation. Sometimes—and probably too often—photomicrographs are made. These have been considered in the preceding chapter.

Thirty years' experience with the illustrations of a prominent botanical periodical makes me bold enough to venture some suggestions not only to beginners but even to my colleagues. Before you begin to make a drawing for publication, get pure, smooth, white cardboard and dead black waterproof India ink. Get good steel pens. Remember that for drawings which are to be reduced one-half, "crow quill" pens are dangerous, because their lines and dots are likely to be too small for successful reproduction, especially if the drawings are to appear as text figures.

Freehand drawings, for most botanists, are difficult and they generally look crude. Drawings of apparatus, where much can be done with a ruler and a compass, are not so bad. Make the lines bold, so that they may be reduced to one-half the size of the drawing. Maps 3 feet long to be reduced to page width (usually about 4 inches) or "the long way of the page," which always irritates the reader, are often sent to journals. Letters $\frac{1}{4}$ inch in height, when such a map is reduced to page width, would be only $\frac{1}{36}$ inch in height—unreadable; and "the long way of the page," only $\frac{1}{24}$ inch in height—still unreadable. To appear $\frac{1}{8}$ inch high in the periodical, the letters must be $\frac{3}{4}$ inch high in the drawing. The author should think how he wants letters, lines, and other things to look in the reproduction and make his drawing of the map accordingly. For very coarse lines, unless they can be made with a ruling pen or a compass, use a "speedball" pen, which makes a line of uniform weight.

In making graphs, never use the yellow- or pink- or blue-lined paper which is so common in class work. If a piece of research is worth publishing, it is worth doing right. Take a piece of smooth white Bristol board and, with a ruling pen set for a heavy line, make the vertical line at the left of the sheet and join it at the bottom with a heavy horizontal line. Some use only these two lines; but it looks better to rule, in lighter lines, the space between. Figures and letters can be pasted on, or may be indicated in pencil and the printer can do the rest. If you choose to do your own lettering, *Exercises in Lettering*, "*Slant Gothic*," by George G. Greene, published by the Bruce Publishing Company, Milwaukee, Wisconsin, will be helpful.

Where several curves are to be shown, the ideal method would be to use different colors; but, in practically all scientific journals the expense makes this method prohibitive. So, use a solid heavy line for one curve, a broken line for another, a dotted line for another, etc.

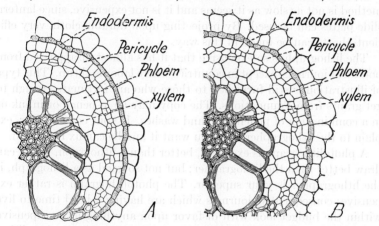

Fig. 35.—Two drawings of a part of a vascular bundle of *Pteris aquilina*, *A* showing a poor style, looking as if the layer of cells just outside the endodermis might be the outer border of the structure; *B*, a better style, showing that the cells just outside the endodermis are not the outer border. ×150.

The camera lucida minimizes the amount of skill required in making highly magnified drawings. Draw first with a pencil, making very light lines which will easily rub out; then ink while you still have the preparation under the microscope for constant reference. Such drawings are almost always reproduced by the zinc-etching process. Pencil drawings can be reproduced by the more expensive photolithographic method, or by the still more expensive lithographic method. They can also be reproduced, although not so satisfactorily, by the halftone process.

In making a detail from a tissue, do not make a border of entire cells so that it will look like an outer margin; but leave it so that it will look like a detail which had more surrounding it (Fig. 35).

If one should need a line drawing of a tree, or flower, or mushroom, a kind of drawing that, ordinarily, requires real artistic ability, there is a way to get an outline with as good proportion and perspective as even the best artist could not surpass. Photograph the object, make a lantern slide, and then throw the object on cardboard and trace with a pencil. It is more convenient to catch the object on a mirror placed at 45° and thus throw the object on the cardboard resting on the table. Drawings can be made from photomicrographs in the same way. Instruments can be bought which will throw the object down directly, saving a lot of time in many cases. However, the projection method is not as slow as it seems and it is not expensive, since lantern slide plates can be used. By projecting upon durable cloth, very efficient charts can be made in this way.

The lithograph is so expensive that it has almost disappeared from botanical journals, except in countries where labor is cheap. This type of illustration is still furnished to those who are fortunate enough to get grants from Foundations. The copy may be in pencil or in ink or in a combination of pencil, ink, and washes. If your copy is poor, explain to the lithographer how you want it and he can fix it for you.

A photolithograph is excellent, better than a lithograph, if you can draw better than the lithographer; but not so good as a lithograph, if the lithographer is your superior. The photolithograph is rather expensive; consequently, journals which are having a hard time to live within the budget look with disfavor upon anything more expensive than the zinc etching and the halftone. The copy for a photolithograph should not be a mixture of pen and pencil work, but should be all in pencil or all in ink. To get different shades with ink, dilute the ink for lighter tones: do not use a pencil. The best reproductions by the photolithographic method are made from copy entirely in dead black ink on pure white cardboard, different shades from light to dark being obtained by dots and lines. Such a photolithograph can be printed in a lithograph colored ink, and the finished product looks like an expensive genuine lithograph.

Photographs of trees, flowers, and landscapes are nearly always reproduced by the halftone process. Remember that there is a screen which makes black lines through light parts and light lines, through black parts, thus reducing the contrasts so that a good print from a good negative will be disappointing. This may be remedied, to some extent, by using a contrasty plate or film, and a contrasty developer with the negative; and a contrasty paper for the print. For good reproduction, the print should look too hard for an artistic picture. Overdo it just enough to offset the flattening which the halftone process cannot avoid. If the page width of the journal in which the illustration is to appear is 4 inches, do not use a negative smaller than 5×7. If you have no camera larger than a $3\frac{1}{4} \times 4\frac{1}{4}$, get an 8×10 enlargement on glossy paper. If your camera is smaller than $3\frac{1}{4} \times 4\frac{1}{4}$, try to describe the situation. Good English will be better than poor illustrations.

There are many other methods of reproducing drawings and photos, but the practical investigator had better learn to make copy for reproduction by the zinc etching and the halftone, and work on reproduction by the photolithographic process to show details of chromosomes and the structure of cytoplasm and similar difficult features.

PART II

SPECIFIC DIRECTIONS

In the preceding chapters the principles and methods of technique have been described in a general way. It is difficult, especially for a beginner, to apply general principles to specific cases, and, besides, the material which he might select for the preparations might not yield the most valuable collection. We have tried to select types involving all kinds of botanical microtechnique and which, at the same time, illustrate fundamentals upon which the theories of evolution, phylogeny, genetics, and physiology are based. An ambitious student, by making preparations, studying them, and reading about them, can become well grounded in comparative morphology without attending any classes. Hofmeister, the father of morphology, got his botanical training in this way while clerking in a store. We shall not discuss morphology, but shall try to answer, by means of sketches and specific directions, the multitudinous questions which confront the instructor in the laboratory. For those who have had a thorough training in general morphology the following suggestions will be in some degree superfluous; but we are asked so often to recommend books which will help the student to interpret the preparations which he has made that a few references may save the student the trouble of asking for this kind of advice. Nearly all of the books are in English.

Algae.—

OLTMANNS, F., Morphologie und Biologie der Algen. Jena: Gustav Fischer, 1927.

WEST, G. S., and FRITSCH, F. E., British fresh water algae. Cambridge University Press. 1927.

YAMANOUCHI, SHIGEO, Morphology and cytology of the algae. University of Chicago Press (to be published in 1932).

SMITH, GILBERT M., Algae (to be published in 1932).

Fungi.—

GWYNNE-VAUGHAN, H. C. L., and BARNES, B., The structure and development of the fungi. Cambridge University Press. 1927.

GÄUMANN, E. A. (trans. by W. D. DODGE), Comparative morphology of fungi. McGraw-Hill Book Co., 1928.

STEVENS, FRANK L., The fungi which cause plant disease. Macmillan, 1919.

197

LISTER, ARTHUR, Mycetozoa. 3d ed. by GULIELMA LISTER. Published by the British Museum. 1925.

Bryophytes.—

CAMPBELL, D. H., Mosses and ferns. Macmillan. 1918.

LAND, W. J. G., Morphology of Bryophytes (in preparation).

Pteridophytes.—

CAMPBELL, D. H., Mosses and ferns. Macmillan. 1918.

BOWER, F. O., The ferns (3 vols.). Cambridge University Press. 1926.

Gymnosperms.—

COULTER, J. M., and CHAMBERLAIN, C. J., Morphology of gymnosperms, University of Chicago Press, 1917.

Angiosperms.—

COULTER, J. M., and CHAMBERLAIN, C. J., Morphology of angiosperms (out of print). Appleton. 1903.

SCHÜRHOFF, P. N., Die Cytologie der Blüthenpflanzen. Stuttgart: Ferdinand von Enke. 1926.

CHAMBERLAIN, Elements of Plant Science. McGraw-Hill Book Co. 1930.

WETTSTEIN, RICHARD, Handbuch der Systematischen Botanik. Leipzig: Franz Deutike. 1926.

JEFFREY, E. C., The anatomy of woody plants. University of Chicago Press. 1917.

EAMES, A. J., and McDANIELS, L. H., An introduction to plant anatomy. McGraw-Hill Book Co. 1925.

STRASBURGER, E., Text-book of botany. 6th English ed. Macmillan, 1930.

SHARP, L. W., An introduction to cytology. McGraw-Hill Book Co. 1926.

SCOTT, D. H., Studies in fossil botany. London: A. & C. Black. 1923.

The directions for collecting and growing laboratory material constitute an important feature of this part of the book.

With a few exceptions, the order in which the forms are presented is that given in Engler's *Syllabus der Pflanzenfamilien.*

CHAPTER XVI

MYXOMYCETES AND SCHIZOPHYTES

MYXOMYCETES

An organism large enough to be seen with the naked eye and so peculiar that biologists do not know whether it is a plant or an animal, should be studied by both botanists and zoölogists. In the sporangium stage of its life-history, the organism looks and behaves like a plant; in the plasmodium stage, it looks and behaves like an animal. Writers who think these organisms are plants, call them myxomycetes; those who think they are animals, call them mycetozoa.

With the exception of a few forms like *Fuligo* (often found on oak, stumps and on oak bark in tanyards), the myxomycetes are small, and are usually overlooked by collectors (Fig. 36). A careful examination of rotting logs in moist woods will usually reveal an abundance of these delicate and beautiful organisms. Various species may be found in spring, summer, and autumn. The plasmodia are most abundant just after a warm shower. A couple of days of dry weather will then bring sporangia in abundance. The specimens should be pinned to the bottom of the box

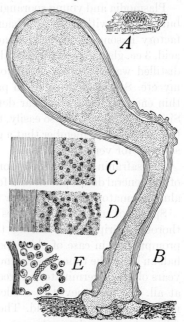

Fig. 36.—*Trichia*, a myxomycete. *A*, habit of a group of sporangia growing on rotten wood. Natural size. *B*, single sporangium with some of the rotten wood. The dots represent fairly well the size and distribution of the nuclei at this stage. ×70. *C*, *D*, and *E*, successive stages, much later than *B*, showing condensation of the wall, origin of elaters (*D*), and mature sporangium (*E*). Preparation stained in safranin, gentian violet, orange. ×320.

for safe carrying. An excellent collecting-box can be made from an ordinary paper shoe-box. On the bottom of the box place a thin piece of soft pine, or a piece of the corrugated paper so commonly used in packing; or, better still, a sheet of cork. At each end nail in a piece of pine half an inch thick and an inch high. Upon these end pieces place a thin piece of pine, thus making a second bottom, which, of course, should not be fastened. A second pair of ends with a third pine bottom nailed to them may rest upon the second bottom. The three bottoms will give a considerable surface upon which the material may be pinned. For most purposes, the specimens are simply allowed to dry, and are then fastened with glue or paste to the bottom of a small box.

Plasmodia and young sporangia may be fixed in chromo-acetic acid, but staining with iron-alum haematoxylin is likely to be more satisfactory if some osmic acid is added. The solution—0.7 g. chromic acid, 3 cc. glacial acetic acid, and 7 c.c. 1 per cent osmic acid to 90 c.c. distilled water—will be good for the younger stages of any myxomycete. Sections cut easily in paraffin. For general structure, 5 μ is thin enough; but for nuclear detail 3, 2, or even 1 μ will be better. Since the material cuts so easily, this is a good place to practice cutting thin sections. Remember that a good sliding microtome is better than a rotary for very thin sections.

The safranin, gentian violet, orange combination is good for a study of the general development and for some cytological features, but iron-alum haematoxylin is better for nuclear details.

Spores of most myxomycetes will germinate as soon as they are thoroughly ripe, and, during the first year, germination is more prompt than in case of older spores. Fresh spores may germinate in half an hour; the time may extend to several hours; spores two or three years old may germinate in three or four days, or may not germinate at all. We have never succeeded in germinating spores which were more than three years old. The longevity is doubtless different in different species. In most cases, spores will germinate in water, if they will germinate at all. For small cultures, the hanging-drop method, described on page 82, may be used.

Plasmodia may be raised by sowing spores on moist, rotten bark or wood and placing the culture under a bell jar, where the moist, sultry condition favorable to their growth is easily imitated. Plasmodia may be got upon the slide by inclining the slide at an angle of about 15°, with one end of the slide at the edge of the plasmodium, and allowing water to flow very gently down from the upper end of the slide to the lower. The proper flow of water could be secured by dropping water from a pipette, but a less tedious plan is to arrange a siphon so as to secure a similar current. The plasmodium will creep up the slide against the current, furnishing an excellent illustration of rheotropism. Enough plasmodium for an illustration may be formed in two or three hours. Examined under the microscope, the preparation should give an excellent view of the streaming movements of protoplasm.

The following is another method for getting the plasmodia upon the slide: Place the slides upon a pane of glass and upon each slide place a small piece of plasmodium-bearing wood. Cover with a bell jar. Wet blotting paper or a small dish of water included under the jar will help to create the warm, sultry atmosphere necessary. The slides may be covered with the plasmodium in a few hours. Permanent preparations may be made by immersing the slide in chromo-acetic acid, then washing and staining without removing the plasmodium from the slide. Acid fuchsin is a good stain for bringing out the delicate strands of the plasmodium. Iron-alum haematoxylin, followed by acid fuchsin or erythrosin, brings out both nuclei and cytoplasmic strands.

Some of the foregoing methods are taken from an article by Professor Howard Ayers in the January and February (1898) numbers of the *Journal of Applied Microscopy*. Other methods, with directions for various experiments, are given in the same article.

In 1931, in the *American Journal of Botany*, Howard published a very effective method of cultivating myxomycete plasmodia. He used oat agar. Cook 30 g. rolled oats, 15 g. agar, and 1 liter of water for 15 minutes in a double boiler. Pour into a flask and autoclave at 15 pounds for 15 minutes. When nearly cool, pour into Petri dishes. Temperatures from 20° to 26° C. are good for the growth of most plasmodia.

If the plasmodia are allowed to dry slowly by exposing them to air, they pass into the sclerotium condition, where they may remain for a year or more. To revive them, place them under moist conditions, but never cover them with water. Within 24 hours they may become active again.

SCHIZOPHYTES (*Fission Plants*)

BACTERIA (*Schizomycetes. Fission Fungi*)

Bacteria are studied almost exclusively from the standpoint of health and disease, and bacteriological methods are, largely, those which have been developed for determining species, structure and phylogeny being incidental. The methods of the medical school will

not contribute much to our knowledge of the internal structure of bacteria.

The methods given here will merely enable the student to study the form and size of those bacteria which are more easily demonstrated.

Foul water at the outlets of sewers and such places will usually afford an abundance of *Coccus, Bacillus, Spirillum,* and *Beggiatoa* forms. Place a drop of water on a slide, heat it gently until the water evaporates, then stain with fuchsin or methyl violet, dehydrate, clear in xylol, and mount in balsam.

The hay infusion is a time-honored method for securing bacteria for study. Pour hot water on a handful of hay, and filter the fluid through blotting paper. Place the fluid in a glass dish, and cover with a piece of glass to keep out the dust. When the fluid begins to appear turbid, bacteria will be abundant. The active movements are easily observed in a mount from the turbid water. As the bacteria pass into the resting condition, they form a scum on the surface of the water. Usually, the first to appear is a somewhat rod-shaped form, the *Bacterium termo* of the older texts. *Spirillum* and *Coccus* forms often appear later. Scrape the inside of your cheek with your finger nail and you are almost sure to find some bacteria. If you let your teeth go without brushing for 24 hours you can get bacteria by scraping your teeth with your finger nail. Throw flies or other insects into water from a pond or ditch and bacteria will soon appear.

From such material or from vigorous cultures smear a *little* on the slide and allow it to dry for 24 hours in a warm place, free from dust; or, if you are in a hurry, dry it by passing it several times over the flame of a Bunsen burner. Then try the following rapid method:

1. Place on a clean cover a drop of water containing the bacteria and dry completely in a flame or on a hot plate.
2. Stain 2–5 minutes in gentian violet or methyl violet.
3. Rinse quickly in water.
4. Dip into 95 per cent alcohol to reduce the stain.
5. Remove most of the alcohol by touching a corner of the cover with filter paper and then dry completely by passing through a flame.
6. Mount in balsam.

Cilia of bacteria can be stained in various ways. In the hay infusion, the first form to appear is likely to be one which goes under the name of *Bacterium termo*. It is a harmless ciliated form. *Bacillus typhosis,* the bacillus of typhoid, is a good ciliated form; but students had

better leave dangerous bacteria alone. Try *Bacterium termo* with the
following solution:

> Ferric chloride, aqueous (1 part ferric chloride to
> 20 parts water)............................. 25 c.c.
> Alum, saturated aqueous solution............... 75 c.c.
> Shake and add a saturated aqueous solution of
> basic fuchsin.............................. 10 c.c.

Filter and allow it to stand for some time; then stain for 5 minutes,
gently warming but not to the boiling point. Rinse in water and stain
lightly in carbol fuchsin. If the cilia are not stained, repeat the process.
Mount in balsam.

Here is another method. After drying the smear, treat with a 10 per
cent aqueous solution of tannin for 2 minutes. Wash in water, 10 seconds. Put a few drops of acid fuchsin on the smear and heat until bubbles begin to appear. Let it cool, wash in water, 1 minute; then to 95
per cent alcohol, 20 seconds; absolute alcohol, 5 seconds; xylol. Mount
in balsam. The cilia should be red.

The following method is much better if the bacteria are vigorous and
the haematoxylin is at its best: make smears from the hay infusion,
invert over fumes of 1 per cent osmic acid, 10 seconds; dry in a warm,
dry room; heat gently; 10 per cent aqueous solution of tannin, 10 seconds; water, 10 seconds; iron-alum 4 per cent, 4 hours; water, 1 minute; ½ per cent haematoxylin, overnight; water, 5 minutes; 1 per cent
iron-alum, until stain is right; water, 2 minutes; 30, 50, 70, 85, 95, and
100 per cent alcohol; xylol. Mount in balsam. The cilia should be
black.

Still another method: After drying the smear, treating with tannin,
and rinsing slightly with water, put on a few drops of acid fuchsin and
heat until bubbles appear. Cool off; wash in water, 1 minute; 95 per
cent alcohol, 20 seconds; 100 per cent, 5 seconds; xylol. Mount in
balsam.

Fine preparations may be obtained by inoculating a mouse with
Anthrax, and then cutting paraffin sections of favorable organs. For
making mounts of a dangerous form like *Anthrax*, secure properly
fixed material from a bacteriologist. Let him cut the liver and spleen
(and any other parts) into small pieces, about 5 mm. square and 2 or
3 mm. thick, and put them into the chromo-acetic–osmic solution
(0.7 g. chromic acid, 3 c.c. glacial acetic acid, 7 c.c. 1 per cent osmic

acid, and 90 c.c. water). Fix 24–48 hours and then follow the usual schedule for imbedding in paraffin. Cut 2–5 μ thick and stain in Haidenhain's iron-alum haematoxylin, or try the following schedule, which is good for *Anthrax* and many other bacteria:

1. Gentian violet, 5 minutes.
2. Rinse in water a few seconds.
3. Gram's solution (iodine 1 g., potassium iodide 2 g., water 300 c.c.) until the color is almost or quite black; this will generally require 1 or 2 minutes.
4. Ninety-five per cent alcohol until the color has nearly disappeared.
5. Rinse in water and examine. If the bacteria are well stained, a counterstain may be added.

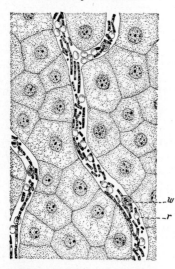

6. Light green or erythrosin, 5 seconds; or Bismarck brown, 5 or 10 seconds.
7. Ninety-five and 100 per cent alcohol, dehydrating as rapidly as possible. Not more than 5 or 10 seconds can usually be allowed.
8. Xylol, 1–5 minutes.
9. Balsam.

After the rinsing in water of stage 5, the preparation may be dehydrated rapidly in 95 per cent and 100 per cent alcohol, and then stained for 5 or 10 seconds in orange dissolved in clove oil. From the clove oil, transfer to xylol and mount in balsam (Fig. 37).

Fig. 37.—*Bacillus anthracis*, from a paraffin section cut from the liver of a mouse and stained in crystal violet; *w*, white blood corpuscle; *r*, red blood corpuscle. ×580.

The bacteria are the only plants in which a nucleus has not been conclusively demonstrated, and some claim that a nucleus is present even in bacteria. In determining the presence or absence of a nucleus in bacteria, the crude method, just given, would be of no value, and even the most critical methods of the bacteriologist, who mounts the organisms whole, would be entitled to only scant consideration. The presence or absence of a nucleus will have to be determined by a study of thin, well-stained sections of perfectly fixed material.

CYANOPHYCEAE. BLUE-GREEN ALGAE (*Schizophyceae. Fission Algae*)

The blue-green algae include unicellular, colonial, and filamentous forms. They occur everywhere in damp or wet places. On the vertical faces of rocks where there is a constant dripping of water, brilliant blue-green forms are abundant. In the Yellowstone National Park the brilliant coloring of the rocks is due in large measure to members of this group. Many forms occur as brownish or greenish gelatinous layers on damp ground or upon rocks, or even upon damp wooden structures in greenhouses. Other forms float freely in water or on the surface of the water.

Oscillatoria.—For most purposes it is best to study *Oscillatoria* in the living condition. It is readily found in watering-troughs, in stagnant water, on damp earth, and in other habitats. The commonest forms have a deep blue-green or brownish color. It is very easy to keep *Oscillatoria* all the year in the laboratory. Simply put a little of a desirable form into a gallon glass jar half filled with water. By adding water occasionally to compensate for evaporation, the culture should keep indefinitely. In a jar with a tightly fitting cover we have kept such a culture for years without renewing the water.

For the purposes of identification and herbarium specimens the material may simply be placed on a slip of mica and allowed to dry. When wanted for use, add a drop of water and a cover, and the mount is ready for examination. After the examination has been made, remove the cover, allow the preparation to dry, and then return it to the herbarium.

Good mounts may be made by the Venetian turpentine method. Species of medium size are more satisfactory for a study of the nucleus than the very large species. Fix in a chromo-acetic–osmic solution (1 g. chromic acid, 3 c.c. acetic acid, and 7 c.c. 1 per cent osmic acid). Stain in iron-alum haematoxylin, and follow the Venetian turpentine method. While the nuclei are easily seen in such preparations, still better views can be secured from sections of paraffin material fixed in the same solution or in Flemming's weaker solution. The section should be 1–3 μ thick. After staining with haematoxylin, stain lightly with orange dissolved in clove oil. In paraffin sections the scattered condition of the material as it appears in thin sections is very annoying. As soon as the material is thoroughly washed in water, arrange it so that the filaments will all have the same general direction. This will enable you to get longitudinal and transverse sections. As you begin with the alcohols, use a Petri dish and lay a slide over the material, and keep it there until you imbed in paraffin. This will keep the filaments from

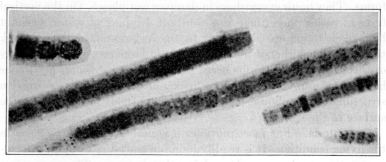

FIG. 38.—*Oscillatoria:* photomicrograph from a paraffin section 3 μ in thickness and stained in iron-alum haematoxylin. ×373.

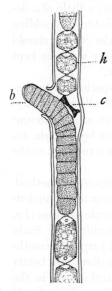

FIG. 39.—*Tolypothrix,* showing "false branching": *h,* heterocyst; *c,* concave cell; *b,* end of false branch with beginning of new sheath. ×620.

spreading out too much, and you will be able to get as much on one slide as you would be likely to get on a dozen slides without such precaution.

Oscillatoria, as it appears in section, is shown in Figure 38.

Tolypothrix.—This form occurs as small tufts, either floating in stagnant water or attached to plants and stones. Some species grow upon damp ground. It furnishes an excellent example of false branching (Fig. 39). Like all small filamentous algae, it may be dried on mica for herbarium purposes. Venetian turpentine mounts and paraffin sections are prepared as in *Oscillatoria. Tolypothrix* is even better than *Oscillatoria* for a study of the nucleus.

Scytonema is a similar form which is fairly common. It is often found as a feltlike covering on wet rocks.

In staining forms like *Tolypothrix* and *Scytonema,* which have a thick sheath, take care not to obscure the cell contents by staining the sheath too deeply. If the sheath is not stained at all, you may not be able to see the nature of the false branching. Iron-alum haematoxylin, with orange in clove oil for the sheath, is good for sections. Phloxine, with light green or anilin blue for the sheath, is good for Venetian turpentine mounts (Fig. 40).

Nostoc.—*Nostoc* is a cosmopolitan form. It occurs on damp earth or floating freely in water. In a fruit can or a battery jar, *Nostoc* is easily kept year after year in the laboratory. Young specimens are generally in the form of gelatinous nodules, but in older specimens the form may be quite various. It is very easy to make sections, since the gelatinous matrix cuts well and holds the filaments together. Chromo-acetic acid is a good fixing agent. Stains which stain the gelatinous matrix make the preparations look untidy, but they show that each filament of the nodule has its own gelatinous sheath. Small nodules may be stained in bulk and be got into Venetian turpentine. Crushed under the cover, they make instructive preparations.

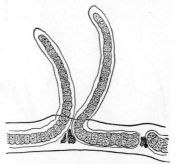

FIG. 40.—*Scytonema:* filament showing thick sheath and characteristic branching. ×640.

Rivularia.—This form is readily found on the underside of the leaves of water-lilies (*Nuphar, Nymphaea*, etc.), but is also abundant on submerged leaves and stems of other plants. It occurs in the form of translucent, gelatinous nodules of various sizes. Chromo-acetic acid gives beautiful preparations, but good results can also be secured from formalin or picric acid material.

The most instructive preparations for morphological study can be obtained by the Venetian turpentine method. Stain in iron-haematoxylin and very lightly in erythrosin, the latter stain being used merely to outline the sheath. When ready for mounting, crush a small nodule under a cover glass. The paraffin method is easily applied, since the gelatinous matrix keeps the filaments in place. Any form of similar habit may be prepared in the same way.

Gloeotrichia.—*Gloeotrichia* (Fig. 41), in its later stages, is a free-floating form. In earlier stages it is attached to various submersed aquatic plants. The nodules, when young, are firm like *Nostoc*, but as they grow older and larger they become hollow and soft. The older forms become so much dissociated that they lose their characteristic form and merely make the fixing fluid look turbid. Allow a drop of such material to spread out and dry upon a slide which has been slightly smeared with albumen fixative. Leave the slide in 95 per cent alcohol 2 or 3 minutes to coagulate the albumen fixative, and then stain in safranin. If the background appears untidy, stain for 24 hours, or longer; you can then extract the stain from the background, and still leave the long spore and some of the other features of the filament well stained. A touch of light green will bring out the sheath. Iron-alum haematoxylin, followed by orange in clove oil, gives a beautiful differentiation. The firmer young nodules can be treated like *Nostoc.*

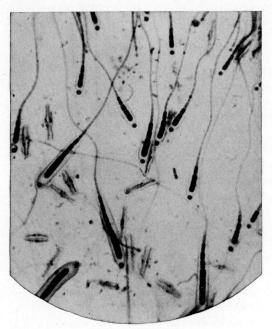

FIG. 41.—*Gloeotrichia:* photomicrograph from a preparation stained in cyanin and erythrosin; negative by Dr. W. J. G. Land.

"Wasserblüthe."— Some of the Cyanophyceae occur as scums on the surface of quiet or stagnant water. The name, *Wasserblüthe,* "water flowers," was given because the scums are often iridescent. Some of the commonest forms are *Coelosphaerium* and *Anabaena* (Fig. 42). Some of the Chlorophyceae also occur as *Wasserblüthe.* Where the material is very abundant, it may be collected by simply skimming it off with a wide-mouthed bottle, but where it is rather scarce, it is better to filter the water through bolting silk and finally rinse the algae off into a

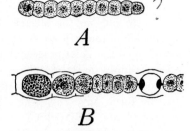

FIG. 42.—*Anabaena: A,* hormogonium showing well-defined nuclei; *B,* older filament showing a spore and a heterocyst.

bottle, adding enough formalin to the water in the bottle to make a 5 per

cent solution. The material may be kept here indefinitely, but after 24
hours it is ready for use. If the forms are small, like *Anabaena*, smear
a slide lightly with Mayer's albumen fixative, as if for paraffin sections,
add a drop of the material and allow it to dry overnight or for 24 hours;
then immerse the slide in strong alcohol for a few minutes, and proceed with the staining. Cyanin and erythrosin form a good combination for differentiating the granules. Delafield's haematoxylin, used
alone, stains some granules purple and others red. Iron-alum haematoxylin is excellent for heterocysts. With patience, these *Wasserblüthe*
forms may be stained in iron-haematoxylin and brought into Venetian
turpentine, from which they will yield much better preparations than
can be secured by the drying-down method.

Sometimes *Anabaena*, mixed with *Gloeothece* or *Gloeocapsa*, occur
floating in gelatinous masses which hold together fairly well so that it
is easy to fix in the chromo-acetic–osmic solution recommended for
Oscillatoria, stain in iron-alum haematoxylin, and follow the Venetian
turpentine method.

With such material we have tried a more expeditious method with
excellent results. After staining in haematoxylin, we have used a series
of alcohols, $2\frac{1}{2}$, 5, 10, 15, 20, 30, 40, 50, 70, 85, 95, and 100 per cent,
allowing only 3 or 4 hours for the entire series. Then use mixtures of
clove oil and absolute alcohol, beginning with 1 part clove oil to 4 parts
alcohol, followed by equal parts clove oil and alcohol, then 3 parts
clove oil to 1 of alcohol. At this point, stain in orange dissolved in
clove oil. Drain off the stain and transfer to pure clove oil. Then place
the material in thin balsam, about 1 part of the balsam used for
mounting to 3 parts of xylol. Here the material may be kept indefinitely. Mounts may be made in balsam from this stock. Figure 42
was drawn from material prepared in this way.

CHAPTER XVII
CHLOROPHYCEAE. GREEN ALGAE

For experiments in most phases of botanical microtechnique, no group of plants affords better material than the green algae, since the killing, fixing, and staining can be watched directly; the effect of the change from one solution to another can be observed; and even the behavior during infiltration with paraffin can be determined with considerable accuracy.

Since the Chlorophyceae furnish our best illustrations of the evolution of the plant body, the origin and development of sex, and also the beginning of alternation of generations, they occupy a prominent place in any well-planned course in the morphology of plants; and, if they were better known, the ease with which the reactions of the individual cell may be observed would make them valuable to the physiologist.

They are found in both fresh and salt water, but are most abundant in fresh water. The ponds, ditches, and rivers of any locality will yield an abundance and variety both of the unicellular and the multicellular members of this group. Most of the algae are independent, but there are epiphytic, endophytic, and saprophytic species. The larger forms and those which grow in tufts or mats are readily recognized in the field. Many of the smaller forms are attached to other water plants. Drain the water plants and then squeeze them over a bottle. The sediment is likely to contain a variety of unicellular and other small algae.

Many of the genera are easily kept in the laboratory. It is not necessary to have very large aquaria. Ordinary glass battery jars holding about a gallon are good for most forms. Jars holding 2 gallons will be as good or better. For some cultures which are to be kept for a long time, like *Scenedesmus*, small glass jars, or dishes, with ground-glass tops are desirable. For a limited amount of material, quart or 2-quart fruit cans are very efficient. Put about an inch of pond dirt in some, clean sand in others, and in still others use a gravel bottom. Many forms grow well without any soil or sand in the bottom of the jar.

When possible, use the water in which the algae were growing, since

210

very few take kindly to a sudden change of water. If the material has been brought to the laboratory in a very small quantity of water, fill the jar about two-thirds full with tap water. Let the water run for 2 or 3 minutes before you fill the jar, since the water standing in the pipes is injurious, or even fatal, to most algae. Add water occasionally, only a little at a time, to compensate for evaporation. If the water has evaporated until the jar is about one-third full and you fill it nearly to the top with tap water, you are likely to kill some of the most desirable forms.

It is a mistake to put too much material into a jar. A wad of *Spirogyra* half as large as one's finger is as much as should be put into a gallon jar. As it grows to ten or twenty times that amount, it is not necessary to keep throwing it out, since it will gradually accommodate itself to conditions; but if the larger amount should be put into the jar when brought in from the field, it would die in a day or two.

Cultures may be started even in the winter. A surprising number of the green algae live through the winter under the ice of ponds and rivers. *Oedogonium* commonly passes the winter in the sporeling stage. *Cladophora* may be found the year around. *Coleochaete*, on stems of plants like *Typha*, can be taken from under the ice and, in a few days, will be fruiting. Many pass the winter in the spore stage.

Bring in some mud over which algae were growing the previous summer or autumn; put it into a jar and fill it two-thirds full of tap water. Also bring in sticks, leaves, and stones from good alga localities and put them into jars of tap water. Cultures may be started either by taking mud and sticks from under the ice or by taking them from places which have entirely dried up during the summer or autumn. A few such jars will be likely to yield a variety of material.

If you have a good jar of *Oedogonium*, or some other desirable form, do not throw it out if the alga should disappear. Remember that temporary disappearances occur in nature. Allow the culture to become dry and then set it aside where it will be protected from dust. After a few months, pour on tap water and it is very likely that you will soon have a good jar of *Oedogonium*. Many algae behave similarly; some, like *Volvox*, appear for a short time and then disappear for a long time; some, like *Cladophora*, may last the whole year, and grow so luxuriantly that the excess material must be removed; and some, like *Ulothrix*, we have not been able to cultivate at all in the laboratory.

Some very useful hints on collecting and growing fresh-water algae for class work will be found in an article by Dr. J. A. Nieuwland in the *Midland Naturalist*, **1**:85, 1909.

Professor Klebs has shown that various phases in the life-histories of many algae and fungi may be produced at will. By utilizing his results, the fruiting condition may be induced in many of the common laboratory types. Knop's solution will be needed in most cases. A stock solution which can be diluted as required may be made as follows:

Potassium nitrate, KNO_3 .... 1 g.
Magnesium sulphate, $MgSO_4$ .... 1 g.
Calcium nitrate, $Ca(NO_3)_2$ .... 3 g.
Potassium phosphate, K_2HPO_4 .... 1 g.

Dissolve the first, second, and fourth ingredients in 1 liter of distilled water, and then add the calcium nitrate. A precipitate of calcium phosphate will be formed. For practical purposes this may be called a 0.6 per cent solution. Whenever a dilute solution is made from the stock solution, the bottle must be shaken thoroughly in order that a proper amount of the precipitate may be included in the diluted solution. To make a 0.1 per cent solution, add 5 liters of distilled water to 1 liter of the stock solution; for a 0.3 per cent solution, add 1 liter of distilled water to 1 liter of the stock solution, etc.

The addition of a liter of a 0.2 per cent solution to 4 or 5 liters of water will often produce a more thrifty growth. Directions for inducing reproductive phases are given in connection with the various types. With a good supply of glass jars, plenty of Knop's solution, a reasonable control over temperature, and the teacher's usual amount of patience, most laboratory types can be studied in the living condition at all seasons of the year.

Collecting algae need not be so laborious as most botanists make it. Forms like *Spirogyra, Zygnema, Cladophora, Vaucheria*, and *Hydrodictyon* may be rolled up in wet newspaper and carried in a botany can. They suffer less from lack of water than from lack of air. Large quantities of material can be brought in and transferred to water after reaching the laboratory. Even after 24 hours in the wet paper, such forms seem to suffer no damage.

Permanent preparations are needed to show details which are not so evident in the fresh material. The unicellular and filamentous members, together with such forms as *Volvox*, are best prepared by the Venetian turpentine method. The structure is so much more complicated than in the Cyanophyceae that it demands far more care and skill to make good preparations.

In many, probably in most of the green algae, nuclear and cell division takes place at night. This is definitely known to be the case in *Spirogyra, Zygnema, Closterium, Ulothrix*, and others. Mitosis is most abundant about midnight, or an hour before midnight, and continues up to three or four o'clock in the morning. The most extensive work on the time of day at which nuclear division occurs is a paper by G. Karsten, "Ueber embryonales Wachstum und seine Tagesperiode," *Zeitschrift für Botanik*, **7**:1-34, 1915. Although the paper is in German, the numerous tables can be understood by those who are unfamiliar with the language. The paper contains a bibliography of the subject.

Chromo-acetic acid, with or without osmic acid, is a good killing and fixing agent for the entire group. We prefer the following formula: Chromic acid, 1 g.; glacial acetic acid, 3 c.c.; 1 per cent osmic acid, 5 c.c.; water, 90 c.c. If material is to be imbedded, it is better to increase the amount of osmic acid up to 7 c.c., since the staining of thin sections is likely to be more brilliant.

With any fixing agent, it is worth while to place a few filaments in the mixture and watch the effect under the microscope. If plasmolysis occurs with the chromo-acetic mixture, weaken the chromic or strengthen the acetic until the suitable proportions are determined. In the previous edition, the usual method was to weaken the chromic acid. While this avoided any shrinking of the cell contents, the fixing was not very thorough, and material often suffered during staining or other subsequent processes. An extensive series of experiments, especially with coenocytic forms which are notoriously difficult to prepare, proved that it is better not to let the chromic acid drop below 0.7 g. to 100 c.c. of water. Generally 3 c.c. of acetic will be enough to avoid any shrinking. If there is still a tendency to shrink with 4 c.c. of acetic, weaken the chromic down to 0.5 and let the solution act for 48 hours. One function of the osmic acid is to make the killing almost instantaneous. If you put the little crustacean, *Cyclops*, into a 1 per cent chromo-acetic solution, it will keep up its characteristic movements for several minutes; but if you add one drop of 1 per cent osmic acid to 25 c.c. of the chromo-acetic solution, the movements stop in a few seconds. Besides, the osmic acid acts as a mordant for some stains, especially haematoxylin. About 24 hours in any of the chromic series and a 24 hours' washing in water will be sufficient for members of this group. Only a few of the most commonly studied will be mentioned.

With marine forms use sea water in making up the fixing agents and for most of the washing; but finish the washing in fresh water and use fresh water in making up alcohols and for the 10 per cent glycerin.

For collecting, use "bolting cloth" or "bolting silk" of the finest mesh available. With a piece of thin cloth about 15 cm. square, laid over an ordinary coffee strainer, you can pour through about 4 liters of water in a minute. In this way you will secure all the *Volvox* in about a barrel of water in half an hour. *Eudorina* may be collected in the same way. Smaller members of the *Volvox* family like *Pandorina*, *Gonium*, and *Chlamydomonas* are too small to be held by the cloth; but if material is very abundant, the water goes through faster than the organisms and you will soon have many times as much material in a bottle as you could get by dipping. Many small organisms are effectively collected in this way, even when they are so small that most of them pass through the cloth.

Material of *Volvox* and all the Volvocaceae may be fixed in the corrosive sublimate–acetic mixture, used hot—85° C. If material is to be stained and mounted whole, use the aqueous mixture; if it is to be imbedded and cut, use the alcoholic. For mounting whole, stain in iron-alum haematoxylin, or in phloxine and anilin blue, following the Venetian turpentine method.

Chlamydomonas is such an important type from the standpoint of evolution and phylogeny, that there should always be a supply of living material as well as some well-prepared slides. It often appears in the greenhouse. A small quantity in a Petri dish on white sand, moist but not flooded with water, may be kept for months. Add a pipette full of water occasionally to keep it from drying up. If there are zygotes, the material may dry up without any damage. If stained in iron-alum haematoxylin, stain one lot heavily to show cilia; another lot, lightly, to show internal structure. Some of each lot, with some in phloxine and anilin blue, and some in iron-haematoxylin, on each slide, make an instructive preparation. Of course, it is assumed that there has been a thorough study of living material. The principal stages in the life-history are shown in Figure 43. The Powers' methods yield beautiful, transparent preparations.

Volvox.— *Volvox* is found in ponds and ditches, and even in shallow puddles. The most favorable place to look for it is in the deeper ponds, lagoons, and ditches which receive an abundance of rain water. It has been claimed that where you find *Lemna*, you are likely to find *Volvox;* and it is true that such water is favorable, but the shading is unfavorable. Look where you find *Sphagnum, Vaucheria, Alisma, Equisetum fluviatile, Utricularia, Typha,* and *Chara.* Dr. Nieuwland reports that *Pandorina, Eudorina* and *Gonium* are commonly found in summer as constituents of the green scum on wallows in fields where pigs are kept. The flagellate, *Euglena,* is often associated with these forms. If you have a culture in the laboratory, do not throw it out

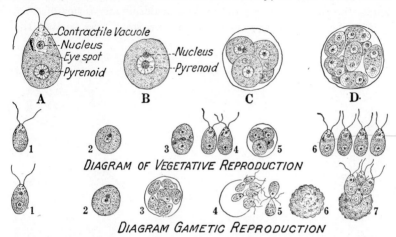

Fig. 43.—*Chlamydomonas: A,* vegetative cell of the zoöspore; *B,* the zoöspore loses its cilia and rounds off; *C,* four new zoöspores are formed within the parent zoöspore; *D,* when eight new individuals are formed within the parent zoöspore, the eight are gametes. ×1,000. The second and third rows are diagrams of vegetative and gametic reproduction. Vegetative reproduction: *1,* zoöspore; *2,* zoöspore has lost its cilia and rounded off; *3,* the rounded cell is dividing; *4,* the rounded cell has divided, producing four zoöspores; *5,* the rounded cell instead of dividing as in *3* and *4* has produced four zoöspores within itself; *6,* the four zoöspores have escaped from the rounded cell. Gametic reproduction: *1,* zoöspore; *2,* the zoöspore has lost its cilia and rounded off; *3,* eight gametes are formed inside the rounded cell; *4,* gametes escaping; *5,* two gametes uniting; *6,* zygote formed by the two uniting gametes; *7,* four zoöspores escaping from the germinating zygote. From Chamberlain's *Elements of Plant Science* (McGraw-Hill Book Co., New York).

when the culture disappears, because new coenobia are likely to develop from the oöspores.

Many fixing agents cause the protoplasmic connections between the cells to be withdrawn. Figure 44 *A,* showing the protoplasmic connections in nearly the living condition, was drawn from material fixed in the hot aqueous corrosive sublimate–acetic acid solution; *B,* fixed in a 1 per cent chromo-acetic solution, does not show the connections; *C* to *E* show details drawn from sections.

For paraffin sections, the material, preferably in sufficient abundance to make a layer 5 mm. deep may be placed in a shell with a bottom rounded like a test tube. The tube should be on top of the bath, with the cork out, to evaporate as much of the xylol as possible. Put it in the bath, standing it in some dish to keep it from tipping over. As soon as the paraffin melts, draw it off with a pipette *just a little* warmer than the paraffin. A *hot* pipette works well, but ruins the material. Change the paraffin four times. Half an hour in the bath should be enough for any of the Volvocales or any forms of similar consistency. Imbed by pouring out into a small tray so that there

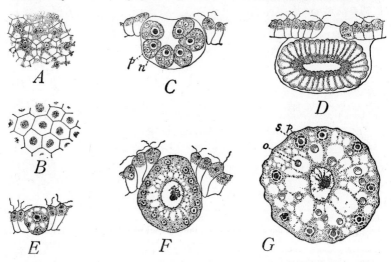

Fig. 44.— *Volvox:* *A*, surface view of several cells, fixed in the hot aqueous corrosive sublimate-acetic acid mixture, stained in iron-alum haematoxylin, and mounted in Venetian turpentine; *B*, fixed in chromo-acetic acid, but otherwise treated like *A*; *C–G*, fixed in 1 per cent chromo-acetic acid, imbedded in paraffin, and cut 5 μ; *C*, *E*, and *F* stained in iron-alum haematoxylin; *D* and *G* stained in safranin, gentian violet, orange; *C*, new colony showing pyrenoids, *p*, and nucleus, *n*; *D*, a nearly mature antheridium; *E*, young egg; *F*, egg before fertilization; *G*, egg after fertilization, showing oil globules, *o*; pyrenoids, *p*; starch cut off from pyrenoid, *s*. All ×780.

shall be a layer of material about 2 mm. thick. If you have trouble in pouring it out, just let it cool in the shell, putting it into luke-warm water for 15 or 20 seconds, then into cold water. Break the shell. There will be some loss of material in getting it ready for cutting. Sections should not be thicker than 5 μ; 3 or 2 μ will be better for details. Safranin, gentian violet, orange, is a good combination for older stages, especially for pyrenoids and starch. Iron-alum haematoxylin is better for nuclei and the younger stages of oögonia, antheridia, and new colonies. ·

Figure 45 shows that even such delicate forms as *Volvox* can be imbedded in paraffin without shrinking.

The Powers' methods.—Professor J. H. Powers' mounts of *Volvox* and other members of the Volvocaceae have been the delight and despair of both botanists and zoölogists for many years. They have never been surpassed and, probably, never equaled. Professor Powers has kindly given me an outline of his methods; but, as in other phases of technique, judgment, skill, and patience must be furnished by the student.

For fixing, Professor Powers uses the aqueous potassium iodide solution used in testing for starch. This solution may be weaker than the usual formula so that it has a light brown color. From 10 to 24 hours is sufficient for fixing, but material may be left here for several days. Wash thoroughly in tap water which has stood long enough to give off all of its excess of air; otherwise bubbles will form on the colonies, causing them to float and hindering subsequent processes. Change after change of water should be made rapidly, using large amounts of water and decanting just as soon as the colonies have settled. From 1 to 3 hours' washing should be sufficient to remove the brown color of the iodine.

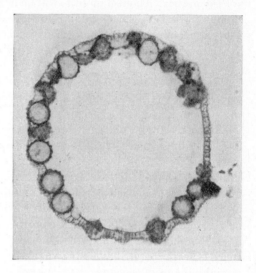

FIG. 45.— *Volvox:* photomicrograph of a section from material fixed in chromo-acetic acid and stained in Delafield's haematoxylin; from a preparation and negative by Dr. W. J. G. Land.

Stain in Mayer's carmalum. Use a pure carminic acid in making the stain, 1 g. carminic acid, 10 g. alum, and 200 c.c. distilled water. Dissolve with heat, filter, and add a crystal of thymol to keep out fungi. After staining, follow the Venetian turpentine method, taking care to wash the glycerin out completely. The 10 per cent turpentine should not be allowed to concentrate too rapidly.

Material fixed in weak osmic acid is even better for protoplasmic connections and cilia. About 4 or 5 drops in 50 c.c. of distilled water is sufficient. From 6 to 24 hours is long enough for fixing.

After either of these fixing agents, following the washing in water, material may be preserved in a nearly saturated solution of alum; or in a dilute aqueous carmalum, with a crystal of thymol to prevent mold. Staining for 3 weeks in a weak carmalum stains the cells but not the matrix. About 3 months will be necessary to stain the matrix enough to make it a background for the cells.

An aqueous solution of nigrosin gives an effect like that of iron-alum haematoxylin. Rose benzol and Lee's pyrogallic acid method were also useful.

When forms so large and so delicate as *Volvox* are to be mounted whole, put a few small pieces of cover glass into the balsam to keep the cover from crushing the specimens.

Diatoms.—Living diatoms are often found clinging in great numbers to filamentous algae, or forming gelatinous masses on various sub-merged plants. *Cladophora* is frequently covered with *Cocconeis*, an elliptically shaped diatom; *Vaucheria* is often covered with small forms. Other algae will pay for examination, especially if they look brown. If stones in the water have a brown, slippery coating, you can be sure of diatoms. Sometimes the brown coating on sticks and stones is so abundant that it streams out with the current. If rushes and stems of water plants have a brown, gelatinous coating, you are likely to find millions of specimens of the same diatom. The surface mud of a pond, ditch, or lagoon will always yield some diatoms. They can be made to come out from the mud by putting a black paper around the jar and letting direct sunlight fall upon the surface of the water. The diatoms, in a day or even less, will come to the top in a scum which can be easily secured.

Since diatoms form an important part of the food of molluscs, tunicates, and fishes, the alimentary tracts of these animals often yield deep-water forms which are not easily secured in any other way.

Fresh water diatoms appear in greatest abundance in spring, are comparatively scarce in summer, and reappear in autumn, though not so abundantly as in the spring.

Marine forms can be secured by scraping barnacles, oyster shells, and other shells. The big *Strombus* shell from the West Indies, which we use to keep the door open, will yield a good collection if you get it before it is cleaned.

The silicious shells of diatoms are among the most beautiful objects which could be examined with the microscope (Fig. 46). To obtain perfectly clean mounts requires considerable time and patience, but when the material is once cleaned, preparations may be made at any time with very little trouble. Diatom enthusiasts have devised numer-

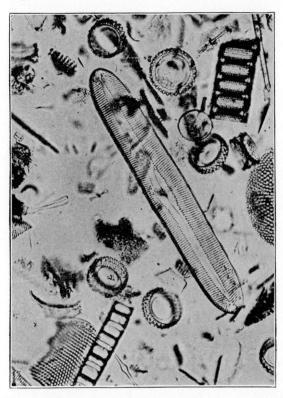

Fɪɢ. 46.—Diatoms: diatomaceous earth from Cherryfield, Maine, a Pleistocene deposit, showing the great variety of forms usually found in such material; photomicrograph by Miss Ethel Thomas from a preparation by Rev. E. L. Little. ×400.

ous methods for cleaning them, and separating the various forms from one another, but we shall give here only a few simple, practical methods.

Dr. Wood's method of mounting frustules of living forms is easy and effective:

Material may be obtained by skimming off the brownish scum found on ponds, by squeezing out water weeds, by scraping sticks and stones which are covered at high water, or from the mud of filter beds and pumping-works, or in other places. The material is put in a dish of water, and after it has settled the water is decanted. This is repeated until the water will clear in about half an hour. The sediment is then treated with an equal bulk of sulphuric acid, after which dichromate of potash is added until all action ceases. After a couple of hours the acid is washed out. To separate the diatoms, place the sediment in a glass dish with water, and when the water becomes clear give the dish a slight rotary motion. This will bring the diatoms to the top, when they may be removed with a pipette and placed in alcohol. To mount, place a number in distilled water, evaporate a few drops of the mixture on a cover-glass, which is then mounted on a slide in balsam.

It is better to use a very slight smear of Mayer's albumen fixative to prevent the diatoms from floating to the edge of the cover.

Many scouring soaps and silver polishes contain large quantities of fossil diatoms, and the diatomaceous earths are particularly rich. Diatomaceous earths from Cherryfield, Maine, and from Beddington, in the same region, are the richest we have seen (Fig. 46). The deposits at Richmond, Virginia, have long been famous. In some of our western states there are deposits 300 feet thick, with 80 per cent of silica, the silica being the valves of diatoms.

Break up a small lump of such material and boil it in hydrochloric acid. An evaporating dish or a test-tube is convenient for this purpose. Let the diatoms settle, pour off the acid, and then wash in water. As soon as the diatoms settle, the water should be poured off. The washing should be continued until the hydrochloric acid has been removed. When the washing is complete, pour on a little absolute alcohol, and after a few minutes pour off the alcohol and add equal parts of turpentine and carbolic acid. The material will keep indefinitely in this condition, and may be mounted in balsam at any time. In making a mount, put a little of the material on a slide and allow it to become dry, or nearly dry, and then add the balsam and cover. If the balsam should be added too soon, the diatoms are likely to move to the edge of the cover.

We have had excellent results with the following method: After washing in water, keep the diatoms in 5 per cent formalin. To make a mount, smear the slide very slightly with Mayer's albumen fixative, add a little of the material, and heat just enough to coagulate the albumen. When perfectly dry, add a drop of balsam and a cover. Or, after coagulating the fixative, dip in absolute alcohol and then in xylol before mounting in balsam. Without the alcohol and xylol, some air is sure to be caught and it may accentuate some markings; but, in general, we prefer to use the alcohol and xylol.

To show the cell contents, diatoms must be fixed and stained. If they are clinging to filamentous algae, the algae with the diatoms attached should be put into chromo-acetic acid (24 hours) and then washed in water for 24 hours. Stain in iron-haematoxylin and proceed by the Venetian turpentine method. When ready for mounting, the diatoms can be scraped off from the algae or other substratum. Safranin gives a beautiful stain, bringing out the radiations and the peculiar centrosomes. This stain has been used very effectively in studying auxospores.

When material is in gelatinous masses or is clinging firmly to some easily cut substratum, it may be fixed and imbedded in paraffin. The knife often breaks the frustules as cleanly as if they were cut.

Desmids.—The desmids are unicellular, free-floating, or suspended algae. They are not found in salt water and are more abundant in soft water than in hard. Deep pools, quiet ponds, and quiet margins of small lakes are good collecting-grounds. Collections of other freshwater algae often contain some desmids. It frequently happens that a single desirable desmid appears during examination of field collections. In such a case, remove it with a fine pipette, and get it into a drop of water on a clean slide, invert it over a bottle of 1 per cent osmic acid for 8 seconds, leave the slide exposed to the air until almost all the water has evaporated, and then add a drop of 10 per cent glycerin. In a few hours (6–24) put on a cover and seal. It requires more time, care, and patience than it is worth to attempt staining in such a case.

Sometimes desmids occur in great abundance. We have found *Micrasterias* so loosely attached to *Chara* that a quart bottle full could be squeezed off in a few minutes. A watering-trough yielded *Cosmarium* in almost equal abundance. They may then be treated like the filamentous algae, except that more care must be taken not to lose them when changing fluids. Four or 5 drops of 1 per cent osmic acid to 50 c.c. of water fixes well, and material from this solution may be placed directly into 10 per cent glycerin and mounted by the Venetian turpentine method. It looks almost as if stained in iron-alum haematoxylin. The iodine solution used in testing for starch gives good results and may be followed by any stains. The larger desmids stain beautifully in iron-alum haematoxylin.

The Venetian turpentine method, with phloxine and anilin blue, will give beautiful preparations. A deep stain with phloxine and a rather light stain with anilin blue is better for the pyrenoids and nucleus, while a light stain in the red and a deep stain in blue is better for the chromatophores.

Material may be fixed and stained as directed for *Volvox.* Formalin 8 c.c., acetic acid 2 c.c., and water 90 c.c. fixes well, and material may stain in the solution indefinitely.

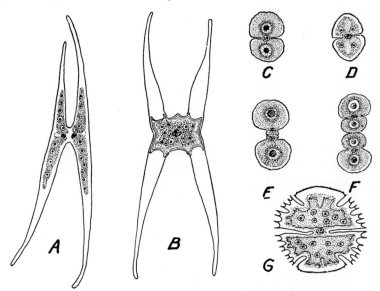

Fig. 47.—Some common desmids. *A* and *B*, *Closterium* conjugating; *C–F*, *Cosmarium*; *C* and *D*, adult cells; *E* and *F*, dividing; the inner half-cells will grow until they reach the size of the outer half-cells; *G*, *Micrasterias*. *A* and *B* ×640; *C–F* ×770; *G* ×640.

Lutman found that nuclear division in *Closterium* takes place at night. This is probably true to a greater or less extent, for most of the Chlorophyceae.

The division is peculiar. When the cell divides, each of the resulting cells gets a half-cell already of adult size; the other half-cell—the inner one—is very small, but it grows rapidly and, in a day or so, becomes as large as the other half.

A few of the most common desmids are shown in Figure 47.

Zygnema.—*Zygnema* is one of the most common algae of the ponds. swamps, and ditches. The mats are very slippery to the touch. In the field it resembles *Spirogyra*, but is distinguished by the two characteristic chromatophores which are readily seen with a good pocket lens. Sometimes conjugation can be induced by bringing the material into the laboratory and placing it in open jars with plenty of water and not too much light.

The chromo-acetic–osmic acid solution is good for fixing. Stain in iron-alum haematoxylin and also in phloxine and anilin blue. Follow the Venetian turpentine method, and in mounting put material from both stains on each slide. Also, have both conjugating and vegetative material on each slide. There will probably be vegetative filaments mixed with those which are conjugating; but these will not be so vigorous and are not so likely to show dividing cells and plastids as material which has not begun to conjugate. Don't forget to run the material up to 85 per cent alcohol and then run it back before staining. To many, this may seem unnecessary, but the results are worth the time and labor.

Textbooks describe "stellate chromatophores" in *Zygnema*. A good preparation should show that the chromatophores have an even outline, with no trace of a stellate form. The boundary between the chromatophore and the protoplasm—often of a stellate form—in which the chromatophore is imbedded, should be seen in well-fixed material with either of the foregoing stains. The large starch grains, extending from the pyrenoid almost to the border of the chromatophore, are better differentiated by the phloxine and anilin blue; the nucleus and pyrenoid are better stained by the iron-alum haematoxylin. Careful staining should bring out the features shown in Figure 48. The chromatophores do not stain as readily as those of *Spirogyra*, and consequently it is necessary to use stronger stains or more prolonged periods. Use the Venetian turpentine method.

For a detailed study, imbed in paraffin and cut thin sections. After washing in water, arrange the filaments so that most of them will have the same general direction; then, in running up through the alcohols, keep the filaments from spreading too much by placing a slide on the material. After imbedding, the material can be cut into blocks about a centimeter square. If sections thinner than 5 μ are wanted, cut out smaller paraffin blocks.

Spirogyra.—Probably no alga has been more studied by pupils, teachers, and investigators than *Spirogyra* (Fig. 49). Nearly all of the numerous species belong to the low, quiet waters of ponds and ditches, where they often form large, flocculent green mats nearly covering the

surface of the water. A few species occur in running water. The mats
are very slippery to the touch—a character which assists in recogniz-
ing the genus in the field. In the larger species the characteristic spiral
chromatophores can be seen with a good pocket lens, thus completing
the identification, as far as the genus is concerned. Mats in which
zygospores have been formed are likely to show a pale, or even a
brownish, color, due to the brownish walls of the zygospores. This

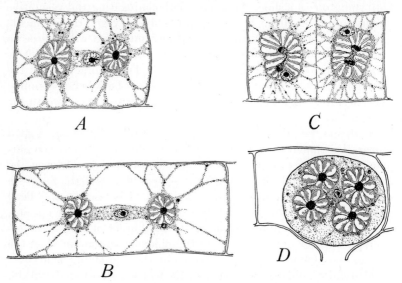

FIG. 48.—*Zygnema:* fixed in the Chicago chromo-acetic–osmic solution: *A* and *B* stained in
Magdala red and anilin blue; *C* and *D* stained in iron-alum haematoxylin. All show the nuclei, the
chromatophores differentiated from the cytoplasm, and the large starch grains arranged radially
about the pyrenoids. In *C*, cell division has just taken place and the pyrenoids and chromatophore
in each new cell are dividing. In *D*, a young zygospore, the two nuclei have not yet fused. ×790.

color, however, is not always, or even usually, due to zygospores, but
is more often due to the death and degeneration of the plants. Mats in
early stages of conjugation and those with young zygospores show as
bright a green as vigorously growing material.

Spirogyra is not easy to keep in the laboratory. The small species
keep better than the larger ones. Put only a small amount of the
material in a jar and use rain water. If it is necessary to use tap water,
let the water run for a minute before taking the water for the culture.
Most metals are poisonous to *Spirogyra*, even the small amount taken
up by the water while standing in the water pipe being detrimental.

The species found in running water will usually conjugate within a week, when brought into the laboratory and placed in rain water or tap water. Species belonging to quiet waters, when brought into the

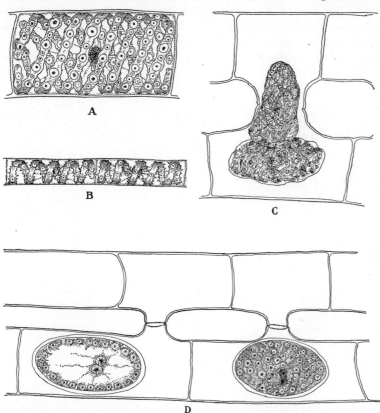

Fig. 49.—*Spirogyra:* A, vegetative cell of a large species, with four spiral chromatophores, containing many large and small pyrenoids. B, a smaller species with only one spiral chromatophore. C, union of gametes: these large, non-motile gametes, consisting of the entire contents of the cell, are characteristic of the group. D, mature zygotes: the one on the right focused on the surface; the one on the left focused for the center, showing the nuclei of the two gametes. All ×300. From Chamberlain's *Elements of Plant Science* (McGraw-Hill Book Co., New York).

laboratory and placed in a 0.2 per cent Knop's solution, are likely to undergo rapid cell division and growth. After the alga has remained in such a culture for a few days or for a week, conjugation may be induced by transferring to rain water or tap water, and keeping the culture in bright sunlight. Conjugation may begin within 3 or 4 days.

Variations in temperature between 1° and 15° C. have little influence upon conjugation.

The Chicago chromo-acetic–osmic solution fixes well. Stain some material in iron-alum haematoxylin and some in phloxine and anilin blue. Use the Venetian turpentine method, and on each slide mount material stained in both ways. With phloxine and anilin blue the spiral chromatophore takes the blue and its pyrenoids the red.

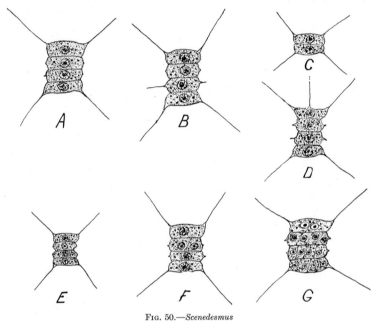

Fig. 50.—*Scenedesmus*

If the material contains figures, stain in iron-haematoxylin. This will stain the figures, but will hardly touch the chromatophore or cell wall, thus allowing an unobstructed view of the figures. While figures occur occasionally in the daytime, collect your material at night, preferably near midnight.

Spirogyra is easily imbedded and cut.

Scenedesmus.—*Scenedesmus* (Fig. 50) is found everywhere as a constituent of the fresh water plankton. It is more abundant in stagnant water. It often appears in considerable quantity in laboratory cultures, where it may be kept for years in a tightly closed glass jar without renewing the water, the lid being removed only when material is needed.

The form is so small that in living material little more than the general form can be distinguished. Excellent mounts are easily and quickly made. Smear a very thin layer of albumen fixative upon the slide, and add a drop of water containing the *Scenedesmus*. The drop may be inverted for 4 or 5 seconds over the fumes of 1 per cent osmic acid. No washing is necessary, and good mounts may be made without any fixing whatever. Allow the drop to dry completely. It is better to leave it for 24 hours before proceed-ing. The usual difficulty with this form, and with many others, is that the back-ground stains and so makes the mounts untidy. The following method by Yam-anouchi will produce beautiful prepara-tions (Fig. 50):

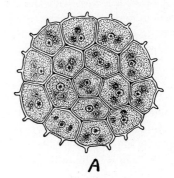

A

1. Dry on the slide, 24 hours.
2. Ten per cent alcohol overnight to re-move chlorophyll.
3. Safranin (alcoholic), 4 days.
4. Water, 5 minutes.
5. Aqueous gentian violet, 2 days.
6. Water, a few seconds.
7. Orange G, aqueous, 3 minutes.
8. Ninety-five per cent alcohol, a few seconds.
9. Absolute alcohol, 1 minute.
10. Clove oil, until the stain is satis-factory. Different collections of *Scenedesmus* stain very differently, but the time in clove oil is likely to be long, even as long as 6 hours.
11. Xylol, 5 minutes.
12. Mount in balsam.

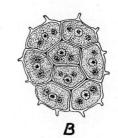

B

Fig. 51.—*Pediastrum: A,* colony with 16 cells; *B,* colony with 8 cells. Both are beginning to form new colo-nies inside each cell. ×770.

Pediastrum.—This is a beautifully regular little alga (Fig. 51). Scattered specimens often occur mixed with other algae and, occasion-ally, one finds it in abundance. Look in small ponds, ditches, and bog pools, where it is associated with other water plants. If it is at all abundant, centrifuging very gently for a few minutes may help you get a hundred specimens in a single drop. If material is scarce, put it into formalin–acetic acid—5 c.c. formalin and 5 c.c. acetic acid to

90 c.c. water. Stain with safranin, fuchsin, or carmine. Avoid stains which need much washing out. However, small scanty material like this can be handled in the following away: strip epidermis from the inner scales of an onion or from a *Sedum* leaf; fix in the above formalin–acetic acid solution; get the material into a drop or two of water on the epidermis; roll it carefully so as to make a little tube; tie the ends of the tube and treat like any macroscopic object. When ready to mount, the ends with the threads can be cut off and the material can be mounted in balsam. Such pieces can be treated like a root-tip, imbedded in paraffin, and cut. The epidermis makes a ring around each section, thus making the objects easier to find.

Hydrodictyon.—This is popularly known as the "water-net." *Hydrodictyon* is found floating or suspended in ponds, lakes, or slow streams. The young nets are formed within the segments of the older nets. Examine segments 4 or 5 mm. in length for the formation of young nets. The old nets may reach a length of 10 cm. Cultures are easily kept in the laboratory. If material which has been growing in a 0.5–1 per cent Knop's solution be brought into tap water or pond water, zoöspore formation may begin within 24 hours. Nets brought from the nutrient solution into a 1–4 per cent cane-sugar solution produce zoöspores for a few days.

Nets of all sizes should be selected for study. The segments are coenocytic, and the nuclei of the older segments are hard to differentiate, except in stained preparations. Only one nucleus will be found in the young segments, but in the older segments the nuclei become very numerous.

For fixing try 0.7 g. chromic acid, 3 c.c. acetic acid, 6 c.c. of 1 per cent osmic acid, and 100 c.c. water. If the cell contents of the vegetative cells shrink away from the wall, reduce the chromic acid to 0.5 g. If there is still some tendency to shrink, increase the acetic acid to 4 c.c., leaving the chromic acid at 0.5 g. If the chromic acid is as weak as 0.5 g., fix for at least 24 hours, using a large amount of the fixing agent. About 100 times the weight of the material is not too much.

For fixing, use the Chicago chromo-acetic–osmic formula. This should not produce plasmolysis in nets of any age. Iron-alum haematoxylin will differentiate the nuclei and pyrenoids, which may look alike with less precise stains. Use the Venetian turpentine method for mounting whole young nets and parts of older nets. Fine scissors should be used freely, because any attempt to arrange the material with needles will make it look as if the whole method of preparation were wrong. Parts of nets mounted whole are shown in Figure 52.

For details of the formation of starch and for the finer details of the development of zoöspores and gametes, *Hydrodictyon* should be imbedded and cut.

Pleurococcus.—This form, which is used everywhere as a laboratory type of the unicellular green algae, is found on the bark of trees, where it is more abundant on the north side and near the ground. It is also found on stones and fences, and in moist situations generally. It is easily secured in nearly all localities and at all seasons.

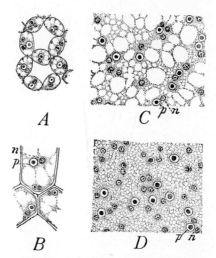

The life-history of *Pleurococcus* is variously described in textbooks, but it is very doubtful whether there is any mode of reproduction except by cell division. The zoöspores and gametes which are sometimes described probably belong to other forms which are occasionally associated with *Pleurococcus*, especially when growing in very moist situations. The life-history was examined very critically by the great algologist, Wille, who not only concluded that cell division is the sole mode of reproduction but

FIG. 52.—*Hydrodictyon: A*, part of young net with segments showing one pyrenoid and one or two nuclei; *B*, parts of three segments with nucleus, *n*, and pyrenoid, *p*, well differentiated; *C*, part of a still older segment with nuclei more numerous than the pyrenoids; *D*, part of a nearly mature segment with nuclei much more numerous than the pyrenoids. Fixed in the Chicago chromo-acetic–osmic solution and stained in iron-alum haematoxylin. ×600.

showed how investigators, even those relying upon cultures, had made their mistakes. Wille's paper was published in 1913 in *Nyt Magazin for Naturvidenskaberne*.

A study of the living material is sufficient for any general course. The bright-green cells, scraped off and mounted in a drop of water, show the rather thick wall, the chromatophores, and usually the nucleus. A drop of iodine will bring out the nucleus, if it does not show already, and will also stain the pyrenoid, if the cell contains one. A mount in Venetian turpentine, stained in phloxine and anilin blue, shows the nucleus very clearly.

Vaucheria.—This form can always be obtained in greenhouses, especially in the fernery, where it forms a green felt on the pots. The greenhouse form is likely to be *Vaucheria sessilis*. Another species, *V. geminata*, is very common in the spring, when it may be found in

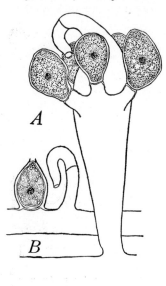

ponds and ditches (Fig. 53). *Vaucheria* is also found in running water, but in this situation is almost certain to be sterile. In the vicinity of Chicago, *V. geminata* appears late in March or early in April and within a few weeks begins to fruit abundantly. The fruiting continues for from 4 to 8 weeks, and then the alga may disappear until later in the season, when some of the oöspores germinate.

Vaucheria sessilis is found at all seasons in the greenhouses, but it is usually in the vegetative condition. Klebs found that the formation of oögonia and antheridia can be induced in *V. repens* (a variety of *V. sessilis*) within 4 or 5 days by putting the material into a 2–4 per cent cane-sugar solution in bright sunlight. The sex organs will not be formed in weak light or in darkness.

Fig. 53.— *Vaucheria: A, Vaucheria geminata*, showing antheridium and five oögonia containing fertilized eggs; from a preparation fixed in formalin, acetic acid, and stained in iron-alum haematoxylin. *B, V. sessilis:* from a preparation fixed in chromo-acetic acid and stained in eosin and gentian violet. ×150.

The formation of zoöspores may be induced in the following way: Cultivate in an 0.1 to 0.2 per cent Knop's solution for a week, then bring the material into tap water, and keep the culture in the dark. Zoöspores may appear within 2 days. Bright light or a temperature higher than 15° C. will check the production of zoöspores. A 2 per cent cane-sugar solution kept in the dark is also likely to furnish zoösporic material. If no zoöspores are formed when the solution is kept in the dark, the nutrition has been too weak: strengthen the nutrient solution and keep the culture in the light for a few days; then put the culture in the dark, and zoöspores should appear. The formation of zoöspores may continue for a couple of weeks.

Aplanospores of *V. geminata* are formed in nature when the plant is growing upon damp ground. The aplanospores may also appear in a 4 per cent cane-sugar solution.

In fresh 0.5 per cent Knop's solution in bright light, cultures remain in the vegetative condition, and the result is the same in weak light if the nutrient solutions are seldom changed. Such cultures may be kept indefinitely by changing the nutrient solution whenever a whitish scum appears on the surface.

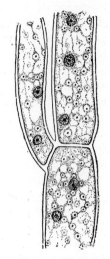

Vaucheria is not easy to fix. Solutions which give fine results with *Spirogyra* and *Zygnema* may be ruinous to *Vaucheria*. We have secured the best results with a formalin-acetic solution (10 c.c. formalin, 5 c.c. glacial acetic acid, and 90 c.c. water). Chromic-acid solutions, even with 4 or 5 per cent acetic acid, cause some plasmolysis. If the chromic acid is weakened enough to prevent plasmolysis, the solution should be allowed to act for 48 hours. The addition of 1 per cent osmic acid up to 6 c.c. to 100 c.c. of the solution does not seem to cause any more shrinking, and nuclei are easier to stain.

Fig. 54.—*Cladophora;* fixed in chromo-acetic acid and stained in iron-alum haematoxylin.

Iron-alum haematoxylin is the best stain. Phloxine and anilin blue give beautiful results, *occasionally*, but preparations are almost sure to fade. Eosin is good for topography, but will not show the nuclei.

Use the Venetian turpentine method. In mounting, use small scissors freely. You cannot untangle a mat of *Vaucheria* so as to give good views.

For the development of the oögonium and antheridium, for fertilization and for the structure and development of the various spores, thin sections are necessary. Imbed in paraffin. For nuclear details, use iron-haematoxylin; for cytoplasm, use safranin, gentian violet, orange.

Cladophora.—This genus is found in both salt and fresh water (Fig. 54). The fresh-water forms are usually attached to sticks or stones in quiet or running water. The mats feel rough and crisp and, even under a pocket lens, show the characteristic branching by which the form is easily recognized. The absence of a mucous coat makes *Cladophora* a convenient host for numerous parasitic algae, among which diatoms belonging to the genera *Cocconeis* and *Gomphonema* are particularly abundant.

For laboratory cultures, select the forms found in quiet water, but for preparations, forms growing where the waves dash hard are better, since you can get a fine display of branches under a small cover. Forms growing in still water or in gently flowing water may look like unbranched filaments, under an ordinary cover.

For fixing, use chromo-acetic–osmic acid, watching the effect of the solution and modifying the constituents until you find just what you need for that lot of material. If it looks all right at the end of 10 minutes, it is likely to remain all right. *Cladophora* is one of the most difficult of all algae to fix well. Iron-alum haematoxylin, followed by the Venetian turpentine methods, gives the best results for nuclei and pyrenoids. Phloxine and anilin blue are better for the cell wall and chromatophores (Fig. 54).

Ulothrix.—Where the problem of the origin and evolution of sex is studied, *Ulothrix* is an indispensable type (Fig. 55). *Ulothrix zonata* is found in springs, brooks, and rivers, occurring in bright green masses attached to stones in riffles, especially in sunny places. It is abundant on stones and piles along the beaches of lakes. Nuclear division takes place at night, most abundantly about midnight, and is followed by a rapid development of zoöspores and gametes, which continue to be discharged throughout the forenoon. In the afternoon the material is largely vegetative. Another species is found in stagnant ponds, ditches, and even in watering-troughs and rain-barrels. It is difficult to keep in the laboratory the forms which are found in rapidly flowing water. However, if they are brought in still attached to stones and placed under a stream of tap water, they may live for a couple of weeks and may produce zoöspores every morning. The production of zoöspores may continue for a few days, if the material is merely put into a jar of water; in a 2–4 per cent cane-sugar solution the production of zoöspores continues a little longer.

No form is better than *Ulothrix* for illustrating to a class the difference between zoöspores and gametes. Even when gametes are not conjugating, their more rapid movement is noticeable; and when conjugating, the awkward, jerky movements of the pair contrast sharply with the graceful movements of the zoöspores.

Fix in chromo-acetic acid—1 g. chromic acid and 2 c.c. acetic acid to 100 c.c. water; or in 0.7 g. chromic acid—3 c.c. acetic acid, and 6 c.c. 1 per cent osmic acid to 100 c.c. water. Formalin–acetic acid—10 c.c. formalin and 5 c.c. acetic acid to 100 c.c. water—is a good fixing agent, especially when followed by phloxine and anilin blue. The anilin blue

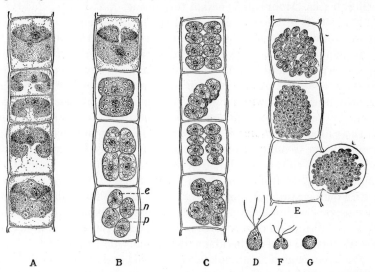

Fig. 55.—*Ulothrix: A,* part of vegetative filament. *B,* a vegetative cell at the top; the cell below has divided and one more division would make 4 zoöspores; the next cell shows 4 young zoöspores, and the bottom cell has 4 zoöspores almost ready to escape; *e,* eye spot; *n,* nucleus; *p,* pyrenoid. *C,* each cell with 8 nearly mature zoöspores. *D,* mature zoöspore. *E,* filament with gametes. *F,* two gametes uniting. *G,* zygote formed by the two uniting gametes. ×535. From Chamberlain's *Elements of Plant Science* (McGraw-Hill Book Co., New York).

should stain the chromatophore and the phloxine the pyrenoids. Iron-alum haematoxylin should stain the chromatophore gray and the pyrenoids black. Mount on each slide material from both lots.

Oedogonium.—Most species are found in quiet waters, especially in ponds and ditches. The best fruiting material is often attached to submerged twigs, rushes, and various plants, where, to the naked eye, it forms only a fuzzy covering. Some species form floating masses, bearing some resemblance to *Spirogyra,* but they are not so slippery.

The fixing agents mentioned for *Ulothrix* are good for *Oedogonium.* The iodine solution used in testing for starch, or a weak aqueous solution of osmic acid (4 or 5 drops of 1 per cent osmic acid to 50 c.c. of water) is good for zoöspores and androspores.

For cell division and the peculiar method of forming the new cell wall, stain in phloxine and anilin blue. Iron-alum haematoxylin is better for most of the other phases; but the fertilized eggs stain very deeply. Consequently, stain some material lightly, for the fertilized eggs; and some more deeply for young eggs, chromatophores, and other phases. Mount in Venetian turpentine.

For details of blepharoplasts and the development of the various motile forms, material should be imbedded and sectioned.

Nanandrous species have antheridia only in the dwarf males; and species with antheridia in the ordinary filaments have no androspores in the life-history. A species with no dwarf males in the life-history (macandrous) is shown in Figure 56 A and B; a species with dwarf males in the life-history (nanandrous) is shown in C of the same figure.

In studying *Oedogonium diplandrum*, Klebs found that a change from a lower to a higher temperature would induce the production of zoöspores. A culture which had been kept in a cold room with a temperature varying from 6° to 0° C., when brought into a warmer room with a temperature varying from 12° to 16° C., produced an abundance of zoöspores within 2 days. Light does not seem to have any influence upon the formation of zoöspores in this species, but light is necessary for the formation of antheridia and oögonia.

We have secured an abundance of oögonia and antheridia by keeping the material for 4 or 5 days in a very weak Knop's solution and then transferring to distilled water. The oögonia appeared in 3 or 4 days. The method seems to succeed with some species, especially those which occur floating or suspended in the water, but we have not succeeded with species which form a fuzzy covering on grasses and twigs under water. Sterile material sometimes fruits when brought into the laboratory and placed in open jars with plenty of water and not too much light.

Coleochaete.—*Coleochaete* is epiphytic upon the stems and leaves of submerged plants. *Sagittaria* is a good host plant. Look on petioles from the surface of the water down to 6 inches below, where the alga begins to get scarce. The well-lighted part of the host is better than the shaded part. Three or four species may be found growing so close together that they all come in the field of the microscope with a 16 mm. objective. *Coleochaete scutata* is the best-known species, but *C. soluta*,

C. orbicularis, and *C. irregularis* are equally common. *C. scutata* is often found on the floating leaves of *Polygonum amphibium*.

Chromo-acetic acid (1 g. chromic acid and 3 c.c. acetic acid to 100 c.c. water) is a good fixing agent. For finer details and for sections, add 6 c.c. of 1 per cent osmic acid.

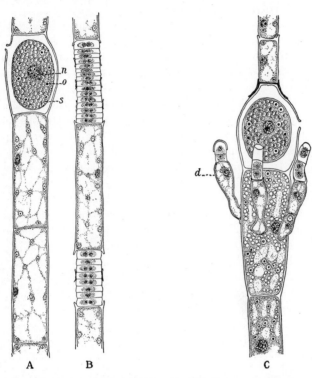

Fig. 56.—*Oedogonium*. *A*, oögonial, and *B*, antheridial filament of a dioecious species; *n*, nucleus; *p*, pyrenoid; *s*, starch. *B* shows two groups of antheridia, with 16 antheridia in the upper group and 8 in the lower. Most of the antheridia contain two nearly mature sperms. *C*, *Oedogonium nebraskense*, a nanandrous species collected by Dr. Elda Walker; *d*, dwarf male. ×300. From Chamberlain's *Elements of Plant Science* (McGraw-Hill Book Co., New York).

The epidermis of the host plants is hard to peel off. With a fleshy plant, like *Sagittaria*, cut parallel to the surface pieces 8 or 10 mm. wide, lay the outer side on a piece of glass, and gently scrape off the hypodermal cells until practically nothing but the epidermis, with the *Coleochaete*, is left. Then fix and mount the epidermis with the *Coleochaete*. Stained in iron-alum haematoxylin and mounted whole, such preparations are very effective. All the species mentioned are flat: *C. pulvinata* is hemispherical and might be mistaken for a small *Rivularia*.

If you overstain with Delafield's haematoxylin and then reduce the stain with hydrochloric acid (about 3 or 4 drops to 100 c.c. water), the alga will stand out sharply against the host. A slight tinge of orange in clove oil will increase the contrast.

Sections are easily cut and, especially in forms with a flat thallus, show features which might escape if one depended entirely upon plants mounted whole. Cut out small pieces of leaf or stem abundantly covered with *Coleochaete*, imbed in paraffin, and cut host and guest together.

Chara.—*Chara* is found in ponds, lagoons, and ditches. Once seen, it is always readily recognized. In the ponds and lagoons along the southern shores of Lake Michigan it fruits so abundantly that the whole pond shows an orange color due to the immense numbers of antheridia. In the lagoons of the Chicago parks *Chara* is so abundant that it must be dredged out every summer.

Chara is easily kept alive throughout the year in the laboratory. A 2-gallon glass jar with an inch of pond dirt, sand, and gravel at the bottom, and nearly filled with tap water, is all that is needed for a successful culture. If the jar is to be covered, it should not be more than two-thirds full of water. Not more than a dozen plants should be put into such a jar.

A rather strong solution should be used for fixing. The following will give good results:

Chromic acid	1 g.
Glacial acetic acid	1 c.c.
Water	100 c.c.

In about 24 hours this not only fixes but dissolves the lime with which most species are coated.

For paraffin sections select the tip of the plant, a piece about a centimeter in length. Sections of this may show, not only the large apical cell, but also various stages in the development of antheridia and oögonia (Fig. 57). For the development of the plant body from the apical cell and also for early stages in the development of oögonia and antheridia, the safranin, gentian violet, orange combination is excellent; for later stages, especially in the development of the antheridia, iron-haematoxylin is much better.

The antheridium of *Chara* stains so rapidly that the beginner uniformly makes poor preparations. In order to get good preparations of the antheridium it is necessary to disregard other structures, which will be stained lightly or not at all when the stain is just right in the antheridial filaments.

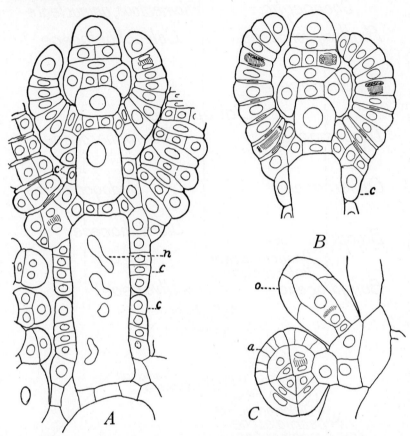

Fig. 57.—*Chara:* fixed in chromo-acetic acid and stained in safranin, gentian violet, orange. *A*, longitudinal section of apex showing five nodes; *c*, corticating filaments; *n*, part of the fragmented nucleus. *B*, note the different condition of the nodes and first branches. *C*, young antheridium, *a*, and young oögonium, *o*. ×230.

If it is desired to mount whole branches showing the antheridium and oögonium in position, use the Venetian turpentine method, staining in phloxine alone, or in phloxine and anilin blue. Good mounts showing shield, manubrium, capitula, and filaments may be obtained by crush-

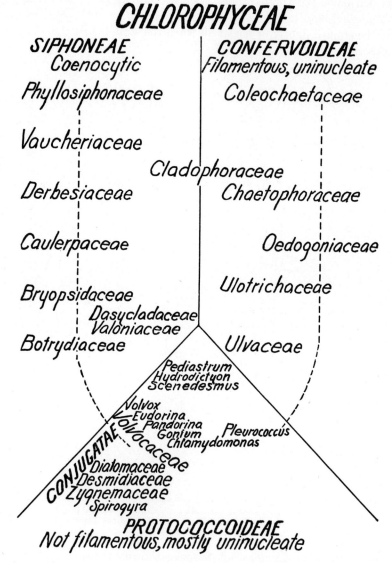

Fig. 58.—A diagram illustrating an opinion in regard to relationships in the *Chlorophyceae*

ing an antheridium under a cover glass. For this it is better to stain in phloxine alone, since any overstaining is easily corrected by exposing the preparation to direct sunlight.

When the fertilized egg of *Chara* germinates, a simple filament is produced, homologous with the protonema of a moss. From this filament, the familiar *Chara* plant arises as a lateral bud. This stage is easily secured. When the pond dries up, collect the dry *Chara* plants, with their hundreds of black zygotes. After a month or two, put the black zygotes in a dish of water and the filamentous stage, with its young *Chara* plants, will soon be abundant. They make effective preparations when mounted whole.

As slides accumulate, the thoughtful student will feel the need of some kind of classification. Of course, one might arrange alphabetically and there would be no need for thought; but we assume that the student who has made enough slides to need a classification will want one which expresses some idea of relationship, even if the idea may be more or less faulty. The classification indicated in Figure 58 is essentially that of Oltmann, and does not differ much from that given in Engler and Prantl's *Die natürlichen Pflanzenfamilien*. If the student would compile similar diagrams in all the groups, his slides would mean, not only proficiency in technique, but an increasing knowledge of the structure, development, and relationship of plants.

CHAPTER XVIII

PHAEOPHYCEAE. BROWN ALGAE

These algae are almost exclusively marine. The plant body ranges from delicate filamentous forms to coarse, leathery plants 150 feet in length. There are no unicellular members of the Phaeophyceae.

For all marine algae, fixing agents should be made up with sea water, never with fresh water; and the washing should begin with sea water. In general, wash in running sea water 24 hours.

For washing, especially when there is a large class, it is not likely that there will be a sufficient number of faucets. A convenient washing-box can be made from an ordinary washtub. Bore a dozen ¾-inch holes in the bottom, insert rubber tubes 6 inches long, and in the end of each tube place the glass part of a pipette. The tub may be elevated by nailing three narrow boards to the sides so as to form a tripod. Place the bottles or cans of material under the pipettes and let sea water flow into the tub. The outlets which are not in use can be closed by placing clamps on the rubber tubes.

After the washing in sea water, wash for 1 or 2 hours in a mixture of equal parts of sea water and fresh water; then, for 1 hour in fresh water. Use fresh water in making up the alcohols.

During cold weather, large coarse forms, like *Fucus, Nereocystis, Laminaria*, etc., can be shipped from either coast to the Mississippi River, without any fixing. Roll the plants in a dozen thicknesses of newspaper, around this put oiled paper, and then wrap in oilcloth. Upon arrival, the material can be studied while it is still alive. Rotation of the egg and fertilization in *Fucus* has been studied satisfactorily in material shipped from the coast to the Mississippi River.

For habit work, material can be put into formalin—about 10 c.c. of formalin to 90 c.c. of sea water—and kept there indefinitely. Material should be washed well in water before handing it to a class, because formalin is irritating to the eyes and nose, and even to the hands. Material, which is not used, can be put back into the preservative.

Large forms, like *Nereocystis*, can be soaked in the formalin mixture for a week, and then the preservative may be poured off and the material can be rolled up, as directed for the living material, and shipped to

240

its destination, where it should be put into the formalin mixture. This method reduces the cost of transportation.

These large forms, after a week in the fixing agent, may be rinsed in water and then soaked in equal parts of glycerin and water, using just enough glycerin to make the plants flexible, not enough to make them wet to handle. In this way, material of *Laminaria*, *Nereocystis*, *Macrocystis*, *Postelsia*, and other coarse forms have been kept for years. When not in use, they should be kept stored in a box.

For habit demonstrations many of the smaller forms can be floated out and dried on paper. *Ectocarpus*, *Desmotrichum*, *Dictyota*, *Cutleria*, and even small specimens of *Laminaria*, *Nereocystis*, and *Macrocystis* are quite useful when prepared in this way. Take a light pine board, a little larger than the standard herbarium sheet, float it in a tub of water, place on the board the paper upon which the material is to be mounted, arrange the material with a toothpick or the blunt end of a needle, dipping all or a part of the board under water whenever necessary. Cover with a piece of cheese-cloth, add a blotter or two, as in case of flowering plants, and dry under gentle pressure, changing the blotters frequently. The algae have enough mucilage to make them adhere to the paper. Coarse forms like *Fucus* and *Ascophyllum* will have to be fastened to the herbarium sheet with gummed paper.

For material to be mounted by the Venetian turpentine method, 10 per cent formalin in sea water is a good fixing agent. There should not be any acetic acid in the reagent, unless you desire to dissolve away the mucilaginous coating which all these algae have, if they feel slippery. Wash in sea water 24 hours, then in equal parts sea water and fresh water for 1 hour, and then for 1 hour in fresh water.

If material is to be mounted whole, it is usually stained at this point and put into Venetian turpentine. A longer method, while tedious, gives so much better results, especially with delicate forms, that it is worth the extra labor. Run the material up through the series of alcohols to 85 per cent, as recommended under the Venetian turpentine method. Leave it in 85 per cent for 2 days to harden; then run it back slowly to water. Stain and put it into 10 per cent glycerin and follow the usual Venetian turpentine method. If phloxine and anilin blue are to be used, the material can be run up to 85 per cent alcohol, then stained in the usual way. Or, after washing in water, the regular Venetian turpentine method can be followed.

Sphacelaria.—The apical cell of *Sphacelaria* or the nearly related

Stypocaulon affords an excellent study of the structure of cytoplasm. The Chicago formula, on page 28, is good for fixing this or any of the small members of the brown algae. The centrosomes and radiations stain particularly well with Haidenhain's haematoxylin or with the safranin, gentian violet, orange combination. For these immense apical cells, it is a good plan, when the material gets into xylol, to break off pieces 6–12 mm. long, which will lie flat in the paraffin. If you try to

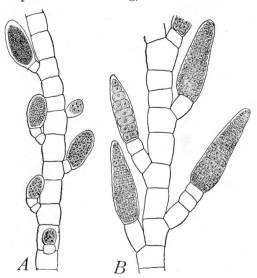

cut a whole tuft, most of the cells will be cut so obliquely that they will be worthless.

Ectocarpus.—During most of the year, *Ectocarpus* will have only gametangia: the sporangia are at their best in December and January. For a short time, during the cold season, the plant bears both sporangia and gametangia. A 10 per cent solution of formalin in sea water is a good fixing agent for all stages, if material is to be mounted whole (Fig. 59). Stain some in iron-alum haematoxylin, and some in phloxine and anilin blue; then mount from both lots under each cover.

Fig. 59.—*Ectocarpus: A*, sporangia of various ages; *B*, gametangia, three of them nearly mature. Fixed in 10 per cent formalin and stained in iron-alum haematoxylin. ×280.

The Chicago formula is better for paraffin sections.

Desmotrichum.—Forms as large as *Desmotrichum* can be handled like *Ectocarpus*, but care must be taken not to overstain.

Laminaria.—In such large forms, small portions showing the structure and development of the thallus and also the reproduction should be cut out with a razor and then placed in the fixing agent. The sporangia of *Laminaria* stain very deeply and quickly. Iron-haematoxylin is good, but be careful not to overstain. After this stain is just right, about 3–5 minutes in alcoholic safranin will stain the mucilaginous structures and add to the value of the preparation.

Zoöspores from sporangia begin to germinate within 24 hours, forming dioecious, filamentous gametophytes bearing oögonia and antheridia. The fertilized egg at once begins to develop into the *Laminaria* plant. If you succeed in getting gametophytes, fix in 10 per cent formalin and follow the Venetian turpentine method.

Nereocystis.—This immense kelp, often more than a hundred feet long, is abundant along our northern Pacific Coast. July and August are good months for sporangia. The immense sori, often more than 30 cm. long, contain millions of sporangia, and sori of various ages are found on a single leaf. The Chicago formula is good for sections of sporangia. Lay one leaf upon another for a support and cut the sori into pieces about 5 mm. square. Sporangia at the shedding stage will be found just as the big sori are dropping out from the leaf. The reduction of chromosomes will take place in sori nearer the tip of the leaf. The Chicago formula, with the iron-alum haematoxylin stain, followed by a minute in safranin to touch up the mucilaginous caps, makes a good mount.

Nereocystis has dioecious, filamentous gametophytes, like *Laminaria*. The zoöspores from sori which are just falling out from the leaves germinate promptly; but antheridia and oögonia appear 10 or 11 weeks later. The young sporophytes, developing from fertilized eggs, continue to be formed for at least a year.

If you should start a culture, sterilize the sea water, take a sorus just as it is dropping out from the leaf, wash it thoroughly to get off as much as possible of the diatoms, bacteria, and other things, and don't put too much of the sorus into the jar; two or three pieces, a centimeter square, is enough. You can save two or three unsuccessful seasons by reading carefully a paper by Dr. Lena A. Hartge, who succeeded in keeping cultures growing for more than a year (*Nereocystis*, Publications of the Puget Sound Biological Station, **5**:207–237, 1928). A paper in the same journal on "Gametophytes of *Costaria costata*," by Miss Laura Angst, was published a year earlier. The gametophytes of *Costaria* mature in half the time required by *Nereocystis;* consequently, the chances for securing gametophytes are more favorable.

Follow the directions given for *Nereocystis.*

Cutleria.—This alga deserves a place in any course in morphology, if the course is thorough enough to permit the study of three members of the Phaeophyceae. These three should be *Ectocarpus* (or *Pylaiella*), *Cutleria,* and *Fucus. Cutleria* is not found on the American coasts, but is abundant at Naples. The habits of gametophyte (known as *Cutleria*) and the sporophyte (known as *Aglaozonia*) are so different that they furnish a good illustration of alternation of generations. Beginners understand such an illustration more readily than they do an illustration like *Dictyota*, with its two generations looking so nearly alike. *Cutleria*, with its large, motile eggs, furnishes a good stage in the evolution of sex, about midway between isogamy and the extreme heterogamy of *Fucus* (Fig. 60).

For habit study, both generations should be mounted upon paper. The gametophyte (*Cutleria*) sticks well, but the sporophyte (*Aglaozonia*) will need some glue or gummed paper.

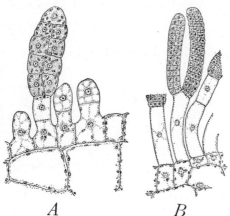

For paraffin sections, use the Chicago formula and cut 10 μ thick. For mitotic figures, cut 2 or 3 μ thick and stain in iron-alum haematoxylin. This stain will also differentiate the cilia-producing organ, which is a modified portion of a plastid.

Fucus.—Material for habit study may be dried, or preserved in formalin, or mounted on paper. In the latter case, glue or gummed

FIG. 60.—*Cutleria multifida: A*, oögonia; *B*, antheridia. Fixed in Flemming's weaker solution, cut 3 μ, and stained in iron-alum haematoxylin. ×470.

paper will be necessary. Most satisfactory of all is to send to Woods Hole, Massachusetts (George M. Gray), for living material. Fertilization occurs at all seasons, but autumn is the most favorable. In summer the material dies before it reaches Chicago, but during the rest of the year a pailful will reach Chicago, and even as far west as the Mississippi River, in good condition for showing the rotation of the egg by the sperms. The eggs and sperms form slimy masses, the antheridia being orange red and that containing the eggs, a dirty green. Mix a drop of the red with a drop of the green. The movements of the egg can be observed, and material for a study of fertilization and later stages is easily secured. In fixing fertilization and preceding stages, Flemming's weaker solution is good.

For the growing points and conceptacles, small pieces should be cut off with a razor. If the fruiting tips be cut through lengthwise before they are cut off, the fixing will be more satisfactory. For sections of the conceptacles it is better not to cut across the whole tip, but to cut off pieces of the rind containing half-a-dozen conceptacles. Such pieces are more easily imbedded and cut. There is no difficulty in cutting such pieces in paraffin. Iron-haematoxylin is a good stain. Safranin and gentian violet are also satisfactory, but care must be taken not to over-stain since *Fucus* usually stains deeply and rapidly.

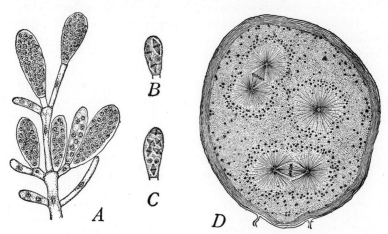

Fig. 61.—*Fucus vesiculosus: A*, antheridial branch with antheridia in various stages of development; *B*, the third mitosis in the antheridium, one figure showing a transverse view in which the chromosomes can be counted; *C*, the fourth mitosis, with two of the eight figures cut transversely but hard to count chromosomes in the figure, which is reduced one-half; *D*, the third mitosis in the oögonium, showing centrosomes and radiations. Fixed in Flemming's weaker solution, cut 3 μ, stained in iron-alum haematoxylin. ×480.

For the cytologist, *Fucus* might be used as a test object for testing proficiency in technique, just as *Pleurosigma angulatum* is used in testing an objective. The nuclear divisions in the antheridium are simultaneous, and at the sixth division, which is the last, there are 32 mitotic figures, each with 32 chromosomes which split so that 32 go to each pole. When you can make a preparation in which these chromosomes can be counted, your technique is adequate for research work in cytology. In a good preparation, the mitotic figures in the oögonium show small but brilliant centrosomes, with a great display of radiations (Fig. 61).

For your test, don't try to stain a 5 μ section; cut at 2 μ, and if you have a good sliding microtome, try 1 μ. Good ribbons of root-tips have been cut at 0.5 μ, in 52° C. paraffin, without icing. The room temperature was −2° C.

Dictyota.—*Dictyota* deserves a place in the series illustrating the evolution of sex, since its large egg has lost all motility, but the difference in size of egg and sperm is not so extreme as in *Fucus*. It also furnishes an excellent example of the development of a thallus from an apical cell.

Mount habit material on paper. For sections, fix in chromo-acetic acid. For figures, cut 3 to 5 μ, but for general views of apical cell and reproductive phases, cut 10 μ. Stain in iron-haematoxylin and counterstain for 2 or 3 minutes in safranin.

CHAPTER XIX

RHODOPHYCEAE. RED ALGAE

The red algae belong almost exclusively to salt water, but a few genera are found only in fresh water, usually in running water, and a few forms occur both in salt and in fresh water. Nearly all are small forms, and for habit work can be floated out and mounted on paper. A few, like *Chondrus crispus*, will need glue or gummed paper. When the floating out is carefully done, the small, filamentous forms, commonly called sea mosses, make beautiful place cards and decorations for letterheads, as well as serviceable herbarium specimens. The first day, the blotters should be changed three times; twice, the second day; and once a day thereafter until the specimens are perfectly dry. This may seem unnecessarily laborious, but specimens prepared in this way keep indefinitely all the brilliancy of their natural colors.

For more critical habit work and for Venetian turpentine mounts, fix in 6–10 per cent formalin in sea water. Just a trace of acetic acid will improve it, and the stock of material for future use will keep better. For the red algae, keep a 1 per cent solution of acetic acid (1 c.c. glacial acetic acid in 100 c.c. sea water). To the 10 per cent formalin add 5 c.c. of this weak acetic acid to 100 c.c. of the formalin solution.

For nuclear detail, material must be imbedded in paraffin. Chromoacetic–osmic is the best fixing agent. The following is a good formula to begin with and is not likely to need much modification:

Chromic acid	0.7	c.c.
Glacial acetic acid	3	c.c.
Osmic acid	7	c.c.
Water	90	c.c.

Always add the osmic acid just before fixing.

In this solution, many of the delicate red algae fix with amazing rapidity. For *Ceramium rubrum*, 1–2 seconds is enough. Even if the material does not break up in the fixing agent, if fixed too long, it will go to pieces in the 50 or 70 per cent alcohol. For *Polysiphonia*, 5–40 seconds is about right. If the time is too prolonged, the material is likely to break up in the fixing agent. For many forms of similar con-

247

sistency, the time must be measured in seconds, rather than in minutes or hours.

For many others, the times are longer. For *Plocamium*, 6–8 hours; *Nitophyllum* and *Rhodymenia*, 8–10 hours; *Gelidium*, overnight; *Bangia* and *Porphyra*, 24 hours; *Nemalion*, 24 hours or longer.

After washing 24 hours in sea water, an hour in equal parts sea water and fresh water, and an hour in fresh water, follow the close series of alcohols described in the chapter on the paraffin method. For filamentous forms, use Petri dishes for the alcohol and xylol series and keep the forms as straight as possible. After 24 hours in 85 per cent alcohol, test the material to determine whether it is sufficiently hardened. With forceps, take the base of a plant like *Polysiphonia* and move it gently back and forth in the direction of the long axis. If it keeps its shape, it is ready to go on: if the branches bend back toward the forceps, keep it in the 85 per cent alcohol until there is no bending. This is also a test for any other filamentous algae or fungi.

Thirty minutes in the bath should be long enough for any of the brown or red algae, whether coarse or filamentous. It takes about 30 minutes to make 4 changes of paraffin, and so the time cannot be shortened much for delicate forms, and it is sufficient for coarse forms like *Gigartina*.

Batrachospermum.—This is a green, fresh-water member of the red algae. It is not very uncommon in small streams. Fix in the formalin solution or in the chromic solution recommended above. It can be left indefinitely in the formalin solution. In the chromic solution, it should fix overnight, or 24 hours. Iron-alum haematoxylin seems to be the best stain, both for material mounted whole and for sections. In mounting whole, tease out small portions and still further dissociate the filaments by tapping smartly on the cover.

Nemalion.—Fix in the formalin solution recommended above. In a 10 per cent formalin solution, *Nemalion* has kept its color for 15 years. In the chromic solutions, fix for 24 hours. *Nemalion* does not break up like so many delicate red algae. For studying fertilization, Wolfe used the following method:

Young tips were crushed in water under a cover glass and on a slide that had previously been treated with fixative; the cover was then removed, and the water on the slide allowed to evaporate. The gelatinous nature of the wall prevents the contents of the cell from being affected by this treatment, even when the albumen has hardened sufficiently to hold the filaments firmly in place.

Stain in safranin and gentian violet, and mount in balsam.

Material killed in 2 per cent formalin in sea water and gradually transferred to glycerin keeps its color.

For material to be mounted whole, we should recommend fixing in 10 per cent formalin and staining in iron-alum haematoxylin. Place the material in 10 per cent glycerin until all the water is out. Mount in glycerin jelly. To make a mount, take a small piece of the material, not more than 3 or 4 mm. long, touch it to filter paper to remove as

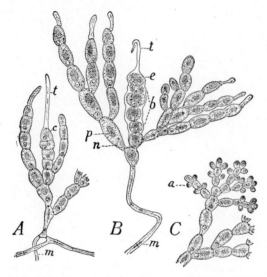

Fig. 62.—*Nemalion multifidum:* A, branch showing carpogonium, *c*; trichogyne, *t*; central strand, *m*. B, somewhat older stage showing two-cell stage immediately following fertilization, *e*; carpogonial branch, *b*. C, branch with antheridia, *a*. Fixed in 10 per cent formalin and stained in iron-alum haematoxylin. ×400.

much of the glycerin as possible, put it into the melted glycerin jelly, add a round cover, and crush by tapping on the cover. The antheridia and procarps are in the slender filaments, and the cystocarps are in the larger filaments. If several slides are to be made, it is a good plan to select slender, medium, and thicker filaments, remove the surface glycerin with filter paper, and then crush the filaments between two slides. There is scarcely any danger of crushing too much. A little of the crushed material, including the various stages, can be put into the melted glycerin jelly. Add a round cover, tap gently until the jelly comes just exactly to the edge of the cover. As soon as the jelly is cool, the mount may be sealed with balsam, but we prefer to leave the mounts for a day or two before sealing. Such mounts would probably keep for a year or two without sealing (Fig. 62).

We have mounted *Nemalion* in Venetian turpentine; but by this method the material becomes hard and behaves like cartilage, so that it cannot be crushed under a cover. However, it can be crushed on a piece of glass with a scalpel.

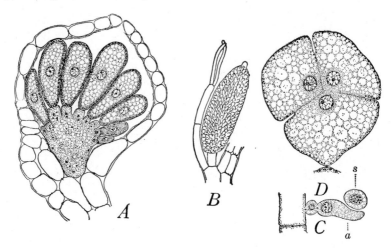

Fig. 63.—*Polysiphonia fibrillosa: A*, nearly mature cystocarp, showing the large cell formed by the fusion of several auxiliary cells with the pericentral cell—the carpospores are large and elongated; *B*, an antheridium—the term "antheridium" is more correctly applied to the structure shown in *C*, *a*, which cuts off one or more sperms, *s*; *D*, young tetraspores. Fixed in Flemming's weaker solution, cut 3 μ, and stained in iron-alum haematoxylin. *A* and *B* ×240; *C* and *D* ×780.

Nemalion, stained in eosin, makes beautiful mounts, but they always fade.

Polysiphonia.—This is a very difficult form to handle, but Dr. Yamanouchi has developed an adequate method, and, by following it, anyone should be able to get good preparations.

For mounting in glycerin, glycerin jelly, or in Venetian turpentine, fix in 10 per cent formalin and stain in iron-haematoxylin.

For sections, fix in Flemming's weaker solution, but omit the osmic acid for spermatogenesis and germination of carpospores. The time should be *very short, 5–40 seconds* being sufficient. If material is left too long, it goes to pieces. The chromo-acetic–osmic solution, mentioned at the beginning of this chapter, may be used.

Wash in a gentle stream of sea water for 24 hours. Stain in iron-haematoxylin, and then for 2–3 minutes in safranin (Fig. 63). This short stain in safranin gives a faint rosy tinge to mucilaginous structures, but does not obscure the fine nuclear detail. In the nucleus of the sperm, the chromosomes remain distinct, so that the number, 20, can be counted from the time the sperm is formed (Fig. 63 C) up to fertilization.

With very delicate forms, like *Callithamnion* and *Griffithsia*, the washing may be in part or even wholly omitted, and the chromic acid extracted by the lower alcohols, the material being kept in the dark.

Corallina.—*Corallina* and other forms whose surface is incrusted with lime need special treatment. The following solution is good:

Chromic acid..............................	1 g.
Glacial acetic acid..........................	1 c.c.
Sea water..................................	100 c.c.

Fix 24 hours, changing the fixing agent 2 or 3 times. Wash 24 hours in sea water.

If carefully applied, the following is a good method: Put the material into 5 per cent glacial acetic acid (in sea water) and watch it. As soon as the vigorous effervescence begins to subside, rinse in sea water and transfer to Flemming's weaker solution, and fix 24 hours. Iron-haematoxylin is best for figures, but for general structure the safranin, gentian violet, orange combination gives beautiful results.

CHAPTER XX

FUNGI

Our principal object is to describe methods of making preparations for a study of the morphology and cytology of the fungi. The whole subject of culture media, especially for those which cause disease, has become so specialized that only the trained pathologist could be expected to know just what is the best medium for each particular fungus.

We shall not attempt to deal with the subject of culture media, but shall simply indicate how a student, not trained in pathology, may secure material for preparations. Professor Kleb's methods make it possible to secure material of many forms in various phases of their life-histories.

In general, filamentous fungi are treated like the filamentous algae, while the fleshy forms are cut in paraffin.

PHYCOMYCETES

Rhizopus (Mucor).—This familiar mold appears with great regularity on bread. The following is a sure and rapid method for obtaining *Rhizopus:* Place a glass tumbler in a plate of water, put on the tumbler a slice of bread which has been exposed to the air for a day, and cover with a glass jar. The bread must not become too wet.

To obtain a series of stages in the development of the sporangium it is better to use living material. For class work, time the cultures so as to have plenty of sporangia which have not yet begun to turn brown.

For permanent preparations, fix for 2 or 3 days in formalin acetic acid—10 c.c. formalin, 5 c.c. glacial acetic acid, and 85 c.c. water—wash 24 hours in water, and follow the Venetian turpentine method. Stain in aqueous eosin 24 or even 48 hours, treat with 2 per cent acetic acid, changing several times, and then put into glycerin, merely pouring off the 2 per cent acetic acid and not rinsing the acid out in water. When washing out the glycerin, do it with alcohol which has about 0.5 c.c. of acetic to the 100 c.c. of alcohol, and leave about 1 c.c. of this slightly acid absolute alcohol on the material when you add the 10 per cent Venetian turpentine.

The Chicago formula is a good chromo-acetic–osmic solution for *Rhizopus*, especially if iron-alum haematoxylin is to be used for material to mounted whole or for sections; but for material to be mounted whole, the osmic acid should be reduced to 2 or 3 c.c. to 100 c.c. of the solution, because material is hard to bleach. A thin section is easier to bleach. Wash for 24 hours and follow the Venetian turpentine method.

To bring out the nuclei, use iron-alum haematoxylin. *Rhizopus* stains very rapidly, so that an hour in iron-alum and an hour in the haematoxylin may be long enough; it may be necessary to stain longer. The time should be such that it will require about an hour for differentiation in the second iron-alum. The sporangia stain more readily than the mycelium; consequently to show the coenocytic character of the mycelium, the action of the second iron-alum must be stopped earlier than when staining for the sporangium. Extract the stain until the nuclei of the mycelium show clearly, and then remove part of the material to wash in water. For the rest of the material, continue to extract the stain until the sporangia are satisfactory. Mount some of each lot on each slide.

The finer details of the sporangium can be seen only in thin sections. *Rhizopus* is the most easily obtained material for showing the progressive cleavage of protoplasm by vacuoles.

The zygosporic stage in the life-history is rarely met in nature or in cultures, but when once secured it may be propagated indefinitely. We had a culture which furnished illustrative material for twenty years. When a particularly good culture appears, lay aside some of it to start the next culture.

Dr. Blakeslee has shown why zygospores are so infrequent. The conjugating filaments belong to different strains of mycelia which he calls "plus and minus strains," and which, for convenience, may be called "female and male strains." The more vigorous mycelium is + and the less vigorous −. When the two strains come together, zygospores are formed along the line of meeting. If + and − strains are started at opposite sides of a dish, they will meet near the middle and form a dark line of zygospores. Through Dr. Blakeslee's generous distribution of material, the + and − strains are now available in practically all of the great universities of the world.

While *Rhizopus* may be grown on bread, it is better to use culture media in Petri dishes. While it grows well on agar media, it is hard to pick it off; and on liquid media, the growth is abnormal. Dr. Alice

A. Bailey has devised a method which is ideal for securing material. She puts about the usual amount of a potato dextrose agar in a Petri dish and pours over it a potato decoction about 2 mm. deep. The + and − strains are then added. The potato decoction is made as follows: Use 300 g. of Irish potatoes and 1,000 c.c. distilled water. Peel and slice the potatoes and boil for 1 hour in the distilled water. Strain off the liquid through cheesecloth and make up to the original quantity by adding distilled water. Flask and sterilize.

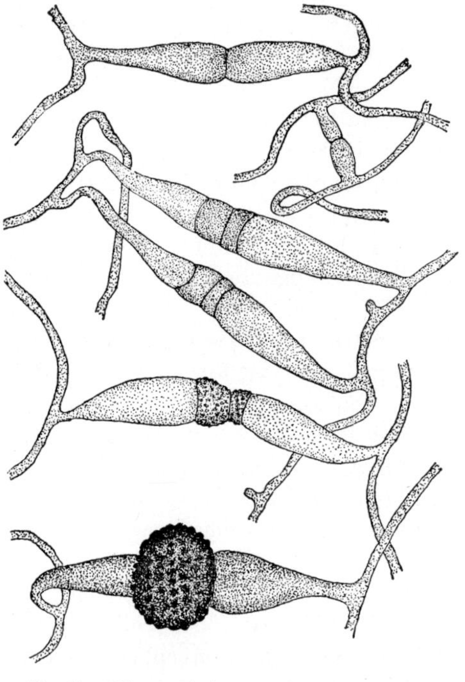

The potato dextrose agar is made as follows: to 1,000 c.c. of potato decoction, add 20 g. of dextrose and 30 g. of agar. Boil $\frac{1}{2}$ hour in a double boiler. Strain, flask, and sterilize.

The potato dextrose agar is an excellent medium, and the thin layer of potato decoction keeps the material from sticking to the agar so that it can be lifted off intact. Rinse it under the tap and fix in the chromo-acetic-osmic solution.

Zygospores may begin to form within 3 days, and mature zygospores may appear within 4 or 5 days, usually at a lower

FIG. 64.—*Rhizopus nigricans:* various stages in the development of zygospores from a culture on bread; preparation stained in eosin and mounted in Venetian turpentine. ×80.

level than the sporangia. Watch the cultures and fix so as to secure a series of stages (Fig. 64).

Paraffin sections should not be thicker than 3 μ, and 2 or even 1 μ is better for nuclear detail. Iron-alum haematoxylin is best for nuclear detail, but safranin, gentian violet, orange will give beautiful preparations.

In the related genus, *Sporodinia*, which is rather common in sum-

mer on fleshy fungi, especially upon *Boletus* and its allies, the zygosporic condition is not infrequent, because *Sporodinia* does not have +
and − strains. *Rhizopus* behaves like a dioecious plant, while *Sporodinia* behaves like a monoecious one. The very damp atmosphere and
the nutrition necessary for the formation of zygospores may be provided in the laboratory in the following way: Put a little water in a
glass battery jar and place filter paper around the inside of the jar so
that it will take up water and thus keep the sides of the jar moist.
Place a small beaker or dish, without any water in it, in the bottom of
the jar, and in the beaker place a small piece of bread dampened with
the juice of prunes. Infect the bread with spores, or use a piece of
bread upon which mycelium is already growing. Sections of the root of
Daucus carota may be used instead of the bread. Put a piece of wet
filter paper on a pane of glass and cover the jar. Begin to examine
after 24 hours. The zygospores may appear in 4 or 5 days. A very full
account of the methods by which the various phases of the life-history
of *Sporodinia* may be produced at will is given by Klebs in the *Jahr-
bücher für wissenschaftliche Botanik*, **32**: 1–69, 1898.

Phycomyces nitens.—This is a relative of *Rhizopus*, with a zygosporic stage characterized by horny processes, which make it easily
recognizable.

Zygorhynchus is another interesting relative of *Rhizopus*, readily
distinguished by having suspensors of very unequal size. Dr. Florence
A. McCormick sent us magnificent zygosporic material, raised on beef
broth and fixed in 10 per cent formalin in water.

No one has been able to germinate the zygotes of any of the above-
mentioned genera.

Saprolegnia.—This is an aquatic mold, very common upon insects
and algae. Cultures are easily and quickly made. Bring in a quart of
water from any stagnant pond or ditch, and into the water throw a
few flies. After 12–24 hours throw the water away, rinse the flies in
clean water, and put them into tap water. The water must be changed
every day to keep bacteria from ruining the culture.

Ants, or the larvae of ants, are often as good as flies. Small pieces of
boiled white of egg are excellent, especially if material is to be imbedded in paraffin. About 1 mm. cubes are large enough, and not
more than 20 cubes should be put into 500 c.c. of water.

Sporangia may appear within 24 hours but may be a day later. Sporangia may be produced in the greatest abundance by cultivating the

mycelium for several days and then transferring it to pure water or to distilled water. As long as the nutrient solution is sufficiently strong and fresh, only sterile mycelium will be produced.

To secure oösporic material, mycelium which has been highly nourished for several days in a nutrient solution is brought into a 0.1 per cent solution of leucin, or into a 0.05–0.1 per cent solution of haemoglobin. Begin to examine after 24 hours.

Oögonia have been produced in great numbers by the following method: cut ordinary corn (*Zea mais*) into small pieces and boil for 20 minutes. When cool, put pieces into a Petri dish and add enough pond water to nearly cover the pieces of corn. Oögonia may appear within 3 or 4 days.

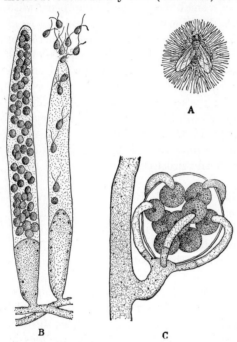

For fixing, the following formula is excellent for material which is to be mounted whole:

Formalin.......... 10 c.c.
Glacial acetic acid... 5 c.c.
Water............. 85 c.c.

Fix at least 24 hours, but material may be left for months in this fixing agent.

Stain some in phloxine and anilin blue, and some in iron-alum haematoxylin. Mount some of each lot on each slide (Fig. 65).

For sections, it is better to fix in the Chicago chromo-acetic–osmic acid solution.

FIG. 65.—*Saprolegnia*: *A*, a fly with three days' growth of *Saprolegnia*, natural size. *B*, two sporangia, the one on the left with nearly mature zoöspores and the one on the right with mature zoöspores escaping. *C*, an oögonium with 9 eggs; 5 antheridia are shown. *B*, *C*, and *D* ×300. From Chamberlain's *Elements of Plant Science* (McGraw-Hill Book Co., New York).

Satisfactory material for general laboratory purposes can be secured as just described. Absolutely pure cultures can be secured only by observing all the precautions necessary in bacteriological work.

Achlya is similar and equally good for illustrative purposes. It is found on insects, fishes, dead fish eggs, and on algae. The zoöspores escape in a mass, which, for a short time, is held together by a transparent pellicle; in *Saprolegnia* the zoöspores swarm separately. In *Saprolegnia*, the new sporangia grow up through the empty ones; in *Achlya*, the later sporangia arise on lateral branches below the earlier ones. *Dictyuchus* and *Olpidium* often appear when one is trying to get

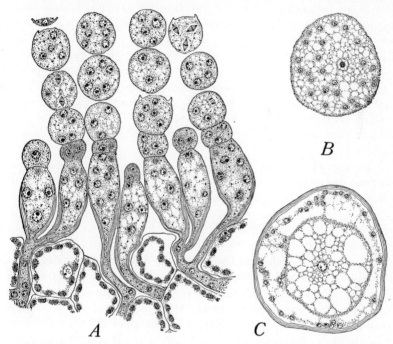

B

A   *C*

Fig. 66.—*Albugo candida: A*, small portion of a section of a blister showing coenocytic mycelium, conidiophores, and multinucleate conidia. *B*, a young oögonium with large coenocentrum and many nuclei. *C*, later stage, after differentiation into a central oöplasm, surrounded by the multinucleate periplasm; all of the nuclei of the oöplasm, except one, have disorganized. Fixed in the special chromo-acetic acid solution and stained in iron-alum haematoxylin and orange. ×780.

Saprolegnia or *Achlya*. The fixing and staining described for *Saprolegnia* will give good results with the other genera.

Albugo.—This fungus is quite common on Cruciferae, where the white "blisters" or "white rust," *Albugo candida*, form quite conspicuous patches. Affected portions of leaves and stems should be fixed in chromo-acetic acid and cut in paraffin. Sections 5 μ or less in thickness will be found most satisfactory. Stain in iron-alum and counter-stain lightly with orange (Fig. 66).

The white blisters cause little distortion, but are easily recognized by their color; the oögonia do not cause any change in color, but they cause great distortion in the pods or stems, so that these organs may reach several times their normal size. Parts only slightly distorted should be selected, as well as the extreme cases; otherwise, you will secure only old fertilized eggs, with very few of the younger stages. The stages between B and C of Figure 62 often have numerous mitotic figures, and the divisions are simultaneous. Sections at 3 μ, or less, are better for these figures. The oösporic phase of *Albugo bliti* is easily recognized on *Amaranthus*, especially on *A. retroflexus*, where the oöspores may be seen with the naked eye by holding the leaf up to the light. The oöspores usually occur in more or less circular patches upon the leaf. When they occur among the floral structures, there is often a slight reddish coloration. Unfortunately for the collector, it is very seldom that any red coloration in *Amaranthus* is due to the desired material.

The oösporic stage of *Albugo ipomeae*, on the morning-glory, causes extreme distortion of the stem. For sections, it is well to cut out small pieces of the cortex, rather than to fix larger pieces of the stem.

HEMIASCOMYCETES

Saccharomyces.—Formerly it was considered rather difficult to demonstrate the nucleus of the yeast cell. With fresh-growing yeast the following method by Wager made the classical demonstration. Fix in a saturated aqueous solution of corrosive sublimate for at least 12 hours. Wash successively in water, 30 per cent alcohol, 70 per cent alcohol, and methyl alcohol. Place a few drops of alcohol containing the cells on a cover, and when nearly dry add a drop of water. After the yeast cells settle, drain off the water and allow the cells to dry up completely. Place the cover, or slide, with its layer of cells in water for a few seconds, and then stain with a mixture of fuchsin and methyl green, or fuchsin and methyline blue. Mount in glycerin or in balsam.

With modern methods, there should be no more difficulty than in demonstrating the nucleus in the Cyanophyceae or in the mycelium of the Phycomycetes. Use an abundance of vigorously budding material, so that you can afford to lose most of it and still have a plenty left: fix in the Chicago chromo-acetic–osmic acid solution and stain in iron-alum haematoxylin. Use the Venetian turpentine method, or imbed in paraffin and cut sections at 2 or 3 μ.

To obtain the spore stage, put a cake of good yeast, free from bacteria, into equal parts of grape juice and distilled water; add 1 g. of peptone and allow to bud freely overnight at 30° C.; place the material

in a plaster-of-Paris cup with a depression, and put the cup in a small Stender dish with water coming nearly to the top of the cup. In 60–70 hours there should be abundant spore formation.

A

ASCOMYCETES

This group, popularly known as the "sac fungi," contains an immense number of saprophytic and parasitic forms. The green mold on cheese and leather, the leaf curl of peach, the black knot of cherry and plum, and the powdery mildews are familiar to everyone. The few objects selected will enable the student to experiment, but he must not be discouraged if success does not crown the first attempt, for some members of the group present real difficulties.

Peziza.—The Pezizas and related forms are fleshy and present but little difficulty in fixing, cutting, or staining. They are abundant in moist places, on decaying wood, or on the ground.

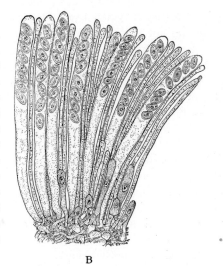

B

Fig. 67.—*Peziza: A*, several specimens growing on rotten wood, natural size. *B*, several mature asci, each with 8 ascospores; some young asci near the base; and some long slender paraphyses. Teased and mounted whole. ×230. From Chamberlain's *Elements of Plant Science* (McGraw-Hill Book Co., New York).

The apothecia have the form of little cups, which are sometimes black and sometimes flesh-colored, but often orange, red, or green.

For general morphological work it is better to tease out fresh or preserved material. The best views for the beginner are obtained in this way (Fig. 67).

For the free nuclear division in the ascus, the Chicago chromo-acetic–osmic formula is excellent. Fix for 24 hours and stain in safranin, gentian violet, orange. The centrosomes show up well and the radiations should have a clear, sharp violet color against an orange background. Sections should not be more than 5 μ thick; 2 μ and even 1 μ sections are worth while, if well cut. Remember that a ribbon which doubles in length when warmed in water is not well cut. When sections lengthen more than 20 per cent, either cut thicker or cool, with ice if necessary, until the stretching of the ribbon is down to 20 per cent or less. With a room temperature of $-2°$ C., 52° Grubler paraffin, a Spencer Student's Sliding Microtome, and a specially hardened Watts safety razor blade, a ribbon of *Peziza* should be cut so smoothly at 1 μ that it will not stretch more than 15 per cent; at 5 μ, there should not be more than 10 per cent of stretching when the ribbon is floated on water and warmed; at 10 μ, there should be practically no stretching.

Iron-alum haematoxylin is better for the centrosomes and for the young "hook" stages in the formation of the ascus, but not so good for the radiations.

Morchella esculenta is very good for the development of the ascus because the nuclei are very large.

For showing the ascogonium, ascogenous hyphae, and the origin of the asci, nothing is better than *Pyronema*. Fix in formalin acetic acid (10 c.c. formalin, 5 c.c. acetic acid, and 85 c.c. water) for 24 hours or more; wash in water and stain in eosin. Or, fix in the Chicago chromo-acetic–osmic solution and stain in iron-alum haematoxylin. In either case, use the Venetian turpentine method and tease the material so as to obtain instructive views.

Eurotium.—*Eurotium* with its conidial stage, *Aspergillus*, is a very common mold found on bread, cheese, decayed and preserved fruit, etc. In the conidial stage it is green and in the ascosporic stage, yellow, reddish yellow, or reddish brown. *Aspergillus* is almost sure to appear upon bread which is kept moderately moist, because the conidia are usually abundant in the atmosphere. If the bread be wet with a 10 per cent solution of cane-sugar or with grape juice, this stage appears sooner and in greater abundance. A temperature of 22° to 30° C. is also a favorable condition.

The perithecial stage is not found so frequently, but can sometimes be secured by examining moldy preserves. The sexual stage has been induced. Soak a piece of bread in a 20 per cent solution of grape-sugar in grape juice; upon this sow the spores and keep at a temperature of

about 28° C. After 4 or 5 days, begin to examine. A 40 per cent solution of cane-sugar in the juice of prunes is also a good nutrient solution.
If you find the perithecial stage, keep the culture going in a test-tube;
and it would be wise to pickle a lot, lest something might happen to the
culture and you might not find the rare stage again.

For class use or for permanent preparations it is best to select
rather young material which shows various stages in development,
from the swollen end of the hypha to the ripe spore (Fig. 68). Permanent preparations of the conidial stage, as shown in Figure 68, and
also of the coiled twisted filaments which initiate the ascosporic stage,
should be made by the Venetian turpentine method or by the glycerin
method.

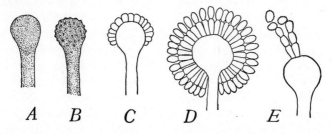

FIG. 68.—*Aspergillus:* from material growing on a hectograph pad; fixed in chromo-acetic acid,
stained in eosin, and mounted in glycerin; *A–E*, successive stages in development. ×375. All such
material is more satisfactory when mounted in Venetian turpentine.

Fix in 1 per cent chromo-acetic acid (1 g. chromic acid, 1 c.c. acetic
acid, and 100 c.c. water) for 24 hours; wash in water 24 hours, stain
sharply in eosin, transfer to 10 per cent glycerin, and follow the Venetian turpentine method.

Material may be fixed in corrosive sublimate–acetic acid (corrosive
sublimate 2 g., glacial acetic acid 2 c.c., and water 100 c.c.). Use it hot
(85° C.). One minute is long enough. Wash in water and add, a few
drops at a time, the iodine solution used in testing for starch. At first,
the brownish color caused by the iodine will disappear, but after a certain amount has been added the brownish color will remain. Stain in
eosin or iron-haematoxylin and follow the Venetian turpentine method.

A very rapid method for this and for similar small filamentous forms
may be added. Forms as large as *Thamnidium elegans* can be mounted
successfully by the following method.

1. One hundred per cent alcohol, 2 minutes.
2. Eosin (aqueous), 2 minutes.
3. One per cent acetic acid, 2–10 seconds.
4. Mount directly in 50 per cent glycerin and seal.

If the material gets through the first three stages without shrinking but collapses at the fourth, put it into 10 per cent glycerin and allow it to thicken, following the Venetian turpentine method.

The earlier perithecial stages are more instructive when mounted whole; but later stages, even before the formation of the asci, are very unsatisfactory by this method, and should be cut in paraffin.

Penicillium.—This green mold is found everywhere upon decaying fruit, upon bread, and upon almost any decaying organic substance. Material is even more easily secured than in case of *Aspergillus*, and *Penicillium* is an easier type for laboratory study. Such a satisfactory study can be made from the living material that it is hardly worth while to fix and stain. The very rapid method described for *Aspergillus* will furnish good mounts if permanent preparations are desired.

The Erysipheae.—The mildews are found throughout the summer and autumn on the leaves of various plants. Some of the most abundant forms are *Microsphaera alni* on the common lilac; *Sphaerotheca castagnei* on *Bidens frondosa* and other species, on *Erechtites hieracifolia*, and on *Taraxacum officinale; Uncinula necatar* on *Ampelopsis quinquefolia*, and *U. salicis* on *Salix* and *Populus; Erysiphe commune* on *Polygonum aviculare;* and *Erysiphe cichoriacearum* on numerous Compositae and Verbenaceae. *Podosphaera* may be found on the leaves of young cherry trees and apple trees, and on young shoots of older trees. The infected leaves are likely to be more or less deformed. *Phyllactinia* is sometimes abundant on leaves of *Alnus incana*. It is also found on *Celastrus, Desmodium, Typha*, and on various members of the Amentiferae. For herbarium purposes they may be preserved by simply drying the leaves under light pressure. When needed for examination the leaf should be soaked in water for several minutes, after which the perithecia may be scraped off and mounted in water. In mounting, great care must be taken not to break off the appendages. The asci may be forced out by tapping smartly on the cover (Fig. 69).

For permanent mounts of entire perithecia with appendages, fix in 5 per cent formalin 24 hours, wash in water 1 hour, stain in aqueous eosin 24 hours, remembering to keep all solutions slightly acid. Use the Venetian turpentine method. If chromic acid, corrosive sublimate, or alcohol be used for fixing, the appendages become brittle and very easily break off. However, the chromo-acetic mixtures are better if it is desired to make paraffin sections showing the developing of the perithecium with its asci and spores. For this purpose the omnipres-

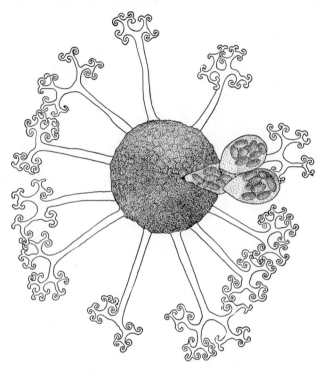

Fig. 69.—*Microsphaera alni*, the Lilac Mildew, on *Syringa vulgaris*. Single perithecium crushed a little, so that the asci, each with 8 ascospores, are coming out. The appendages are beautifully branched at the tip. Stained in eosin, which stains the appendages. ×300. From Chamberlain's *Elements of Plant Science* (McGraw-Hill Book Co., New York).

ent *Erysiphe commune* on *Polygonum aviculare* is exceptionally favorable, because, after the material has been fixed and has been brought into alcohol, the whole mycelium, with the developing perithecia, may be stripped from the leaf without the slightest difficulty, thus avoiding the necessity of cutting the leaf in order to get the fungus. Material in which the perithecia are still white or yellowish contain stages up to the formation of the uninucleate ascus; brownish perithecia show the development of ascospores, and dark brown or black perithecia contain the mature asci with fully developed ascospores. In early stages while the perithecia are still yellow or very slightly brownish, the material can be stripped off from the leaves before fixing. An air-pump will remove any air. Use iron-alum haematoxylin and orange, or the safranin, gentian violet, orange combination. Sections thicker than 5 μ will be hard to stain effectively. *Erysiphe commune* also grows on *Polygonum erectum*, from which it can be stripped even before fixing.

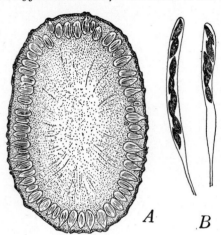

FIG. 70.—*Xylaria: A*, transverse section of a young stroma, showing perithecia; ×8. *B*, two asci with ascospores; ×245.

The Xylariaceae.—Most of these forms, in their mature condition, are black. In younger stages the color is lighter, often showing gray, brick-red, or brownish tints. *Nummularia* is common on dead branches of beech, elm, oak, locust, and other trees. It is generally flat, orbicular, or elliptical in form. *Ustilina* is a crustaceous form, rather diffuse and irregular in shape. It is most common on the roots of rotten stumps. *Hypoxylon* is more or less globose in form, and the color is brick-red, brown, or black. It is found on dead twigs and bark of various trees, especially beech, and is more abundant in moist situations. *Xylaria* (Fig. 70) is found on decaying stumps and logs, and often apparently on the ground, but really growing on twigs, wood, and bark just under the surface. When mature it is black outside and white or light-colored within. When young, it is easily cut in paraffin; in some forms the ascospores are fully formed before the stroma becomes hard enough to occasion any difficulty in cutting. Even in the forms which become the hardest in their mature stages, the young stages, up to the ascogonium or a little later, the stroma is not hard to fix or cut. With iron-alum haematoxylin and orange, the ascogonium becomes sharply outlined against the vegetative hyphae.

When the stroma becomes black, many members of the Xylariaceae become very hard and brittle, so that sections are likely to be unsatisfactory. For general morphological study it is better to break the stroma transversely and examine with the naked eye and with a pocket lens. The asci with their spores can be teased out and mounted in water. For permanent preparations, soak the stroma for a month in equal parts of 95 per cent alcohol and glycerin; then cut sections, and, after leaving them in glycerin for a day or two, mount in glycerin jelly. It is better not to stain the old stages. For illustrative purposes, select forms which can be cut in paraffin. The method just given merely shows that such material can be cut.

LICHENS

For habit study, the lichens are best kept dry in a box. When wanted for use, they can be taken out and sprinkled with water, which will give them a bright, fresh appearance, besides making them less brittle to handle. *Evernia (Letharia) vulpina*, the most beautiful of all the lichens, and so abundant on California conifers, makes a splendid demonstration specimen when wet in this way.

Attractive pieces of lichens like *Ramalina reticulata* can be stained in eosin and mounted whole. *Dichonema cincinnatum, Coenogonium interpositum*, and similar forms in which the algal and fungal elements are loosely associated, can be stained in eosin, teased a little, and mounted whole, making much more effective mounts than could be obtained by sectioning.

Lichens are generally regarded as difficult forms to cut. If they are dry, soak them well before fixing. Formalin (5 c.c.), acetic acid (5 c.c.), and water (90 c.c.) fixes in 2 or 3 days, but material may be left here indefinitely.

The lichens are usually regarded as difficult forms. In younger stages they occasion no trouble, but an old apothecium or a leathery thallus often fails to cut well. By employing the gradual processes already described on page 115, satisfactory sections should be obtained from thalli and mature apothecia of *Physcia, Usnea, Sticta, Parmelia*, and *Peltigera. Collema* and other lichens of such gelatinous consistency, while they cut readily, show a strong tendency to wrinkle.

Cyanin and erythrosin is a very good stain for lichens. The algae stain blue, and the filaments of the fungus take the red.

BASIDIOMYCETES

This is an immense group, of which the smuts, rusts, mushrooms, toadstools, puffballs, and bracket fungi are the most widely known representatives.

The smuts (Ustilagineae).—The smuts are abundant on wheat, oats, corn, and various other plants.

The smuts may be studied in the living material. The following method, described by Ellis, is worth remembering: A supply of smutted barley may be obtained by sowing soaked, skinned barley that has been plentifully covered by *Ustilago* spores. In such material it is easy to trace stages in the development of spores. Freehand sections of ears about 12 mm. long show the mycelium and spore clusters. If smutted ears be removed and kept floating on the water, the spores continue to develop and often germinate. For paraffin sections desirable stages should be fixed in Flemming's fluid or picro-acetic acid. Delafield's haematoxylin, followed by a very light touch of erythrosin or acid fuchsin, will give a good stain.

For a study of the germinating spores and conidia, cultures may be made in beerwort on the slide or in watch crystals. Harper's method of making preparations from such material is ingenious and is valuable in making mounts of various small plant and animal forms. A drop of the material is taken up with a capillary tube and is then gently blown out into a drop of Flemming's weaker solution (from 15 minutes to 1 hour was sufficient for the fungus spores). Cover a slide with albumen fixative, as if for sections. A drop of the material, without previous washing, is drawn up into the capillary tube and touched lightly and quickly to the surface of the albumen. A series of such drops, almost as small as the stippled dots in a drawing, may be applied to the slide. The fixing agent may now be allowed to evaporate somewhat, but the preparation must not be allowed to dry. As the slide is passed rapidly through the alcohols, the albumen is coagulated, and the preparation may be treated just as if one were dealing with ribbons of sections.

The rusts (Uredineae).—*Puccinia graminis*, the common rust of wheat and oats, is familiar to everyone. The urediniospores, or summer spores, known as the red rust, and the winter spores, known as the black rust, are found in unfortunate abundance, but the aecium stage on the barberry is not necessary for the vigorous development of rust in the United States, and it is not nearly so prevalent as the red- and

black-rust stages. When found, it may be so abundant that most of
the leaves of the barberry are spotted with the cluster cups. It is a
curious fact that wheat and oats may be quite free from the red and
black rust in localities where the aecium stage is very abundant, and
that the rust stages may be most destructive where there are no barberry bushes. But not all rusts of wheat and oats are *Puccinia graminis*, and other rusts have other hosts than the barberry for the aecium stage. However, *Puccinia graminis* is so prevalent and destructive
that there is some excuse for the campaign for eradicating the common

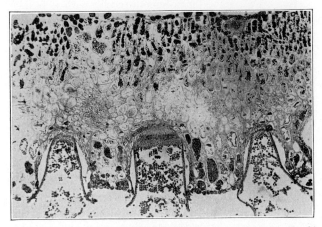

Fig. 71.—*Puccinia graminis:* photomicrograph of aecium stage on barberry. Fixed in chromo-
acetic acid and stained in cyanin and erythrosin. Eastman Commercial Ortho film, Wratten E
filter (orange); arc light; Spencer 16-mm. objective, N.A. 0.25; Bausch and Lomb projection eye-
piece; exposure, ½ second. ×47. Negative by Dr. P. J. Sedgwick.

barberry. No one doubts that the aecium on barberry is a stage in the
life-history of *Puccinia graminis*.

The aecium on barberry cuts easily in paraffin (Fig. 71). Formalin
acetic alcohol (formalin 10 c.c.; acetic acid, 5 c.c.; 70 per cent alcohol,
85 c.c.) fixes well. If a chromic solution is used, cut a piece from each
side of the sorus, keeping about the middle third, since the fixing agent
does not penetrate well. Iron-alum haematoxylin is the best stain to
bring out the binucleate condition in the aeciospores.

If the aecium stage is not easily available, there are various aecia
which are just as good, or even better, for morphological study. The
aecia growing on *Euphorbia maculata* (spotted spurge) are abundant
and are very easy to fix and cut. The infected plants are also very

easily recognized, normal plants having the prostrate habit, while infected plants become erect and the internodes become greatly elongated. Aecia growing on *Arisaema triphyllum* (Jack-in-the-pulpit) are also easy to cut. The *Aecium* on *Hepatica* has large nuclei and affords particularly good views of the intercalary cells, and the origin of the binucleate stage.

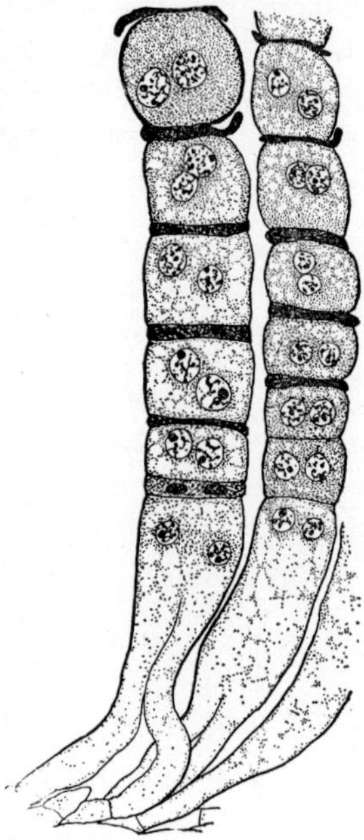

The Chicago chromo-acetic–osmic acid solution is recommended for fixing, and iron-haematoxylin with a faint touch of orange is a satisfactory stain (Fig. 72).

Without special treatment, it is practically impossible to get good sections of sori of urediniospores and teliospores, on account of the silica. Fix in formalin (10 c.c.), acetic acid (5 c.c.), and 70 per cent alcohol (85 c.c.) for at least 2 days, preferably 1 week. Material may be left in the fixing agent indefinitely. When wanted for imbedding, rinse in 70 per cent alcohol and treat with hydrofluoric acid (10 c.c. hydrofluoric acid and 90 c.c. of 70 per cent alcohol) for 2 days, or even 3 or 4 days. Wash in 70 per cent alcohol, at least 3 changes, to get rid of the hydrofluoric acid. Then proceed in the usual way.

If a chromic fixing agent has been used, treat with hydrofluoric acid after washing in water.

FIG. 72.—Aecium on *Hepatica:* fixed in chromo-acetic acid with a little osmic acid, and stained in safranin, gentian violet, orange; from a preparation by Dr. Wanda Pfeiffer Vestal. ×950.

Everyone who studies the rusts should attempt to germinate the urediniospores and teliospores. For this purpose the hanging drop culture may be employed, as described in the chapter on temporary mounts (chap. v). The urediniospores germinate readily all summer but in most forms teliospores will germinate only in the spring following their maturity. However, the teliospores of "lepto" species, like *Puccinia xanthii* on *Xanthium canadense* (cocklebur), will germinate as soon as they ripen, and will serve equally well for study. If a particularly good specimen is secured, it may be preserved by the method previously described for desmids, except that in this case it might be worth while to attempt staining with Mayer's haem-alum or with eosin.

Gymnosporangium, which is rather common on *Juniperus virginiana* (red cedar), forms its basidia in the "cedar-apple" stage. Bring the cedar apples into the laboratory in late winter or early spring and put some into a dish of water. The yellowish, gelatinous strands with the germinating teliospores may appear within 24 hours. The various stages are easily recognized under a low-power dry lens without even

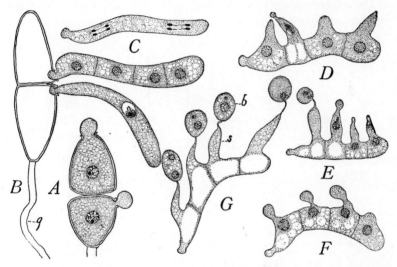

Fig. 73.—*Gymnosporangium*: *A*, beginning of germination of teliospore. *B*, later stages, the lower basidium showing the nucleus in the synapsis stage of the heterotypic mitosis, and the upper basidium showing the four-cell stage following the homotypic mitosis. *C*, the two figures of the homotypic mitosis; *D*, *E*, *F*, and *G*, later stages showing the formation of basidiospores, many of the basidiospores being binucleate—*g*, gelatinous stalk; *b*, basidiospore; *s*, sterigma. Fixed in 10 per cent formalin and stained in iron-alum haematoxylin. ×800.

crushing the gelatinous masses. The teliospores germinate readily and one soon gets the stages shown in Figure 73. The basidiospores may be germinated on apple seedlings (the Jonathan apple is particularly good), and aecium stages may be obtained in this way.

Fix in 10 per cent formalin for 2 or 3 days. If any acetic acid is used in the formula, the soft, gelatinous material is dissolved, and the material goes to pieces. In chromic fixing agents, the material also breaks up. In germinating stages, however, the basidia, in which reduction of chromosomes takes place, can be seen. One of the soft, gelatinous horns can be put into a piece of onion-leaf epidermis, as described on page 228. The material can then be stained whole or imbedded in paraffin. Stain in iron-alum haematoxylin. If mounting whole, when thick glycerin is reached, mount in glycerin jelly and seal. Fewer basidia are torn out from the teliospores, and fewer basidiospores are torn off from the basidia than when mounting in Venetian turpentine. However, with extreme care, material can be got into Venetian turpentine, and the mounts are firmer.

The interesting nuclear conditions in the life-history of a rust which has urediniospores, teliospores, basidiospores, and aeciospores, and

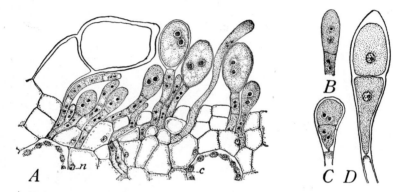

Fig. 74.—*Puccinia graminis: A*, uredospores on oats, showing binucleate mycelium and binucleate uredospores with binucleate stalk cells; *c*, chloroplasts, and *n*, nuclei of host cells. *B*, *C*, and *D*, stages in the development of the teleutospore; the two nuclei of the binucleate cells in *C* fuse to form the uninucleate cells of *D*. ×780.

also pycniospores in the life-history, are not difficult to demonstrate (Fig. 74). Basidia may be mounted whole. The mycelium from the basidiospore, which (in *Puccinia graminis*) germinates on the barberry leaf, is uninucleate. The binucleate stage begins in the aecium and continues up to the reduction of chromosomes in the basidium, so that the aeciospores, urediniospores, and young teliospores are binucleate. The two nuclei fuse in the teliospore. Reduction of chromosomes takes place during the two divisions in the basidium, and the uninucleate stage begins with the basidiospore. Iron-alum haematoxylin is the best stain for the whole series.

The fleshy fungi.—For habit study, nothing is equal to fresh material; for second choice, buy canned "mushrooms" (usually *Agaricus campestris*) at the grocery; forms not readily available in field or grocery may be preserved in formalin alcohol (6 c.c. of formalin to 100 c.c. of 50 per cent alcohol.) When formalin is used in water, the fungi become too soft. Larger forms of the mushroom, puffball, and bracket types may be dried in an oven. The circulation of air should be good, and the temperature should be kept at about 50° C. After drying, the fungi should be poisoned.

For sections, Gilson's fluid deserves more recognition than it has received. It is particularly good for soft forms, like *Tremella*.

Gilson's fluid.—

Ninety-five per cent alcohol	42 c.c.
Water	60 c.c.
Glacial acetic acid	18 c.c.
Concentrated nitric acid	2 c.c.
Corrosive sublimate (saturated solution in water)	11 c.c.

Fix about 48 hours and wash in 60 or 70 per cent alcohol.

Coprinus micaceus is particularly good for a study of gills, basidia, and the formation of basidiospores, because it is so small that a single section may show a fine series of stages. Gills which are becoming brownish at the tip, but which are still white toward the top of the cap, will show a splendid series of stages, as will also pieces cut from gills which are brownish at the edge, but white farther back. For fixing, cut out pieces 1 cm. long and 3 mm. thick. If pieces are taken into the mouth and wet with saliva for 30 seconds, the fixing agent penetrates better and there is scarcely any danger that air may be caught between the gills. The Chicago chromo-acetic–osmic formula is good for fixing any of the fleshy fungi.

To show the four basidiospores attached to the basidium, sections should be 10–15 μ thick; but to show nuclear detail, 2 or 3 μ is thick enough (Fig. 75).

In *Hydnum* and *Polyporus*, cut out pieces about 3 or 4 spines or 3 or 4 pores in width and about 1 cm. long. A rectangular piece which will allow the transverse sections of the spines or pores to be about 4 mm. wide and 1 cm. long cuts better than a piece which will give square sections.

In *Boletus*, simply strip off the hymenium and cut into pieces which will give transverse sections of the tubes.

In *Lycoperdon*, *Bovista*, *Geaster*, and *Scleroderma*, longitudinal sections of the entire fructification can be cut in paraffin as long as the fresh material is easily sliced with a safety razor blade.

Young stages of *Cyathus*, *Crucibulum*, and *Nidularia* cut easily in paraffin; somewhat older stages can be cut in celloidin, but mature stages fail to cut by any of our present methods.

It is often desirable to secure differential staining of the fungus and its host. Some of the methods previously mentioned secure this result and give excellent detail, but do not make the mycelium stand out sharply in contrast with the tissues of the host. A special method by B. T. Dickson generally gives a good differentiation. He uses Magdala red and light green, using the Magdala red in a 2 per cent solution in 85 per cent alcohol, and the light green in a 2 per cent solution in clove oil to which have been added a few drops of absolute alcohol. His schedule is as follows:

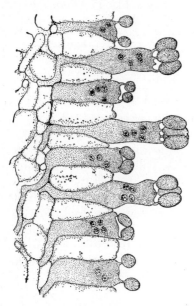

Fig. 75.—*Coprinus:* young basidia with four nuclei which, later, pass into the spores; fixed in chromo-acetic acid and stained in safranin, gentian violet, orange. ×780.

1. Dissolve paraffin in xylol and wash in absolute alcohol.
2. Wash in 95 and 85 per cent alcohol.
3. Stain with Magdala red 5–10 minutes.
4. Remove surplus stain and wash in 95 per cent alcohol.
5. Stain in light green in clove oil for 1–3 minutes.
6. Wash in absolute alcohol, or in carbol turpentine.
7. Clear in xylol and mount in balsam.

The time factors will vary slightly with different material. If the light green overstains slightly it may not interfere much with the differentiation. Mycelium, spores, amoebae, and bacterioidal tissue stain red, and the host tissues, green. If tissues do not stain readily, mordant in a 1 per cent solution of potassium permanganate in water for 2–5 minutes, wash in water, pass through the alcohols to 85 per cent alcohol, and stain. The mordant does not keep.

This combination has given good results with the following material: *Plasmodiophora brassicae*, legume tubercles, *Albugo candida*,

Phytophthora infestans, Uromyces caryophyllinus, Puccinia graminis, and many others.

We should suggest phloxine instead of "Magdala red" since the Magdala red which succeeds is probably phloxine.

A method by Stoughton produces a fine differentiation in many cases. He used it, originally, for *Bacterium malvacearum* in a study of the disease which it causes in cotton. The stain is thionin and orange G. The thionin was made as follows: thionin, 0.1 g., 5 per cent solution of phenol in 100 c.c. of distilled water. The orange was dissolved in absolute alcohol. Schedule for paraffin sections:

1. Stain in thionin, 1 hour.
2. Through grades of alcohol to 100 per cent.
3. Differentiate in a saturated solution of orange G in absolute alcohol, about 1 minute.
4. Wash thoroughly in absolute alcohol.
5. Xylol-alcohol.
6. Xylol.
7. Mount in balsam.

The parasite should be violet-purple; cellulose walls, yellow or green; lignified walls, blue; chromosomes, blue; and spindle, purple.

Freehand sections may be stained very quickly:

1. Sections in water.
2. Stain in carbol-thionin, 5 minutes.
3. Wash in water.
4. Ninety-five per cent alcohol.
5. Differentiate in orange G, several minutes.
6. Wash well in absolute alcohol.
7. Xylol.
8. Mount in balsam.

We should suggest that, to get the best results, different stains may be necessary for different forms. It would be worth while to experiment. If the host is woody, select a good stain for xylem. Safranin is generally good. Then try various blue and green stains until you find one which suits that particular case. Or, take iodine green for the xylem, and try various red stains for the fungus. If the host has cellulose walls, try Delafield's haematoxylin or light green or anilin blue for the host, and find a red stain for the fungus.

CHAPTER XXI

BRYOPHYTES

The Bryophytes, comprising the two groups, liverworts (*Hepaticae*) and mosses (*Musci*), present a great diversity of structure, some being so delicate that good preparations are very uncertain, while others are so hard that it is difficult to get satisfactory sections. Between these extremes, however, there are many forms which readily yield beautiful and instructive preparations.

If but one fixing agent should be suggested for the entire group, it would be chromo-acetic acid with 1 g. chromic acid and 2 c.c. acetic acid to 100 c.c. of water. Wherever nuclear detail is desirable, particularly in fertilization and the reduction of chromosomes, the addition of 6 or 7 c.c. of 1 per cent osmic acid to this solution will improve both the fixing and the staining. Fix for at least 24 hours: 48 hours may be an optimum, but material, which has been in this solution for 3 or 4 days, still gives good results. Since this fixing agent is not a good preservative, nothing should be left in it for more than 4 or 5 days.

Professor Land used a formalin alcohol solution (6 c.c. commercial formalin to 100 c.c. of 50 per cent alcohol) which he had tested in extensive collections in tropical Mexico and in various islands of the South Seas, where it was impracticable to use the chromic series, with its tedious washing and changing of alcohols. Material may be left in this solution until needed for use, a convenience which will hardly be appreciated by those who are always within reach of a laboratory. Material left for more than 20 years in this solution, in well sealed containers, when opened recently, was found to be in excellent condition for paraffin sections. Professor Land, in his more recent work, adds some acetic acid to his original mixture. His formula, with various modifications, is now the most generally used fixing agent for tropical work and is widely used, even when the chromic series is practicable.

For general study, the small, delicate forms, like *Cephalozia, Fossombronia*, and *Geocalyx*, may be stained in eosin and mounted whole in Venetian turpentine.

Instead of treating forms in a taxonomic sequence, we shall consider first the gametophyte structures under the headings *thallus, antheridia,* and *archegonia,* and shall then turn our attention to the *sporophyte.*

HEPATICAE

Some of the liverworts are floating aquatics, but most of them grow on logs or rocks or upon damp ground. They are found at their best in damp, shady places. Many of them may be kept indefinitely in the greenhouse. *Riccia, Marchantia, Conocephalus, Preissia,* and many others vegetate luxuriously, and often fruit if kept on moist soil in a shady part of the greenhouse, and they do fairly well in the ordinary laboratory if covered with glass and protected from too intense light. *Riccia natans* is a valuable type for illustrative purposes. It floats freely on the surfaces of ponds and ditches. Early in the spring (during April in the Chicago region) it produces antheridia; then, for a short time (about the first of May), both antheridia and archegonia; and still later, only archegonia. Sporophytes then appear as black dots along the grooves. After the spores are shed, the thallus remains sterile for the rest of the season. *Marchantia* and similar forms are not difficult to establish out of doors. A rather damp, shady spot close to the north side of a building is best. Scrapings from a board wich has been nearly burned up make the best fertilizer to scatter on the soil, if one is to cultivate *Marchantia.* Such freezing as *Marchantia* receives in the vicinity of Chicago does not prevent it from appearing again the next spring. If it is desirable to have material throughout the year, the out-of-door culture may be made in a box which can be brought into the laboratory or greenhouse in the winter. A box 3 feet long, 2 feet wide, and 1 foot deep will be convenient. An old window will do. It should have a glass cover. There should be about 6 inches of dirt in the box. A mixture of sand, loam, and charred scrapings will make a good substratum for *Marchantia.* If one is to raise liverworts in the laboratory, it is absolutely necessary to note carefully the conditions under which they grow in the field.

Marchantia can be grown very satisfactorily on pots in the greenhouse. Pots as small as 4 inches in diameter are all right. Have a little black, charred wood mixed with the soil and sow gemmae on the surface. If you take care to sow only gemmae from antheridial plants on one pot and gemmae from archegonial plants on another, you will get only one kind of plant on a pot. If well lighted, the cultures develop faster.

Spores of *Marchantia polymorpha* germinate as soon as they are shed, but can be kept about a year in envelopes at room temperature. The young sporelings, looking like young fern prothallia, are very small. It is convenient to grow them on porcelain plates kept moist with Knop's solution under a glass bell jar.

If even a small room in a greenhouse is available, liverworts can be grown in great variety and abundance. On one side of the room, have a pile of rocks. Half of this space should be occupied by limestone rocks, held in place with as little mortar as possible. There should be some shale and some porous red brick. The whole should be arranged so that water may trickle down from above. A pipe with holes $\frac{1}{16}$ inch in diameter will furnish enough water. The other three sides may be built up of various rocks, and some clay, so as to form a table about 1 m. high. A small fountain, with a bowl a couple of feet in diameter, built of rocks, will add to the efficiency. If a few well-supported cement tanks be placed above the principal pile of rocks, *Isoetes* and all the water ferns may be grown there, besides *Elodea, Myriophyllum, Chara,* and other forms constantly needed in laboratory work.

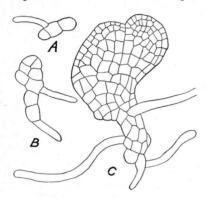

Fig. 76.—*Marchantia polymorpha*, early stages, looking like fern prothallia. From spores germinated on porcelain plates. *A* and *B* ×150; *C* ×100. After Sister Mary Ellen O'Hanlon.

The thallus.—Young stages in the thallus are usually neglected. They should receive much more attention from advanced classes. Spores of many liverworts germinate so readily that there is no difficulty in getting material. *Marchantia* is so universally used for adult stages of the thallus that a study of its early stages is very appropriate (Fig. 76).

For the adult thallus in many cases it will not be necessary to make a special preparation for the study of the thallus, since preparations of antheridia, archegonia, or sporophytes may include good sections of vegetative portions. This is particularly true of forms like *Riccia,* where the various organs are not raised above the thallus. In forms like *Marchantia,* where the antheridia, archegonia, and sporophytes are borne upon stalked receptacles, it is better to make separate preparations to show the structure of the mature thallus. Sections intended to show the structure of the mature thallus should be 15 to 25 μ in thickness, but sections to show the growing point and development of the thallus should not be thicker than 10 μ. The apical region of the Jungermanniaceae (Figs. 77, 78) affords an excellent opportunity for studying the development of the plant body from a single apical cell.

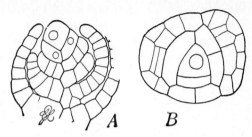

Fig. 77.—*Ptilidium ciliare:* A, longitudinal section, and B, transverse section of the apical region of the leafy gametophyte. Fixed in chromo-acetic acid and stained in Delafield's haematoxylin. ×420.

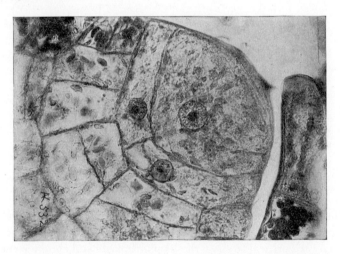

Fig. 78.—*Pellia epiphylla:* photomicrograph of apex of gametophyte showing apical cell and segments; fixed in chromo-acetic–osmic acid and stained in safranin, gentian violet, orange The negative was made by Dr. Köhler at the Zeiss factory in Jena, Germany.

Safranin, gentian violet, orange, is good for forms like *Pellia*, where even the apical cell is vacuolated, since it not only brings out the cell walls but stains the plastids and other cell contents (Fig. 78). The chloroplasts and leucoplasts are well differentiated by this stain.

Antheridia.—It is not difficult to get good preparations showing the development of antheridia. In forms like *Conocephalus, Preissia, Pellia,* etc., cut out small portions of the thallus bearing the antheridia. The piece should not be more than 1 cm. long and 5 mm. wide, preferably smaller. For the development of the antheridia of *Marchantia,* select young antheridiophores which still lie close to the thallus. With the antheridiophore, cut out a small piece of the thallus, about 5 mm. in length. For general development, cut 5 μ, but, for details of spermatogenesis, sections should not be thicker than 1 or 2 μ (Fig. 79).

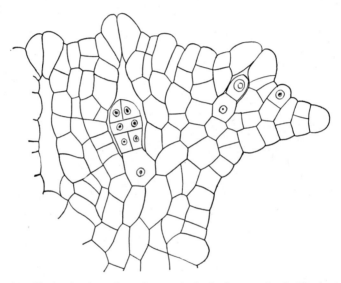

Fig. 79.—*Marchantia polymorpha:* early stages in the development of antheridia; from an unpublished drawing by Dr. W. J. G. Land. ×600.

Sections should be stained in iron-alum haematoxylin. The cells are very small and the contents very dense; consequently, the staining must be very critical to show the blepharoplasts and chromosomes or, in later stages, the transformation of spermatids into sperms. If the material is perfectly infiltrated and imbedded, there should be no difficulty in getting sections as thin as 1 μ. We have never seen a rotary microtome with which anyone except Dr. Land can cut a good ribbon at 1 μ; but the comparatively cheap sliding microtome, shown in Figure 2, cuts readily at 2 μ; and a modified type, a little more expensive, with a wheel for 1 μ, makes even ribbons at 1 μ. With Grübler

52° C. paraffin, Watts safety razor blade, and a room temperature of −2° C., this microtome cuts translucent ribbons of root-tips at 0.5 μ. The ribbons should not stretch more than 20 per cent when warmed on the slide. It is a good thing to practice cutting ribbons at 1 and 0.5 μ, since the extreme care, so absolutely necessary for these very thin sections, will develop a technique which will make 2 and 3 μ sections seem easy.

If sperms are found escaping, transfer them to a small drop of water on a clean slide, invert the drop over a 1 per cent solution of osmic acid for ten seconds, allow the drop to dry up, pass the slide through the flame 2 or 3 times, as in mounting bacteria, and then stain sharply in acid fuchsin. This should show the general form of the antherozoid, and will usually bring out the cilia.

The archegonia.—The methods for archegonia are practically the same as for antheridia. Too much stress cannot be laid upon the importance of carefully selecting the material. Use very small pieces, and, before placing them in the fixing agent, trim them to such a shape that the position of the archegonia will be known accurately even after the pieces are imbedded in paraffin. Since air is likely to be caught between the perigynium and the archegonium, it is worth while to use an air pump or an aspirator as soon as the material is put into a chromic fixing agent. With the formalin-alcohol–acetic solution, material is likely to sink promptly, and the pump is not necessary.

For the younger stages, 3–5 μ is a good thickness; but for older stages, after the necks of the archegonia have begun to curve, 10 or even 15 μ may be necessary if the egg, ventral canal cell, and neck canal cells are to appear in one section (Fig. 80).

For stages in the cutting off of the ventral canal cell and fertilization of the egg, sections should not be thicker than 5 μ.

In *Riccia natans* the direction of the axis of the archegonium at every stage in the development must be known; otherwise, there will be few good longitudinal sections.

In forms like *Porella* and *Scapania*, the involucre covering the archegonia is likely to hold a bubble of air, which will delay or even prevent fixing. The best plan is to cut off the offending leaf with a pair of slender-pointed scissors. Sometimes the air can be got out with an air-pump.

The sporophyte.—Sporophytes in early stages of development often yield good preparations without very much trouble, but in the later stages of some forms, like *Riccia natans*, they may be difficult to cut on account of the secondary thickening of the capsule wall and the stubborn exine of the mature spores. Great care must be taken to get

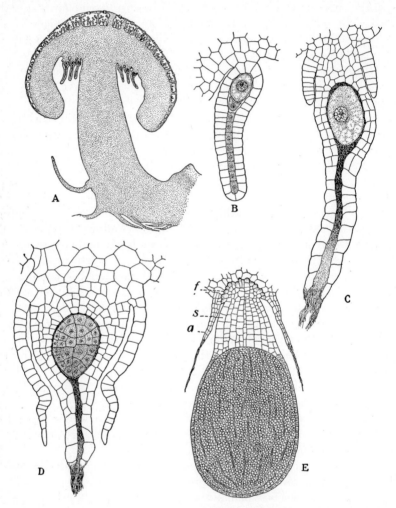

Fig. 80.—*Marchantia polymorpha: A*, section through archegonial head. ×30. *B*, an archegonium shortly before fertilization, showing egg, ventral canal cell, and 8 neck canal cells. ×300. *C*, egg after fertilization. ×300. *D*, young embryo; the spores will come from the more deeply shaded part; the lightly shaded part will produce the foot and seta. ×300. *E*, nearly mature embryo with foot (*f*), stalk (*s*), and remains of ruptured archegonium (*a*). ×45. From Chamberlain's *Elements of Plant Science* (McGraw-Hill Book Co., New York).

Riccia natans into paraffin without shrinking, and the same thing may be said of other forms which have such loose tissue with large air

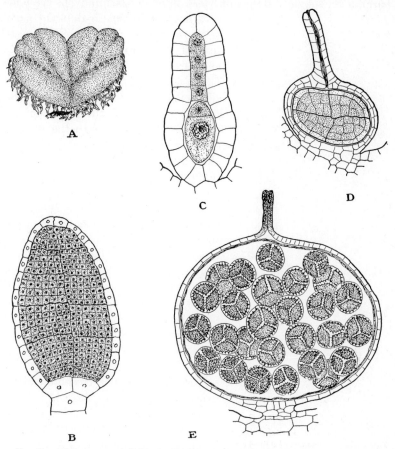

FIG. 81.—*Riccia natans: A*, habit sketch showing four rows of sporophytes. ×2. *B*, nearly mature antheridium. ×345. *C*, nearly mature archegonium, with egg, ventral canal cell, and 4 neck canal cells. ×720. *D*, young sporophyte inclosed in the swollen archegonium: the inner cells (endothecium) shaded; the outer layer (amphithecium) only one layer of cells thick, lightly shaded. ×200. *E*, nearly mature sporophyte, inclosed by the greatly swollen venter of the archegonium. The broken-down amphithecium represented only by a line. Spores in tetrads. ×100. From Chamberlain's *Elements of Plant Science* (McGraw-Hill Book Co., New York).

cavities. Formerly, we resorted to celloidin for stages like that shown in Figure 81. The gradual processes already described have obviated the difficulty, so that the student should be able to get thin paraffin sections as free from distortion as were the old celloidin sections. But even with well-fixed material great care must be taken not to let the paraffin get too hot. Remember that in most paraffin ovens the temperature is different in different parts of the oven. Do not let the temperature of the paraffin go above 53° C., and, preferably, not above 52° C. In *Riccia natans* it is even more difficult to get median longitudinal sections of the sporophyte than of the archegonium. Sections perpendicular to the groove, whether longitudinal or transverse, are almost sure not to give median longitudinal sections of the sporophyte, and these are the sections the beginner is sure to cut. Examine the material and note very exactly the orientation of the sporophyte; then, for fixing, cut out sections about 2 mm. thick, taking these sections in such a plane that paraffin sections parallel to the thick section will give the desired median longitudinal sections of the sporophyte.

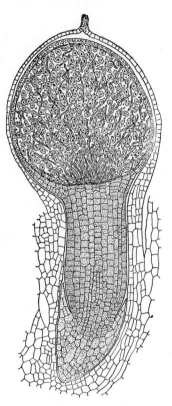

FIG. 82.—*Pellia epiphylla:* sporophyte nearly mature but still inclosed within the archegonium. ×40. From Chamberlain's *Elements of Plant Science* (McGraw-Hill Book Co., New York).

In forms like *Pellia* and *Aneura*, it is desirable to show the sporophyte still inclosed in the calyptra (Fig. 82). For such sections, we should recommend fixing in formalin acetic alcohol.

For cytological studies, the calyptra must be removed and a thin slab should be cut from opposite sides of the capsule to facilitate fixing and infiltration. Chromo-acetic acid, with the addition of a little osmic acid, is best for fixing. In *Pellia* and *Conocephalus* the spores are very large and have a rather thin wall. Both these genera show a peculiar intrasporal development of the gametophyte, i.e., the gametophyte develops to a considerable extent before it ruptures the spore wall and before it is shed from the capsule (Fig. 83). Mitotic figures during the first three divisions in these spores are exceptionally beautiful and are very easy to stain with the safranin, gentian violet, orange combination, the chromosomes taking a very brilliant red, while the asters take the violet. Achromatic structures are very prominent during these three divisions, but become less and less conspicuous as division progresses; and before the intrasporal stage is over, the radiations are scarcely demonstrable.

For the older sporophytes of *Marchantia*, it is better not to cut the whole receptacle. Remove the radiating branches. The sporophytes are in radiating rows, alternating with the branches. A piece 2 mm. wide can be cut so as to include two of the radiating rows, one on each side of the stalk, and such a piece will include early stages in other rows. By taking such care, you can get median longitudinal sections of nearly all the sporophytes. For class work, 5 to 10 μ is a good thickness, but

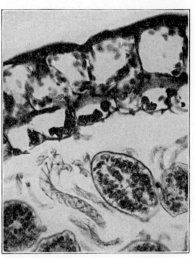

Fig. 83.—*Pellia epiphylla:* photomicrograph of spore germinating while still within the capsule. Fixed in chromo-acetic–osmic acid, and stained in safranin, gentian violet, orange. Negative by Miss Ethel Thomas. ×276.

for figures, especially the reduction mitoses in the spore mother-cells, the sections should not be thicker than 1 or 2 μ.

Among the Bryophytes no form affords a better opportunity for studying the development of spores than *Anthoceros*, since a single longitudinal section of the sporophyte may show all stages, from earliest archesporium to mature spores (Fig. 84). The sporophyte is even more difficult to orient than that of *Riccia natans*. Cut a slice 1 or 2 mm. thick, so as to orient the visible portion of the sporophyte, and trust to luck for the orientation of the foot. The starch grains in the chloroplasts take a beautiful violet color with the safranin, gentian violet, orange combination. With so many stages in a single section, it will be impossible to stain all of them well. A stain which will show the mother-cells and their divisions will be too deep for the mature spores, and a stain which shows the spores well will be too faint for the mother-cells. It is better to stain some preparations for one feature and others for another. It is not worth while to steer a median course.

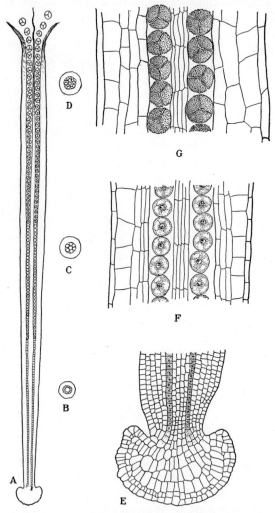

Fig. 84.—*Anthoceros laevis:* A, diagram of a longitudinal section of the sporophyte. ×5. *B, C,* and *D,* cross-sections at these three levels. *E,* early sporogenous cell (shaded) near the foot; *F,* spore mother-cells at the level shown in *C. G,* ripe spores at the level shown in *D. E, F,* and *G* ×150. From Chamberlain's *Elements of Plant Science* (McGraw-Hill Book Co., New York).

CHAPTER XXII

BRYOPHYTES

MUSCI

In general, the mosses are more conspicuous than the liverworts and easier to collect. Many of the most desirable forms fruit only in the spring, but something can be found throughout the summer and autumn and some, like species of *Sphagnum,* pass the winter with the antheridia and archegonia in advanced stages of development.

For herbarium specimens, mosses should be pressed *very* lightly, changing the blotters 3 or 4 times the first day, otherwise the plants will have a dull brown color. Some prefer to keep the mosses in boxes, without any pressing.

Material is more troublesome to fix than in the liverworts because small bubbles of air hinder the penetration of the fixing fluid. Use the air pump or aspirator. Older archegonia and capsules which have turned brownish add to the difficulties of the technique.

The Chicago chromo-acetic–osmic acid formula, or this formula without the osmic acid, fixes well. If neither an air pump nor an aspirator is available at the time of fixing, Land's formalin alcohol solution (6 c.c. commercial formalin to 100 c.c. of 70 per cent alcohol) will be more satisfactory. Dr. Land probably would now add about 3 c.c. acetic acid to the mixture.

Protonema.—Protonema of some moss can be found at any season. Look between the sidewalk and the curb, in shady places close to buildings, in the field and in the woods. Greenish patches resembling *Vaucheria* may be moss protonema with buds of the young leafy plants. Where there are recognizable leafy plants, there may be some good protonema, but young buds are likely to be scarce. The brownish bulbils, which are quite common in mosses, can be seen with a pocket lens. Some of the very small leaved mosses found on pots in the fernery or on benches in greenhouses, often show this mode of reproduction. Protonema is easily grown from spores.

Fresh green moss protonema will stand, without damage, what might seem to be very rough treatment. Scrape a thin layer off from the soil, put it in the palm of your hand, let water drip on it, and pat it with your finger. Nearly all of the soil will soon be removed. Put it in a bottle of water and shake. Pour it out into a flat dish and transfer the protonema to clean water. If there is still some soil, pat it with your finger. In this way you can soon clean enough for a thousand mounts.

Permanent mounts are very easily made. Simply wash away the dirt with water and put the material into 50 per cent glycerin, and let the glycerin concentrate. Mount in glycerin or glycerin jelly for permanent mounts. Seal thoroughly. Such mounts, with no fixing or staining, may retain the green color for many years.

If you do not insist upon keeping the green color, much clearer mounts can be made by fixing in formalin acetic acid, about 10 c.c. of formalin and 5 c.c. of acetic acid to 100 c.c. of water, and staining in eosin or in phloxine and anilin blue. A good stain in Delafield's haematoxylin gives a beautiful purple color and is permanent. Mount in Venetian turpentine.

Antheridia.—It is easy to find material for a study of antheridia, because, in so many cases, the antheridial plants can be detected at once without even a pocket lens. *Funaria*, with its bunch of antheridia as large as a pinhead, is extremely common everywhere. Spring is the best time to collect it, but it is found fruiting in the autumn and sometimes in summer; besides, it is easily kept in the greenhouse, where it may fruit at any time. *Bryum roseum* has a large cluster of antheridia surrounded by radiating leaves, making it easy to recognize. Other species of *Bryum* and species of *Mnium*, like *M. cuspidatum*, make good sections. *Polytrichum* has a large cluster of antheridia surrounded by reddish leaves, so that the whole is sometimes called the moss "flower." In fixing this or the closely related *Atrichum* (*Catharinea*), cut a small slab from two sides, so as to leave a flat piece to cut for longitudinal sections. This trimming will greatly facilitate fixing and infiltration. A single antheridial plant of *Polytrichum* often furnishes a fairly complete series of stages in the development of antheridia. Transverse sections show not only the antheridia but also good views of the peculiar leaf of this genus. In all cases the stem should be cut off close up to the antheridia, for many of the moss stems, after they have begun to change color, cut like wire.

Sections to show the development of the antheridium should be 5 to 10 μ in thickness. The safranin, gentian violet, orange, is a good combination (Fig. 85 A). For details of spermatogenesis, sections should not be thicker than 3 μ. Iron-haematoxylin is a better stain for the chromatin and blepharoplasts.

Although sections 20–50 μ in thickness can be cut to show topography, it is far better to study such stages in the fresh material. When a particularly fine view is secured in this way, a permanent preparation may be made by putting the piece into 10 per cent glycerin without any fixing or staining, and allowing the glycerin to concentrate. Then mount in glycerin jelly.

Archegonia.—The younger stages in the development of the archegonium, up to the time of fertilization, present no difficulties in technique. Trim away the leaves which usually cover the cluster of archegonia, fix in the Chicago chromo-acetic-osmic solution, and cut about 5 μ thick (Fig. 85*B*).

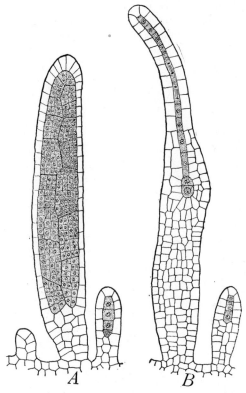

As soon as the necks of the archegonia begin to turn brown, troubles begin. The hardened necks are like wire and they pry the sections

FIG. 85.—*Mnium cuspidatum: A,* nearly mature antheridium in the center, with a young archegonium at the right, and at the left a still younger stage which may develop into either an antheridium or an archegonium; *B,* a nearly mature archegonium with a young archegonium at the right. Fixed in formalin–acetic alcohol (formalin 10 c.c., acetic acid 5 c.c., 50 per cent alcohol 100 c.c.) and stained in safranin, gentian violet, orange. ×240.

loose from the slide. Besides, the necks, even as early as the fertilization stage, are usually long and curved, so that it is necessary to cut as thick as 15 to 30 μ to get the egg, ventral canal cell, and neck canal cells in one section. Use Land's fixative. Haupt's fixative also holds some of the refractory objects to the slide, when they wash off if Mayer's albumen fixative has been used.

There is a general impression that the antheridia and archegonia of *Sphagnum* are rare and hard to find. Dr. George Bryan, who made an extensive study of *Sphagnum subsecundum*, found that antheridia appear in August and archegonia in September. In examining acres of this species, he did not find a sterile plant.

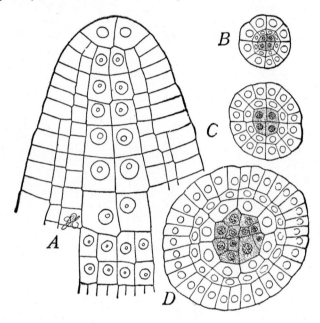

Fig. 86.—*Funaria hygrometrica:* A, apex of young sporophyte showing endothecium and amphithecium—chromo-acetic acid and Delafield's haematoxylin; 10 μ; ×420. B, C, and D, transverse sections of a sporophyte of the same age as A, taken at different levels; ×255.

Sporophyte.—It is often difficult to get good mounts of sporophytes. In the younger stages the calyptras are likely to interfere with cutting, while in the older stages the peristome, or hard wall of the capsule, occasions the trouble. If an attempt is made to remove the calyptra in young stages, like A of Figure 86, the apex of the sporophyte usually comes with it. With patience and a dissecting microscope, you may be able to snip off the brown neck of the archegonium which tops the calyptra and makes all the trouble. Land's fixative may hold the sections to the slide. Remember that the dichromate of potassium in this fixative is sensitive to light; so don't let the light strike it at the wrong time. The stage shown in Figure 87 stains beautifully in Delafield's haematoxylin. It is not difficult to cut; because, at this stage, the calyptra can be pulled off without injuring the top of the sporophyte. From this stage, there is no difficulty until the peristome gets

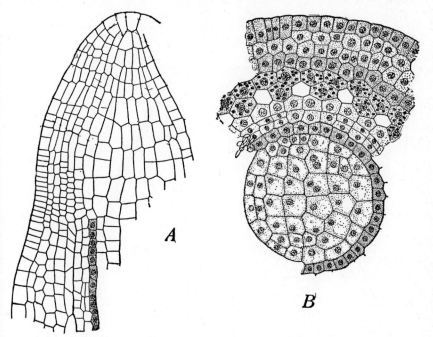

FIG. 87.—*Funaria hygrometrica: A*, longitudinal section of capsule; *B*, transverse section of capsule of about the same age as *A*—Delafield's haematoxylin and erythrosin; 10 μ. The columella, archesporium, outer spore case, two layers of chlorophyll-bearing cells, and the beginning of the air spaces can be distinguished at this stage. ×420.

hard and the capsule begins to get brown (Fig. 88). As soon as the brownish color begins to appear, it is hard to get good fixing in the chromic series: better try formalin 10 c.c., acetic acid 5 c.c., and 70 per cent alcohol 85 c.c. Remember that there should be a couple of days in 85 per cent alcohol to insure perfect hardening. Safranin and Delafield's haematoxylin, or the triple stain, will be good for these later stages.

Beautiful mounts of the peristome are easily and quickly made. Take a capsule at the stage when the operculum is just ready to fall off, or has just fallen off; with a sharp razor cut off the end of the capsule just below the line of the annulus; put it into absolute alcohol for an hour, change the alcohol, clear in clove oil, transfer to xylol, and mount

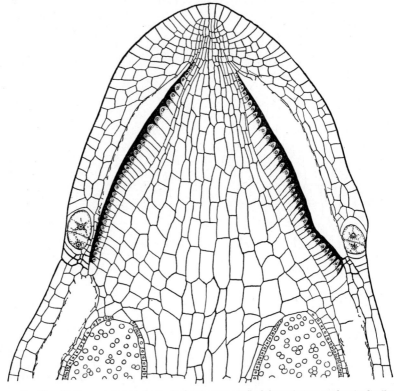

Fig. 88.—*Mnium:* upper part of capsule showing two teeth of the peristome cut longitudinally. Fixed in formalin alcohol and stained in safranin and light green. ×120.

in balsam. Cut some off without removing the operculum. The views will not be quite as clear, but the perfect regularity of the teeth will not be disturbed. No staining is either necessary or desirable (Fig. 89). If some are mounted one side up, and some the other, it will make the preparation more instructive.

The mature sporophytes of *Sphagnum* are exceptionally hard to cut. It will be worth while to prick the capsule with a needle when the material is collected. This will allow the fixing agent to penetrate readily, and will also facilitate the infiltration of paraffin or celloidin. The puncture causes only a slight damage, and need not reach the really valuable portion which is to furnish the median longitudinal sections.

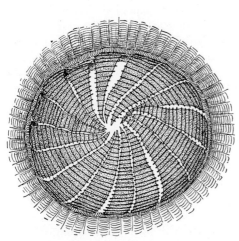 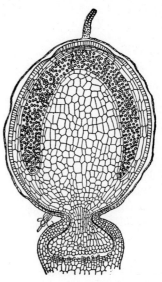

FIG. 89.—*Funaria hygrometrica:* bird's-eye view of the peristome after the operculum has fallen off. ×35. From Chamberlain's *Elements of Plant Science* (McGraw-Hill Book Co., New York).

FIG. 90.—*Sphagnum:* longitudinal section of sporophyte showing also the upper portion of the pseudopodium and the calyptra—Delafield's haematoxylin. ×24.

The younger stages in the sporophyte of *Sphagnum*, like that shown in Figure 90, and also the antheridia, archegonia, and the peculiar development of the leaves cut easily in paraffin.

CHAPTER XXIII

PTERIDOPHYTES

This group includes the Lycopodiales, Sphenophyllales, Psilotales, Pseudoborniales, Equisetales, and Filicales. The Sphenophyllales and Pseudoborniales occur only as fossils and the Psilotales are confined to tropical and subtropical regions. The Lycopodiales are commonly called club mosses or ground pines, the Equisetales are called horsetail rushes or scouring rushes, and the Filicales are the common ferns. The Ophioglossaceae, a family of the Filicales, are often treated as an order. Two of its genera, *Ophioglossum* and *Botrychium*, are widely distributed and well known. Material of the living forms, except in the Psilotales, is abundant and so easily recognized that anyone who pays a little attention to collecting can, in a single season, get a fine supply for a study of the group. Some desirable forms may not be present in all localities, but these will be few, and can be secured at a reasonable price from those who make a business of collecting.

The technique for Sphenophyllales will be found in chapter xiii. Nothing but impressions has yet been found in Pseudoborniales. Gametophytes of Psilotales have been found only recently. Their young sporangia cut easily, but older stages are very refractory and should receive extreme care in dehydrating, clearing, and infiltration. No further directions will be given for these rather inaccessible orders.

LYCOPODIALES

Lycopodium.—The genus is evergreen, and consequently some stage in development can be secured at any season. In general, the tropical species are easier to cut than the temperate. Without any regard to taxonomic sequence, we shall consider the vegetative structure, the strobili, and the prothallia.

Vegetative structure.—For stems and roots we recommend formalin 10 c.c., acetic acid 5 c.c., and 70 per cent alcohol 85 c.c., as a successful fixing agent.

The growing points of stems and roots cut easily in paraffin; and some stems, like those of *Lycopodium lucidulum* and *L. inundatum*, cut well even after the metaxylem has become lignified. Cut at 5 or

10 μ and stain in safranin and Delafield's haematoxylin. Safranin and anilin blue or light green is good, and the light green gives particularly clear views of the phloem.

Lycopodium lucidulum is exceptionally good for a study of stem structure, because one can pick out one-, two-, and three-year-old por-

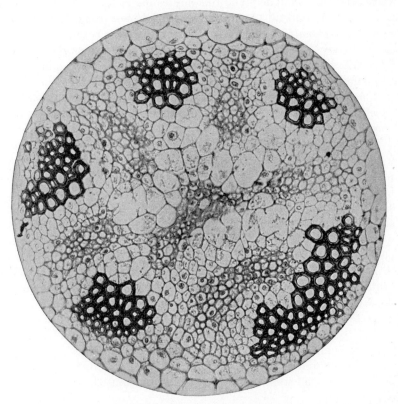

Fig. 91.—*Lycopodium lucidulum:* photomicrograph of transverse section of stem near the apex. The five deeply staining groups of thick-walled cells are the protoxylem, and alternating with them are groups of phloem cells; the large, thin-walled cells are metaxylem. Eastman Commercial Ortho film, Wratten E filter (orange); arc light; Spencer 4-mm. objective. N.A. 0.65; ocular ×6; exposure, 6½ seconds. Slide by Dr. J. J. Turner, negative by Dr. P. J. Sedgwick. ×360.

tions of the stem at a glance, by looking at the alternating groups of sporophylls and vegetative leaves. During the first year, only the protoxylem, and not quite all of that, will be lignified. Early in the second year, the lignification of the protoxylem is complete (Fig. 91).

During the second year most of the metaxylem becomes lignified; and in the third year, lignification is completed. The first-year and beginning second-year stems cut easily in paraffin and are splendid for showing protoxylem, metaxylem, and phloem. The third-year stem can be cut, but not so easily. Dr. Turner's paper should be read by those who wish to understand this interesting stem.

Stems more difficult to cut, like those of *L. obscurum, L. clavatum,* and *L. complanatum,* after fixing and washing, had better be treated for 2 or 3 days with 10 per cent hydrofluoric acid. Sections of stem and root of *L. complanatum,* mounted on the same slide, show an interesting parallelism of structures. Transverse sections of the stem of *L. pithyoides,* a Mexican species, show not only the stem structures but excellent transverse sections of roots which grow down through the cortex.

If young sporelings are available they afford a beautiful example of a very primitive type of stele, in transverse section showing an exarch protostele with 4 or 5 radiating arms of metaxylem, each tipped with a comparatively large group of protoxylem cells. In most species, this simple radial stele of the sporeling passes into a complicated, banded stele in the adult plant. Even in the adult plant the protoxylem and metaxylem are easily distinguished in sections near the growing point of the stem or root.

The strobilus.—For longitudinal sections, cut a slab from each side of the strobilus to insure fixing and infiltration. If a strobilus, or similar organ, is simply halved, both pieces are likely to curve. Among north temperature species, *Lycopodium inundatum* is the most easily cut. A young strobilus 1 cm. in length may show all stages from the archesporium to the spore mother-cell. Iron-haematoxylin is the best stain for differentiating the archesporial cells. The divisions in the spore mother-cell stain intensely, so that care must be taken not to overstain.

Strobili of *Lycopodium dendroideum* or *L. obscurum* 6 or 7 mm. in length show a beautiful series in the development of the sporangium from the earliest stages up to tetrads. They fix well in the Chicago chromo-acetic–osmic formula.

The gametophyte.—In most species the gametophyte, or prothallium, is subterranean, tuberous, and has no chlorophyll; in other species the prothallium is partly subterranean and partly aerial, the aerial portion being green and bearing the archegonia and antheridia.

In those species which have the green aerial portion, the spores germinate at once, soon produce archegonia and antheridia, and the sporeling becomes established by the end of the season. *L. inundatum* is our only species with this kind of prothallium. In this country, as far as we know, prothallia have not been found growing wild, and no one has germinated the spores. The spores germinate in 10 days to 6 months, develop up to the 8- or 10-cell stage, and die, doubtless from the lack of the proper fungus. No one but Bruchmann has had any notable success in germinating the species with subterranean tuberous prothallia.

In some species, the spores do not germinate for several years, but when the prothallia are once developed they continue to bear archegonia and antheridia for several years. The spores of *L. Selago* germinate in 3–5 years after shedding; those of *L. clavatum* and *L. annotinum* in 6–7 years. In *L. clavatum* and *L. annotinum* archegonia and antheridia develop in 12–15 years after the spores are shed.

Botanists in *Lycopodium* localities should look for prothallia. Since the subterranean forms are perennial and as large as a grain of wheat, some reaching a length of 1.5 cm., it would seem as if they should be found wherever *Lycopodium* grows.

In the third edition of this book, published in 1915, the statement was made that no one had yet discovered prothallia of *Lycopodium* in the United States. Two years later, a teacher in the high school at Marquette, Michigan, Dr. E. A. Spessard, announced the discovery of the prothallia of four species and gave such clear directions for finding prothallia that already two papers have appeared, announcing the discovery of prothallia. One of these papers, by Dr. Alma Stokey and Dr. Anna Starr, describes seven stations for prothallia in Massachusetts; and the other, by O. Degener, adds four more stations in Massachusetts and mentions the finding of prothallia near the crater of Kilauea, Hawaii. Both papers appeared in the *Botanical Gazette* of March, 1924. With such a start, others began to find prothallia. Look for tiny sporelings, just above ground. They may still be attached to the prothallia. Where you find a sporeling, take a layer of soil 2 or 3 inches deep and examine it carefully for younger stages. Prothallia are more likely to be found at the edges of a patch than where *Lycopodium* is very abundant.

The archegonia and antheridia are borne on cushions on the upper part of the prothallium (Fig. 92).

Once found, the technique is easy. Fix in the Chicago chromo-acetic–osmic solution, or this solution without the osmic acid.

Stain in iron-alum haematoxylin and orange for the development of archegonia and antheridia. Use safranin, gentian violet, orange, for the development of the embryo. For the endophytic fungus which stains well with the last-named combination, try the method of differentiation of pathogen and host, described at the close of the chapter on fungi.

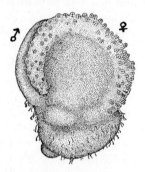

FIG. 92.—*Lycopodium volubile:* prothallium showing crown with numerous antheridia ♂, and archegonia ♀. ×14.

Selaginella.—Material of *Selaginella*, in all phases of the life-history, is easy to secure, but not so easy to handle after it is obtained. As many as 340 species, mostly tropical, have been described, only 3 of which are common in the range of Gray's *Manual.* Of these 3, *Selaginella apus* is best for sections. It is found in moist or wet situations on the borders of ponds, along ditches, or on moist meadows. While the plant is very small, it has large spores. Several of the tropical species are common in greenhouses, and they fruit abundantly.

Vegetative structure.—Growing points and root-tips are easily cut in paraffin. In most species the older parts of the stem are too hard and brittle to cut in paraffin and are too small to cut well freehand.

After fixing, treat for 2 or 3 days in 10 per cent hydrofluoric acid, and then try paraffin.

Some of the tropical species, like *Selaginella wildenovii,* have stems nearly as large as a lead pencil, with polystelic structure, and are not hard to cut. The vascular cylinder is an exarch protostele or, when polystelic, each bundle is an exarch protostele. It is exceptionally easy to get a brilliant, differentiated stain when once the sections are cut.

The strobilus.—Very young strobili cut easily in paraffin, but after the megaspore coats begin to harden, there are few objects which make more trouble than the strobili of *Selaginella.* For stages up to the young megaspores, fix in chromo-acetic acid, with or without the addition of osmic acid. For later stages, use formalin 10 c.c., acetic acid 5 c.c., and 70 per cent alcohol 85 c.c. The cutting of the later stages is likely to be more satisfactory if, after fixing and washing, the strobili are treated for 24–48 hours with a 10 per cent solution of hydro-fluoric acid in 70 per cent alcohol.

The strobili of most species are square in transverse section. To get longitudinal sections showing the relations of sporangia, sporophylls,

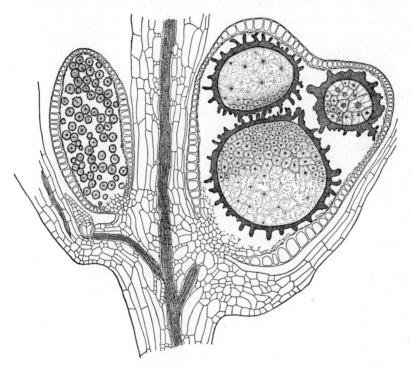

Fig. 93.—*Selaginella apus:* longitudinal section of strobilus showing a microsporangium with germinating microspores on the left; on the right, three of the four megaspores with gametophytes near the archegonium initial stage; fixed in formalin alcohol, cut in paraffin, and stained in safranin and light green; from a preparation by Dr. W. J. G. Land. ×80.

and axis, cut diagonally, from corner to corner, never parallel to the flat side.

Sometimes sections of the difficult later stages stay on the slide with Mayer's albumen fixative. Even stages like that shown in Figure 93 should always stay on with Land's fixative.

For archesporial cells, use iron-haematoxylin; for young megaspores and the development of spore coats, use safranin, gentian violet, orange; for later stages use safranin and light green.

The gametophytes.—In most cases the spores germinate while still within the sporangium and, in some cases, like *Selaginella apus,* the female gametophyte develops up to the archegonium initial stage before shedding. If strobili of this species at the stage shown in Figure 93 be broken off and laid down on moist ground so as to keep the sporangium moist, dehiscence may not be vigorous enough to discharge the megaspores; but development of archegonia and antheridia will continue, fertilization will take place, and an embryo will be developed while the megaspore is still inclosed within the sporangium. Such a structure satisfies the definition of a seed. Ordinarily, to get the later stages, shake the spores out from the older strobili into a Petri dish with the bottom covered by several thicknesses of wet filter paper. There is enough nutritive material in the spores to carry them up to the sperm and egg stage. The female gametophytes within the old spore coats generally orient themselves in the paraffin, the base of the spore being down and the archegonium end of the gametophyte being up. A little of some nutrient solution, added to the water, will carry the development up to the cotyledon stage. All stages after the megaspore has fallen out from the sporangium may be fixed in the Chicago chromo-acetic–osmic solution. After washing in water, the very hard outer spore coat may be softened somewhat by treating with 5 per cent hydrofluoric acid for 2 days. The gametophyte is so delicate at this stage that a stronger acid will injure the tissues. Wash for 24 hours to remove all traces of hydrofluoric acid.

The young embryo, with its two cotyledons, its root, and the megaspore still attached, makes an instructive preparation when mounted whole in Venetian turpentine.

The various stages of the female gametophyte and embryo are not hard to stain; but the walls throughout the development of the male gametophyte are very thin and extremely hard to stain. Safranin and light green is a good combination. Light green in clove oil is more satisfactory than the alcoholic solution.

Isoetes.—This peculiar genus is widely distributed, and 16 of its 64 species occur within the United States. It looks so much like a sedge that it is easily overlooked, even when rather abundant. As a genus, it is hydrophytic, growing in wet places or even under water. A monograph by Dr. Norma Pfeiffer not only gives an ecological, morphological, and taxonomic account (with keys in English) but gives hundreds of stations, a feature which will enable many to find material.

Vegetative structure.—The short, thick stem, even in old plants, cuts easily in paraffin. Fix in formalin acetic alcohol and stain in safranin, gentian violet, orange; or in safranin and light green.

Sporelings with stems about 2 mm. in diameter and young plants with stems up to 5 mm. in diameter are best for a study of the peculiar vascular system of this plant. These young stages fix well in chromo-acetic acid and are not hard to cut.

Sporangia.—All the sporangia of the plant may be said to constitute a single strobilus of the *Selago* type. Both longitudinal and transverse sections should be cut. The stem is so short that, in a plant of medium size, a longitudinal section may include the stem, the sporangium, and the sporophyll, up to the top of the ligule. Such sections, 10–15 μ, or even 20 μ, in thickness, are best for demonstration. Early stages in the development of the sporangium should not be thicker than 5 μ and should be stained in iron-alum haematoxylin.

Transverse sections through the whole cluster of sporophylls show the arrangement of megasporophylls and microsporophylls and also the relations of the sporangia to sporophylls.

The gametophytes.—The spores are shed in the uninucleate stage, and consequently it is not so easy to find the germination as in the case of *Selaginella*. When the large megasporangium begins to decay, let the megaspores dry naturally. They retain their power of germination for a year at least. Simply wet them with tap water and the earlier stages are easily secured, quite clean and ready for cutting. There must be soil in the dish for later stages. Try a similar method for microspores. Also, look at the top of the stem of old plants for stages developing naturally. The cell walls of the male gametophyte, as in the case of *Selaginella*, are rather hard to differentiate. Use anilin blue or light green.

CHAPTER XXIV

PTERIDOPHYTES

EQUISETALES

This order was large and prominent in the Carboniferous age, but now only a single family, the Equisetaceae, survives. Its only genus, *Equisetum*, contains 24 pieces, 10 of which occur within the Gray's *Manual* range. *Equisetum* means "horse bristle," and the name "Horsetail Family" is given in the manuals. The name, "scouring rush," is more appropriate, because the rough stems have been used for scouring kettles. The roughness is due to silica. Species, like *E. hiemale*, which contain much silica, must be treated with hydrofluoric acid before the older parts can be cut in paraffin.

Vegetative structure.—The roots are very small, but have large cells and easily yield good preparations. If a handful of *Equisetum fluviatile* or *E. hiemale* growing in water be pulled up, scores of root-tips may be secured in a few minutes. Fix in the Chicago chromo-acetic–osmic solution.

In case of such small objects it is a good plan to add a few drops of eosin to the alcohol during the process of dehydrating, in order that the material may be seen more easily. The slight staining does no damage, even if more critical stains are to be used after the sections are cut. Longitudinal sections of the roots may also be obtained by cutting transverse sections of the nodes.

The growing points of stems may be cut with ease in paraffin. *E. arvense* is particularly favorable on account of the numerous apical cells which may be found in a single preparation. Dissect away very carefully the scale leaves covering the growing point. To show the segmentation, building up the root or the stem from a single apical cell, the sections should not be too thin; 10 or 12 μ is not too thick.

The "fertile" stem of *Equisetum arvense* is so free from silica that it can be cut in paraffin without any difficulty. The adult vegetative stem of *E. arvense*, and all stems which contain so much silica, should be fixed in formalin acetic alcohol and—after washing in 70 per cent alcohol—should be treated with 20 per cent hydrofluoric acid in 70 per cent alcohol for 2 or 3 days. The acid must then be washed out with 70 per cent alcohol.

The strobilus.—*E. arvense* affords the most favorable material for a study of the development of sporangia, since the strobilus contains almost no silica and, even in its latest stages, is easily cut in paraffin. In this species, the young strobili, in the Chicago region, can be distinguished from vegetative buds in July; sporogenous tissue is well advanced by the middle of August; and the reduction divisions occur

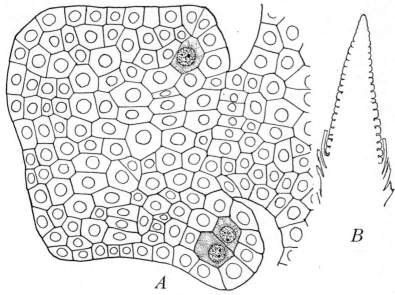

FIG. 94.—*Equisetum arvense: A*, section of a sporangiophore showing beginning of sporogenous tissue, early August condition; *B*, topography of the strobilus at this stage. *A* ×580; *B* ×8.

late in August or early in September (Fig. 94). The spores are not shed until the following April. If you know a patch of this species which "fruits" every year, dig up the horizontal underground stem in July. The tip of the main axis is almost sure to be a strobilus. Dissect away the scale leaves and fix the strobilus in chromo-acetic acid with a little osmic acid. August and September stages are easy to recognize. If strobili are brought into the laboratory in December or January, they shed their spores within a week.

Equisetum telmateia, of our Pacific states, has the strobilus on a comparatively soft, early shoot, as in *E. arvense*; the vegetative shoot

coming later from a bud near the base of the fertile shoot. The immense strobilus, 2 or 3 inches in length, cuts easily in paraffin.

In the other species, the strobilus is borne at the top of the vegetative shoot. It appears in the spring, develops, and sheds its spores the same season. The younger stages may be fixed in chromic solutions, imbedded in paraffin, and cut without difficulty. Later stages, if they show much silica, as is likely to be the case in such species as *E. hiemale*, had better be fixed in formalin acetic alcohol and treated with hydrofluoric acid.

The spores of *Equisetum* are excellent for illustrating hygroscopic movements. Shake out the spores from the strobili and let them dry thoroughly. They can be kept dry for years. When wanted for demonstration, put a few on a slide, moisten a little, and watch the movements under the microsope.

The gametophytes.—The spores of *Equisetum* germinate as soon as they are shed, but, like all spores with a considerable amount of chlorophyll, they do not long retain the power of germination. A comparatively small percentage will germinate a week after shedding, and after a month, there may be no germination at all. There is no difficulty in growing prothallia to maturity and securing stages in the embryo, if fungi or blue-green algae do not appear and ruin the cultures. Use Costello's method for fern prothallia, as described on page 316.

Dr. Elda Walker's papers on *Equisetum* give directions for finding prothallia in the field and raising them from spores; besides, they correct some current misconceptions in regard to gametophytes of *Equisetum* and contain a full account of the gametophyte of *E. laevigatum*.

If you should not succeed with this much-condensed summary of Dr. Walker's methods, consult the full papers. Boil *Sphagnum* 45 minutes, pack in boiled moist chambers to a depth of 2 inches and press out surplus water. Cover until cool and then sow the spores by tapping on the strobilus. Cover with glass and place in a north window. If fungi appear, water with a solution of potassium permanganate, putting enough crystals into distilled water to give the solution a dark purple color. This does no damage and may save cultures, even after fungi get in. Some algae do no damage. Cultures of *Equisetum telmateia* and *E. kansanum* grew two years, and of *E. arvense*, 9 months. Antheridia may appear in 3 weeks; archegonia, a week or two later (Fig. 95).

In another method an ordinary greenhouse flat was filled with sifted

loam and sand, smoothed and pressed down until a hard surface was
obtained. This was flooded and allowed to stand until the water
soaked into the soil. Then spores were sown, the flat was covered with
glass and placed in a sunny room of the greenhouse. No more water
may be needed until the plants are 1 mm. high. Water with potassium
permanganate if there is any tendency to damp off.

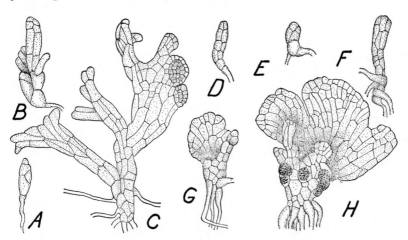

Fig. 95.—*Equisetum* prothallia: *A–C, Equisetum arvense: C* shows two antheridia. *D–H, E.
telmateia; H* shows six antheridia. After Walker. ×30.

The prothallia fix well in chromo-acetic acid. The younger stages
may be stained in iron-alum haematoxylin and mounted in Venetian
turpentine. The older stages, even of *E. arvense*, are too large for such
mounts. *E. laevigatum* has prothallia a centimeter in diameter.

For the development of antheridia, the blepharoplast, and the development of the sperm, fix in the Chicago chromo-acetic–osmic solution and stain in iron-alum haematoxylin. For oögenesis, and spermatogenesis, especially the centrosome situation, the sections should not
be thicker than 3 μ. The sperm of *Equisetum* is the largest in Pteridophytes.

CHAPTER XXV

PTERIDOPHYTES

FILICALES

This order includes the common ferns and also the Ophioglossaceae, which was treated as an order, co-ordinate with Filicales, until Chrysler showed that it was only a family under the Filicales. Some of the ferns are sure to be available in almost any locality, and all stages in the life-history are easily secured, except early stages in the Ophioglossaceae.

Vegetative structure.—From a technical standpoint, the vegetative structures of Filicales present a wide range of conditions, some being so soft that the greatest care must be taken to get them into paraffin, while others are so hard that it is almost impossible to cut them at all.

The stem.—Growing points, even of the largest ferns, can be cut in paraffin. If the growing point is covered with dense hairs or ramentum, either remove the covering entirely or, in case of rather fleshy ramentum, remove only the scales which are beginning to turn brownish. The white scales will fix and cut. Use chromo-acetic acid (1 g. chromic acid and 3 c.c. acetic acid to 100 c.c. water). Unless mitotic figures are desirable, it is just as well not to add any osmic acid. For illustrating the development of the stem from the apical cell, sections 10, 15, or even 20 μ are not too thick.

Older portions of the stem, or rhizome, in most ferns are easily cut while fresh, the sections being transferred to 95 per cent alcohol after cutting. But even fairly well-developed rhizomes, after the xylem has become lignified sufficiently to stain sharply in safranin, can be cut in paraffin, and much finer sections can be obtained than by cutting without imbedding (Fig. 96). In digging up rhizomes, do not merely dig down until the rhizome can be grasped and then pull it up, for such material is sure to show the pericycle of the bundles torn away from the parenchyma. Dig carefully around the rhizome and then with a very sharp knife cut off pieces which are perfectly free. The pieces can be wrapped in wet paper and taken to the laboratory. Then, if they are to be cut without imbedding, cut into pieces about 3 cm. long; but material which is to be imbedded should be in pieces not longer than 1 cm.

Pteris aquilina is a good form to practice with. For freehand sections, cut as thin as possible, which will probably be 20 μ or thicker.

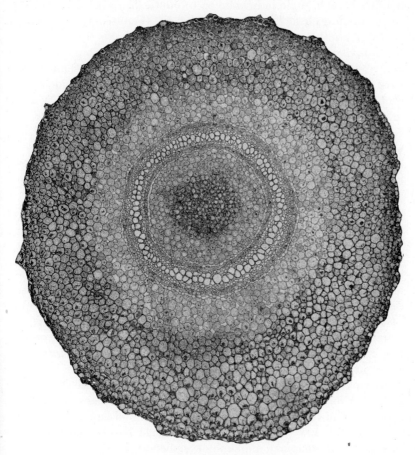

FIG. 96.—*Dicksonia punctilobula:* photomicrograph of transverse section of rhizome. Fixed in formalin–acetic alcohol, and stained in safranin and light green. Paraffin section 10 μ thick. Eastman Commercial Ortho film, Wratten E filter (orange); arc light; J. Swift and Son 1-inch lens; exposure, 1 second. Negative by Dr. P. J. Sedgwick. $\times 33$.

Put the sections into water, changing several times to wash out as much of the mucilage as possible. From this point, there are rapid and slow methods of arriving at the finished mount. For a very rapid method, try this. Transfer the sections from water to 95 per cent alcohol and leave them for 30 minutes. Stain in safranin for two hours. Rinse in 50 per cent alcohol until most of the safranin is washed out from cellulose walls. Then in 70, 85, and 95 per cent alcohol 10 minutes in each. Stain in light green 1 minute. Rinse in 95 per cent alcohol; absolute alcohol, 10 minutes; clove oil, 2 minutes; xylol; balsam.

Here is another method, not so rapid, but better. Fix the sections in formalin-alcohol–acetic acid, for 24 hours. Rinse in 50 per cent alcohol. Stain in safranin overnight or 24 hours: 50 per cent alcohol until most of the stain is drawn from the cellulose walls: 70, 85, and 95 per cent alcohol, 1 hour each; 100 per cent alcohol, 1 hour; crystal violet in clove oil, 1 minute; xylol, balsam.

Here is a still better, and slower, method. Fix the sections in chromo-acetic acid (1 g. chromic acid, 3 c.c. acetic acid) overnight or 24 hours. Wash in water 24 hours. Run the sections through the alcohols as slowly as if for imbedding in paraffin. Allow the 85 per cent to act overnight or 24 hours. Then 70 per cent, 30 minutes and 50 per cent, 10 minutes. Stain in safranin and light green. With this very slow method, the protoplasm should not shrink away from the walls.

However, it is better to imbed in paraffin and cut thinner sections. The rhizome of *Pteris aquilina*, cut 10 μ and stained in safranin and light green, or in safranin, gentian violet, orange, will show the superiority of this method in everything except speed. Sections a short distance back from the apical cell, at the region where lignification is just beginning to take place, will show the protoxylem stained red with safranin, while the rest of the xylem (metaxylem) is still in the cellulose condition and staining green. The rhizome of *Pteris* affords an excellent illustration of a mesarch polystele.

Dicksonia punctilobula has a small rhizome, often on the surface of the soil or rock, so that it is easy to get good clean pieces. About 2 or 3 cm. back of the growing point, the xylem is well lignified, but the material still cuts well in paraffin. One could hardly find a better illustration of a mesarch amphiphloic siphonostele (Fig. 96).

Botrychium is widely distributed, but individual plants are not abundant. The stem is erect, subterranean, and has an endarch siphonostele with secondary wood. Trim away the roots, which are very thick and fleshy in *B. obliquum*, fix in formalin-alcohol–acetic acid, and imbed in paraffin. Even the older parts of old stems can be cut in paraffin if you are sufficiently careful (Fig. 97). Transverse sections from the base of the bud down to the secondary wood will give a beautiful series in the development of the stele.

The bud at the top of this rhizome is an interesting object. The leaf is in its fourth year when it appears above ground, and, consequently, the bud contains young leaves of three successive seasons. Two of the three show a differentiation into sterile and fertile portions.

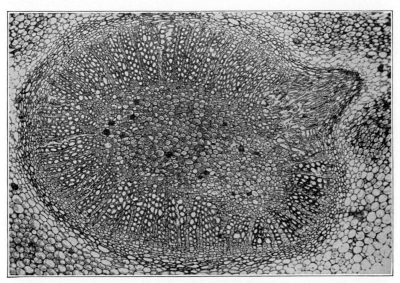

Fig. 97.—*Botrychium obliquum:* photomicrograph of transverse section of rhizome. Fixed in formalin–acetic-acid alcohol, and stained in safranin, gentian violet, orange. Paraffin section, 10 μ. Eastman Commercial Ortho film, Wratten E filter (orange); arc light; J. Swift and Son 1-inch lens; exposure, 1 second. Negative by Dr. P. J. Sedgwick. ×45.

In *Osmunda*, and in many other ferns of similar habit, the rhizome is surrounded by the very hard leaf bases. Good sections of the central cylinder can be secured only by dissecting away these hard leaf bases and any hard portions of the cortex before attempting to cut sections. A short distance back of the growing point will be found a region which will show practically all the structures of the mature stem, which will be easy to cut. Even in this region the leaf bases should be dissected away. From the apical cell back to the region where the sclerenchyma is beginning to turn brown, the material is easily cut in paraffin. Older portions should be cut freehand. *Osmunda* affords an excellent illustration of the mesarch siphonostele (Fig. 98).

The rhizome of *Adiantum* affords a good illustration of leaf gap and leaf trace. The vascular cylinder is a mesarch siphonostele; but there are few sections like Figure 96, because the cylinder is so interrupted by leaf gaps. This rhizome cuts well without imbedding. The petiole of *Botrychium*, in transverse sections below the fertile spike, shows the interesting leaf-trace situation which proves that the fertile spike consists of a pair of pinnae fused together.

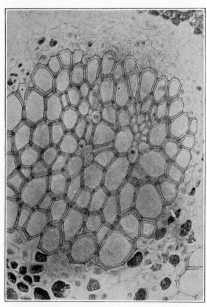

FIG. 98.—*Osmunda cinnamomea:* photomicrograph of single bundle of the mesarch siphonostele. Stained in safranin and anilin blue. Eastman Commercial Ortho film, Wratten C filter (blue-violet); Bausch and Lomb 4-mm. objective, N.A. 0.65; exposure, 4 seconds. Negative by Dr. P. J. Sedgwick. ×108.

The ferns of the Gray's *Manual* range afford no very satisfactory material for illustrating the protostele, although protosteles occur in *Lygodium* and *Trichomanes*. The most satisfactory material is *Gleichenia*, a very common and very beautiful fern in tropical and subtropical regions, but almost never seen in greenhouses or even in botanical gardens. Formalin-alcohol material can be cut without imbedding and is easy to stain.

The *Gleichenia* rhizome is one of the most difficult of all fern rhizomes to imbed in paraffin and cut. The most beautiful sections of this rhizome we have ever seen were cut in paraffin by Dr. Fredda Reed. This is the method:

1. Cut the rhizome into pieces 1 cm. long.
2. Twenty per cent hydrofluoric acid, 3 or 4 days.
3. Wash well in water.
4. Dehydrate in 10, 20, 30, 40, 50, 70, 85, 95, and 100 per cent alcohol, 24 hours in each.
5. One-fourth xylol, $\frac{3}{4}$ absolute alcohol, 12 hours.
   One-half xylol, $\frac{1}{2}$ absolute alcohol, 12 hours.
   Three-fourths xylol, $\frac{1}{4}$ absolute alcohol, 12 hours.
   Pure xylol, 12 hours.

Xylol and paraffin, saturated at room temperature, 2 days.

Xylol and paraffin, saturated on top of oven, 3–4 days.

6. In the oven until infiltrated, generally about 24 hours.

7. Imbed.

8. Soak the paraffin cake in water for a few hours before cutting.

Such material will cut at 10 μ or less. Let the sections dry on the slide for at least 24 hours; a month will do no harm.

Probably most fern rhizomes could be cut by this method. Even the *Adiantum pedatum* rhizome is not harder than that of *Gleichenia*.

The stems of tree ferns require special treatment. With the large leaf bases partly cut away with a sharp razor, transverse sections are easily cut for a considerable distance below the apex. Material fixed in formalin acetic alcohol cuts very well. If fresh material is to be cut, the softer portions should be flooded with alcohol after each section. Farther down, there will be a region where sections can be cut without any flooding, and still farther down, it will be difficult or impossible to cut sections across the whole stem. Sections 1 or 2 cm. thick, cut smooth on the ends, may be kept in 95 per cent alcohol or in glycerin in large glass dishes of the Petri dish pattern. Better still, clear such sections in xylol and preserve in cedar oil.

The root.—The roots of Filicales develop from a strong apical cell. For mitotic figures and the development of the root from the apical cell, fix in the Chicago chromo-acetic–osmic acid solution. None of the fern roots need any treatment with hydrofluoric acid. If the development of the root is the principal object, stain in safranin and light green, or in the safranin, gentian violet, orange combination; if mitotic figures are to be studied, stain in iron-haematoxylin with a very light counter-stain in orange. The comparatively large root-tips of *Botrychium* are excellent for the apical cell and its segments. *Dicksonia punctilobula* can also be recommended; but even the very small root-tips of most of our ferns will yield good preparations.

Roots of tree ferns are sometimes available in greenhouses. In some species the stem is covered by a dense felt of small roots, some of which will be white and soft at the tip. These roots are likely to have about the diameter of onion root-tips, and the beauty of preparations made from them could hardly be excelled. In the tropics, where the plants are often in the spray of cataracts and the lower part of the trunk is often washed by mountain streams, a thousand tips might be secured from a single tree fern.

The older roots of *Botrychium*, especially the large fleshy roots of *B. obliquum*, cut very easily and show a simple exarch protostele with 4 or 5 protoxylem points.

The roots of *Angiopteris* and *Marattia*, which become as large as a lead pencil, may be secured in some greenhouses. Since fine large roots are exposed above the soil, gardeners will generally furnish a root, although they might hesitate to dig into the soil for such a large root. They cut easily after fixing in formalin alcohol and furnish a fine example of the exarch protostele, common to all roots (Figs. 99 and 100). Even such big roots as these need no treatment with hydrofluoric acid.

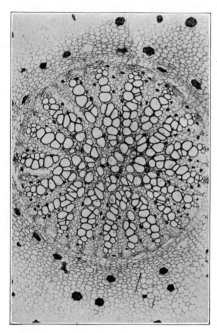

FIG. 99.—*Angiopteris evecta:* photomicrograph of a transverse section of a root, showing the polyarch, exarch siphonostele. Eastman Commercial Ortho film, Wratten E filter (orange); arc light; J. Swift and Son 1-inch lens; exposure, ¾ second. Negative by Dr. P. J. Sedgwick. ×25.

The structure of the leaf will appear in sections cut to show the sporangia.

The sporangia.—To illustrate the character of the annulus, select sporangia which are just beginning to turn brown and mount them whole. Fix in formalin acetic alcohol, and dehydrate as if for paraffin sections; after the absolute alcohol, transfer to 10 per cent Venetian turpentine. Staining is neither necessary nor desirable. The various kinds of annulus which characterize the seven time-honored families—the vertical, oblique, apical, equatorial, and rudimentary—are easily demonstrated in such mounts.

The various relations of sorus and indusium are best illustrated by rather thick sections (10–20 μ) of material in which the oldest sporangia have barely reached the spore stage. Fix in formalin alcohol and stain in safranin and anilin blue.

For the development of sporangia any of our common ferns will furnish good material. *Pteris* is easy to orient, because a transverse section of the leaf will always give longitudinal sections of the sporangia. *Aspidium* is good for the sorus covered by a peltate indusium. *Cyrtomium falcatum*, very common in greenhouses, is even better, and the receptacle is so elongated that there is a fine series of stages in a single sorus (Fig. 101).

For the youngest stages, take the circinate tips of the leaves. While many sporangia will be cut obliquely, many will show perfect longitudinal sections.

Marattia, a tropical fern which is likely to be found in botanical gardens, will illustrate the "synangium" type of sporangium. *Angiopteris*, another tropical fern, more likely to be found in greenhouses than *Marattia*, has a sporangium which furnishes an easy transition to that of the Cycadales.

For the reduction of chromosomes, the sections should not be thicker than 5 μ. *Osmunda* is particularly good for this purpose because the number of chromosomes is comparatively small. The young sporangia of *Osmunda cinnamomea* and *O. claytoniana* show

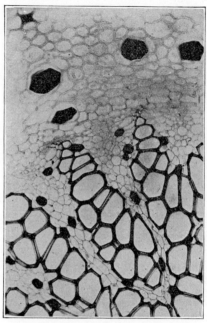

Fig. 100.—*Angiopteris evecta:* photomicrograph showing a detail of the stele shown in Figure 99. Stained in safranin. Eastman Commercial Ortho film, Wratten E filter (orange); Bausch and Lomb 8-mm. objective, N.A. 0.50; exposure, 1¼ seconds. Negative by Dr. P. J. Sedgwick. ×60.

the mother-cell stage in the autumn, but the division into spores does not occur until the following spring, in the vicinity of Chicago, the mitotic figures being found during the latter part of April (Fig. 102). *O. regalis* does not reach the mother-cell stage in the autumn. Material for mitosis should be collected during the first two weeks in May.

For the development of a typical sporangium of the eusporangiate type, nothing is better than *Botrychium*. Buds of *B. virginianum* taken in September or October show sporangia with well-marked sporoge-

nous tissue. From the underground bud, cut off the fertile portion of
the leaf and fix it separately. The reduction divisions in the spore
mother-cell take place soon after the leaf appears above ground. The
later sporogenous stages and the reduction stages furnish excellent
illustrations of the "tapetal plasmodium."

For all stages in sporangia, until they begin to turn brown, use the
Chicago chromo-acetic–osmic solution. Stain in safranin, gentian violet, orange, for morphological study; and in iron-alum haematoxylin
with a light tinge of orange for mitotic figures.

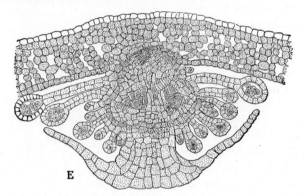

E

FIG. 101.—*Cyrtomium falcatum:* various stages in the development of sporangia, covered by a
peltate indusium. Chromo-acetic–osmic; safranin, gentian violet, orange. ×90. From Chamberlain's *Elements of Plant Science* (McGraw-Hill Book Co., New York).

Prothallia.—The best prothallia are those found growing naturally.
In *Sphagnum* bogs and on damp shaded banks, and on rotting logs,
they are sometimes found in abundance, and may be so large that
they look like *Pellia.* It is easier to find them in the ferneries of greenhouses on pots and on the benches.

Prothallia are easily grown from spores. Ripe spores of some fern
or other can be obtained at any time of the year either in the field or in
the greenhouse. Spores usually germinate promptly and produce good
prothallia, even if the sowing is not made for several months after the
spores have been collected.

Fine prothallia of *Pteris aquilina* have been grown two years after
the spores were gathered. Some, however, must be sown at once, or
they will not germinate at all. Spores which are large and contain
enough chlorophyll to make them appear greenish should be sown at
once. The spores of the common *Osmunda regalis,* and of the other

members of the genus, must be sown as soon as ripe, or they fail to germinate. The prothallia of *O. regalis*, if carefully covered with glass, may be kept for a long time, and they become quite large. Prothallia of this fern in the writer's laboratory produced ribbon-like outgrowths 5 mm. wide and more than 5 cm. in length. These prothallia continued to produce archegonia, antheridia, and ribbon-like outgrowths for more than a year, when they suddenly "damped off." Lang watered

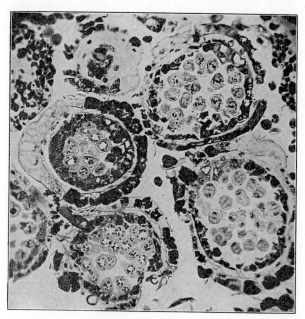

FIG. 102.—*Osmunda cinnamomea:* photomicrograph of sporangia with spore mother-cells in various stages of division; fixed in Flemming's weaker solution and stained in iron-alum haematoxylin; from a preparation by Dr. S. Yamanouchi. Negative by Miss Ethel Thomas. ×114.

prothallia with a weak solution of permanganate of potash, which kills the fungi but does not injure the prothallia. He does not state the strength of the solution, but 4 or 5 crystals to 1 liter of water seems to be effective. Enough should be added to give the water a deep purple color.

The prothallia of most ferns will grow for a long time under such conditions. *Pteris aquilina* and many other ferns often furnish a good supply of antheridia 3 weeks after sowing, and the archegonia appear soon after, but it is well to make sowings 6 weeks before material is needed for use. In *P. aquilina* and in many others, if the spores are sown too thickly only antheridial plants will be obtained (Fig. 103). If crowded, fern prothallia often have peculiar shapes and produce antheridia very early (Fig. 104). If they are to produce archegonia, they must have sufficient room and nutrition.

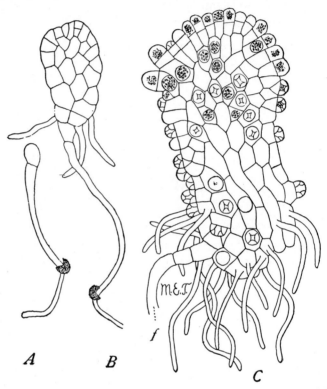

A   *B*   *C*

FIG. 103.—*Pteris aquilina: A*, filamentous stage, *B*, the apical cell has been established and several segments have been cut off; the figure shows the initial rhizoid and also three rhizoids coming from the main body of the prothallium; *C*, an older prothallium covered with antheridia in various stages of development. From a drawing by Miss M. E. Tarrant.

The best method we have ever seen for growing fern prothallia was devised by M. J. Costello, head gardener at the University of Chicago. The diagrammatic Figure 105 will make the method clear. Select a clean flower-pot, as porous as possible, and pack it full of wet *Sphagnum*. Wet the outside of the pot and invert it in a pan of water. Sow the spores on the surface of the pot and cover with a bell jar. No further wetting is necessary, except to take care that the water in the pan does not dry up. With *Pteris longifolia* there may be antheridia in 2 weeks; archegonia in 3 or 4 weeks; and in 5 or 6 weeks, abundant sporophytes in various stages. Prothallia grown by Costello's method are entirely free from soil and, consequently, very convenient for cutting or for mounting whole.

While there should always be a study from living material, it is worth while to make permanent mounts, even for habit study. For such study, the prothallia should be mounted whole. Fix in the Chicago

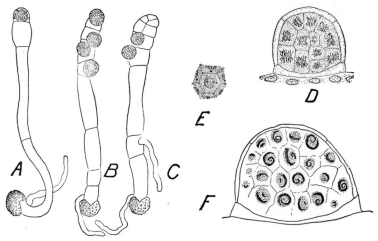

Fig. 104.—Fern prothallia: *A–C, Pteris longifolia*, bearing antheridia at an early stage; ×230. *D–F, Nephrodium molle: D*, mitosis in the antheridium; *E*, young sperm mother-cell and parts of 6 others, 3 of them showing the blepharoplast from which the cilia will develop; *F*, antheridium with nearly mature sperms. *D–F* ×580.

chromo-acetic–osmic solution. If the material shows any tendency to break up, use 2 c.c. of acetic acid instead of 3 c.c. In cities where water is treated with copper or other substances, the difficulty may sometimes be due to the water rather than to any excess of acetic acid. Formalin–acetic acid (10 c.c. formalin, 5 c.c. acetic acid to 100 c.c. water) is good for material which is to be mounted whole. Stain some in iron-alum haematoxylin, and some in phloxine and anilin blue. Mount in Venetian turpentine, using material from each stain for each mount. Select stages so that each preparation will show the filamentous stage, the apical cell stage, the group of initials stage, and also antheridia and archegonia.

For sections, use the Chicago formula. If the gradual processes of dehydrating, clearing, and infiltrating at room temperature and on the top of the bath have been observed, about 20 minutes in the bath may be sufficient; not more than 30 minutes should be needed for any prothallia. About 10 μ is a good thickness for such views of the archegonium as are shown in Figures 106, 107, and 108. Safranin, gentian violet, orange is a good stain.

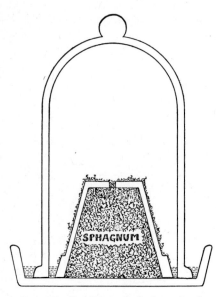

FIG. 105.—Costello's method of growing fern prothallia.

For the development of the antheridium and sperm, and especially for the blepharoplasts and their transformation, cut 2 or 3 μ in thickness and use iron-haematoxylin (Fig. 104, *D, E, F*); for the development of archegonia, cut at 5 μ and stain in the safranin, gentian violet, orange combination.

The gametophyte of *Botrychium* is subterranean and tuberous. It sometimes reaches a length of 7–12 mm. and a thickness of 4–5 mm. Usually, it is not more than 5 or 6 mm. long and 2 or 3 mm. thick. Gametophytes showing the development of antheridia and archegonia are not likely to be more than 2 or 3 mm. long and 1 or 2 mm. thick. Near large plants, look for small sporelings, not more than 1 or 2 cm. in height. Dig very carefully and you may find the gametophytes attached. The soil should be examined for smaller specimens. Most of the gametophytes will be found at a depth of 1–3 cm. Fix in chromo-acetic acid.

No one has yet succeeded in raising the prothallia from the spores. The prothallia always contain an endophytic fungus, but even when this is present no one has succeeded in raising prothallia. Perhaps there is long-delayed germination and development, as in *Lycopodium*, and no one has followed cultures for 5 or 6 years.

The prothallium of *Ophioglossum* is harder to find or, perhaps it would be better to say, harder to recognize, for it is also subterranean and tuberous and, besides, looks so much like the root that you may not recognize it, even when you have it in your hand.

The embryo.—Instructive mounts of the whole embryo, with the prothallium still attached, can be made by the Venetian turpentine method. Iron-alum haematoxylin, with the stain not too deep, is good; phloxine and anilin blue are more transparent and will show the structure of the root, if the two stains are well balanced.

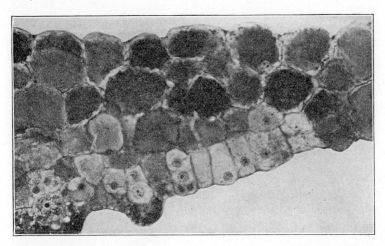

Fig. 106.—*Osmunda cinnamomea:* photomicrograph of vertical section from the notch toward the base of the prothallium showing four stages in the development of the archegonium. Chromoacetic acid; safranin, gentian violet; from a preparation by Dr. W. J. G. Land. Negative by Miss Ethel Thomas. ×425.

For sections, cut longitudinally, perpendicular to the prothallium. *Pteris longifolia* may show the young embryo within 3 or 4 weeks; *Osmunda*, somewhat later.

Nephrodium molle, often found in greenhouses, is generally parthenogenetic, the embryos developing from vegetative cells of the prothallium. The prothallia are very small, but they can be piled up like little sheets of paper. It is better to dehydrate in a Petri dish, piling the prothallia into little groups and weighting them down a little with a thick cover glass or very thin slide. A whole group can then be cut at one time, yielding many stages with comparatively little labor. *Pteris cretica*, an omnipresent greenhouse form, is also very often parthenogenetic.

The heterosporous filicales.—The four genera, *Pilularia*, *Marsilia*, *Salvinia*, and *Azolla*, are aquatic, the first two growing rooted but more or less submerged, and the other two floating freely on the water. *Marsilia* is the most available and convenient laboratory type of this group. It is easily grown in a pond or in an aquarium in the green-

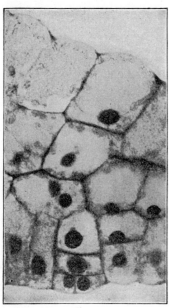

Fig. 107.—*Osmunda cinnamomea:* photomicrograph of vertical section of prothallium with an early stage in the development of the archegonium, showing the basal cell, two neck cells, and, between them, the cell which is to give rise to the neck canal cell, the ventral canal cell, and the egg. Chromo-acetic acid; safranin, gentian violet; from a preparation by Dr. W. J. G. Land. Negative by Miss Ethel Thomas. ×425.

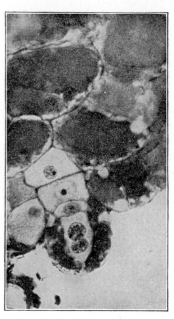

Fig. 108.—*Osmunda cinnamomea:* photomicrograph of a vertical section with a young archegonium, showing the neck canal cell with two nuclei, the ventral canal cell, the egg, and the basal cell. Chromo-acetic acid; safranin, gentian violet; from a preparation by Dr. W. J. G. Land. Negative by Miss Ethel Thomas. ×293.

house. In setting it out in a pond, select a place with a gently sloping bank, so that part of the material may be under water and part may creep up the bank. In the greenhouse, a rectangular aquarium may be tilted to secure the same conditions. The portions which are not under water will continue to fruit during the summer and autumn. The whole sporocarp cuts easily in paraffin during the development of sporangia, the division of the spore mother-cells, and even during the earlier stages in the formation of spores. Except in the case of the youngest sporocarps, it is better to cut off a small portion at the top and at the bottom to facilitate fixing and infiltration. The mother-cell stage and the young spores will be found in sporocarps which are just beginning to turn brown. In nature, no further nuclear divisions take place within the sporangium until the next spring, but the wall of the sporocarp becomes extremely hard. Sporocarps for germinating should not be collected until they are so hard that it is impossible to crush them between the thumb and finger. They can be kept in a box until needed for use. When you find them in good condition, make a big collection, for they retain their power of germination almost in-

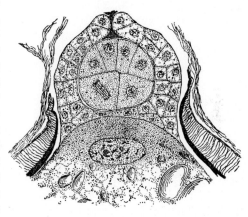

Fig. 109.—*Marsilia quadrifolia:* upper portion of megaspore with an archegonium containing a young embryo. ×212.

definitely, sporocarps from poisoned herbarium specimens 50 years old germinating readily. Sporocarps which have been kept in 95 per cent alcohol for years germinate almost as quickly as those which have been kept in a dry box.

To germinate sporocarps, cut away a portion of the hard wall along the front edge and place the sporocarp in a dish of water. The gelatinous ring with its sori will sometimes come out in a few minutes. In less than 24 hours, sometimes within 10 or 12 hours, microspores, starting from the one-cell stage, will produce the mature sperms; and the development of the female gametophyte is equally rapid. Starting with the uninucleate megaspore, the stage found when the gelatinous ring comes out, the archegonium may be developed and fertilization may occur within 12 hours; and within 36 hours, stages like that shown in Figure 109 may be reached. At the end of a week, there may be green sporophytes more than a centimeter in length.

It is obvious that material should be fixed at frequent intervals if

one is to secure a series of stages in the development of the gametophytes and embryo.

For young sporocarps, up to the pale brown stage, try Gourley's
basic fuchsin method. Take a small piece of rhizome with a leaf and
sporocarps; cut, under the stain, and after the solution has stained all
the vascular system of the sporocarp, fix in 95 per cent alcohol, 24
hours; absolute alcohol, 24 hours; treat with the xylol mixtures and
then with pure xylol. Finally, put it into a very small bottle with
equal parts of xylol and carbon disulphide. Such a preparation can be
mounted in balsam in a shallow cell.

For sections showing the development of the antheridium and
sperms, it is better to remove the megaspores from the sorus,
since they occasion considerable difficulty in cutting. Fix in the
Chicago chromo-acetic–osmic solution and stain in iron-alum haematoxylin.

The older megaspores, with archegonia or embryos at the apex, are
very hard to cut. Fix in formalin-alcohol–acetic acid; wash in 50 per
cent alcohol; treat with 10 per cent hydrofluoric acid in 50 per cent
alcohol for 2 days; wash thoroughly in 50 per cent alcohol; 70 per cent
alcohol, 24 hours; 85, 95, and 100 per cent alcohol, 24 hours each; then
the usual xylol series. The need for a good paraffin is more urgent in
such a case than for material which is not so hard to cut. A little bayberry wax will improve a paraffin which is not quite up to grade. If
sections come loose from the slide, use Land's fixative.

The sperm, which in *Marsilia* has an unusually large number of
turns in the spiral, is easily mounted whole. When the sperms have
become numerous, put several megaspores upon a slide and heat gently
until dry. Then wet the preparation in any alcohol and stain sharply
in acid fuchsin. Dehydrate in absolute alcohol for 2 or 3 hours, changing 2 or 3 times; clear in clove oil, and mount in balsam. Such a preparation will often show a score of sperms in the gelatinous funnel leading down to the neck of the archegonium.

Azolla is not difficult to obtain, and it is easy to get a series of stages
in the development of the micro- and megasporangia; but it is not at
all easy to find the gametophytes, since the spores germinate only
after they have been set free by the decay of the plant. *Azolla* does
not fix well in any of the chromic-acid series, because it catches so
much air that it will not sink. Alcohol-formalin–acetic, or hot alco-

holic corrosive sublimate–acetic acid, formalin (4 g. corrosive sublimate, 5 c.c. formalin; 5 c.c. acetic acid, 100 c.c. of 50 per cent alcohol)
can be recommended for both *Azolla* and *Salvinia*. Both of these
forms grow well in the greenhouse, floating on the water in tanks or
aquaria; but *Azolla* seldom fruits under such conditions. *Salvinia*
sometimes produces microsporangia in the greenhouse, but megasporangia are comparatively rare.

CHAPTER XXVI

SPERMATOPHYTES

If one were a master of all phases of technique needed for a microscopic study of seed plants, one would need nothing more for the groups below, for material ranges from structures so delicate that they need more skill and patience than the coenocytic algae to structures so hard that the method for rock sections is the best way to get mounts.

We cannot hope to give even approximately complete directions for making preparations, but must be content to give a few hints which may prove helpful in collecting material and in securing mounts of the more important structures. We shall consider the gymnosperms and the angiosperms separately, although in many respects the technique is the same for both.

GYMNOSPERMS—CYCADALES

Cycas revoluta, the Sago Palm, can be found in almost any large greenhouse which keeps decorative plants. The large conservatories of city parks may keep, in addition, some species of *Ceratozamia* or *Encephalartos*. Only one cycad, *Zamia*, occurs in the United States, and it is confined to Florida. In *Encephalartos* and *Ceratozamia* the development of the ovule, and even the development of the female gametophyte up to the fertilization period, takes place quite naturally in the greenhouse, where pollination is not likely to occur; but in other genera, the female cones, or at least their ovules, nearly always abort unless pollination takes place. *Cycas revoluta* is so abundant as a decorative plant on lawns in our Gulf states that artificial pollination is quite practicable. Shake pollen from a male cone into a box, carry it to a female plant, put some of the pollen on a piece of paper and puff it over the young female sporophylls. In the greenhouse, if cycads of different species, or even different genera, but of different sexes, are coning, cross-pollination is likely to be successful. Even if there should be no fertilization, the pollination is likely to stimulate the ovule so that it may develop to nearly full size, with good archegonia. The vegetative structures are natural enough, but, with the exception of leaves and small roots, are not so available, since it would kill or, at least, damage the plant to take pieces of the stem.

The vegetative structures.—All the vegetative structures cut rather easily.

The stem.—*Zamia*, which grows in various parts of Florida, is the most available material. Directions for handling the stem are given on page 140.

Stems of the larger cycads are not likely to be obtained, except in the field, and they are confined to tropical and subtropical regions.

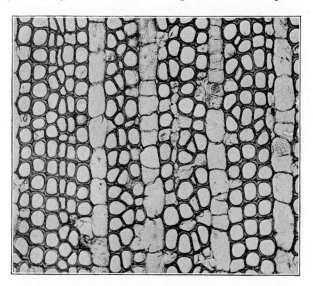

Fig. 110.—*Dioon spinulosum:* photomicrograph of transverse section of wood, cut from fresh material. ×105.

Cycad stems cut better while fresh (Fig. 110) but, fixed in formalin (10 c.c.), acetic acid (5 c.c.), and water (85 c.c.), fleshy stems like *Zamia* and *Ceratozamia* cut well, even after years in the solution.

A piece of cycad trunk 15–30 cm. in diameter and 20 cm. in length will survive a journey of 6 weeks or even 2 months, if care be taken to coat the exposed ends with a mixture of melted paraffin and moth balls, using 3 or 4 moth balls as large as marbles to half a kilo of paraffin. If material is to be fixed before cutting, use 6–10 per cent formalin in water.

Dr. La Dema Mary Langdon succeeded in cutting paraffin sections of the adult wood of *Dioon spinulosum*. She fixed 1–2 cm. cubes of adult wood in formalin–acetic acid–alcohol (6 c.c. formalin, 3 c.c.

acetic acid, 100 c.c. of 50 per cent alcohol). After thorough washing, 24–48 hours in running water, the blocks were softened for 3–6 weeks in 50 per cent hydrofluoric acid in water. With dry material, the cubes were boiled and cooled repeatedly to remove air. The usual gradual processes of dehydrating, clearing, and infiltrating were then followed and sections were cut with a sliding microtome, with the knife placed obliquely, as in cutting celloidin. The sections are likely to curl. With the forefinger of the left hand touching the section gently as it is being cut, the curling can be prevented and the section sticks to the finger enough to facilitate transferring the sections to the slide as fast as they are cut. In this way, it is easy to cut sections 10 or 15 μ thick, while 20–30 μ is the usual thickness of a similar section cut without imbedding.

The course of the vascular bundles, as they pass to the cones, is quite peculiar. Instructive preparations may be made by cutting longitudinal sections, about 3 mm. thick, through the apex of the stem and, without staining, clearing thoroughly and mounting in balsam. In this way we have mounted sections 5 cm long, 15 cm. wide, and 3 mm. thick.

The course of the bundles in the xylem zone and in the cortex may be traced by clearing the cubes in xylol and then transferring to equal parts of xylol and carbon disulphide. Placed on a glass plate with an electric light bulb beneath, the bundles are quite distinct.

The root.—Roots up to 3 cm. in diameter are easily cut freehand, but cycad roots are so exceptionally easy to cut that they should be imbedded in paraffin (Fig. 111). Formalin–acetic acid–alcohol is good for anatomical preparations; but it is better to use the Chicago chromo-acetic–osmic solution for root-tips and for the peculiar aerial, apogeotropic roots. These aerial roots, which are very common in greenhouses, have a zone of *Anabaena* in the cortex and also have bodies looking like bacteria (bacterioids). For general structure and for the *Anabaena*, stain as for any root-tip. For the bacterioids, it is better to fix in 10 per cent neutral formalin and stain as for chondriosomes.

Transverse sections of roots up to 4 cm. in diameter can be cut while fresh, by flooding the root with alcohol for every section.

The leaves.—Young tender leaves should be fixed in formalin acetic alcohol and cut in paraffin. The adult leaves are rigid and can be cut without imbedding. Pile leaflets, one on top of another, and tie them together with a string, letting about a centimeter project beyond the string. Dip the whole thing in paraffin 2 or 3 times. There will be no infiltration, but the paraffin will hold the leaflets in place. Cut on a sliding microtome with an oblique stroke, placing the sections in a dish of cold water as fast as they are cut. The sections fall out from the paraffin, which is easily skimmed away. Fix the sections in formalin acetic alcohol for 24 hours; harden in 85 per cent alcohol, 24 hours; 70 and 50 per cent alcohol, 1 hour each. Stain in safranin and light green. Don't make the periods too short, if you want the best preparations.

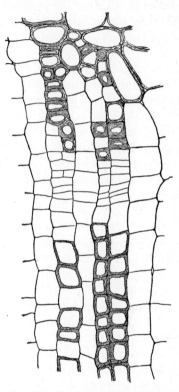

Spermatogenesis.—Except in the earliest stages, the staminate cones are too large to be cut whole. The individual sporophylls, with their sporangia, cut easily up to the formation of microspores; then the sporangium wall hardens rapidly and cutting becomes difficult. Up to the young microspore stage, fix in chromo-acetic–osmic-acid solution (1 g. chromic acid, 2 c.c. acetic acid, 6 c.c. 1 per cent osmic acid to 100 c.c. water). With a larger proportion of acetic acid, our results have not been satisfactory.

Up to the stage when the micro-spores become free, stain in iron-alum haematoxylin. As soon as the microspore mother-cells become

FIG. 111.—*Encephalartos altensteinii:* part of transverse section of root, showing cambium, with 3 rows of xylem cells below, and phloem above; the latter with several thick-walled suberized cells. ×230.

free, the Belling method, as modified by Dr. McClintock, can be used. Try this: Squeeze the microspore mother-cells out into a thin smear, on a slide with a very thin coat of Mayer's albumen fixative. Invert for 2–5 seconds over the mouth of a bottle containing 1 per cent osmic acid. Put on very gently with a pipette a couple of drops formalin acetic alcohol (formalin 1 c.c., acetic acid 1 c.c., absolute alcohol

4 c.c.). Renew the fixing agent. Don't let it dry up. After an hour, run down gradually through the alcohols to water and stain in iron-alum haematoxylin.

Fix later stages in formalin acetic alcohol. Transverse sections are easier to cut since the peripheral end of a sporophyll can be cut only in early stages. Sporogenous tissue appears first at the base of the cone and last at the top; but pollen ripens first at the top and last at the bottom.

In all genera of cycads, the microspore germinates while still within the sporangium, the pollen grain, at the time of shedding, consisting of a prothallial cell, a generative cell, and a tube cell. For preparations at the shedding stage, shake the cone over a piece of paper and pour the pollen into water. After 15 or 20 minutes, put it into the fixing agent. In wind-pollinated plants, the pollen would look shriveled if you put it into a fixing agent before it regained its turgidity.

The pollen, mounted whole, makes beautiful preparations. Fix in formalin–acetic acid (formalin 10 c.c., acetic acid 5 c.c., water 100 c.c.), and let it remain here for a week, shaking it gently once in a while. Stain in iron-alum haematoxylin and follow the Venetian turpentine method. Or, run it up to 85 per cent alcohol and, after 2 days, run it back to water. Then stain and follow the Venetian turpentine method. Since the pollen makes fine preparations when cut at 2 to 5 μ in paraffin, the lot may be run up to 85 per cent alcohol and then part may be taken back to water, while the rest goes on to paraffin. Powers' methods, described on page 217, are satisfactory for pollen to be mounted whole.

If some material is put into a 5 or 10 per cent sugar solution for 2 or 3 days, early stages in the formation of the pollen tube may be added. In a week or two the tubes may reach several times the length of the pollen grain; but, as far as we know, the generative cell has never divided in culture solutions (Fig. 112 A).

The development of the pollen tube and its structures must be studied in sections of the nucellus. As soon as the integument is removed the nucellus is exposed and the position of the pollen tubes is easily determined, since the haustorial portions of the tubes form brownish lines radiating from the nucellar beak. Having learned the location of the pollen tubes, it is better not to remove the integument, but to remove the female gametophyte; then cut from the underside of the nucellus against the hard, stony layer of the integument so as to remove a small piece of the nucellus 5–7 mm. square, according to the species. Fix in chromo-acetic–osmic acid (1 g. chromic acid, 2 c.c. acetic acid, 6 c.c. 1 per cent osmic acid to 100 c.c. water). Nothing surpasses iron-alum haematoxylin for all the stages in the development of the male gametophyte (Fig. 112 A–C). By using a 2 per cent iron-alum for 5 or 6 hours and staining overnight, or even 24 hours, the stain can be drawn so precisely that the portion of the cilia between

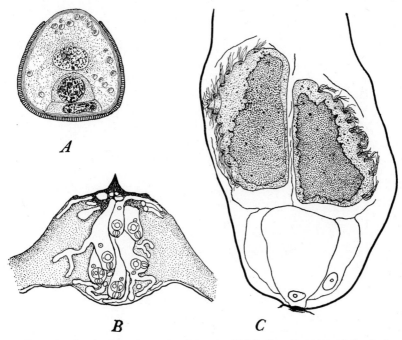

A

B C

Fig. 112.—*Ceratozamia mexicana:* A, pollen grain which has been in a sugar solution for two days; $\times876$. B, nucellus with numerous pollen tubes; $\times17$. C, basal end of pollen tube showing the persistent prothallial cell; outside it the stalk cell; and, above, the two sperms still inclosed in the sperm mother-cells; $\times156$.

the blepharoplast and the surface can be differentiated from the free portion (Fig. 113).

The pollen tubes, with their sperms, make instructive preparations when mounted whole. Fix the nucellus, with its pollen tubes, as if for paraffin sections. About 6 per cent formalin in water has proved successful. Wash in water for 2 hours and stain in aqueous safranin, 4 or 5 hours. Extract the stain until it is satisfactory, and then transfer to

10 per cent glycerin and follow the Venetian turpentine method. When the turpentine becomes thick enough for mounting, tease the pollen tubes from the nucellus and mount with pieces of cover glass

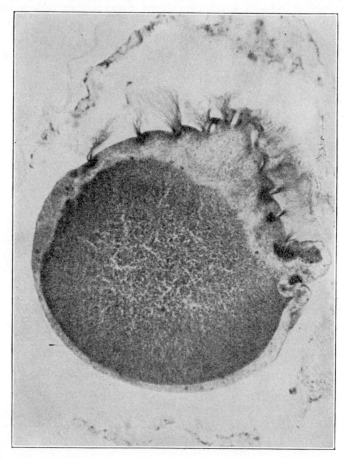

Fig. 113.—*Ceratozamia mexicana:* photomicrograph of a longitudinal section of a sperm, showing the very large nucleus, thin sheath of protoplasm which is thicker at the apical end, and blepharoplast cut across in various places and bearing numerous cilia. At this stage, the sperm is swimming in the pollen tube. Cramer contrast plate. Negative by Miss Ethel Thomas. ×506.

under the cover to prevent crushing. Iron-alum haematoxylin, which is so satisfactory for staining sections of sperms, is the most unsatisfactory stain we have tried for staining the cycad pollen-tube structures whole.

The immense sperms of the cycads, more than 100 μ in diameter, can be seen with the naked eye. If the tip of the nucellus with the pollen chamber be removed when the sperms are mature, the large pollen tubes, 300 to 500 μ in diameter, are very conspicuous. Even with the naked eye, the movements of the sperm can be seen; and with a pocket lens one can see some details. Place the piece of nucellus on a slide in a drop of water, but without any water on the pollen tubes, and examine with a 16 mm. objective. The amoeboid movements of the sperm, and also a quick movement reminding one of the sudden jerky movement of *Vorticella*, are easily seen; and, by closing the diaphragm a little, some movement of the cilia should be distinguishable. *Zamia* is the only genus available in the United States; but even its rather small female cones, as they near the fertilization stage, will keep 4 or 5 weeks after they have been removed from the plant.

In the region of Miami, Florida, pollination takes place late in December or early in January; blepharoplasts appear in March, and swimming sperms are found during the first 2 weeks of June. In northern Florida, all stages are 2 or 3 weeks later. If one is so fortunate as to get cones of *Ceratozamia*, the sperms should be found from the last week in June through the second week in July.

Oögenesis.—The ovules of the Cycads and *Ginkgo* are very large, and, when mature, thin sections cannot be cut by any method yet discovered. In younger stages it is not difficult to get good sections of the entire ovule. Slabs should be cut from two sides of the ovule to facilitate fixing and infiltration. During free nuclear stages in the endosperm, and even during earlier stages in the formation of walls, care must be taken that the slabs may not cut into the endosperm, or even too near to it, for the endosperm is so turgid that it may even break out or, at least, will be distorted. Even after the ovule approaches its full size, it can be cut entire, until the stony layer begins to harden. Paraffin sections of the entire ovule, cut 15–20 μ thick, and stained rather lightly in safranin, gentian violet, orange, make very instructive preparations. When the fresh ovule can no longer be cut easily with a razor, it is not worth while to try to cut it in paraffin. Interesting preparations may be made by cutting from the median longitudinal portion of the ovule a slab about 5 mm. thick. The slab should be fixed, washed, dehydrated, and cleared in xylol. It should then be kept in a flat-sided bottle. Such a preparation shows the integument, micropyle, nucellus with its beak, pollen tubes, the stony and fleshy layers, general course of vascular bundles, and the female gametophyte with its archegonia.

If living cones should be available, it would be worth while to try Gourley's basic fuchsin method. Under the liquid, cut the ovule off, with a little of the sporophyll. After 14 hours, fix the ovule in absolute alcohol, changing once or twice. After clearing, keep it in equal parts of xylol and carbon disulphide.

For thin sections of the archegonia, a cubical piece with an edge of 6 or 8 mm. should be cut from the top of the endosperm with a very sharp, thin blade. Since the slightest pressure upon the archegonia

Fig. 114.—*Zamia floridana:* photomicrograph of a small portion of a proembryo showing simultaneous free nuclear division. Fixed in chromo-acetic–osmic acid and stained in safranin, gentian violet, orange. Cramer contrast plate; Spencer 4-mm. objective, N.A. 0.65; ocular ×4; yellowish-green filter; camera bellows 50 cm.; arc light; exposure, 6 seconds. Negative by Miss Ethel Thomas. ×413.

will ruin the preparations, it is better not to cut closer to the archegonia than 2 mm. After the material is in 85 per cent alcohol, the sides of the cube can be shaved off with a safety razor, making the piece much smaller to cut, so that as many sections can be mounted on 2 slides as on 3, without the trimming.

Chromo-acetic–osmic acid (1 g. chromic acid, 2 c.c. acetic acid, and 6 c.c. of 1 per cent osmic acid to 100 c.c. of water) is a good fixing agent for all stages in oögenesis. During the free nuclear stage and early wall stage in the female gametophyte, some plasmolysis is to be anticipated. Hot alcoholic corrosive sublimate–acetic acid sometimes fixes these stages with less distortion.

Sporophyte.—During the period of simultaneous free nuclear division, which follows the fertilization of the egg, the mitotic figures are quite striking and are easily stained (Fig. 114).

After the embryos begin to grow down into the endosperm, oblong pieces containing the embryos should be cut out.

After the cotyledons appear, useful preparations may be made by dissecting out the entire embryos, which may be fixed in chromo-acetic acid, washed, stained in eosin or in Delafield's haematoxylin, placed in 10 per cent glycerin, and mounted by the Venetian turpentine method. Since the suspensors become long and irregular, each embryo should be placed in a separate dish, lest the suspensors become entangled and broken.

After the stony layer becomes hard, it is better to use a small fret saw for opening the ovule. Before the embryo has pushed down into the endosperm, the ovule should be sawed in two transversely. The endosperm and nucellus can then be picked out and treated as desired. After the tip of the embryo reaches the middle of the endosperm, the ovule should be sawed open longitudinally.

GYMNOSPERMS—GINKGOALES

From the standpoint of technique the Ginkgoales, now represented only by *Ginkgo biloba*, are less difficult than the Cycadales, but the difficulties are somewhat similar.

The vegetative structures.—The adult stem is harder to cut than *Pinus*, but good sections should be secured by boiling in water for 24 hours, soaking in equal parts 95 per cent alcohol and glycerin for a couple of weeks, and using the steam method.

Transverse sections of the "spur" shoots are easily cut. They have a comparatively large pith and narrow zone of wood, thus contrasting sharply with a long shoot of the same diameter, which has a small pith and wide zone of wood.

The petiole of the leaf and the peduncle of the ovule look alike; but transverse sections show two bundles in the petiole and four in the peduncle. On this account, it is thought that the peduncle consists of two petioles fused together, each bearing a blade (collar) with an ovule. The fact that, in "abnormal" cases, the collar becomes leaflike, is responsible for this interpretation. Both petiole and peduncle cut easily in paraffin.

Spermatogenesis.—The entire staminate cone, even at the time of shedding pollen, can be cut in paraffin. For the latest stages, however, it is better to remove the sporophylls and cut them separately, since the sections must not be thicker than 5 μ, if they are to show the internal structures of the pollen grain.

The young staminate cones become recognizable in June; by September, they have nearly or entirely reached the spore mother-cell stage, but the division of the spore mother-cell does not take place until the following April. In these early stages the bud scales should be carefully dissected away before fixing. Pollen is shed early in May. Fix in chromo-acetic acid, with or without a little osmic acid, cut 5 μ thick, and stain in iron-alum haematoxylin. There are four cells in the pollen grain at the time of shedding (Fig. 115).

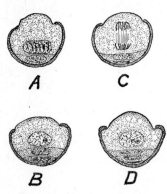

FIG. 115.—Microspores of *Gingko biloba: A*, first prothallial cell. *B*, first and second prothallial cells. *C*, the two prothallial cells and the mitosis which will give rise to the body cell and tube cell. *D*, the two prothallial cells, the lower nearly disintegrated, the body cell, and the tube cell. Pollen is shed in the condition shown in *D*. ×770.

For the development of the microsporangium, consult Dr. Starr's paper.

Pollen tubes and their structures must be studied in sections of the nucellus. Fertilization, in the Chicago region, occurs about the middle of September.

Oögenesis.—Young ovules about 0.25 mm. in length are found about the middle of April; the megaspore mother-cell and its division into four megaspores are found about the first of May; the free nuclear stage in the development of the female gametophyte extends from the first week in May to the first week in July; during July, walls appear; then come the archegonium initials and the growth of the archegonium, the ventral canal cell being cut off the second week in September; fertilization, free nuclear division in the sporophyte, and the beginning of walls may all be found before the end of September; cotyledon stages belong to October, and when the seeds fall in November the embryo extends throughout nearly the entire length of the endosperm. This is the winter resting stage, but, planted in the greenhouse, the seeds germinate without any resting period, as in the case of cycads.

For all stages in oögenesis and development of the embryo, use the Chicago chromo-acetic–osmic solution. If the gametophyte in early free nuclear stages should shrink, increase the acetic acid up to 4 c.c. and decrease the chromic acid to 0.7 or even 0.5 c.c. If the chromic acid is decreased, lengthen the time to 48 hours. Free nuclear stages, like this, in a thin layer of protoplasm surrounding a large central vacuole are the most difficult structures to fix well that the botanist encounters. They occur in various groups of plants.

For sections of the entire ovule, use safranin, gentian violet, orange; for free nuclear stages in both gametophyte and sporophyte, use iron-haematoxylin with a touch of orange; for the megaspore membrane, safranin seems to be the best stain.

The entire ovule, even at a late embryo stage, makes an effective demonstration when cleared whole in equal parts of xylol and carbon disulphide. If living material is available, it would be worth while to try Gourley's basic fuchsin method.

GYMNOSPERMS—CONIFERALES

Since *Pinus* is an available laboratory type, we shall describe methods for demonstrating various phases in the life-history of this genus, hoping that the directions will enable the student to experiment intelligently with similar forms. The dates are for *Pinus laricio* in the vicinity of Chicago, but dates will be different for different species and even for the same species in different regions; *P. laricio*, at Chicago, sheds pollen about the middle of June, but *P. maritima* at Auckland, New Zealand, sheds its pollen about the first of October. After a year's collecting in any region, there should be no difficulty, since the dates do not vary much from year to year.

The vegetative structures.—The stem, root, and leaf will be treated separately.

The stem.—The vascular cylinder is an endarch siphonostele, a type which, with few exceptions, is found throughout the living gymnosperms.

The young stem in its first year's growth is green and soft and is easily cut in paraffin. The best time to collect material is soon after the young shoot has emerged from the bud scales in the spring. Resinous material, like these young stems, do not fix well in aqueous media. With a thin safety razor blade, cut the stem transversely into pieces about 5 mm. in length; fix in formalin (10 c.c.), acetic acid (5 c.c.), 70 per cent alcohol (85 c.c.), for several days, or until needed for use. Imbed in paraffin, and stain in safranin and light green, or in safranin and Delafield's haematoxylin.

Longitudinal sections of the buds in winter or early spring condition are instructive for comparison with longitudinal sections of the ovulate cone. Trim away most of the bud scales and cut a slab from oppo-site sides, leaving a piece 2 or 3 mm. thick to be imbedded. The bud, and also selected pieces of the young stem, will show the structure of the young leaf.

Toward the end of the season, the first-year shoot is rigid enough to be cut without imbedding. This shoot and also two-, three-, and four-year shoots are generally cut without imbedding. When living mate-rial is cut in this way, the sections should be placed in water as they are cut, and then fixed in formalin–acetic acid for 24 hours. Run them up through close grades of alcohol to 85 per cent, where they should be left for 24 hours. Then, after $\frac{1}{2}$ hour in 70 and $\frac{1}{2}$ hour in 50 per cent alcohol, they can be stained. With this care, which is seldom taken, the protoplasm should not pull away from the cell walls of the cortex.

It is quite possible to cut paraffin sections of two-, three-, and four-year pine stems. Cut into pieces not more than 1 cm. long; fix in for-malin–acetic–alcohol for several days—or months; wash in 70 per cent alcohol, 8 hours; 85 per cent alcohol, overnight; 95 per cent, overnight; 100 per cent, overnight. Make the transfer to xylol *very* gradual. Place the pieces of stem in absolute alcohol at one side of a large Petri dish and put a few drops of a mixture of equal parts of xylol and absolute alcohol into the dish at the side opposite the material. Every half-hour or so, put in several drops of the alcohol-xylol mixture. When the quantity of liquid has nearly doubled, pour off about half of it, and continue the dropping. Then drop with pure xylol. When the material looks as if it were nearly cleared, transfer to pure xylol. Pieces of stem 1 cm. in diameter and 5 mm. thick should be cleared in about 24–36 hours. Then put some paraffin into the xylol, about 3 hours at room temperature; put in more and leave it on the bath for 3 hours; then inside the bath, 30–36 hours, with three changes of paraffin. Imbed. The time for mixtures of paraffin and xylol is the minimum.

For the structure of the adult stem, select a clear board (*Pinus strobus* is very good); and for transverse sections, cut out pieces 2 cm. long and trimmed to give sections 5×8 mm.; for longitudinal sections, use pieces 2 cm. long, with 5 and 10 mm. for the other two faces.

Cut from the face which will give sections 5×10 mm. Orient care-fully, so that the longitudinal radial sections shall be exactly parallel with the rays, and the longitudinal tangential sections exactly tan-gential to the rays.

Pinus strobus needs no preliminary treatment except a few hours' soaking in water; but harder pines and most of the other conifers should be boiled in water for 24 hours—there is no harm in letting it cool overnight—and transferred to equal parts 95 per cent alcohol and glycerin. Even soft pine may remain in this mixture for at least a week, and it is a good plan to keep in this mixture, as long as possible, all woody material which is to be sectioned. Cut by the hot steam method. The Durham duplex blade cuts better in the Spencer holder, as now made; but the "Gem" or "Star" blade, with the back broken off, is still better. The "Gem Double Life Razor Blade," without the back, can be obtained from The American Safety Razor Corporation, Jay and Johnson Streets, Brooklyn, N.Y. There is no extra charge for these blades. With the much thinner safety razor blades, the holder is likely to hit the block. Unless you can cut the transverse sections of mature wood of *Pinus strobus* (white pine) at 20 μ or thinner, there is something the matter in preparing the wood, in the microtome, in the knife, the angle of the knife, the steam, or the technician. Safranin and Delafield's haematoxylin is a good stain for any mature wood.

If you are in a hurry, soak the blocks in hot water 30 minutes, cut as thin as you can, treat with 95 per cent alcohol for 15 minutes, 50 per cent alcohol for 5 minutes, safranin for 2 hours (or overnight); rinse in 50 per cent alcohol, 85 per cent for 1 minute, light green for 2 minutes, 95 per cent for 10 seconds, absolute alcohol, for 10 seconds, clove oil until clear (a few seconds), xylol, balsam.

Every preparation of wood should show transverse, longitudinal radial, and longitudinal tangential sections.

Safranin and Delafield's haematoxylin should show the bars of Sanio clearly, as should also the safranin and crystal violet, or gentian violet. A 50 per cent alcoholic safranin may be allowed to stain for a week; and crystal violet, either in water or clove oil, may stain several hours or overnight. With care in differentiation, the long periods give splendid results. A little orange in clove oil usually improves the stain. If a preparation shows the bars of Sanio and differentiates the bordered pit, the technique is good (Fig. 116).

Jeffrey's maceration method will isolate the tracheids and other cells, which can then be stained and mounted in balsam. Be careful to wash out all acid before staining. Such preparations show features which are likely to be overlooked in sections.

FIG. 116.—*Pinus strobus:* photomicrograph of longitudinal radial section of mature wood of stem, showing bordered pits and bars of Sanio. Safranin and crystal violet. Eastman Commercial Ortho film, Wratten B filter (green); Spencer 4-mm. objective, N.A. 0.65; arc light; exposure, ½ second. Negative by Dr. P. J. Sedgwick. ×166.

The root.—The primary root should be studied in the embryo while it is still contained in the seed. Collect material in September, October, or at any later date. If material is collected in winter, the seeds should be soaked in water for a day or two before fixing. In any case, remove the testa and cut a thin slab from opposite sides of the endosperm to facilitate fixing and infiltration. For secondary roots and also for the structure of the stele in the primary root, germinate the seeds and fix material after the hypocotyl has reached a length of 3 or 4 cm. The

Fig. 117.—*Picea nigra:* photomicrograph of transverse section of root. Fixed in alcohol and stained in safranin and Delafield's haematoxylin. Eastman Commercial Ortho film, Wratten B filter (green); J. Swift and Son 1-inch objective; arc light; exposure, ¾ second. Negative by Dr. P. J. Sedgwick. ×28.

seeds of *Pinus edulis*, commonly called Piñon, or edible pine, can be obtained in most cities. They are particularly good for a study of the mature embryo and the seedling.

The older roots are treated like the stems. The structure of roots 2 or 3 mm. in diameter is wonderfully regular (Fig. 117).

The leaves.—Good sections of mature leaves of our common gymnosperms may be obtained in great quantities with little trouble by the following method: Make a bunch of the needles as large as one's little finger, wrap them firmly together with a string, allowing about ¼ inch of the bunch to project above the wrapping; dip 2 or 3 times into melted paraffin; and then dip into cold water to harden the paraffin. While there is no infiltration, the paraffin holds the needles in place for cutting. Fasten in a sliding microtome and cut with the knife placed obliquely. Place the sections in water as they are cut and the paraffin can be easily skimmed away. Then fix the sections in 95 per cent alcohol for half an hour; transfer to 70 per cent alcohol, where they should remain for about 5 minutes; then to 50 per cent alcohol, where they should be kept until the green color, due to chlorophyll, disappears. Stain in safranin and light green.

The young leaves cut easily in paraffin. But the mature leaves which, we used to think, must be cut freehand, can be got into paraffin. Then thinner and better sections can be made than are possible by the freehand method.

Take leaves at the end of their first growing season. They will have all the structures of leaves two or three years old and will cut better. With a safety razor, cut the needles into pieces about 1 cm. long. Fix in formalin acetic alcohol for several days: 70 per cent, overnight or 24 hours; 85 per cent, 2 days; 95 per cent, overnight or 24 hours; 100 per cent, overnight or 24 hours. Then use the close series of xylols. The time in the bath is likely to be 24 or 48 hours.

Spermatogenesis.—In October the clusters of staminate cones which are to shed their pollen in the coming spring are already quite conspicuous. The cones should be picked off separately, and the scales should be carefully removed so as to expose the delicate greenish cone within. At this time the sporogenous cells are easily distinguished. Material collected in January, or at any time before growth is resumed in the spring, shows about the same stage of development. If it is desired to secure a series of stages with the least possible delay, a branch bearing numerous clusters of cones may be brought into the laboratory and placed in a jar of water. Growth is more satisfactory in case of branches broken off in the winter than in those brought in before there has been any period of rest. The material can be examined from time to time, and a complete series is easily secured. The mitotic figures in the pollen mother-cells furnish exceptionally instructive preparations. The two mitoses take place during the last week in April and the first week in May. Staminate cones which will yield mitotic figures can be selected with certainty by examining the fresh material. Crush a microsporangium from the top of the cone and one from the bottom, add a small drop of water and a cover to each, and examine. If there are pollen tetrads at the bottom, but only undivided spore mother-cells at the top, it is very probable that longitudinal sections of the cone will yield the figures. If a drop of methyl green be allowed to run under the cover, it will enable one to see whether figures are present or not. When desirable cones are found, slabs should be cut from two sides, in order that the fixing agent may penetrate more rapidly and that infiltration with paraffin may be more thorough.

The later stages, showing the germination of the microspores, furnish better sections if the cones are cut transversely into small pieces about 5 mm. thick. It is very easy to get excellent mounts of the pollen just at the time of shedding, which, in *Pinus laricio* in the vicinity of Chicago, occurs near the middle of June. Shake a large number of cones over a piece of paper, thus securing an abundance of material; slide the pollen off from the paper into a bottle half-full of water and shake a little to wet the pollen grains, because pollen of wind-pollinated plants is likely to be more or less shriveled at the time of shedding. A few minutes in water will make the pollen turgid. Fix in formalin-alcohol–acetic acid. If material is so abundant that you can lose much of it and still have plenty left, fix in chromo-acetic–osmic acid. Staining, especially the staining of mitotic figures, is likely to be more brilliant after fixing in the chromic series. However, most of the mitoses take place before the pollen is shed or after it reaches the nucellus. Infiltration in the bath will not require more than 30 minutes. When the infiltration is complete, pour out into a paper tray or an imbedding dish, just warm enough to allow the pollen to settle to the bottom. A layer of pollen 3 mm. thick, with enough paraffin to make the cake about 5 mm. thick, will be satisfactory for cutting. Or, the paraffin may be poured out upon a piece of cold glass. Still another method is to leave the paraffin in a shell or vial during infiltration in the bath, and then let it cool in the bottle. After the paraffin is hard, break the bottle. Break the bottle carefully, cut off the lower portion of the paraffin containing the pollen, mount it on a block in the usual manner, and trim away some of the paraffin so that two parallel surfaces will make the sections ribbon well. Sections should not be thicker than 5 μ, and 3 μ is better.

Material in this stage shows a large tube nucleus, a somewhat lenticular (generative) cell with a more deeply staining nucleus, and, lastly, two small prothallial cells quite close to the spore wall. The prothallial cells cannot always be detected at this stage, and there may be some doubt as to whether two such cells are always present. The division of the lenticular cell into "stalk cell" and "body cell," and also the division of the body cell into the two male cells, must be looked for in sections of the nucellus of the ovule. As stated before, the dates are for *Pinus laricio* in the vicinity of Chicago. In *P. banksiana*,

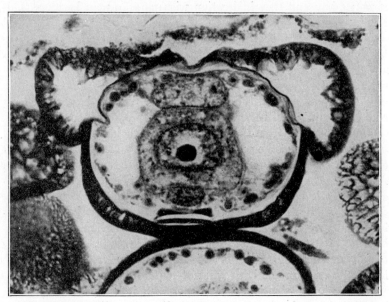

Fig. 118.—*Abies balsamea:* photomicrograph of pollen; one complete section showing two prothallial cells, the stalk cell, generation cell, and tube cell with starch grains. Fixed and cut while still within the microsporangium. Stained in safranin and gentian violet. Eastman Commercial Ortho film, Wratten B filter (green); Spencer 4-mm. objective, N.A. 0.66; ocular ×6; arc light; exposure, 6 seconds. Preparation by Dr. A. H. Hutchinson, negative by Dr. P. J. Sedgwick. ×784.

stages come about 2–3 weeks earlier. In pines in the Gulf states, the dates are still earlier. No pines are native in the Southern Hemisphere, but in cultivated specimens, which are very common, the dates are about 6 months from the Northern Hemisphere dates.

Abies balsamea is a better type for illustrating spermatogenesis, since the pollen mother-cells and the pollen grains are much larger and the division of the generative cell into the "stalk" and "body" cells takes place before the pollen is shed (Fig. 118).

Araucaria and *Agathis* are the best forms for illustrating numerous prothallial cells. *Podocarpus* and *Taxodium* are also good. *Thuja* or *Juniperus* may be used to illustrate the entire absence of prothallial cells, a very advanced condition; while both these genera have highly developed sperms, like those of the cycads and *Ginkgo*, except that they lack cilia. This is a good illustration of the fact that one structure may advance while another remains primitive.

Oögenesis.—In *Pinus laricio* the rudiment of the ovulate strobilus, which is to be pollinated in June, can be detected in the preceding October. The collection of this stage is very uncertain, because there seems to be no mark distinguishing buds containing ovules from buds which are only vegetative. By collecting numerous buds from the tops of vigorous trees which are known to produce an abundance of strobili, a few buds containing the desired stages may be obtained. In May, after the strobili break through the bud scales, material is easily collected. Up to the time of pollination the entire ovulate strobilus cuts easily in paraffin. Longitudinal sections of the cone at this time give good views of the bract and ovuliferous scale bearing the ovules. The integument is very well marked, and in the nucellus one or more sporogenous cells can usually be distinguished. The young cones of *Pinus contorta* are very interesting since the megasporangium often contains several megaspore mother-cells, most of which may divide, so that the structure really looks like a sporangium.

As soon as the scales close up after pollination, the cone begins to harden and soon makes trouble in cutting. Even before the scales close up, it is better to cut a slab from opposite sides of the cone; after the scales close, it is almost a necessity. For sections of the whole cone, fix in formalin acetic alcohol. Dr. Hannah Aase succeeded in cutting complete series of paraffin sections from cones of *Pinus banksiana* more than 2 cm. in length.

She fixed them in formalin alcohol, and used prolonged periods in dehydrating, clearing, and infiltrating. Land's dichromate of potash and glue fixative was used in fixing the sections to the slide. Such series of sections of large cones were necessary for an investigation of the vascular anatomy.

For a study of the ovule and the structures within it, cut the pair of ovules off from the scale with extreme care, because the young megagametophyte is so difficult to prepare without shrinking that it would be a pity to have any imperfections due to careless pressure. These difficult free nuclear stages begin in the autumn, are interrupted by winter, and are completed in May.

After walls appear there is less danger. From the middle of May to
the first of July collections should be made at intervals of two or three
days, since during these six weeks the gametophyte completes the free
nuclear stage and develops cell walls, the archegonium completes its
entire development, the egg is fertilized, and the sporophyte may
reach the suspensor stage.

At the stages shown in Figure 119 B–D, it is a good plan to remove
the female gametophyte with its proembryos from the ovule; but at

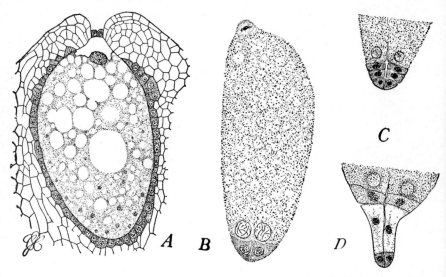

Fɪɢ. 119.—*Pinus laricio:* A, top of prothallium, with an archegonium just before the cutting
off of the ventral canal cell; fixed in Flemming's weaker solution and stained in Haidenhain's iron-
alum haematoxylin; collected June 18, 1897. B, C, D, early stages in the development of the embryo; fixed in chromo-acetic acid and stained in safranin, gentian violet, orange; collected July 2,
1897. ×104.

the stages shown in Figures 119 A and 120 the pollen tubes with their
contents are rapidly working their way through the nucellus toward
the archegonia, and consequently, in some of the material, it is better
to retain enough of the tissues of the ovule to keep the nucellus in
place. In later stages, after fertilization has taken place, the developing testa should be removed with great care, for a very slight pressure
is sufficient to injure the delicate parts within.

With any fixing agent of the chromic-acid series, the free nuclear
stages of the female gametophyte and, later, the archegonia and pro-

embryo stages, like those shown in Figure 119, are likely to show plasmolysis; but, by reducing the chromic acid to 0.5 c.c. and increasing the acetic acid to 3 c.c., and fixing for 48 hours, there is less danger.

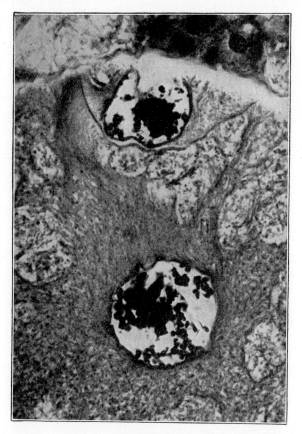

FIG. 120.—*Pinus laricio:* photomicrograph showing the formation of the ventral canal cell; usually this cell is not so large in proportion to the egg; fixed in Flemming's weaker solution and stained in safranin, gentian violet, orange; the preparation was made in 1897, the photomicrograph in 1915; Cramer contrast plate; 4-mm. objective; ocular ×4; Abbé condenser; yellowish-green filter and also a strong filter used in outdoor photography; camera bellows, 75 cm.; arc light; exposure, 7 minutes. Negative by Miss Ethel Thomas. ×587.

Stages, like those shown in Figure 119*B–D*, without any shrinking, were secured by Miss Ethel Thomas by using hot alcoholic corrosive sublimate–acetic acid with formalin (4 g. corrosive sublimate, 5 c.c.

acetic acid, 5 c.c. formalin, 100 c.c. 70 per cent alcohol). Figures like that shown in Figure 120 are better in chromo-acetic–osmic acid.

The period at which the various stages may be found varies with the species, the locality, and the season. In *Pinus laricio* the megaspore mother-cells appear as soon as the young strobili break through the bud scales. At Chicago, in the season of 1897, material collected May 27 did not yet show archegonia; the ventral canal cell was cut off about June 21 (see Fig. 120), the fusion of the egg and sperm nuclei occurred about a week later, and stages like Figure 119*B*, *C*, and *D*, were common in material collected July 2. In the season 1896 all the stages appeared about 2 weeks earlier. In *Pinus sylvestris* the stages appeared a little earlier than in *Pinus laricio*.

After the stage shown in Figure 119 *A* has appeared, it is necessary to collect every day until the stage shown in Figure 119*D* is reached. If collections are made at intervals of 3 or 4 days, the most interesting stages, like the cutting off of the ventral canal cell, fertilization, and the first divisions of the nucleus of the fertilized egg, may be missed altogether. It should be mentioned that all the ovules of a cone will be in very nearly the same stage of development; consequently, it is worth while to keep the ovules from each cone separate. Stages like that shown in Figure 120 are rare in miscellaneous collections, but if ovules from each cone are kept separate and this figure is found, the rest of the ovules from that cone will be likely to show some phase of this interesting mitosis.

Thuja and *Juniperus* are good types to illustrate the archegonium complex and the large, highly organized sperms. In *Thuja occidentalis*, in the Chicago region, a series from the appearance of archegonium initials to young embryos may be collected between June 10 and June 20. In *Juniperus virginiana*, in the same locality, pollination occurs late in May and fertilization takes place 12½ months later. The megaspores are formed late in April, and the development of the female gametophyte occupies about 6 weeks.

The embryo.—The early stages of the sporophyte, usually designated as the proembryo, have been mentioned already.

From the time when the suspensors begin to elongate up to the appearance of cotyledons, instructive preparations can be made by mounting the embryo whole. Dr. J. T. Buchholz has developed a method for handling these small objects. Remove the testa and then, under water, hold the endosperm gently with forceps and press the neck and upper part of the archegonium with a needle, pressing, and at the same time drawing, the needle away, so as to pull the young embryo out. Some of the embryos will be broken, but by care-ful manipulation more than half should be entirely uninjured. Fix in formalin (5 per cent in water), stain in Delafield's haematoxylin, transfer to 10 per cent glycerin, and continue with the Venetian turpentine method. A preparation made in this way is shown in the photomicrograph (Fig. 121).

These stages, and all subsequent stages, are easily cut in paraffin without removing the embryo from the endosperm. Cut a thin slab from opposite sides of the endosperm, fix in chromo-acetic acid, with or without osmic acid, imbed in paraffin, and stain in safranin and gentian violet. This will give a good view of the abundant starch and other food stuff, and at the same time will bring out sharply the cell walls of the embryo.

FIG. 121.—*Pinus banksiana:* photomicrograph of young embryos teased out by the method described in the text; from a preparation by Dr. J. T. Buchholz; Cramer contrast plate; 16-mm. objective; no ocular or Abbé condenser; camera bellows, 75 cm.; safranin filter; arc light; exposure, 17 seconds. Negative by Miss Ethel Thomas. ×54.

GYMNOSPERMS—GNETALES

Of the three peculiar genera belonging to this order only one, *Ephedra*, occurs in the United States. *Welwitschia* is found only in Damaraland, South Africa, and *Gnetum* is tropical and subtropical.

Gnetum thrives in the greenhouse, but the other two have not been cultivated successfully. The wood of *Ephedra* and *Gnetum* is extremely hard, but can be cut by the hot steam method. The wood of *Welwitschia* consists, principally, of a delicate parenchyma tissue, with numerous, large, rigid, spicular cells. Dr. Langdon cut beautiful sections by treating with 50 per cent hydrofluoric acid for 3–6 weeks and imbedding in paraffin. There should be no haste. Allow 24 hours for each grade of alcohol and for each grade of the paraffin mixtures. Allow at least 24 hours for the xylol-paraffin mixtures, half of the time at room temperature and half, on the top of the bath. Put the material in an open dish in the bath. About 2 or 3 days will be required, and the paraffin should be changed 3 or 4 times.

All of the Gnetales show vessels in the secondary wood, an angiosperm character.

The strobili can be fixed in formalin-acetic-alcohol, but in *Ephedra* the dry chaffy scales must be dissected away before completing the dehydration and infiltration with paraffin. If you can secure material of *Ephedra*, Dr. Land's researches present a very complete life-history, with dates of various stages and suggestions for fixing and staining.

CHAPTER XXVII

SPERMATOPHYTES

ANGIOSPERMS

This immense group demands knowledge and skill in the whole field of histological technique, for embryo sacs are so delicate that they are as difficult as the free nuclear stage in the female gametophyte of a gymnosperm, while the peach stone needs a petrotome rather than a microtome. Between these extremes there is everything imaginable in structure, chemical composition, and consistency.

Some hints will be given, but the student will gradually learn what should be cut freehand and what should be imbedded, what stages in floral development, what stages in the development of the embryo sac, or what stages in spermatogenesis are likely to be correlated with easily recognized field characters; and what fixing agents are likely to give the best results with various kinds of material.

The vegetative structures.—In stems, roots, and leaves the more delicate structures should be imbedded in paraffin and the more rigid structures should be cut without imbedding at all; but it should be remembered that the range of structures which can be imbedded in paraffin can be increased by the use of hydrofluoric acid and improvements in the paraffin method.

The stem.—The vascular cylinder of the angiosperms is either an endarch siphonostele, or a polystele derived from it. For a study of the development of the stem, the common geranium (*Pelargonium*) may be recommended. Near the base of a fresh stem, about 1 cm. in diameter, cut freehand sections and fix them in formalin acetic alcohol for 24 hours. The sections may be left here for months. Transfer to 50 per cent alcohol and leave them here until all chlorophyll is extracted. Probably 24 hours will be sufficient. Then stain in safranin and light green, or safranin and Delafield's haematoxylin. Such sections will show both primary and secondary structures in both stele and cortex. Higher up, there will still be secondary structures in the stele, but none in the cortex; and still higher up will be found the origin of interfascicular cambium. All of these can be cut without imbedding, but the earlier stages showing the differentiation of protoxy-

347

lem, metaxylem, and the origin of secondary xylem are too soft for successful freehand sections. Cut into pieces about 5 mm. long and fix in formalin acetic alcohol (10 c.c. formalin, 5 c.c. acetic acid, and 100 c.c. of 50 per cent alcohol). Imbed in paraffin.

The vascular system can be traced very successfully by Gourley's basic fuchsin method. Take a small plant of *Pelargonium* (*Geranium*), *Coleus*, or *Tropaeolum*; use only 6 or 8 inches of the tip. Cut off the base—under the stain—and when the stain has reached the tips of the highest leaves, fix and clear.

For a study of woody stems, *Tilia americana* (basswood) is good, and shoots from 5–10 mm. in diameter are easy to cut. Very hard stems like *Hicoria* (hickory) and *Quercus* (oak) must be boiled and treated with hydrofluoric acid, if you expect to cut shoots more than 5–7 mm. in diameter. *Tilia* stems, up to 5 or 6 mm. in diameter, can be cut in paraffin. Fix for 3 or 4 days in formalin acetic alcohol; treat with 10 or 20 per cent hydrofluoric acid for 4 or 5 days, wash thoroughly, and proceed as usual. About 24–48 hours in the bath should be sufficient.

Harder stems, up to 2 cm. in diameter, should be fixed in the same way, treated with 20 per cent hydrofluoric acid, washed thoroughly, and put into equal parts of 95 per cent alcohol and glycerin, where they may remain indefinitely, but should remain at least a week. Cut by the hot steam method.

Of course, veneer machines with very sharp knives cut large sections of the most refractory woods.

While a random selection of stems would furnish material for practice in technique we suggest that the stem of *Clintonia* shows a good siphonostele in a monocotyl; the rhizome of *Acorus calamus* is a good type for the amphivasal bundle and, although a monocotyl, still shows a differentiation into stele and cortex; *Zea mays*, universally used but not characteristic of monocotyls, shows scattered bundles, but not the amphivasal condition, *Aloe*, *Dracaena*, or *Yucca* will illustrate secondary wood in monocotyls. *Iris* has a highly developed endodermis in the rhizome; and *Nymphea* or *Nuphar* will show scattered bundles in a dicotyl.

Lenticels and *tyloses* are abundant and typical in *Menispermum*, and very thin sections can be cut without imbedding; but both these structures are well developed while the stem can still be cut in paraffin without previous treatment in hydrofluoric acid.

The sieve tubes of the phloem are easily demonstrated in *Cucurbita pepo*, the common pumpkin; other members of the family furnish good material. Take pieces of stem about 1 cm. long and not too hard to cut in paraffin, fix in formalin-acetic–alcohol, and stain in safranin, gentian violet, orange. Beautiful sections of the sieve tubes and sieve plates can be obtained by cutting out, very carefully with a thin safety razor, a single vascular bundle with a little of the surrounding parenchyma, and imbedding it in paraffin.

The tropical *Tetracera*, one of the Dilleniaceae, has sieve plates so large that they are easily seen with a pocket lens. The phloem area is so large in the larger stems that it can be cut out, practically free from the xylem, and imbedded in paraffin.

It was once thought that these large sieve tubes afforded an obvious illustration of the continuity of protoplasm; but, as a matter of fact, the actual protoplasmic connections are scanty and hard to demonstrate. Iron-alum haematoxylin and orange will differentiate the strands if you are careful.

Roots.—It has long been known that the root-tip furnishes constantly available material for a study of mitosis (Fig. 122). An onion thrown into a pan of water will soon send out numerous roots. Soak beans in water for several hours and then plant them in loose, moist sawdust. In a greenhouse, with "bottom heat," the primary root will be long enough in 2 or 3 days. The large, flat beans, especially *Vicia faba*, are very favorable. The root-tips of various species of *Trillium*, *Tradescantia virginica*, *Podophyllum peltatum*, *Arisaema triphyllum*, and *Cypripedium pubescens* may be mentioned as known to be favorable; but it is very possible that the best root-tip has not yet been tried.

Cell division does not proceed with equal rapidity at all hours of the day. Kellicott has shown that in the root-tips of *Allium* there are in each 24 hours two periods at which cell division is at the maximum, and two at which it is at the minimum. The maximum periods are shortly before midnight (11:00 P.M.), and shortly after noon (1:00 P.M.). The minima, when cell division is at the lowest ebb, occur about 7:00 A.M. and 3:00 P.M. When cell division is most vigorous, there is little elongation, and when cell division is at the minimum, cell elongation is at the maximum. Consequently, root-tips of *Allium* should be collected about 1:00 P.M. or 11:00 P.M. Lutman, later, made observations upon periodicity of mitosis in the desmid, *Closterium*; and in

1915, Karsten made a comparatively extended study of periodicity in various stems and roots, together with notes on algae.

It is safe to say that the maximum number of mitoses in root-tips will be found shortly after noon (1:00 P.M.) and shortly before midnight (11:00 P.M.). It is certain, however, that abundant mitoses may be found at other times—even at 3:00 P.M.—in sporangia of ferns, in

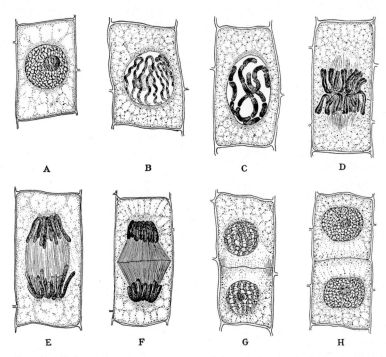

Fig. 122.—Nuclear and cell division in root-tip of onion. *A*, resting nucleus; *B*, spirem stage; *C*, spirem divided into chromosomes; *D*, metaphase, with chromosomes split; *E*, late anaphase; *F*, early telophase; *G*, late telophase; *H*, resting nucleus. ×1,200. From Chamberlain's *Elements of Plant Science* (McGraw-Hill Book Co., New York).

anthers of angiosperms, in endosperm, and in free nuclear stages of the embryo of gymnosperms.

Mitotic figures play such an important part in the development of the plant and in modern theories of heredity that it is worth while to acquire a critical technique in fixing and staining these structures (Fig. 122).

During the past two years we have made an extensive series of experiments with root-tips of *Trillium sessile*, obligingly furnished by my friend, Dr. R. C. Spangler, who fixed the tips, shortly after noon, in chromo-acetic–osmic solutions. With a stock solution of chromic acid 1 g., and acetic acid, 1 c.c., osmic acid was added in various proportions—1 c.c. up to 10 c.c. to 100 c.c. of the stock solution. Fixing was excellent in all; but staining was best with 6, 7, or 8 c.c. of osmic to 100 c.c. of the solution. A long series of trials on onion root-tips indicated that, with the acetic acid raised to 2 c.c., the results were better. We recommend chromic acid 1 g., acetic acid 2 c.c., 1 per cent osmic acid 6–8 c.c., and water 90 c.c. For convenience, this may be called the Chicago formula. Try the various fixing agents. Remember that no matter how good the fixing may be, material can be ruined in dehydrating, in clearing, or in the bath. Make yourself master of Haidenhain's iron-alum haematoxylin; then add the safranin, gentian violet, orange combination; then safranin and anilin blue; and then experiment for yourself, but remember that the triumphs of modern cytology have been won with iron-haematoxylin and that you cannot read intelligently the literature of the past twenty-five years until you have gained at least an approximate mastery of this stain. Of course, dehydration, clearing, and infiltration must be very gradual. The schedule by Yamanouchi on page 47 will repay careful study.

When chromo-acetic–osmic solutions have been used for fixing, there is a relation between the time needed in the second iron-alum and the amount of 1 per cent osmic acid. If the time required for differentiation in 2 per cent iron alum is less than 30 minutes, the percentage of osmic acid was too low; if more than 2 hours, it was too high. About 1 hour in 2 per cent iron-alum, followed by 20–30 minutes in 1 per cent (or weaker) is about right. It is somewhat like an exposure in photography, except that an overexposure develops too fast, while an overfixing in osmic acid comes out too slowly. If the iron-alum haematoxylin is preceded by an overnight stain in safranin, and the safranin is drawn until it has almost disappeared from the chromosomes, the figures will look as if stained only in iron-alum haematoxylin, but the nucleoli will show the red and the cytoplasm will have a slight tinge of pink.

In staining with safranin, gentian violet, orange, allow the alcoholic safranin to act for 16–24 hours; then extract it with 50 per cent alcohol, slightly acidulated with hydrochloric acid, if necessary, until the stain has almost disappeared from the spindle; then pass through 70, 85, 95, and 100 per cent alcohol; stain in gentian violet dissolved in clove oil, or in a mixture of clove oil and absolute alcohol, for 5–20 minutes; follow with orange dissolved in clove oil, remembering that this will weaken the safranin and sometimes the gentian violet; finally use pure clove oil to differentiate the gentian violet. Leave the slide in xylol for 2–5 minutes to remove the clove oil and to hasten the hardening of the balsam.

If you use aqueous gentian violet or crystal violet, use the anilin oil formula. When the safranin is satisfactory, transfer to water and then to the violet. After staining in violet, dip in water to remove the excess of stain, and then dehydrate rapidly in 95 per cent and absolute alcohol, differentiate in clove oil, and then transfer to xylol.

The structure and development of the young root will be shown, to some extent, in preparations made for mitotic figures. The origin of dermatogen, periblem, plerome, and also of protoxylem, is well shown in *Zea mays*. An ear of sweet corn, as young and tender as you can find on the market, will furnish material. Cut out carefully pieces 2 or 3 cm. long, with two rows of grains and fix in formalin acetic alcohol. When needed for paraffin sections, cut out from the grain a rectangular piece about 2×3 mm. and 4 or 5 mm. long; if you want to show also the structure of the entire grain, take a section the entire length of the grain, perpendicular to the flat side of the grain, and about 2 mm. wide. Cut the latter longitudinally; the rectangular pieces are sufficient for transverse sections. This is better than to try to cut out the grains before fixing.

The roots of various cereals will repay study.

The roots of *Ranunculus repens* and *Sambucus nigra* furnish good illustrations of the radial arrangement of xylem and phloem. *Smilax* shows the radial arrangement, with a large number of poles and a very highly differentiated endodermis. Cut it in paraffin. The mature root will need 2 or 3 days' treatment with 10 or 20 per cent hydrofluoric acid. The origin of secondary xylem and phloem is well shown in *Sambucus nigra*. *Vicia faba* is good for the origin of secondary roots. *Pistia stratiotes*, sometimes found on lily ponds in greenhouses, and common in Cuba and Southern Mexico, is unexcelled for showing the origin of secondary roots. On account of the hard root cap, it needs 48 hours in 5 or 10 per cent hydrofluoric acid. The arrangement of cells in the young roots of aquatic or semi-aquatic plants often shows a geometric regularity (Fig. 123).

The leaf.—Young and tender leaves should be fixed in formalin alcohol and cut in paraffin. Cut sections freehand whenever there is sufficient rigidity. Resort to pith only when necessary. In cutting sections of a leaf like that of *Lilium*, lay one leaf on another until you have a bundle of them which will be nearly square in transverse section. Wrap the bundle with string for about 15 mm.; cut the bundle transversely so that about 5 mm. of the bundle will project beyond the

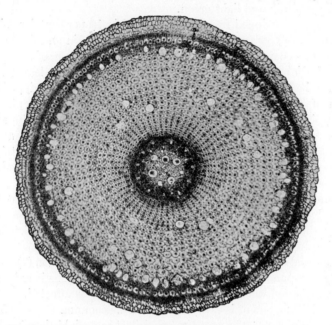

FIG. 123.—*Sparganium eurycarpum:* photomicrograph of transverse section of young root; fixed in chromo-acetic acid and stained in Bismarck brown; Cramer contrast plate; 16-mm. objective; ocular ×4; no Abbé condenser; yellowish-green filter; camera bellows, 1 meter; exposure, 8 seconds. ×90.

tied portion. Dip in melted paraffin, as already suggested for *Pinus*, fasten the tied portion in the sliding microtome, and cut with the knife placed obliquely. About 15–20 μ is a good thickness for general leaf structure. In case of large leaves, cut out pieces 1 cm. wide and 3 cm. long and tie them together to make a good bundle for cutting.

For the finest preparations, imbed in paraffin. The common lilac, *Syringa*, has a good leaf to illustrate palisade and spongy parenchyma: the privet, *Ligustrum*, is even better. *Ligustrum japonicum* has so few cells between the upper and lower epidermis that it is a good type for students to draw.

Buds will furnish beautiful preparations of young leaves and, at the same time, will show the vernation. Cut the bud transversely, a little above the middle; remove the bud scales, if they promise to cause trouble; retain only enough tissue at the base of the bud to hold the parts in place. Fix in formalin acetic alcohol; imbed in paraffin; and stain in safranin and light green.

Epidermis, stripped from the leaf, fixed in 10 per cent formalin in water for a day or two, and then stained in safranin and light green, will give excellent views of stomata. The development of stomata is particularly well shown in *Sedum purpurascens*, even in leaves which have reached the adult size. The epidermis is very easily stripped from a leaf of *Sedum*. If the big *Sedum maximum* is available, pieces of epidermis 6 or 7 cm. long and 2 or 3 cm. wide are easily stripped off, almost free from any underlying tissue. The epidermis of *Lilium* and *Tradescantia* shows fine, large stomata, but it is not so easy to strip off. In these two genera the stomata, as in nearly all leaves, show only the adult structure.

Floral development.—For a study of floral development very young buds are necessary, and it is best to select those forms which have rather dense clusters of flowers, in order that a complete series may be obtained with as little trouble as possible.

The usual order of appearance of floral parts is (1) calyx, (2) corolla, (3) stamens, and (4) carpels; but if any of these organs is reduced or metamorphosed, their order of appearance may be affected.

Floral development is easily studied in the common *Capsella bursa-pastoris* (Fig. 124). The best time to collect material is late in March or early in April. Dig up the plant, carefully remove the leaves, and in the center of the rosette a tiny white axis will be found. A series of these axes from 3 to 9 mm. in length, and from 1.5 to 3.5 mm. in diameter will give a very complete series of stages in the development of the floral organs. Preparations from the apex of the shoot taken after the inflorescence appears above ground are not to be compared with those taken early in the season, because the pedicels begin to diverge so early that median longitudinal sections of the flowers are comparatively rare. Fix in chromo-acetic acid and stain in Delafield's haematoxylin. The sections should be longitudinal and about 5 μ thick. *Capsella* shows the hypogynous type of development. The order of appearance of floral parts is (1) calyx, (2) stamens, (3) carpels, and (4) petals. The ovary is compound (syncarpous).

With its 6 stamens (2 of them shorter than the other 4), 2 carpels, and 4 nectaries marking the place of the missing parts, *Capsella* shows an interesting transition from the pentacyclic to the tetracyclic type of flower. Transverse sections of single flowers, just before the small petals expand, are best for this study.

Ranunculus, which is also hypogynous, will illustrate the development of the simple (apocarpous) ovary. The ovules appear quite early, so that the archesporial cell, or even the megaspores, may be

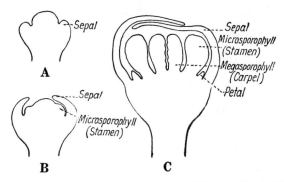

Fig. 124.—*Capsella bursa-pastoris:* floral development. ×85. From Chamberlain's *Elements of Plant Science* (McGraw-Hill Book Co., New York).

seen while the carpel is still as open as in any gymnosperm. The whole structure is a simple strobilus (Fig. 125).

Rumex crispus (yellow dock) is also a good hypogynous type, and the densely clustered flowers afford a fine series of stages. Besides, in transverse sections, the early stages in spermatogenesis are very clear.

In the willows, *Salix*, the bud scales must be removed and the copious hairs should be trimmed off as much as possible with scissors, after which the catkin should be slabbed a little on opposite sides to facilitate penetration. This is a fine illustration of a compound strobilus.

The cat-tail, *Typha*, presents a simple type of floral development. The leaves should be dissected away long before the flowers can be seen from the outside. The cylindrical clusters, varying in diameter from 2 or 3 mm. up to the size of one's finger, will afford a complete series of stages. Until the spike reaches the diameter of a lead pencil, transverse sections are easily cut. For later stages, the outer part of the spike should be sliced off so that only enough spike is retained to hold the florets in place.

Prunus and many other members of the Rosaceae furnish examples of the perigynous type of development. In many of them the floral parts do not occur in the usual succession.

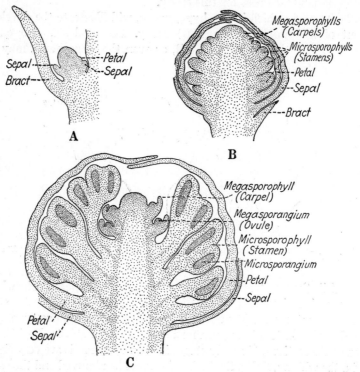

FIG. 125.—*Ranunculus acris.* floral development. ×70. From Chamberlain's *Elements of Plant Science* (McGraw-Hill Book Co., New York).

The epigynous type is well shown in the Compositae. The order of appearance is (1) corolla, (2) stamens, (3) carpels, and (4) calyx (pappus).

The common dandelion, *Taraxacum officinale*, affords an excellent series with little labor. Examine vigorous plants which have, as yet, no flowers or buds in sight. Dig up the plant and dissect away the leaves. If there is a white cluster of flower buds, the largest not more than 4 mm. in diameter, cut out the cluster, leaving only enough tissue at the base to hold the buds in place. Larger heads should be cut separately.

Our most common thistle, *Cirsium lanceolatum*, shows the floral development with unusual clearness, but the preparation of the material is somewhat tedious. The involucre, which is too hard to cut, must be carefully dissected away. Retain only enough of the receptacle to hold the developing florets in place. A series of sizes with disks varying from 3 to 10 mm. in diameter will show the development from the undifferentiated papilla up to the appearance of the archesporial cell in the nucellus of the ovule. The Canada thistle, *Cirsium arvense*, is equally good, but it is more difficult to dissect out the desirable parts. In the common sunflower, *Helianthus annuus*, the young floral parts, like the mature head, are so very large that a satisfactory study may be made with a low-power objective. As in the case of the thistle, the involucre must be trimmed away and only enough of the receptacle retained to hold the florets together.

Erigeron philadelphicus furnishes a beautiful example of epigynous floral development, and the heads are so densely clustered that, in a single section, one may find various stages from heads with undifferentiated disk up to heads with florets showing pappus, corolla, stamens, and carpels (Fig. 126). In the Chicago region, the last two weeks in May are best for these stages.

Spermatogenesis.—The earlier stages in spermatogenesis will be found in the preparations of floral development. The origin of the archesporium, the origin of sporogenous tissue, and the formation of the tapetum are beautifully shown in longitudinal and in transverse sections of the anthers of *Taraxacum* and many other Compositae. Transverse sections of the head of *Taraxacum*, or any similar head at the time when pollen mother-cells are rounding off in the center of the head, will show various stages from the mother-cells in the center to the tetrads of spores at the periphery. Transverse sections of the anther of *Polygala* give exceptionally well-defined views of the archesporial cells and sporogenous areas.

Lilium, *Trillium*, *Galtonia*, *Iris*, *Tradescantia*, *Vicia*, and *Podophyllum* can be recommended for demonstrating the nuclear changes involved in the formation of spores from the mother-cell (Fig. 127). Several species of *Lilium* are common in greenhouses, and these may be used where wild material is not available. In early stages, where

the sporogenous cells have not yet begun to round off into spore
mother-cells, it is sufficient to remove the perianth, retaining just
enough of the receptacle to hold the stamens in place. Transverse sections show the six stamens and also the young ovary. After the spore
mother-cells have begun to round off, each stamen should be removed
so as to be cut separately. In securing the desirable stages showing the
division of the mother-cell into microspores, much time and patience
will be saved by determining the stage of development before fixing

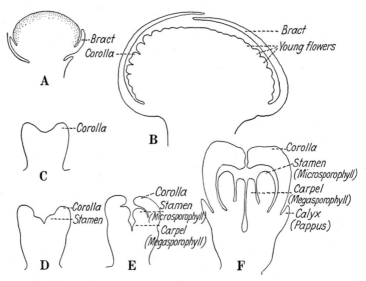

Fig. 126.—*Erigeron philadelphicus:* floral development. *A* and *B* ×35; *C, D, E,* and *F* ×150.
From Chamberlain's *Elements of Plant Science* (McGraw-Hill Book Co., New York).

the material. Mitosis is more or less simultaneous throughout an anther. Long anthers are particularly favorable, since they may show a
very closely graded series of the various phases of mitosis. An anther
of *Lilium* may show mother-cells with nuclei in synapsis at the top,
while the mother-cells at the bottom have reached the equatorial plate
stage of the first division; or, the mother-cells at the top may show
the first division, while those at the bottom show the second. Determine the stage by examining a few mother-cells before fixing.

From what has been said, it is evident that longitudinal sections
should be cut to show mitosis. Transverse sections should be cut to
show the general structure of the anther. It is not necessary to cut the

stamens into pieces before fixing, since they are easily penetrated and infiltrated; in later stages the stamens *must* not be cut into pieces, since the pollen grains and even the pollen mother-cells are easily washed out.

The problem of fixing spore mother-cells has received much attention. In fixing mother-cells and the two mitoses by which spores are

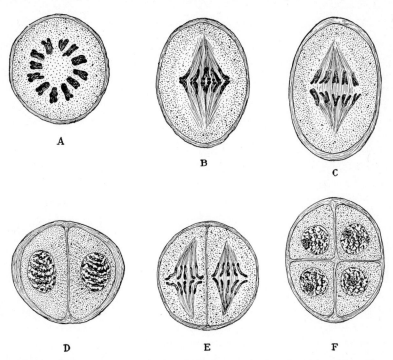

FIG. 127.—*Lilium martagon:* reduction of chromosomes in the microspore mother-cells; *A*, bird's-eye view of metaphase showing 12 pairs of chromosomes; *B*, one chromosome of each pair is starting for one pole and the other for the opposite pole; *C*, anaphase, each of the 12 chromosomes starting for the pole in *B* is seen to be made up of 2 chromosomes, so that 24 chromosomes are going to each pole; *D*, each nucleus of this two-cell stage contains 24 chromosomes. *E*, the 24 chromosomes of each nucleus of *D* are being distributed, 12 to each pole, so that each nucleus of *F* contains 12 chromosomes; the 4 cells of *F* are young microspores. ×530. From Chamberlain's *Elements of Plant Science* (McGraw-Hill Book Co., New York).

formed, investigators have used almost exclusively the chromo-osmo–acetic acid solutions of Flemming, some preferring the weaker solution and some the stronger. These solutions were used in nearly all of the work done under Strasburger at the Bonn (Germany) school.

Professor Grégoire and his students have made this their principal fixing agent.

In spite of the weight of authority, we believe that the Chicago chromo-acetic–osmic formula is better. In the Flemming's weaker formula we believe the chromic acid is too weak; the acetic acid, with its tendency to cause swelling, is too strong; and the osmic acid, unnecessarily strong.

The osmic acid undoubtedly accelerates the killing of the protoplasm. This is seen more readily in animals. If *Cyclops* be brought into 30 c.c. of the solution A, the animals will swim for a while; if 5 or 6 drops of 1 per cent osmic acid be added to the solution, the animals cease their movements almost instantly. Doubtless the osmic acid has the same effect upon plant protoplasm. Where fixing is slow, very few mitotic figures are found with the chromosomes midway between the equator and the poles.

Farmer and Shove, in studying these mitoses and also vegetative mitoses in *Tradescantia*, claimed better results with a mixture of 2 parts of absolute alcohol and 1 part glacial acetic acid. They allowed the fixing agent to act 15–20 minutes, then washed in absolute alcohol, and imbedded by the usual methods. This proportion of acetic acid seems entirely too large for any accurate work with chromatin, and we doubt whether the structure of the cytoplasm is normal when so much acetic acid is used.

The entire pollen mother-cell may be stained and mounted without sectioning. Two descriptions of technique appeared in 1912, one by Mann and the other by Pickett. Mann removes the pollen mother-cells before fixing and staining; Pickett fixes and stains the anther *in toto* and teases out the pollen mother-cells just before mounting.

In Mann's method, the anther is placed in a drop of water and the tip is cut off; a gentle tapping with a needle will then cause the pollen mother-cells to float out into the drop. Fix in Bouin's fluid, 4–8 hours, wash in 50 per cent alcohol until no color remains, and then stain in iron-haematoxylin. At this stage we should put the material into 10 per cent glycerin and follow the Venetian turpentine method.

Pickett fixed entire anthers in chromo-acetic acid for 30 hours, washed in water for 24 hours, and then passed up to 80 per cent alcohol. At this point, he stained in strong cochineal or Kleinenberg's haematoxylin for 5 days, then completed the dehydration, cleared in cedar oil, teased out the mother-cells, and mounted in balsam.

The Belling method, as modified by Dr. McClintock, is more rapid and gives good permanent preparations.

The pollen grain at the time of shedding generally consists of two cells, the tube cell and the generative cell, which afterward divides and forms two male cells or two male nuclei. *Lilium* and *Erythronium* furnish good illustrations of pollen shed in the two-cell stage
(Fig. 128). In *Silphium, Sambucus,* and *Sagittaria* the generative nucleus divides before the
pollen is shed. The division of
the generative cell to form the
two sperms takes place just before fertilization; consequently,
in forms like *Silphium,* fertilization is likely to occur within less
than 72 hours after the division
of the generative cell.

Sections should not be more
than 5 μ thick, if they are to
show a clear differentiation of
exine, intine, starch, and other
structures. If sections have been
stained in iron-haematoxylin,
staining in safranin for from 3
to 7 minutes will give the exine
a bright red color and will not
obscure the haematoxylin. A
rather sharp stain in gentian
violet will stain the starch and
also the intine. In *Asclepias*
and many orchids, in which a
common exine surrounds the

Fig. 128.—*Erythronium americanum:* photomicrograph of mature pollen grains; the one at the
top, which is cut longitudinally, shows both the
tube nucleus and the conspicuous generative cell;
the other is cut transversely and shows the generative cell, but not the tube nucleus. Stained in
safranin and gentian violet; from a preparation by
Dr. Lula Pace. Cramer contrast plate; 4-mm. objective; ocular ×4; yellowish-green filter; bellows,
85 cm.; exposure, 3 minutes. ×615.

entire mass of pollen grains, care must be taken not to overstain.

In many cases the pollen grains will put out their tubes in a 2–5 per cent solution of cane-sugar in water. Where the interval between pollination and fertilization is known (about 72 hours in *Lilium phila-
delphicum* and 96–100 hours in *L. canadense*), pieces of the stigma and style showing pollen tubes can be selected with some certainty.

Oögenesis.—As in spermatogenesis, the early stages will be found in preparations of floral development. The preparations of *Capsella* will show the origin and development of the nucellus (megasporangium) and also the megaspore mother-cell. The division of the megaspore mother-cell to form four megaspores takes place shortly before the bud begins to unfold. A massive megasporangium with several

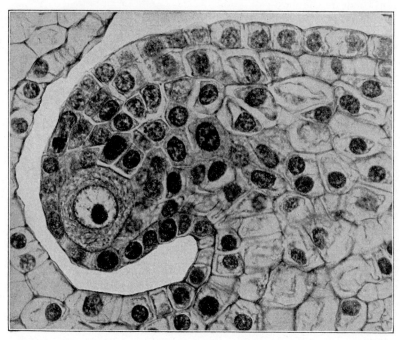

FIG. 129.—*Lilium canadense:* photomicrograph of part of transverse section of ovary, showing longitudinal section of ovule with megaspore mother-cell, just before the formation of integuments. Fixed in chromo-acetic acid and stained in iron-alum haematoxylin. Eastman Commercial Ortho film, Wratten H filter (blue); Spencer 4-mm. objective, N.A. 0.66; ocular ×6; arc light; exposure, 2 seconds. Negative by Dr. P. J. Sedgwick. ×400.

megaspore mother-cells may be found in *Ranunculus*; a megasporangium with only one megaspore mother-cell and only one layer of cells surrounding it may be found in any of the Compositae. *Erigeron philadelphicus* is very good. Head from 4–6 mm. in diameter will show the stages from the megaspore mother-cell to the four megaspores. *E. strigosus* and *E. annuus* are equally good. In *Trillium* and in *Cypripedium* the embryo sac is formed from two megaspores, which are not separated by walls. In *Lilium, Tulipa, Fritillaria, Erythronium,* and many others, the embryo sac is formed by all four megaspores, which are not separated by walls. In *Peperomia,* the Peneaceae, and some species of *Euphorbia,* the sac is formed by the four megaspores, not separated by walls, and the sac has 16 free nuclei. In *Plumbagella* the four megaspores, not separated by walls, constitute the mature sac,

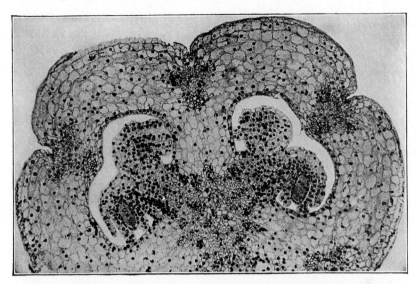

FIG. 130.—*Lilium philadelphicum:* photomicrograph of transverse section of ovary showing, in one of the ovules on the left, the first mitosis in the megaspore mother-cell; and, in one of the ovules on the right, the second mitosis which gives rise to the four megaspore nuclei. Chromo-acetic acid; safranin, gentian violet, orange. Cramer contrast plate; 16-mm. objective; ocular ×4; yellowish-green filter and also a strong filter such as is used in outdoor work; camera bellows, 30 cm.; exposure, 2 minutes. Negative by Miss Ethel Thomas. ×64.

one of the megaspores functioning as the egg, two more fusing to form the endosperm nucleus, while the fourth megaspore aborts; so that the embryo sac, ready for fertilization, contains only two nuclei.

The reduction of chromosomes takes place during the two mitoses by which the mother-cell gives rise to four megaspores. The figures are much larger than in the corresponding mitoses in spermatogenesis but so much more tedious to secure that most studies in reduction have been based upon divisions in the pollen mother-cell. *Lilium* is quite favorable for a study of oögenesis, but it must be remembered that it is exceptional in having an embryo sac formed from four megaspores.

In very young stages, before the appearance of the integument, the ovary may be removed from the flower and placed directly in the fixing agent, but at fertilization and later stages, strips should be cut off from the sides of the ovary in order to secure more rapid fixing and more

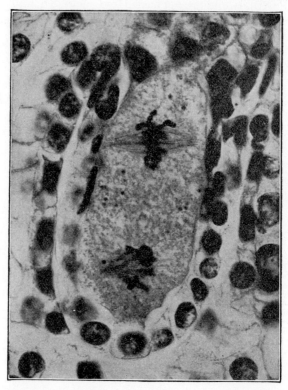

Fig. 131.—*Lilium philadelphicum:* photomicrograph of second mitosis in megaspore mother-cell. Chromo-acetic acid; safranin, gentian violet, orange. Cramer contrast plate; 4-mm. objective; ocular ×4; Abbé condenser; camera bellows, 1 m.; yellowish-green filter and also a strong filter such as is used in outdoor work; exposure, 7 minutes. Negative by Miss Ethel Thomas. ×626.

perfect infiltration with paraffin. The dotted lines in Figure 132*C* show about how much should be cut off. This is a much better plan than to secure rapid fixing and infiltration by cutting the ovary into short pieces, because the ovules will be in about the same stage of development throughout the ovary, and when one finds desirable stages like those from which these photomicrographs were taken, it is gratifying to have these pieces as long as possible.

The Chicago chromo-acetic–osmic formula is good for the entire series. Iron-alum haematoxylin, with a light touch of orange in clove oil, is best for the chromatin. For general beauty and for the achromatic structures, the safranin, gentian violet, orange combination has not been excelled. The photomicrographs (Figs. 129–131) illustrating the series from the archesporial cell (which, in this case, is also the primary sporogenous cell and the megaspore mother-cell) to the four megaspore nuclei will repay a careful study. One more mitosis produces the 8-nucleate embryo sac, but *Lilium* is not a good type for illustrative purposes, since the egg apparatus is not very definitely organized.

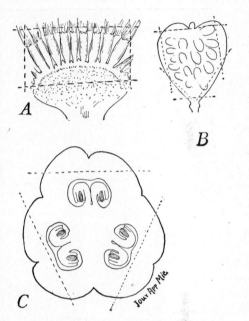

For the embryo sac at the fertilization stage, many of the Compositae are good. *Senecio aureus* is quite favorable, because it is easy to cut and the akenes do not spread. *Aster* gives an exceptional view of the antipodal region, but is rather hard to cut. Before fixing, trim the head as indicated

FIG. 132.—*A*, head of *Aster*; *B*, pod of *Capsella*; *C*, transverse section of ovary of *Lilium*. The dotted lines show how the material should be trimmed before fixing.

in Figure 132. *Silphium*, especially *S. laciniatum*, furnishes an ideal view of the embryo sac. With thumbs and fingers grasp the two wings of the akene and carefully split it, exposing the single white ovule inside. This is rather tedious, but every ovule will yield a perfectly median longitudinal section of the embryo sac, and there is not the slightest difficulty in cutting. When the rays look their best, the embryo sac is ready for fertilization, or the pollen tubes may be entering; as the rays begin to wither, you will find fertilization or early stages in the embryo and endosperm. Sections should be about 10 μ thick.

The *Ranunculaceae*, especially *Anemone patens var. wolfgangiana*, show a rather large, broad embryo sac, with highly organized egg apparatus and antipodals. Sections should be 10–20 μ thick.

For general views of the embryo sac, the safranin, gentian violet, orange combination is recommended.

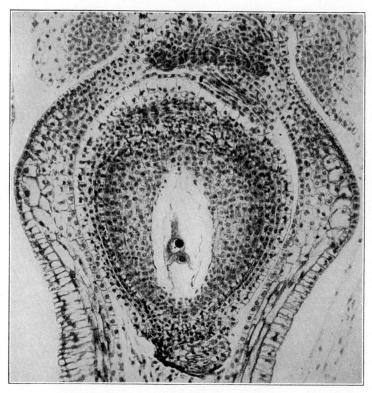

Fig. 133.—*Plumbagella micrantha:* longitudinal section of ovule showing the embryo sac, with the egg and endosperm nucleus ready for fertilization. Stained in iron-alum haematoxylin. Eastman Commercial Ortho film, Wratten E filter (orange); Bausch and Lomb 8-mm. objective, N.A. 0.50; Spencer ocular ×6; arc light; exposure, 1 second. Preparation by Dr. K. von O. Dahlgren and negative by Dr. P. J. Sedgwick. ×208.

The peculiar embryo sac of *Plumbagella*, with only two nuclei—the egg nucleus and the endosperm nucleus—when ready for fertilization, is shown in Figure 133.

Fertilization.—The later stages cut to show the mature embryo sac will often show fertilization. The male and female nuclei almost invariably show a difference in staining capacity when the male nuclei are just discharged from the pollen tube. With cyanin and erythrosin, the male nucleus stains blue and the female, red; hence the obsolete terms "cyanophilous" and "erythrophilous." With safranin, gentian violet, orange, the egg nucleus stains more with safranin and the male with gentian violet; but as the two nuclei come into contact within the egg, they begin to stain alike, the male nucleus staining more and more like the female. As fertilization progresses, it becomes difficult or, at present, impossible to distinguish any difference between the two nuclei. The male nucleus which takes part in the "triple fusion" to form the endosperm nucleus behaves in the same way.

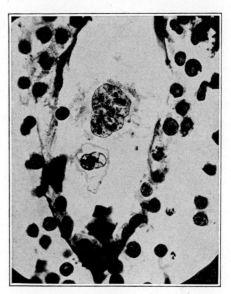

Lilium is a very good and always available type for illustrating fertilization (Fig. 134). Take ovaries from flowers whose petals have withered but have not yet fallen off. Though their embryo sacs and nuclei are smaller, *Silphium* and *Helianthus* are good types, because their

Fig. 134.—*Lilium philadelphicum:* photomicrograph of section showing fertilization and also the triple fusion; from a preparation and negative by Dr. W. J. G. Land. ×585.

curved or twisted male nuclei are easily distinguished from the spherical nuclei in the embryo sac. The embryo sacs of orchids are very small, but ovules are extremely numerous and the chances for securing the fusion of nuclei are correspondingly good. In *Cypripedium* the nuclei do not fuse in the resting condition, but the chromosomes of the two parents are perfectly distinct in the egg. The general statement that nuclei fuse in the "resting condition" is not correct, and probably the chromosomes of the two gametes never fuse.

The endosperm.—Some of the preparations intended for fertilization will be likely to show early stages in the development of endosperm.

In rather long, narrow embryo sacs, a cell wall is likely to follow even the first division of the endosperm nucleus, so that the endosperm is cellular from the beginning. *Ceratophyllum, Monotropa,* and *Verbena* will furnish material of this type.

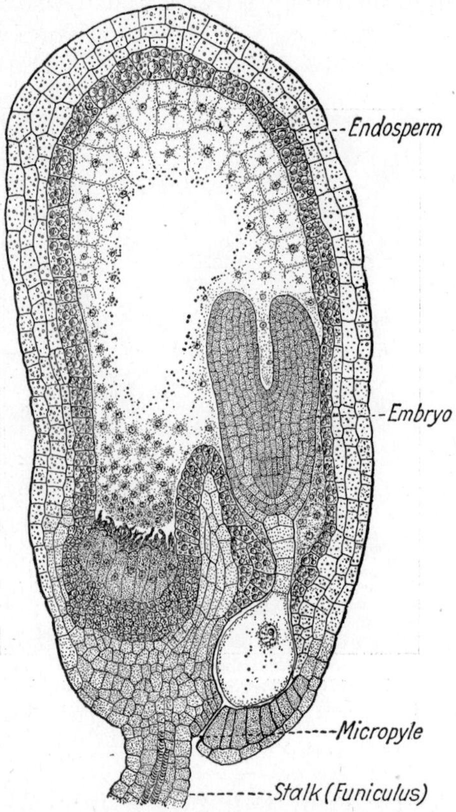

In large, broad embryo sacs, the formation of endosperm is almost sure to be initiated by a series of simultaneous free nuclear divisions. This is a difficult condition to fix well, since the layer of protoplasm, with its free nuclei, surrounding a big vacuole, is likely to shrink away from the surrounding cells. As the free nuclear period comes to a close, walls appear at the periphery, and wall formation gradually advances toward the center until the entire sac is filled with tissue. *Lilium, Capsella,* and *Ranunculus* furnish examples of this type (Fig. 135).

An intermediate condition is seen in somewhat elongated embryo sacs of medium size, like those of Compositae. After a few free nuclear divisions, walls appear simultaneously throughout the entire sac. *Silphium laciniatum* is particularly good. Akenes from which the corolla has just fallen will furnish material.

The embryo.—In most angiosperms the endosperm divides earlier than the fertilized egg and in some cases, like *Asclepias* and *Casuarina,* the free nuclear stage of the endosperm is completed and the cellu-

FIG. 135.—*Capsella bursa-pastoris:* ovule (megasporangium) with embryo and endosperm, the embryo with plerome, periblem, and dermatogen differentiated. Cell walls are appearing in the endosperm. ×60. From Chamberlain's *Elements of Plant Science* (McGraw-Hill Book Co., New York).

lar stage is well advanced before the first division of the egg. In some forms, like the aroids, the embryo is massive, and differentiation into dermatogen, periblem, and plerome comes comparatively late; while in others, like the Cruciferae, the differentiation occurs very early. *Capsella* is a standard example of the latter type (Fig. 136). The stages shown in Figure 136 *A–F* will be found in pods about 3 mm. in length. These may be put directly into the fixing agent, but later stages, which are found in pods 5 mm. or more in length, should be trimmed, as indicated in Figure 132*B*, before fixing. Formalin-alcohol–acetic acid is a good fixing agent; the Chicago chromo-acetic–osmic acid

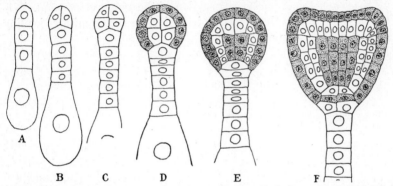

Fig. 136.—*Capsella bursa-pastoris:* development of embryo. In *D*, dermatogen is shaded; in *E*, both dermatogen and the plerome of the root are shaded, and the periblem of the root is completed; in *F*, dermatogen of root is completed. ×520. From Chamberlain's *Elements of Plant Science* (McGraw-Hill Book Co., New York).

with 3 c.c. of acetic acid instead of 2 c.c., is also very good, and Delafield's haematoxylin stains better after the chromic series. Cut 5–10 μ thick and parallel to the flat face of the pod.

For a study of the monocotyl embryo, *Iris*, and especially *I. pseudacorus*, can be recommended. The embryo is straight, and cotyledon, stem-tip, and root are clearly differentiated before the endosperm becomes too hard to cut in paraffin. Fix pieces about 3 mm. wide cut perpendicular to the face of the cheese-shaped seed. Do not try to cut the whole pod.

Sagittaria has been used quite extensively. It is easily obtained, the whole head can be cut with ease, even after the cotyledon and stem-tip are clearly differentiated, and the endosperm is instructive; but, in later stages, the embryo is curved, like that of *Capsella*, so that good views of the stem-tip are rare.

Zea mays, especially the sweet corn, is a good type to illustrate the peculiar embryo of the grasses. Directions have been given on page 352.

In many forms good preparations of late stages may be secured by soaking the seeds in water until the embryo bursts the seed coat. Young seedlings furnish valuable material for a study of vascular anatomy.

Parthenogenesis.—Many embryos are developed without fertilization. *Taraxacum,* the common dandelion, is an omnipresent example. Other widely distributed illustrations are *Hieracium* and practically all species of the *Eualchemilla* section of the genus *Alchemilla.* Parthenogenetic forms show various irregularities in the mitoses leading up to the formation of the egg.

CHAPTER XXVIII

USING THE MICROSCOPE

To use any instrument effectively, one should know something about its structure. The optical principles of the microscope are presented in any textbook of physics. Excellent practical hints are given in two booklets published by the leading American optical companies. These booklets tell the beginner how to set up the microscope, how to keep it in order, and give directions concerning illumination, dry and immersion objectives, mirror, condenser, diaphragm, and various other things (Fig. 137). They were written for advertising purposes, but since they advertise by giving directions for securing the best results with the microscope, the information is very practical. The Spencer Lens Company, Buffalo, New York; and the Bausch and Lomb Optical Company, Rochester, New York, furnish these booklets free of charge.

A cheap microscope with a 16 mm. objective and one ocular can be used for examining preparations while they are wet with alcohols, oils, or other reagents. If it is necessary to use a better instrument for such work, cover the stage with a piece of glass—a lantern slide is of about the right size—and be extremely careful not to get reagents upon the brass portions.

MICROMETRY

One should learn to make some estimate of the size of a microscopic object just as one can make an estimate of the size of larger objects; but, in addition, everyone who uses a microscope should become able to determine just how much it magnifies and should learn how to measure microscopic objects. In any measurement one should note the tube length, which is usually 160 mm. Some companies still make the tube so short that it must be pulled out to reach the desired length of 160 mm., even when the nosepiece is in place. Where there is no nosepiece, the draw tube is simply pulled out until the length is 160 mm. (Fig. 138). Where a nosepiece is used, its height should be measured, and the draw tube should be pushed in a distance equal to the height of the nosepiece.

There are in general use two practical methods of measuring microscopic objects; one by means of the ocular micrometer; and the other, by means of camera lucida sketches.

Measuring with the ocular micrometer.—A stage micrometer and an ocular micrometer are necessary. A stage micrometer should be ruled in tenths and one-hundredths of a millimeter. It does not matter

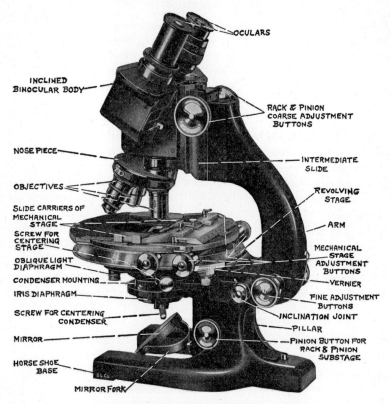

OCULARS

INCLINED BINOCULAR BODY

RACK & PINION COARSE ADJUSTMENT BUTTONS

NOSE PIECE

INTERMEDIATE SLIDE

OBJECTIVES

REVOLVING STAGE

SLIDE CARRIERS OF MECHANICAL STAGE

ARM

SCREW FOR CENTERING STAGE

MECHANICAL STAGE ADJUSTMENT BUTTONS

OBLIQUE LIGHT DIAPHRAGM

VERNIER

CONDENSER MOUNTING

IRIS DIAPHRAGM

FINE ADJUSTMENT BUTTONS

SCREW FOR CENTERING CONDENSER

INCLINATION JOINT

PILLAR

MIRROR

PINION BUTTON FOR RACK & PINION SUBSTAGE

HORSE SHOE BASE

MIRROR FORK

Fig. 137.—A modern microscope

what the spacing in the ocular micrometer may be, except that the lines must be at equal distances from one another. As a matter of fact, the ocular micrometer is generally ruled in tenths of a millimeter, but this ruling is more or less magnified by the lens of the ocular.

Place the stage micrometer upon the stage and the ocular micrometer in the tube, and arrange the two sets of rulings so that the first line in the ocular micrometer will coincide with the first line of the stage micrometer, and then find the value of one space in the ocular micrometer. The method of finding this value is shown in the following case in which the tube length was 160 mm.; the ocular, a Zeiss ocular micrometer 2; and the objective, a Leitz 3. In the ocular micrometer, ninety-eight spaces covered just fifteen of the larger spaces of the stage micrometer. Since the stage micrometer is ruled in tenths and one-hundredths of a millimeter, the fifteen spaces equal 1.5 mm., or 1,500 μ.[1] Then ninety-eight spaces of the ocular micrometer equal 1,500 μ; and one space in the ocular equals $\frac{1}{98}$ of 1,500 μ, or 15.3 μ. This value being determined, there is no further use for the stage micrometer. To measure the diameter of a pollen grain put the preparation on the stage, using the same objective and ocular micrometer, and note how many spaces a pollen grain covers. If the pollen grain covers five spaces, its diameter is five times 15.3 μ, or 76.5 μ. In the same way, the value of a space in the ocular when used with the other objectives should be determined. The values for three or four objec-

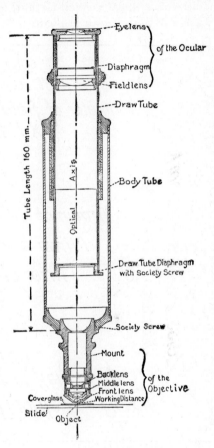

FIG. 138.—Tube length

tives may be written upon an ordinary slide label and pasted upon the base of the microscope for convenient reference.

This method is the best one for measuring spores and for most measurements in taxonomy.

[1] One millimeter=1,000 μ. The Greek letter μ is an abbreviation for μικρόν, or micron.

Measuring by means of camera lucida sketches.—This method is of great importance in research work, because various details can be measured with far greater rapidity than by the other method. Upon a piece of cardboard, about as thick as a postal card, draw a series of scales like those shown in Figure 139.

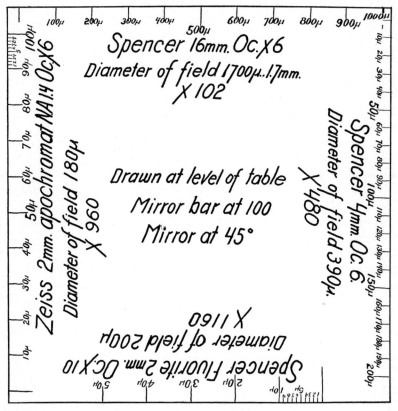

Fig. 139.—Card scale for practical use

Make a scale for each objective. It is not necessary to make scales for all the oculars, but only for the one in most constant use. It is absolutely necessary to note the tube length, length of the bar of the camera mirror and inclination of the camera mirror, and the level at which the scale is made. A variation in any of these details will change the scale.

In using the stage micrometer, place the cardboard on the table, and with the aid of the camera lucida sketch the rulings of the micrometer. In Figure 139 note, for example, the scale drawn with Spencer 16 mm. objective, ocular ×6. The spaces are drawn from the tenths of a millimeter rulings of the stage micrometer. Therefore, each space on the card represents one-tenth of a millimeter or 100 μ, and the ten spaces shown on the card represent 1 mm., or 1,000 μ. By measuring with a metric rule the ten spaces upon the card, it is found that the scale is 102 mm. in length. The magnification of any drawing made with the same ocular and objective, under the same conditions, will therefore be 102 diameters. This does not mean that the magnifying power is 102 diameters, for the magnification of this combination is much less. A scale drawn at the level of the stage would show more nearly the magnifying power of the combination, but would still give too large a figure. The exact size of any object which has been sketched with this combination can now be measured by applying the cardboard scale, just as one would measure gross objects with a rule.

The diameter of the field with this combination is 1,700 μ. By knowing the diameter of the field with the various combinations, one can guess approximately the size of objects.

Other combinations are made in the same way. An excellent check on the accuracy of the computations is to measure the same object by means of the ocular micrometer and by the scale card. If the results are the same, the computations are correct.

In making sketches, it is a good plan to add the data which would be needed at any time in making measurements, e.g., Spencer objective 16 mm., ocular ×6, table, 110, 45°, would show that the sketch was made at the level of the table, with the mirror bar at 110, and the camera mirror at an angle of 45°.

ARTIFICIAL LIGHT

During a considerable part of the year daylight is often insufficient for successful work with the microscope. Numerous contrivances for artificial illumination have been devised, some of them fairly good, but most of them thoroughly unsatisfactory. The best illuminator is the one which will give the most light with the least heat.

More than two hundred years ago Hooke used a device for artificial illumination which probably suggested the apparatus used by the late Professor Strasburger at Bonn. The apparatus consists, essentially, of a hollow sphere filled with liquid. A fairly good and practical light can be got with an ordinary lamp by allowing the light to pass through a wash bottle filled with a weak solution of ammonia copper sulphate. A piece of dark paper with a circular hole in it serves as a diaphragm and at the same time protects the eyes from the direct light of the lamp. With a good electric bulb, this not only furnishes a good light, without any glare, and with no appreciable heat, but throws a good light on the pencil, which is an important consideration in drawing with a camera lucida.

Optical companies are now making excellent lights for microscopes. These lights furnish good illumination and most of them have the effect of good daylight; but there is still too much heat.

If laboratory tables are small, seating only one student, there should be a plug to attach the table to some convenient outlet; and also another outlet on the table for the microscope lamp. If the table is large, seating four or more students, there should be one or two outlets on the table for each student, and a single plug by which the whole table may be connected with a convenient outlet.

For elementary classes, which are not likely to use higher powers than a 4 mm. objective with an ocular magnifying five or six times, individual lamps are not necessary in a well-lighted laboratory. Splendid lights are now available for elementary work, almost as good as daylight, and strong enough for ordinary dry lens microscopic work.

CHAPTER XXIX

LABELING AND CATALOGUING PREPARATIONS

THE LABEL

The *first* thing to write upon a label is the genus and species of the plant; the next thing would be the name of the organ or tissue, and then might be added the date of collection, e.g., *Marchantia polymorpha*, young archegonia, January 10, 1915. The date of making the preparation is of no value unless the student is testing the permanence of stains or something of that sort. It is hardly worth while to write upon the label the names of the stains used, for the student will soon learn to recognize the principal stains. A hasty sketch on the label will often indicate any exceptionally interesting feature in the preparation. To facilitate finding such a feature, it is a good plan to mark the particular section or sections with ink, or better, with a diamond or carborundum point, the marking being always on the underside of the slide so as not to cause any inconvenience if an immersion lens should be used.

Where there are 2, 3, or more rows of sections on a slide, a desirable feature may be found very quickly by marking on the label, 2d row, 4th, etc.

CATALOGUING PREPARATIONS

As a collection grows, the student will need some device for locating readily any particular preparation. Some have their slides numbered and catalogued, but all devices of this sort are too cumbrous and slow for the practical worker in the laboratory. After forty years' experience with a collection which now numbers more than thirty thousand preparations, we recommend the following system:

Four wooden slide boxes of the usual type will do for a beginning; they should be labeled: THALLOPHYTES, BRYOPHYTES, PTERIDOPHYTES, and SPERMATOPHYTES. As the collection grows and new boxes are needed, the classification can be made more definite, e.g., there should be a box labeled BRYOPHYTES *Hepaticae* and one labeled BRYOPHYTES *Musci*. As the liverwort collection grows, three boxes will be necessary, and should be labeled BRYOPHYTES *Hepaticae Marchantiales*, BRYOPHYTES *Hepaticae* Jungermanniales, and BRYOPHYTES *He-*

paticae Anthocerotales. It will readily be seen that the process can be continued almost indefinitely, and that new slides may be at any time dropped into their proper places. A rather complete label gradually built up in this way is shown in Figure 140.

BRYOPHYTES

HEPATICAE

Jungermanniales

Porella platyphyllum

Archegonia

Fig. 140.—Label for slide box

Since there should be some system in the classification, we should recommend the Engler-Gilg *Syllabus der Pflanzenfamilien.*

The beginner will often find that the mere placing of a slide in the proper box and the box in its proper place on the shelf will refresh or increase his knowledge of classification.

CHAPTER XXX

A CLASS LIST OF PREPARATIONS

Where a regular course in histology is conducted, it is a good plan to give each student at the outset a complete list of the preparations which he is expected to make. In a three months' course a fairly representative collection of preparations can be made. The availability of material determines what a list shall be. Besides gaining an introduction to the use of the microscope and its accessories, a class meeting ten hours a week for ten weeks should be able to do as much work as is outlined below.

In making the mounts, the order indicated in the list should not be followed. Begin with temporary mounts, and then study, in succession, freehand sections, the glycerin method, the Venetian turpentine method, the paraffin method, the celloidin method, and special methods. A large proportion of the time should be devoted to the paraffin method.

It is neither possible nor desirable that each student should in every case go through all the processes from collecting material to labeling. Some of the material may be in 85 per cent alcohol, some in formalin, some in glycerin, some in Venetian turpentine, and some in paraffin. One student may imbed in paraffin enough of the *Anemone* for the whole class; another may imbed the *Lilium* stamens; and by such a division of labor a great variety of preparations may be secured without a corresponding demand upon the time of the individual.

LIST OF PREPARATIONS
THALLOPHYTES
MYXOMYCETES

1. *Trichia varia.*—Paraffin sections 5 μ. Safranin, gentian violet, orange.

SCHIZOPHYTES
SCHIZOMYCETES

2. *Bacteria.*—*Coccus, Bacillus*, and *Spirillum* forms. Stain on cover glass or slide.
3. *Bacillus anthracis.*—In liver of mouse. Paraffin sections, 5 μ. Stain in gentian violet, Gram's method.

4. *Oscillatoria.*—Fix in special chromo-acetic–osmic acid and stain in iron-alum haematoxylin to show nuclei. Venetian turpentine method.

5. *Tolypothrix.*—Use the Venetian turpentine method. Should show heterocysts, hormogonia, and false branching.

6. *Nostoc.*—Venetian turpentine method.

7. *Wasserblüthe.*—The principal forms in this material are:

   a) *Coelosphaerium kützingianum.*—Colonies in the form of hollow spheres.

   b) *Anabaena gigantea.*—Filaments straight. Preparations should show vegetative cells, heterocysts, hormogonia, and spores.

   c) *Anabaena flos-aquae.*—Filaments curved. Stain on the slide and mount in balsam. If material is abundant, stain in iron-alum haematoxylin and mount in Venetian turpentine.

8. *Gloeotrichia.*—Smear on the slide, stain in safranin and gentian violet, and mount in balsam; or use the Venetian turpentine method, staining in phloxine and anilin blue and crushing under the cover glass.

ALGAE

CHLOROPHYCEAE

9. *Volvox.*—Use the Venetian turpentine method. If paraffin material is available, cut 2–5 μ in thickness and stain in safranin, gentian violet, orange.

10. *Scenedesmus.*—Let a drop containing the material dry upon the slide, stain, and mount in balsam.

11. *Hydrodictyon.*—Use the Venetian turpentine method.

   Each preparation should contain pieces of old and of young nets, and also at least one young net developing within an older segment. The greatest care must be taken not to injure the older segments while arranging the mount.

12. *Ulothrix.*—Use the Venetian turpentine method. Each mount should show various stages in the development of spores and gametes.

13. *Oedogonium.*—Stain in phloxine and anilin blue and mount in Venetian turpentine.

14. *Coleochaete.*—Stain in Delafield's haematoxylin and mount in balsam.

15. *Cladophora.*—Stain some in iron-haematoxylin and some in phloxine and anilin blue. Mount both together in Venetian turpentine.

16. *Diatoms.*—Make mounts of the frustules and also stained preparations showing the cell contents.

17. *Desmids.*—Make mounts of available forms. Use the Venetian turpentine method if material is sufficiently abundant.

18. *Zygnema.*—Stain in iron-haematoxylin and mount in Venetian turpentine.

19. *Spirogyra.*—Stain in phloxine and anilin blue and mount in Venetian turpentine.

20. *Vaucheria.*—Stain in iron-alum haematoxylin and mount in Venetian turpentine.
21. *Chara.*—Cut paraffin sections of the apical cell, oöginia, and antheridia.

PHAEOPHYCEAE

22. *Ectocarpus.*—Stain some in iron-haematoxylin and some in phloxine and anilin blue. Mount both together in Venetian turpentine.
23. *Cutleria.*—Sections of oögonia, antheridia, and sporangia. Cut 10 μ thick and stain in iron-haematoxylin with about 7 minutes in safranin.
24. *Fucus vesiculosus.*—Antheridial conceptacle with paraphyses and antheridia; oögonial conceptacle with oögonia. Cut 10 μ thick and stain in iron-haematoxylin with about 5 minutes in safranin. For details of antheridia, cut 1 or 2 μ.

RHODOPHYCEAE

25. *Nemalion.*—Stain some in iron-haematoxylin and some in eosin. Each preparation should show trichogyne, carpogonium, and cystocarp. You cannot mount it in Venetian turpentine; use glycerin or glycerin jelly.
26. *Polysiphonia.*—Stain in iron-haematoxylin or phloxine and anilin blue. Mount whole in Venetian turpentine. Each mount should show tetraspores, antheridia, and cystocarps. If material is in paraffin, cut sections about 7 μ thick.

FUNGI
PHYCOMYCETES

27. *Rhizopus nigricans.*—Stain young sporangia in eosin, dilute Delafield's haematoxylin, or in phloxine and anilin blue. Some zygosporic material should be stained strongly in eosin: some should be stained in iron-alum haematoxylin, and in reducing the stain, some should be taken out early to show the coenocytic character of the mycelium, and some should be drawn farther to show the structure of the zygospores and suspensors. Venetian turpentine.
28. *Saprolegnia.*—Stain some in phloxine and anilin blue, and some in iron-alum haematoxylin. Each mount should show sporangia and oögonia. Venetian turpentine.
29. *Albugo candida.*—Select white blisters which have not yet broken open. Paraffin 8 μ. Iron-alum haematoxylin and orange. Oögonia and antheridia, 2–5 μ, same stain.
30. *Albugo bliti* on *Amarantus retroflexus.*—Cut out small portions of leaves in which the oögonia can be seen in abundance. Paraffin, 2–5 μ.

ASCOMYCETES

31. *Peziza.*—Paraffin sections of young apothecia, 5 μ or less; sections of older apothecia, 10 or 15 μ. Safranin, gentian violet, orange.
32. *Aspergillus, Eurotium.*—Stain in eosin and mount in Venetian turpentine.

33. *Penicillium.*—Treat like Aspergillus.
34. *Erysiphe commune* on *Polygonum aviculare.*—Strip the fungus from the leaf. Paraffin, 5 μ or less. Safranin, gentian violet, orange.
35. *Uncinula necator* on *Ampelopsis quinquefolia.*—Stain in phloxine and anilin blue. Mount whole in Venetian turpentine and break the perithecia under the cover.
36. *Xylaria.*—Paraffin sections of younger stages. Delafield's haematoxylin and erythrosin. Be sure that some section in each mount shows the opening of a perithecium.

LICHENS

37. *Physcia stellaris.*—Cut in paraffin, 5 μ. Stain in cyanin and erythrosin.

BASIDIOMYCETES

38. *Puccinia graminis.*—Aecium stage on barberry leaf. Urediniospore and teliospore stage on oats. Cut 3 μ and stain in iron-haematoxylin.
39. *Coprinus micaceus.*—Paraffin. Transverse sections of gills showing trama, paraphyses, basidia, and spores. To show the basidium with four spores, the sections should be 15 μ thick. For development of the spores, cut 5 μ or less. Safranin, gentian violet, orange. *Boletus, Hydnum,* and *Polyporus* are treated in the same manner.

BRYOPHYTES
HEPATICAE

40. *Riccia natans.*—Paraffin, 10 or 15 μ. Delafield's haematoxylin. Archegonia, antheridia, and sporophytes imbedded in the gametophyte.
41. *Marchantia polymorpha.*—Paraffin, 5 or 10 μ. Archegonia, antheridia, and sporophytes.
42. *Anthoceros laevis.*—Paraffin, 5 or 10 μ. Longitudinal and transverse sections of sporophyte. Safranin, gentian violet, orange.
43. *Pellia epiphylla.*—Paraffin, 5 or 10 μ. Longitudinal sections of sporophyte attached to gametophyte. Safranin, gentian violet, orange.
44. *Porella platyphylla.*—Paraffin, 10 μ. Delafield's haematoxylin. Archegonia, antheridia, sporophyte, and apical cell.

MUSCI

45. *Sphagnum.*—Leaf buds. Cut 5 μ and stain in safranin and anilin blue.
46. *Sphagnum.*—Capsule. Paraffin. Delafield's haematoxylin and erythrosin.
47. *Funaria hygrometrica.*—Paraffin. Longitudinal and transverse sections of young capsules. Delafield's haematoxylin.
48. *Funaria hygrometrica* or any favorable form. Protonema. Place the well-cleaned material directly into 50 per cent glycerin and allow it to concentrate. Mount in glycerin or glycerin jelly.
49. *Bryum.*—Paraffin. Antheridia, 10 μ; archegonia, 15–20 μ; capsule, 10 μ. Peristome mounted whole.

PTERIDOPHYTES

LYCOPODIALES

50. *Lycopodium lucidulum.*—Transverse section of stem. Paraffin sections. Safranin and Delafield's haematoxylin.
51. *Lycopodium inundatum.*—Paraffin. Longitudinal sections of strobilus.
52. *Selaginella.*—Paraffin. Longitudinal sections of rather mature strobili. Safranin, gentian violet, orange.
53. *Isoetes echinospora.*—Transverse section of stem. Paraffin. Safranin and Delafield's haematoxylin.
54. *Isoetes echinospora.*—Paraffin. Longitudinal sections of microsporangia and megasporangia. Safranin, gentian violet, orange.

EQUISETALES

55. *Equisetum arvense.*—Prothallia in Venetian turpentine. Stem-tips in paraffin. Transverse section of stem.

FILICALES

56. *Botrychium virginianum.*—Paraffin. Stain rhizome, stipes, and root in safranin and Delafield's haematoxylin. Stain sporangia in iron-haematoxylin.
57. *Protostele.*—Use *Gleichenia.* Cut freehand or in paraffin and stain in safranin and anilin blue.
58. *Solenostele (amphiphloic siphonostele).*—Use *Adiantum* or *Dicksonia punctilobula.*
59. *Ectophloic siphonostele.*—Use *Osmunda cinnamomea.*
60. *Polystele.*—Use *Pteris aquilina* or any species of *Polypodium.*
61. *Sporangia.*—For development, use *Pteris, Aspidium, Cyrtomium,* or try any available species. For mitosis, *Osmunda* is exceptionally good.
62. *Antheridia and archegonia.*—Mount whole in Venetian turpentine. Iron-alum haematoxylin. Sections should be 5–10 μ thick. Stain in iron-haematoxylin and orange.
63. *Embryo.*—*Pteris* and *Adiantum* are good. Cut longitudinal vertical sections 10 μ thick.

SPERMATOPHYTES

GYMNOSPERMS

CYCADALES

64. *Zamia.*—Freehand sections of stem. Safranin and light green. Transverse sections of microsporophyll, 5 or 10 μ. Longitudinal sections of entire ovule, 10–15 μ; stain in safranin, gentian violet, orange. Longitudinal sections of nucellus with pollen tubes, 3–10 μ. Iron-haematoxylin and orange.

GINKGOALES

65. *Ginkgo biloba.*—Longitudinal sections of endosperm showing archegonia or young embryos. Paraffin 10 μ.
Sections of microsporangia with nearly mature pollen, 2–5 μ.

CONIFERALES

66. *Pinus laricio.*—Transverse sections of needles and young stem. Freehand. Safranin and light green.
67. *Pinus strobus.*—Freehand sections of well-seasoned wood. Safranin and Delafield's haematoxylin.
68. *Pinus laricio.*—Paraffin. Longitudinal section of mature staminate strobilus. Safranin, gentian violet, orange.
69. *Abies balsamea* or *Pinus laricio.*—Pollen at shedding stage shaken out and imbedded in paraffin; 5 μ. Stain in safranin, gentian violet, orange.
70. *Pinus laricio.*—Paraffin. Ovule with archegonia. Safranin, gentian violet, orange.
71. *Pinus sylvestris* or *P. laricio.*—Paraffin. Embryos. Cyanin and erythrosin, or safranin and anilin blue.

GNETALES

72. Transverse section of stem of *Ephedra.* Freehand, steam method.
73. Longitudinal section of the ovule of *Ephedra.*

ANGIOSPERMS
DICOTYLS

74. *Pelargonium.*—Transverse sections of stem to show phellogen and intrafascicular cambium. Freehand. Endarch siphonostele.
75. *Tilia americana.*—Celloidin or freehand. Transverse sections of small stems from 3 mm. to 6 mm. in diameter. Safranin and Delafield's haematoxylin. Endarch siphonostele with annual rings.
76. *Sambucus nigra.*—Transverse section of primary root to show origin of secondary structures.
77. *Cucurbita.*—Longitudinal section of stem to show sieve tubes.
78. *Capsella bursa-pastoris.*—Paraffin. Floral development, 5 μ. Stain in Delafield's haematoxylin, without any contrast stain; or in iron-alum haematoxylin and orange.
79. *Erigeron philadelphicus* and *Taraxacum officinale.*—Paraffin. Floral development, 5 μ; megaspores, 10 μ; embryo sac, 10 μ.
80. *Ranunculus.*—Floral development, 5 μ; megaspore mother-cells and megaspores, 5 μ; embryo sac, 10 μ.
81. *Silphium.*—Longitudinal sections of the ovule at the fertilization period. Longitudinal sections of staminate flowers just before the shedding of pollen.
82. *Anemone patens.*—Paraffin. Embryo sac, 10 μ.

MONOCOTYLS

83. *Clintonia.*—Transverse section of stem to show siphonostele. Paraffin. Safranin and anilin blue.

84. *Acorus calamus.*—Transverse sections of rhizome, freehand or paraffin, to show amphivasal bundles.

85. *Zea mays.*—Transverse section of stem to show scattered bundles; also good for companion cells. Paraffin. Safranin and anilin blue.

86. *Tradescantia virginica.*—Longitudinal sections of root-tip. Paraffin, 3 and 5 μ. Stain for mitosis.

87. *Smilax herbacea.*—Transverse section of adult root. Freehand. Shows exarch, radial structure, and a highly developed endodermis. Safranin and Delafield's haematoxylin.

88. *Lilium.*—Transverse section of leaf. Freehand. Transverse section of ovaries in various stages from megaspore mother-cell to fertilization; transverse sections of anthers to show microspore mother-cells and reduction of chromosomes; also later stages with nearly mature pollen. Paraffin 5 to 10 μ.

89. *Iris.*—Section of young seeds to show embryo with cotyledon and stem-tip.

90. *Sagittaria.*—Longitudinal sections of ovulate flowers of various stages to show development of the embryo and endosperm.

91. *Zea mays.*—Longitudinal and transverse sections of embryo (sweet corn, roasting-ear condition) to show structure of root and beginning of protoxylem.

CHAPTER XXXI

FORMULAS FOR REAGENTS

FIXING AGENTS

Absolute alcohol.—Used alone without any mixtures.

Carnoy's fluid.—

Absolute alcohol	2 parts
Chloroform	3 parts
Glacial acetic acid	1 part

Farmer's fluid.—

Absolute alcohol	3 parts
Glacial acetic acid	1 part

Formalin alcohol (Dr. Lynds Jones's formula).—

70 per cent alcohol	100 c.c.
Commercial formalin	2 c.c.

Formalin alcohol (Dr. Land's original formula).—

50 per cent alcohol	100 c.c.
Commercial formalin	6 c.c.

Dr. Land now adds some acetic acid.

Formalin acetic alcohol.—

70 per cent alcohol	85 c.c.
Commercial formalin	10 c.c.
Glacial acetic acid	5 c.c.

Formalin acetic acid.—

Commercial formalin	10 c.c.
Glacial acetic acid	5 c.c.
Water	85 c.c.

Formalin.—

Commercial formalin	3 to 10 c.c.
Water	100 c.c.

Stock chromo-acetic solution.—

Chromic acid	1 g.
Glacial acetic acid	1 c.c.
Water	100 c.c.

Schaffner's chromo-acetic solution.—

Chromic acid	0.3 g.
Glacial acetic acid	0.7 c.c.
Water	99.0 c.c.

Chromo-acetic solution (for marine algae).—

Chromic acid	1.0 g.
Glacial acetic acid	0.4 c.c.
Sea-water	400.0 c.c.

Material must be washed in sea water.

Strong chromo-acetic solution.—

Chromic acid	1 g.
Glacial acetic acid	3 c.c.
Water	100 c.c.

Licent's formula.—

1 per cent chromic acid	80 c.c.
Glacial acetic acid	5 cc..
Formalin	15 c.c.

Flemming's fluid (weaker solution).—

A	1 per cent chromic acid (in water)	25 c.c.
	1 per cent glacial acetic acid (in water)	10 c.c.
	Water	55 c.c.
B.	1 per cent osmic acid (in water)	10 c.c.

Keep the mixture A made up, and add B as the reagent is needed for use, since it does not keep well.

Flemming's fluid (stronger solution).—

1 per cent chromic acid	45 c.c.
2 per cent osmic acid	12 c.c.
Glacial acetic acid	3 c.c.

Chicago chromo-acetic–osmic solution.—

Chromic acid	1 g.
Glacial acetic acid	2 c.c.
1 per cent osmic acid	6 to 8 c.c.
Water	90 c.c.

Merkel's fluid.—

1.4 per cent solution of chromic acid	25 c.c.
1.4 per cent solution of platinic chloride	25 c.c.

Benda's fluid.—

1 per cent chromic acid	16 c.c.
2 per cent osmic acid	4 c.c.
Glacial acetic acid	2 drops

Hermann's fluid.—

1 per cent platinic chloride	15 parts
Glacial acetic acid	1 part
2 per cent osmic acid	4 or 2 parts

Nawaschin's fluid.—

A

Chromic acid	1.5 g.
Glacial acetic acid	10 c.c.
Distilled water	90 c.c.

B

Commercial formalin	40 c.c.
Distilled water	60 c.c.

Mix equal parts A and B just before using. Used for mitosis. Try it for embryo sacs and for free nuclear stages in pteridophytes, gymnosperms, and angiosperms.

Picric acid.—

Picric acid	1 g.
Water or 70 per cent alcohol	100 c.c.

Bouin's fluid.—

Commercial formalin	25 c.c.
Picric acid (saturated solution in water)	75 c.c.
Glacial acetic acid	5 c.c.

Corrosive sublimate and acetic acid.—

Corrosive sublimate	3 g.
Glacial acetic acid	5 cc..
70 per cent alcohol (or water)	100 c.c.

Corrosive sublimate, formalin, acetic acid.—

Corrosive sublimate	4 g.
Formalin	5 c.c.
Glacial acetic acid	5 c.c.
Water (or 50 per cent alcohol)	100 c.c.

For material to be mounted in Venetian turpentine, use the aqueous solution; for imbedding, use the alcoholic. Both this and the preceding solution should be used hot (85° C.).

Zenker's fluid.—

Corrosive sublimate	5 g.
Glacial acetic acid	5 c.c.
Potassium dichromate	2 g.
Distilled water	100 c.c.

Fix 12–24 hours or even a couple of days. Wash in water and add iodine, as in all reagents containing mercury. This is good for embryo sacs and for free nuclear stages in endosperm of gymnosperms and angiosperms.

Bensley's formula (for chondriosomes).—

$2\frac{1}{2}$ per cent corrosive sublimate in water	4 parts
2 per cent osmic acid	1 part

Yamanouchi's formula (for chondriosomes).—

Neutral formalin	10 c.c.
Water	90 c.c.

Gilson's fluid.—

95 per cent alcohol	42 c.c.
Water	60 c.c.
Glacial acetic acid	18 c.c.
Concentrated nitric acid	2 c.c.
Corrosive sublimate (saturated solution in water)	11 c.c.

Bensley's formula (for canal system).—

1. Dichromate of potash	$2\frac{1}{2}$ g.
2. Corrosive sublimate	5 g.
3. Water	90 c.c.
4. Formalin (neutral)	10 c.c.

Make a solution of 1, 2, 3, and then add the neutral formalin.

Osmic acid (stock solution).—

Osmic acid	1 c.c.
Distilled water	1 c.c.

The bottle in which the solution is to be kept, and also the glass tube in which the acid is sold, must be thoroughly cleaned. Break off the end of the tube, and drop both tube and acid into the distilled water, or simply drop the tube into the bottle and shake the bottle until the tube breaks.

Unicellular forms in a drop of water, inverted over the neck of the bottle, fix in 2–5 seconds.

Osmic acid.—

Five or six drops of the stock solution to 50 c.c. of water is good for unicellular and colonial algae. In many cases 1 or 2 c.c. to 100 c.c. of water is better.

STAINS

Delafield's haematoxylin.—

To 100 c.c. of a saturated solution of ammonia alum add, drop by drop, a solution of 1 g. of haematoxylin dissolved in 6 c.c. of absolute alcohol. Expose to air and light for one week. Filter. Add 25 c.c. of glycerin and 25 c.c. of methyl alcohol. Allow to stand until the color is sufficiently dark. Filter and keep in a tightly stoppered bottle.[1]

The solution should stand for at least 2 months before it is ready for using.

Erlich's haematoxylin.—

Distilled water..............................	50 c.c.
Absolute alcohol............................	50 c.c.
Glycerin....................................	50 c.c.
Glacial acetic acid..........................	5 c.c.
Haematoxylin..............................	1 g.
Alum in excess.	

Keep it in a dark place until the color becomes a deep red. If well stoppered, it will keep indefinitely.

Boehmer's haematoxylin.—

A	Haematoxylin...........................	1 g.
	Absolute alcohol.........................	12 c.c.
B	Alum....................................	1 g.
	Distilled water..........................	240 c.c.

The solution A must ripen for 2 months. When wanted for use, add about 10 drops of A to 10 c.c. of B. Stain 10–20 minutes. Wash in water and proceed as usual.

Mayer's haem-alum.—

Haematoxylin, 1 g., dissolved with heat in 50 c.c. of 95 per cent alcohol and added to a solution of 50 g. of alum in a liter of distilled water. Allow the mixture to cool and settle; filter; add a crystal of thymol to preserve from mold (Lee).

It is ready for use as soon as made up. Unless attacked by mold, it keeps indefinitely.

[1] Stirling and Lee.

Heidenhain's iron-haematoxylin.—

This stain was introduced by Heidenhain in 1892 and, for cytological work and much morphological work, has become the most widely and efficiently used of all stains. Two solutions are used, and they are never mixed:

A. $1\frac{1}{2}$ to 4 per cent aqueous solution of ammonia sulphate of iron. Use the ferric (violet) crystals, not the ferrous (green) crystals.

B. $\frac{1}{2}$ per cent solution of haematoxylin in distilled water.

The crystals of haematoxylin will dissolve in the distilled water in about 10 days; the stain reaches its greatest efficiency in about 6 weeks. About 3 months from the time it is made up, it begins to deteriorate. A stain made by dissolving the crystals in strong alcohol and then diluting with water so as to get a practically aqueous solution is not so good.

Greenacher's borax carmine.—

Carmine	3 g.
Borax	4 g.
Distilled water	100 c.c.

Dissolve the borax in water and add the carmine, which is quickly dissolved with the aid of gentle heat. Add 100 c.c. of 70 per cent alcohol and filter (Stirling).

Alum carmine.—

A 4 per cent aqueous solution of ammonia alum is boiled 20 minutes with 1 per cent of powdered carmine. Filter after it cools (Lee).

Alum cochineal.—

Powdered cochineal	50 g.
Alum	5 g.
Distilled water	500 c.c.

Dissolve the alum in water, add the cochineal, and boil; evaporate down to two-thirds of the original volume and filter. Add a few drops of carbolic acid to prevent mold (Stirling).

Picro-carmine.—

Picro-carmine (picro-carminate of ammonia)	1 g.
Water	100 c.c.

Myer's carmalum.—

Carminic acid	1 g.
Alum	10 g.
Distilled water	200 c.c.

Dissolve with heat; decant or filter, and add a crystal of thymol to avoid mold.

This is the stain recommended for *Volvox.*

Carmalum (Alum Lake).—

Carmalum	1 g.
Water	100 c.c.
Ammonia	1 c.c.

Filter, if there is any precipitate.

Aceto-carmine.—

Heat a 45 per cent aqueous solution of glacial acetic acid to the boiling-point, with an excess of powdered carmine. Cool and filter.

Iron aceto-carmine.—

Add a trace of ferric hydrate, dissolve 45 per cent acetic acid, to a quantity of acetic carmine until the liquid becomes bluish red, but no precipitate forms. Then add an equal amount of ordinary acetic-carmine.

Eosin.—

Eosin	1 g.
Water, or 70 per cent alcohol	100 c.c.

General formula for anilins.—

Make a 3 per cent solution of anilin oil in distilled water; shake well and frequently for a day; add enough alcohol to make the whole mixture about 20 per cent alcohol; add 1 g. of cyanin, erythrosin, safranin, gentian violet, etc., to each 100 c.c. of this solution.

Cyanin.—

This general formula is not at all successful with Grübler's cyanin, but gives satisfactory results with an immensely cheaper cyanin, sold by H. A. Metz and Company, 122 Hudson Street, New York.

Anilin blue.—

Anilin blue	1 g.
85 or 90 per cent alcohol	100 c.c.

For staining before mounting in Venetian turpentine, this stain should be made up in strong alcohol, even if the dry stain is intended for aqueous solution.

Iodine green.—

Iodine green	1 g.
70 per cent alcohol	100 c.c.

Methyl green.—

Methyl green	1 g.
Glacial acetic acid	1 c.c.
Water	100 c.c.

If the preparation is to be mounted in balsam, a slight trace of acetic acid and also a trace of methyl green should be added to the absolute alcohol used for dehydrating.

For staining vascular bundles, the acid may be omitted, even from the formula.

Light Green.—

Light green	1 g.
90 per cent alcohol	100 c.c.

or

Light green	1 g.
Clove oil	100 c.c.

or

Light green	1 g.
Clove oil	75 c.c.
Absolute alcohol	25 c.c.

Fuchsin.—

Fuchsin	1 g.
95 per cent alcohol	100 c.c.
Water	100 c.c.

Gourley's basic fuchsin.—

Basic fuchsin	50 mg.
95 per cent alcohol	2 c.c.
Tap water	100 c.c.

Dissolve the fuchsin in the alcohol and add the water. Gourley used two lots of fuchsin, both successful; one from Coleman and Bell, the other from the Will Corporation.

Acid fuchsin.—

Acid fuchsin	1 g.
Water	100 c.c.

Use this formula when staining woody tissues in methyl green and acid fuchsin.

Ziehl's carbol fuchsin.—

Fuchsin.....................................	1 g.
Carbolic-acid crystals.......................	5 g.
95 per cent alcohol..........................	10 c.c.
Water......................................	100 c.c.

Fuchsin and iodine green mixtures.—

Two solutions are kept separate, since they do not retain their efficiency long after they are mixed.

A $\begin{cases} \text{Fuchsin (acid)}.......................... & 0.1 \text{ g.} \\ \text{Distilled water}.......................... & 50.0 \text{ c.c.} \end{cases}$

B $\begin{cases} \text{Iodine green}........................... & 0.1 \text{ g.} \\ \text{Distilled water}.......................... & 50.0 \text{ c.c.} \end{cases}$

C $\begin{cases} \text{Absolute alcohol}....................... & 100.0 \text{ c.c.} \\ \text{Glacial acetic acid}..................... & 1.0 \text{ c.c.} \\ \text{Iodine}............................... & 0.1 \text{ g.} \end{cases}$

Stain in equal parts of A and B. Transfer from the stain directly to solution C, and from C to xylol.

Another formula.—

A $\begin{cases} \text{Acid fuchsin}.......................... & 0.5 \text{ g.} \\ \text{Water}................................ & 100.0 \text{ c.c.} \end{cases}$

B $\begin{cases} \text{Iodine green}........................... & 0.5 \text{ g.} \\ \text{Water}................................ & 100.0 \text{ c.c.} \end{cases}$

Mix a pipette full of A with a pipette full of B; stain 2–8 minutes; dehydrate rapidly and mount in balsam.

Phloxine.—

Phloxine....................................	1 g.
85 or 90 per cent alcohol....................	100 c.c.

This behaves like the better lots of the stain described under the name of Magdala red, in previous editions of this book, and may be identical with those better lots.

Safranin.—

In previous editions it was recommended that in making a 50 per cent alcoholic safranin, two safranins should be mixed, one dissolved in absolute alcohol and the other in water. I am reliably informed that the results averaged better because safranins varied and the method gave two chances to get some good safranin, instead of only one. The certified American safranins give good results whether dissolved in water, anilin water, 50 per cent alcohol, or stronger alcohols.

Safranin...................................	1 g.
Alcohol, 50 per cent.........................	100 c.c.

or

Safranin...................................	1 g.
Water....................................	100 c.c.

or

Safranin...................................	1 g.
Anilin (3 per cent anilin oil in water)...........	100 c.c.

Gentian violet.—

Gentian violet.............................	1 g.
95 per cent alcohol.........................	20 c.c.
Water....................................	80 c.c.
Anilin oil	3 c.c.

A 1 per cent solution in water keeps better, but does not stain the achromatic structures of mitotic figures so well.

A solution in clove oil is made by dissolving 1 g. gentian violet in 100 c.c. of absolute alcohol, and adding 100 c.c. of clove oil. Let the alcohol evaporate until there is practically a clove oil solution.

Crystal violet.—

This is a very pure violet. It can be substituted for gentian violet in all formulas.

Methyl violet (for flagella).—

20 per cent aqueous solution of tannin..........	10 c.c.
Cold saturated solution of ferrous sulphate......	5 c.c.
Saturated solution of methyl violet (or fuchsin)..	1 c.c.

Add the sulphate to the tannin and then add the violet.

For *Bacillus typhosis*, add to the mixture a few drops of caustic soda. For *Bacillus subtilis*, add 30 drops.

Pyoktanin.—

This is sold by E. Merck, in Darmstadt, Germany.
Dissolve 1 g. of pyoktanin in 30 c.c. of water.

Orange G.—

Orange G..................................	1 g.
Water....................................	100 c.c.

For most purposes a solution in clove oil is preferable. It is easier to get a solution by dissolving 0.1 g. of orange in 100 c.c. of absolute alcohol; then add 100 c.c. of clove oil. Let the absolute alcohol evaporate until there is left about 100 c.c. of the solution.

Gold orange.—

Gold orange............................... 0.1 g.
Clove oil................................. 100 c.c.

Dissolve the 0.1 g. of gold orange in 100 c.c. absolute alcohol, add 100 c.c. clove oil and let the alcohol evaporate until there is about 100 c.c. of the solution. Gold orange dissolves more readily than orange G.

Bismarck brown.—

Bismarck brown............................ 2 g.
70 per cent alcohol....................... 100 c.c.

Nigrosin.—

Nigrosin.................................. 1 g.
Water.................................... 100 c.c.

Gram's solution.—

Iodine................................... 1 g.
Iodide of potassium...................... 2 g.
Water.................................... 300 c.c.

MISCELLANEOUS

Mayer's albumen fixative.—

White of egg (active principle)............ 50 c.c.
Glycerin (to keep it from drying up)....... 50 c.c.
Salicylate of soda or carbolic acid (to keep out bacteria, etc.)............................. 1 g.

Shake well and filter through linen.

Land's gum fixative.—

Gum arabic............................... 1 g.
Potassium dichromate..................... 1 g.
Water.................................... 98 c.c.

Dissolve the gum in water and add the dichromate of potash; or dissolve the gum in half the quantity of water and the dichromate of potash in the other half, and mix just before using. Le Page's liquid glue may be used instead of the gum arabic.

Haupt's gelatin fixative.—

Gelatin	1 g.
Phenol	2 g.
Glycerin	15 c.c.
Water	100 c.c.

Dissolve the gelatin in distilled water at 30° C.; add 2 g. phenol crystals and the glycerin. Stir well and filter. In smoothing ribbons, flood the slide with 2 per cent formalin, which makes the gelatin insoluble.

Szombathy and also Artschwager have described gelatin fixatives.

Schultze's maceration fluid.—

The ingredients are nitric acid and potassium chlorate. They are mixed only as the reagent is applied. See chapter on "Special Methods" (chap. xii).

Jeffrey's maceration fluid.—

Nitric acid (10 per cent in water)	50 c.c.
Chromic acid (10 per cent in water)	50 c.c.

For directions, see chapter xii.

Bleaching fluid.—

Potassium chlorate (dry)	0.1 g.
Hydrochloric acid	0.5 c.c.
Alcohol (30 or 50 per cent)	100 c.c.

Put the potassium chlorate on the bottom of a dry Stender dish, drop the hydrochloric acid on with a pipette, and after 20 or 30 seconds pour on the alcohol.

This can always be made fresh and is as good or better than hydrogen peroxide for bleaching osmic acid material.

Fehling's solution.—

A	Cupric sulphate	3 g.
	Water	100 c.c.
B	Sodium potassium tartrate (Rochelle salts)	16 g.
	Water	100 c.c.
C	Caustic soda	12 g.
	Water	100 c.c.

Keep it in three bottles labeled A, B, and C. When needed for use, add 10 c.c. of water to 5 c.c. from each of the three bottles.

Millon's reagent.—

Mercury	1 c.c.
Concentrated nitric acid	9 c.c.
Water	10 c.c.

Cuprammonia.—

Prepare by pouring 15 per cent ammonia water upon copper turnings or filings. Let it stand in an open bottle.

Phloroglucin.—

Use a 5 per cent solution in water or alcohol.

Celloidin.—

To make a 2 per cent solution, add one tablet of Schering's celloidin and enough ether-alcohol (equal parts absolute alcohol and ether) to make the whole weigh 2,000 g.

Where only a small quantity is needed, shave off 2 g. of celloidin and add 100 c.c. of ether alcohol.

Eycleshymer's clearing fluid.—

Mix equal parts of bergamot oil, cedar oil, and carbolic acid.

Cellulose acetate.—

Cellulose acetate	12 g.
Pure acetone	100 c.c.

Mrs. Williamson recommends the cellulose acetate sold by Cellon, Ltd., 22 Cork Street, London, W. I., England.

Glycerin jelly.—

One part (by weight) of finest French gelatin is left for 2 hours in 6 parts (by weight) of distilled water. Add 7 parts of glycerin and for every 100 g. of the mixture add 1 g. of concentrated carbolic acid. Warm the whole mixture for 15 minutes, stirring all the time, until all the flakes produced by the carbolic acid have disappeared. Filter, while still warm, through a fine-meshed cheesecloth.

Venetian turpentine.—

To make a 10 per cent solution, add 90 c.c. of absolute alcohol to 10 c.c. of thick Venetian turpentine. Stir it with a glass rod. Guess at the amount of turpentine, for it is not easy to clean things which have contained Venetian turpentine.

Cleaning fluid.—

Dichromate of potash........................ 20 g.
Sulphuric acid.............................. 30 c.c.
Water...................................... 250 c.c.

This is excellent for cleaning slides, covers, glassware, developing trays, etc.

The following need no formulas: acetic acid, hydrochloric acid, nitric acid, sulphuric acid, carbolic acid, hydrofluoric acid, acetone, chloroform, ether, xylol, cedar oil, clove oil, bergamot oil, turpentine, glycerin, paraffin, balsam.

For photographic formulas see pages 181 to 188.

BIBLIOGRAPHY

It is not our purpose to give a complete list of literature which might be useful, but merely to call attention to some papers and books which will extend the student's knowledge in various directions. Some of the papers are cited because they will aid in collecting material and in studying the preparations rather than for any specific technical methods, for we assume that preparations are made to study and not merely for the pleasure of making a good mount.

It will be worth while to watch the reports which are being published in *Science* by the Committee on the Standardization of Biological Stains. The reports which have been published as this book goes to press are given below under the name of H. J. Conn, the chairman of the Committee. His principal collaborators are L. W. Sharp, F. B. Mallory, S. L. Kornhauser, J. A. Ambler, W. C. Holmes, and R. W. French.

The book, *Biological Stains*, by H. J. Conn, and the journal, *Stain Technology*, are invaluable for all who wish to keep their technique up to date.

ANGST, LAURA, Gametophytes of *Costaria costata*. Publ. Puget Sound Biol. Station **5**:293–308. 1927.

ARTSCHWAGER, E. F., A new fixative for paraffin sections. Bot. Gaz. **67**: 373–374. 1919.

AYERS, HOWARD, Methods of study of the myxamoebae and plasmodia of Mycetozoa. Jour. Applied Microscopy **1**:15–17. 1898.

BAILEY, I. W., Microtechnique for woody structures. Bot. Gaz. **49**:57–58. 1910.

BELLING, JOHN, On counting chromosomes in pollen mother cells. Amer. Nat. **55**:573–574. 1921.

———, The use of the microscope. New York: McGraw-Hill Book Co. 1930.

BENEDICT, H. M., An imbedding medium for brittle or woody tissues. Bot. Gaz. **52**:232. 1911.

BLACKMAN, V. H., Congo red as a stain for Uredineae. New Phyt. **4**:173–174. 1905.

BOYCE, J. S., The imbedding and staining of diseased wood. New Phyt. **8**: 432–436. 1918.

BRUCHMANN, H., Über die Prothallien und die Keimpflanzen mehrerer Europäischer Lycopodien. Pp. 119. *Pls*. 1–8. Gotha: Friederich Andreas Perthes. 1898.

BRYAN, GEORGE S., The archegonium of *Sphagnum subsecundum*. Bot. Gaz. **59**:40–56. 1915.

———, The archegonium of *Catharinea angustata*. Bot. Gaz. **64**:1–20, 1917.

BUGNON, M. P., Sur une nouvelle méthode de coloration élective des membranes végétales lignifiées. C. R. Acad. Sci. Paris **168**:62–64. 1919.

CARTWRIGHT, K. ST. G., A satisfactory method of staining fungi mycelium in wood sections. Amer. Bot. **43**:412–413. 1929.

CHAMBERLAIN, C. J., Prothallia and sporelings of three New Zealand species of *Lycopodium*. Bot. Gaz. **63**:51–65. 1917.

———, Elements of Plant Science. New York: McGraw-Hill Book Co. 1930.

CHURCH, MARGARET, Celloidin paraffin method. Sci. N.S. **47**:640. 1918.

CONN, H. J., An investigation of American stains. Jour. Bact. **7**:127–148. 1922.

———, Dye solubility in relation to staining solutions. Sci. N.S. **57**:638–639. 1923.

———, History of staining. Logwood dyes. Stain Technology **4**:37–48. 1929.

———, Haematin and acid fuchsin. Stain Technology **4**:97. 1929.

——— (Chairman) and Commission on Standardization of Biological Stains have published the following reports in Science:
The standardization of biological stains. January 13, 1922.
The production of biological stains in America. **53**:289–290. 1921.
The present supply of biological stains. **56**:562–563. 1922.
Collaborators in the standardization of biological stains. **56**:594–596. 1922.
Preliminary report on American biological stains. **56**:August 11, 1922.
American eosins. **56**:689–690. 1922.
The preparation of staining solutions. **57**:15–16. 1923.
Safranin and methyl green. **57**:304–305. 1923.
Dye solubility in relation to staining solutions. **57**:41–42. 1923.
Standardized nomenclature of biological stains. **57**:743–746. 1923.
Certified methylene blue. **58**:41–42. 1923.

COUPIN, H., Sur le montage de quelques préparations microscopiques. Rev. Gén. Bot. **31**:109–114. 1919.

COWDRY, E. V., Microchemical constituents of protoplasm. Carnegie Inst. Wash. Publ. 271. 1918.

CROCKER, E. C., An experimental study of the significance of "lignin" color reactions. Jour. Indust. and Eng. Chem. **13**:625–627. 1921.

DAVIS, W. H., Staining germinating spores. Phytopath. **12**:492–494. 1922.

DEGENER, O., Four new stations of *Lycopodium* prothallia. Bot. Gaz. **77**:89–95. 1924.

DE ZEEUW, R., The value of double infiltration in botanical microtechnique. Papers Mich. Acad. Sci. **1**:83–84. 1923.

DICKSON, B. T., The differential staining of plant pathogen and host. Sci. N.S. **52**:63–64. 1920.

Dowson, W. T., A new method of paraffin infiltration. Ann. Bot. **36**:577–578. 1922.

Durand, E. J., The differential staining of intercellular mycelium. Phytopath. **1**:129–130. 1911.

Farmer, J. B., and Shove, Dorothy, On the structure and development of the somatic and heterotype chromosomes of *Tradescantia virginica*. Quart. Jour. Mic. Sci. **48**:559–569. 1905.

Gerry, E., and Diemer, M. E., Stains for the mycelium of molds and other fungi. Sci. N.S. **54**:629–630. 1921.

Gourley, J. H., Basic fuchsin staining for vascular bundles. Stain Technology **5**:99–100. 1930.

Hartge, Lena A., *Nereocystis*. Publ. Puget Sound Biol. Station **5**:207–237. 1928.

Haupt, A. W., A gelatin fixative for paraffin sections. Stain Technology **5**:97–98. 1930.

Hill, J. B., A method for dehydration of histological material. Bot. Gaz. **51**:255–256. 1916.

Hoskins, J. H., Transfer method for thin rock sections. Bot. Gaz. **89**:414–415. 1930.

Howard, Frank L., Laboratory cultivation of Myxomycete plasmodia. Amer. Jour. Bot. **18**:624–628. 1931.

Hubert, E. E., A staining method for hyphae of wood-inhabiting fungi. Phytopath. **12**:440–441. 1922.

Jeffrey, E. C., Technical contributions I. Improved method of softening hard tissues. Bot. Gaz. **86**:456–457. 1928.

Karston, G., Über embryonales Wachstum und seine Tagesperiode. Zeitsch. für Bot. **7**:1–34. 1915.

Kellicott, W. E., The daily periodicity of cell division and of elongation in the root of *Allium*. Bull. Torrey Bot. Club. **31**:529–550. 1904.

Kisser, J., Die Dampfmethode, ein neues Verfahren zum Schneiden härtester pflanzlicher Objecte. Zeitsch. wiss. Mikr. **43**:346–354. 1926.

Kleinenberg, Haematoxylin method. Quar. Jour. Micr. Sci. **19**:208. 1879.

Kornhauser, S. I., Celloidin paraffin method. Sci. **44**:57–58. 1916.

Land, W. J. G., A morphological study of *Thuja*. Bot. Gaz. **34**:249–259. 1902.

———, Spermatogenesis and oögenesis in *Ephedra trifurca*. Bot. Gaz. **38**:1–18. 1904.

———, Fertilization and embryogeny in *Ephedra trifurca*. Bot. Gaz. **44**:273–292. 1907.

———, Microtechnical methods. Bot. Gaz. **59**:397–401. 1915.

———, A method of controlling the temperature of the paraffin block and microtome knife. Bot. Gaz. **57**:520–523. 1914.

LANGDON, LADEMA MARY, Sectioning hard woody tissues. Bot. Gaz. **70**:82–84. 1920.

LEE, H. N., The staining of wood fibers for permanent microscopic mounts. Bot. Gaz. **62**:318–319. 1916.

MANN, ALBERT, The preparation of unbroken pollen mother cells and other cells for studies in mitoses. Sci. **36**:151–153. 1912.

METZ, C. W., A simple method for handling small objects in making microscopic preparations. Anat. Record **21**:373–374. 1921.

McCLINTOCK, BARBARA, A method for making aceto-carmine smears permanent. Stain Technology **4**:53–56. 1929.

MOLLENDORF, W. VON, Vitale Färbungen an tierischen Zellen. Ergebn. Physiol. **18**:141–306. 1920. (Bibliography.)

NEMEC, B., Gentian method for starch. Ber. Deu. Bot. Ges. **24**:528–531. 1906.

NIEUWLAND, J. A., The mounting of algae (preserving the green color). Bot. Gaz. **47**:237. 1909.

PFEIFFER, NORMA E., Monograph of Isoetaceae. Annals Mo. Bot. Garden **9**:79–218. 1922.

PICKETT, F. L., Preparation of whole pollen mother cells. Sci. **36**:479–480. 1912.

———, A study of the stability of staining solutions. Trans. Amer. Mic. Soc. **42**:129–132. 1923.

PLOWMAN, A. B., Celloidin method with hard tissues. Bot. Gaz. **37**:456–461. 1904.

RUCKES, H., Washing microscopic organisms. Sci. N.S. **48**:44–45. 1918.

SAMPSON, H. C., Chemical changes accompanying abscission in *Coleus blumei*. Bot. Gaz. **66**:32–53. 1918. (Summarizes microchemical tests.)

SANDS, HAROLD C., The structure of the chromosomes in *Tradescantia virginica*. Amer. Jour. of Bot. **10**:343–360. 1923.

SCHAEDE, R., Über das Verhalten von Pflanzenzellen gegenüber Anilinfarbstoffen. Jahrb. wiss. Bot. **62**:65–91. 1923.

SEIFRIZ, W., A method for inducing protoplasmic streaming. New Phytol. **21**:107–112. 1922.

SHARP, L. W., An introduction to cytology. New York: McGraw-Hill Book Co. 1926.

SINNOTT, E. W., and BAILEY, I. W., Some technical aids for the anatomical study of decaying wood. Phytopath. **14**:403. 1914.

SMITH, G. M., The preservation of fresh water algae. Plant World **16**:219–230. 1913.

SPALTEHOLZ, WERNER, Über das Durchsichtigmachen von menschlichen und tierischen Präparaten. Leipzig: S. Hirzel. 1911.

SPESSARD, E. A., Prothallia of *Lycopodium* in America. Bot. Gaz. **63**:66–76. 1917; **65**:362. 1918; **74**:392–413. 1922.

STARR, ANNA M., The microsporophylls of *Ginkgo*. Bot. Gaz. **49**:51–55. 1910.

STEIL, W. N., Method for staining antherozoids of ferns. Bot. Gaz. **65**:562–563. 1918.

STEVENS, F. L., The fungi that cause disease. New York: Macmillan Co. 1919.

STEWART, A. B., The mounting of celloidin sections in series. Sci. **42**:872. 1915.

STOKEY, A. G., and STARR, A. M., *Lycopodium* prothallia in western Massachusetts. Bot. Gaz. **77**:80–88. 1924.

STOUGHTON, R. H., Thionin and orange for the differential staining of bacteria and fungi in plant tissues. Annals of Applied Biology **17**:162–164. 1930.

STRASBURGER, E., Das botanische Prakticum, siebente Auflage bearbeitet von Max Koernicke. Jena, Germany: Gustav Fischer. 1923.

SZOMBATHY, K., Neue Methode zum Aufkleben von Paraffinschnitten. Zeitsch. wiss. Mikr. **34**:334–336. 1918. Review in Bot. Gaz. **67**:373–374. 1919.

TAYLOR, W. R., A method for demonstrating the sheath structure of a desmid. Trans. Amer. Micr. Soc. **40**:94–95. 1921.

TISON, A., Méthode nouvelle de coloration des tissus subéreux. Compt. Rend. Assoc. Franc. Avanc. Sci. **28**:Pt. II, 454–456. 1899. (See Phytopath. **9**:483–496. 1919.)

TOBLER-WOLFF, G., Zur Methodik der mikroskopischen Pflanzenfaseruntersuchung. Zeitschr. wiss. Mikr. **32**:129–136. 1916.

TURNER, J. J., The origin and development of the vascular system of *Lycopodium lucidulum*. Bot. Gaz. **78**:215–225. 1924.

VAUGHAN, R. E., A method for the differential staining of fungus and host cells. Ann. Mo. Bot. Garden **1**:241–242. 1914.

WALKER, ELDA, The gametophytes of *Equisetum laevigatum*. Bot. Gaz. **71**:378–391. 1921.

——, Gametophytes of three species of *Equisetum*. Bot. Gaz. **92**:1–22. 1931.

WALTON, JOHN, Improvements in the peel method of preparing sections of fossil plants. Nature. October 13, 1928; and March 15, 1930.

WILLIAMSON, H. S., A new method of preparing sections of hard vegetable structures. Ann. Bot. January, 1921.

WOLFE, JAMES J., Cytological studies in *Nemalion*. Annals of Botany **18**:607–630. 1904.

Wood, D. B., Diatoms. Trans. Vasser Bros. Inst. and Its Scientific Section. **7**:66–86. 1894–1896.

Woods, A. F., Method of preserving the green color of plants for exhibition purposes. Bot. Gaz. **24**:206. 1897.

———, Preserving the green color of algae, protonema, etc. Quar. Jour. Mic. Sci. **14**:225–228. 1921.

The journal, *Stain Technology*, published by the Commission on Standardization of Biological Stains, and originally devoted almost entirely to stains, is publishing an increasingly large number of excellent articles on microtechnique.

INDEX

INDEX

[References are to pages. Italic figures indicate illustrations.]

A

Abies balsamea, pollen, *340*
Acetic acid, 20, 21
Acetic alcohol, 20
Achlya, 257
Acid fuchsin, 59; with iodine green, 70; with methyl green, 70
Acid green, 64
Acorus calamus, 348
Adiantum, leaf gap, 308
Aecium, on *Hepatica*, 268
Agaricus, 270
Agathis, prothallial cells, 340
Albugo, *257*, 258, 272
Albuminoids, 21, 34
Alcannin, 86
Alchemilla, 370
Alcohol, 19; waste, 35; formulas for grades, 36; labels, 36; absolute, 19, 37
Algae (marine), 213
Alisma, 215
Allium, 349; mitosis in root, *350; A. cepa*, 29
Aloe, 348
Alum carmine, 54
Alum cochineal, 55
Ammonia, 51
Ammonia sulphate of iron, 45
Anabaena, *208*, 209, 324
Androspores, 234, *235*
Anemone, Embryo sac, 366
Angiopteris, root, *310, 311*
ANGIOSPERMS, 347
    Vegetative structures, 347
        Stem, 347
        Root, 349
        Leaf, 353
        Buds, 354
        Epidermis, 354
    Floral development, 354

Spermatogenesis, 357
Oögenesis, 362
Fertilization, 366
Endosperm, 367
Embryo, 368
Parthenogenesis, 370
Angst (*Costaria*), 243
Anilin, 56
Anilin blue, 64
Antheridia, of Hepaticae, 278; of Musci, 286, *287;* of Pteridophytes, *303, 314, 315*
Anthoceros, 283, *284*
Anthrax, 203, *204*
Apparatus, 7
Araucaria, prothallial cells, 340
Archegonia, of Hepaticae, 279, *280, 281;* of Musci, *287*
Archesporial cell, 52, *362*
Arisaema triphyllum, 349
Artifact, 5
Artificial light, 375
Asclepias, pollen, 361; endosperm, 368
Ascomycetes, 259
Ascophyllum, 241
Aspergillus, 104, 260, *261*
Aspidium, sorus, 311
Aspirator, 34
Aster, embryo sac, 365
Atrichum, 286
Azolla, 318, 320

B

Bacillus anthracis, 204
Bacteria, 201
Bacterium malvacearum, 273
Bangia, 248
Barberry, 267
Basic fuchsin, 59
Basidia, 269
Basidiomycetes, 266

409